# The Evolution of the US Airline Industry

# Studies in Industrial Organization

**Volume 25**

---

*The titles published in this series are listed at the end of this volume.*

# The Evolution of the US Airline Industry

## Theory, Strategy and Policy

by

Eldad Ben-Yosef

 Springer

A C.I.P. Catalogue record for this book is available from the Library of Congress.

1+

ISBN 0-387-24213-9 (HB)
ISBN 0-387-24242-2 (e-book)

Published by Springer,
P.O. Box 17, 3300 AA Dordrecht, The Netherlands.

*Printed on acid-free paper*

Printed in the Netherlands.

# CONTENTS

# List of Figures

# List of Tables

*In memory of*
*Asher Ben-Yosef, my father*
*and*
*Amos Ginor, my mentor*
*Aviation Pioneers*

# FOREWORD

For over three decades the airline industry has continued to maintain a high profile in the public mind and in public policy interest. This high profile is probably not surprising. There does seem to be something inherently newsworthy about airplanes and the people and companies that fly them.

The industry was one of the first major industries in the United States to undergo deregulation, in 1978. It thereby transitioned from a closely regulated sector (the former Civil Aeronautics Board tightly controlled everything from prices to routes to entry) to one that is largely market oriented. The incumbent carriers transformed themselves from the point-to-point operators that the CAB had required to the hub-and-spokes structures that took better advantage of their network characteristics. Further, they transformed their pricing from the quite simple structures that the CAB had required to the highly differentiated/segmented pricing structures ("yield management") that reached an apogee in the late 1990s. Some carriers, like American, Delta, and United, were better at this transition; others, like Pan American, TWA, and Eastern, were not.

What the incumbent carriers did not do, however, was deal with their costly wage and work rules structures, which were an enduring legacy of their regulatory period. This legacy, when combined with the high-fare end of the yield-management pricing structure, has made them vulnerable to entry by new carriers with lower cost structures. This vulnerability—compounded by high variability in fuel prices—has yielded large and widespread losses since 2001, immersion in bankruptcy proceedings for some carriers, and work forces that (understandably) have been slow to yield the gains of the regulated era and are unhappy in having to do so. The public policy concerns continue.

Eldad Ben-Yosef has written an intriguing book about the modern airline industry. He offers a unique perspective, being able to combine the expertise of a trained economist with the experience of someone who has been involved in the business of the industry for over 20 years. Though some readers may not agree with some points, his positions are definitely well-reasoned and worthy of serious consideration or debate. Readers will surely find the journey through this book to be interesting and worthwhile.

Lawrence J. White
Stern School of Business, New York University
November 2004

# INTRODUCTION

How has the airline industry managed to surprise us once again? Why do airlines buy an enormous number of very expensive new aircraft just when demand drops and revenues can't support their operation? Why do they do it time and again? Why do airlines pay labor and other resources so much when they know they can't afford it? Why do they build excess capacity? Why have low-cost startup entries succeeded just when industry observers are convinced that such entry is doomed to fail?

Many observers claim airline management failures are directly responsible for most of the industry's malaise. Why, then, do management failures continue to be so common and so much a part of the industry?

This industry has attracted so much scholarly attention, yet many important issues and conceptual debates have remained unresolved. In past analyses we were so often confident in our understanding of the industry only to learn later on that we had missed some obvious waypoints that sent it in a completely different direction. Is the industry naturally competitive—as certain observers argued? Or perhaps naturally monopolistic—as argued by others? There is still no clear consensus regarding whether imposing regulation on the industry over sixty years ago was justified. Was deregulation a success story—as certain observers argue? Or a failure—as argued by others? Certain observers have called for reregulating or even for nationalizing the airlines.

At times observers believed too much competition is leading the industry toward economic destruction. It was even suggested that the industry reflects a case of an *empty core*—a theoretical construct of a market that cannot sustain itself over time. At other times the major airlines were assumed to be too strong, earning monopolistic premiums. Industry players, however, know quite well that it is almost impossible to make money in the airline business even if an airline possesses significant market power. In fact, no airline, except for one, has been able to consistently stay out of the red. Yet plans and actual attempts of new entry have always been present and entrepreneurs are always attracted to this industry, ignoring the overwhelming historic evidence of failures and the very small chance of success.

It seems the industry has a life of its own, a life that is at once spontaneous and at times self-destructive.

This book tells the story of the airline industry, mostly in intuitive economic terms. I am particularly interested in market structures, government regulation and related institutions, and the theoretical concepts and models that are created to interpret, predict, and effect them over time. These issues have played an important role in my day-to-day business activities and represent the context within which I interpret events and make business decisions. This approach differs from the more

1

common approaches that emphasize extensive statistical treatment, or that tell about the people or events that have shaped the industry's history.

Mine is an inside observer's view using metaphors and the language of economic theory in an attempt to describe and interpret how things evolved. My business role as an aircraft owner, lessor, and trader, as well as my involvement in airline startups, privatizations, bankruptcies, and ownership for more than two decades, provides me with a different, insider's perspective on the industry. As a real-world market participant with theoretical economics training, I hope to contribute to the ongoing dialogue and interactions among academic researchers, real-market participants, and policymakers dealing with the airline industry.

An intriguing issue that I emphasize in the book is the role that aircraft—as an input—and the aircraft manufacturers play in shaping the travel industry's structure and strategy. This important role has often escaped the attention of observers of the airline industry who have usually focused on labor as the most critical input. The most striking example is that the strategy adopted by aircraft manufacturers impeded airline competition and made startup entry more difficult during the 1990s. Increased competition between Boeing and Airbus for market share and a shift in their strategies encouraged an unprecedented global wave of low-cost startup entries in the early 2000s. In the late 1980s and 1990s aircraft manufacturers helped build the major incumbent airlines that then became the victim of their new strategy in the 2000s.

There are so many books about the airline industry, so why another one? Why now? Two general reasons are particularly important. First, new economic thinking—emphasizing strategic interaction and complex dynamics—provides us with new tools to look at the market, observe, and analyze aspects that have often escaped the traditional perspective, and shed a different light on its evolution. Second, during the early 2000s, it became apparent that the industry is evolving along a different trajectory from that expected in the late 1990s. This shift deserves a serious discussion with respect to the future tendency of the industry. For this purpose it is important to reevaluate the history and evolution of the industry and related government policies with hindsight. It is important to understand where we are and how we got here in order to identify the possible courses of the future.

Two major general and recurrent themes must be identified at the outset. The first has to do with the surprises related to the unexpected path that industry structure has taken. As we look at the evolution of the industry, we cannot escape a conclusion that the dominant set of assumptions and models adopted at any particular time to interpret the industry's behavior and to shape government policies in fact failed to explain or predict the major shifts in this evolutionary path. More often than not, the major trends that seem so obvious in retrospect were largely unexpected before, and it is only with hindsight that we can see the handwriting on the wall.

The prime example is that—despite the dominant view in the 1970s and early 1980s—the industry responded to the introduction of free competition by consolidating into an oligopoly with a very small number of winners. Each one of the major winning airlines is operating complex hubs with regional monopolistic characteristics, taking advantage of economies of scale, scope, and density. This is absolutely contrary to the pre-deregulation mainstream view that the airline industry is inherently naturally competitive, and that economies of scale would play only a negligible role, if any.

American Airlines—considered the most financially vulnerable airline prior to deregulation and in danger of exiting the market immediately after deregulation—surprisingly became an industry leader by adopting the hub-and-spoke network as a prime strategy in the early 1980s. While we once thought the least efficient firm would exit the market, in fact American's almost desperate struggle for survival drove its management to adopt this new winning strategy. This network nature of the industry and its economic impact that now look so obvious were not fully understood by most observers, and were largely ignored for several decades. It is hard to conceive that the term *network*, which dominates current industry discourse, was seldom mentioned before the late 1980s.

This notion of surprise, not to mention errors in prediction, can be explained by the nature of the airlines' strategic behavior, which often changes the assumptions on which we base our expectations and also the complex dynamic nature of the industry's evolution. This notion is at odds with traditional economics and antitrust thinking and poses major theoretical and policy challenges as well as serious antitrust dilemmas. The history-specific nature of the industry's evolution makes universal theoretical claims and traditional empirical generalization and prediction highly questionable, if relevant at all.

The second recurrent major theme is somewhat surprising as well. The deregulation movement in general, particularly its application to the airline industry in the late 1970s, relies on a conviction that government intervention in most markets does not fulfill expectations. The assumption has been that government intervention is very costly, and that markets, while imperfect; often operate better without such intervention. The deregulation of the airline industry was thus perceived as a significant step toward eliminating costly government intervention from the market.

In fact, however, price and entry regulation may have been largely eliminated, but new patterns of safety and environmental (social) regulations emerged, substituting one form of regulation for another. The new government intervention through social regulation has become more apparent and more pervasive than before. It affects market prices and structure mostly through its impact on production costs and its potential negative impact on the ease of entry.

This regulation is different from that contemplated by standard economic principles. Regulation like this in fact dictates standards and methods of compliance, elements in an industry that are not directly related to market signals. Moreover, regulation is achieved through a political process of negotiations, responding to complex interest structures and political power. Contrary to textbook arguments (and perhaps naïve expectations), deregulation did not replace an imperfect government intervention regime with perfect free market forces. Instead it changed the methods and institutions by which an imperfect government interacts with imperfect markets. Deregulation replaced one imperfect social arrangement with another.

The book consists of an overview, nine chapters, and an epilogue. The overview briefly sketches the major trends of the industry's evolution. The epilogue offers concluding comments. Each of the nine chapters was inspired by and responds to a major new trend in the deregulated industry's evolutionary path. There is a certain amount of repetition across the chapters in order to keep each one of them a coherent unit if read on a stand-alone basis. The chapters are organized by the chronological order of the appearance of each trend, in three parts.

The evolution of the deregulated industry can be broken into two major periods with the yearend 2000 serving as a possible divide. During the first period the major incumbent network airlines continually increased their dominance. The new century brought about a new reality and serious questions regarding the continuing dominance of these airlines and skepticism regarding their traditional business strategy. The first two parts of the book focus on the first period. Part 1 focuses on the air travel market. Part 2 discusses safety and environmental regulation. Part 3 looks at the origins of the breakdown of the dominant business model of the 1990s and the new unfolding market reality.

## 1. PART 1: ECONOMIC DEREGULATION

Chapter 1 deals with the major incumbent airlines' move to create complex hub-and-spoke network systems as the major post-deregulation strategy and the continuing trend of consolidation that characterized the industry during the 1980s and 1990s. This trend involves downstream and upstream, vertical and horizontal, integration arrangements among domestic airlines, as well as global interlining—mostly through cross-border alliances—that divide the world into three or four major global airline networks, each associated with a major US airline operating regional dominant hubs.

This structure raised barriers to entry by tying up resources and access to markets, and raising scale and scope requirements and sunk costs, so it attracted much antitrust attention, especially in the late 1990s. Antitrust proponents viewed this trend as leading toward a monopolistic structure and called for renewed antitrust enforcement. On the opposite side of the debate, other observers viewed this trend as a desirable consequence of exploiting production and demand-side network advantages. The first group emphasized empirical findings of a "monopolistic premium" relating to certain hub routes. The latter questioned the extent and doubted the social cost of such a premium, noting that average real fares have declined consistently since deregulation, and the industry's overall profit has been anything but super-normal.

Chapter 2 deals with aspects of the market for aircraft as input. It discusses the recurrent mismatch between business cycles and aircraft acquisition cycles, focusing in particular on specific industry behavior during the last quarter of the 1980s. At this time the major airlines placed an unprecedented number of orders for new aircraft, disregarding both general economic conditions and air travel demand. In parallel, the airlines, the manufacturers, and the regulator initiated unprecedented efforts focusing on previous-generation aircraft as a major target of safety and environmental regulation. The orders for new aircraft resulted in an enormous number of deliveries of new aircraft to an industry struggling with a severe crisis and surplus capacity in the early 1990s.

The traditional explanation for capacity overshooting has been airlines' forecasting error. I suggest that the *increasing return* characteristics of aircraft production and air travel networks and the associated strategic games played by the airlines and aircraft manufacturers (both groups seeking to increase market share and reduce high average fixed costs) can explain at least some of the capacity overshooting. In this and subsequent chapters, I argue that aircraft manufacturers and the strongest incumbent airlines created an ad hoc coalition with a mutual interest of diminishing the market for the previous-generation aircraft. The manufacturers' objective was to expand the market for new aircraft by disparaging the still very efficient and competitive older ones. The major incumbents' objective was to raise the cost of acquiring and operating previous-generation aircraft by the financially weaker incumbents and startup airlines.

Chapter 3 was inspired by the major industry crisis associated with the Gulf War in the summer of 1990. This crisis, which persisted for a few years, is best known for the demise of Pan American, Eastern, and Midway, and the bankruptcy reorganization of Continental, TWA, and America West, as well as industry-wide staggering losses. A notable characteristic of this period was "fare wars," when airlines priced their seats at lower rates than required for long-term industry survival, raising an old question regarding whether destructive competition is a real problem in aviation markets.

*Destructive competition* was a major rationale the airlines and the government used to justify regulation of the industry in the late 1930s. It was rejected, however, by most deregulation proponents and economists, who argued that the industry is naturally competitive and lacks the major prerequisites for destructive competition— high fixed and sunk costs (relative to overall cost), and long sustained and recurrent periods of excess capacity. The events of the early 1990s suggested otherwise. In this chapter I look at the events of the late 1930s (regulation), the late 1970s (deregulation), and the crisis of the early 1990s, from the perspective that the industry is inherently associated with high fixed and sunk costs, increasing returns, and recurrent overcapacity.

## 2. PART 2: NOISE AND SAFETY REGULATIONS

The three chapters in Part 2 focus on environmental and safety regulations that were introduced during the late 1980s and early 1990s, with compliance mandated throughout the 1990s. The enactment of these "social" regulations was as important and ambitious a regulatory effort as the economic deregulation in the late 1970s, yet it did not attract much attention outside the industry. These regulation initiatives dominated the industry's agenda for several years and have had a long-term impact on its structure and conduct. I introduce a new set of issues, arguments, and theories focusing on regulation of externalities and their implementation. They include an extensive discussion and analysis of the nature of aircraft noise and safety issues and their regulation. Readers interested in continuing to read about airline behavior in the air travel market and about the evolution of pricing strategy, should go directly to Part 3 and may return later to read these three chapters, which were placed here for chronological reasons, but can otherwise be read on their own.

Chapter 4 discusses general aspects of social regulation as applied to the airline industry.

Chapter 5 deals with noise regulation. Aircraft noise represents a textbook example of production externality—an environmental cost that is not properly reflected in the free market system. According to economists, the proper definition of property rights or efficient government regulation ought to correct for noise damage in otherwise incomplete markets. In reality, however, the judicial system has not granted rights for a noise-free environment to most negatively affected airport neighbors, and therefore forecloses most possible transactions between airlines or airports and residents. In addition, uncertainty and information problems inherent in both specifying and enforcing efficient noise regulation and interest group politics have interacted to yield complex "order and command" regulations that are quite different from those recommended by economists.

The global nature of the air travel industry further complicates the situation by introducing a new set of conflicting interests and complex patterns of rivalry and cooperation. Aviation requires global coordination and unified operational standards, yet it provides diverse economic costs and benefits on local, national, and international levels. It also inflicts diverse and difficult-to-measure noise damages on local communities that have different thresholds for bearing noise and varying political, judicial, and administrative institutions and power. This necessarily creates complex interactions of interest groups and regulatory institutions at local, federal, and global levels that make regulation less likely to resemble economic principles.

Chapter 6 discusses safety regulation. The general premise is similar to that suggested in the noise regulation chapter. That is, information imperfections, strategic behavior, and interest group politics have moved regulation away from the ideal economic principles. The economic rationale for safety regulation is associated mostly with problems of information imperfections and risk-sharing that are expected to cause a failure of free market mechanisms. The government's regulation is expected to provide airlines with incentives to take the "proper" safety efforts in the absence of efficient free market signals. In reality, however, safety regulation is a complex and dynamically evolving set of negotiated rules that are affected by industry strategic behavior, technology, and public perception of the risks.

In Chapter 6 I argue that the manufacturers and the stronger major airlines accommodated public misperceptions regarding flying risks, all the while supporting inefficient regulation that served their strategic interests. The very costly safety regulations that became effective in the early 1990s were inefficient on two primary counts if judged by traditional economic standards. First, more resources were allocated to aviation safety than justified on the basis of other comparable risks. Second, intraindustry safety efforts were misplaced, and resources were misallocated across safety targets. In particular, older aircraft and startup airlines became major regulatory safety targets at the very time the industry was actually struggling with the quite prominent safety challenges of new technology automated flight systems. Moreover, *controlled flight into terrain*—and not aircraft age—was recognized by the industry as the major safety challenge of the time.

# 3. PART 3: COMPETITION

During the first half of the 1990s, the industry struggled through a devastating economic crisis. By the mid-1990s, the three major incumbent airlines, United, American, and Delta, emerged stronger and larger than ever, well-positioned to recover and to reap most of the benefits of an ultimately impressive economic upturn at the end of the decade. In the last years of the century, the majors came to make unprecedented use of sophisticated pricing techniques with the advantage of computerized reservation and pricing systems that had been developed, installed, and tested since the late 1980s. This enabled the airlines to maximize their revenues based on passenger demand elasticity.

Chapter 7 discusses *yield management*, which is the term the industry uses to describe its pricing strategy. The rich economic theory on price discrimination is particularly useful to characterize the general techniques the airlines have used to price their seats. A major implication of airline yield management strategies in the late 1990s and early 2000s is that a relatively small group of demand inelastic business and other time-sensitive passengers generated a disproportionate portion of the major network airlines' revenues. The severe negative impact of the dwindling numbers of high-fare paying passengers called into question the very survivability of these airlines.

The economic downturn of the early 2000s, the impact of the September 11, 2001, events and the looming war in Iraq had a dramatic effect on the industry's strategy and structure. Yield management could no longer generate sufficient revenues to cover the enormous cost of running high-frequency hub networks. Cost cutting became the order of the day. Yet, extensive labor negotiations between 1998 and 2002, involving an unprecedented number of labor work actions and presidential interventions, resulted in a significant increase in labor costs for the major network airlines. Cost cutting became even more challenging and forced managements to plea for labor concessions in or out of bankruptcy courts. The dominant network airlines—United, American, and Delta—suffered enormously, while Southwest and other mostly point-to-point airlines significantly increased their market share, becoming for the first time a serious threat to the major incumbents' hegemony. The serious antitrust concerns that had characterized the regulator's view in the late 1990s were replaced with new concerns regarding the long-term viability of the major network airlines.

In Chapter 8, I undertake the challenge of answering the question: What next for the industry? Are the major network airlines—as certain observers suggest— doomed to go the way of the dinosaur?

Chapter 9 concludes by analyzing some major policy issues. I challenge some aspects of the traditional mainstream view and some of the current economic theories of oligopoly, particularly those related to the "new economy." Even though aviation is an old rather than new economy industry, it shares many features with the new economy, including high fixed costs relative to a low marginal cost, economies of scale from production and demand-side network effects, and strong innovative competition. My analysis adapts some of these new theories (or sometimes new formulations of old ideas) to interpret today's competition in the aviation market, basically to question the wisdom of basing antitrust action on the traditional *structure-performance-conduct* concept.

The Epilogue offers concluding thoughts.

# OVERVIEW

*From Economic Regulation to Social and Antitrust Regulation*

> Until we realize that we are choosing between social arrangements, which are all more or less failures, we are not likely to make much headway.[1]

I joined the aviation industry in 1980. As a young economist, I was proud of the fact that one of our own, Alfred Kahn, was leading a most fascinating real-life experiment—deregulation of the aviation industry. Professor Kahn, a graduate of New York University and Yale University, was nominated in 1979 as the chairman of the Civil Aeronautics Board (CAB). He led the industry into deregulation with enthusiasm and conviction.

This was a gratifying moment for me as an economist, since the principles of our profession were sure to provide the intellectual basis for a major economic reform of an entire industry. The idea of *contestable markets* represented a positive economic model that was to play an important role in deregulation, perhaps far beyond the dreams of the scholars who developed it.

There was no doubt in my mind (or in almost everyone else's) that deregulation would bring about an efficient, highly competitive airline industry that would offer passengers significantly more aircraft seats for significantly lower fares. The traditional wisdom had suggested that atomistic competition of small firms would promote efficiency. The *contestable markets* concept suggested that similar results could be expected in certain oligopolistic or even monopolistic markets, especially in the air travel market.

A dramatic expansion of the industry at the time, including new entries and plummeting fares during the first half of the 1980s, further strengthened the conviction that we were moving toward a long-run, competitive equilibrium. I was sure I was to witness the transformation of a rigid and government-regulated cartel into an efficient textbook market structure.

Prior to deregulation, it had been widely held that passengers were paying too much for an inadequate number of aircraft seats. Fixed regulated fares encouraged competition as to quality of service. Subsequently, a vicious cycle of cost increases followed by pressures on the regulator to increase fares squeezed airlines' profits and made air travel more expensive. Flying was targeted to the affluent (hence the

---

[1] Ronald Coase, The regulated industries: Discussion, *American Economic Review*, 1964, 54 (May): p.195. Cited in Williamson (1985, p. 327).

phrase, "jet set"). It is said that when the idea of pursuing airline deregulation was first suggested to Massachusetts Senator Edward Kennedy—who led the political process of deregulation—he dismissed it as largely an upper middle class issue of little interest to the vast majority of the Democratic Party's constituency.

As I sit in an uncomfortable seat (nervously tossing down way-too-salty peanuts) in a crowded cabin (after having waited in a long queue for takeoff clearance, upset that the passenger on my left paid only half my fare, concerned that my luggage be lost), it is hard to conceive that under regulation it was not uncommon for airlines to provide in-flight live entertainment, with piano bars (pianists on real pianos installed in the cabin playing cool jazz, most probably) and stand-up comedians and ... bunnies (of the human variety).

## 1. ECONOMIC DEREGULATION: CONSOLIDATION, CONCENTRATION, AND GLOBALIZATION

Starting in the early 1980s, the major airlines embarked on a consolidation trend. They merged with and acquired other domestic airlines and assets, and entered into passenger-feeding or other integration arrangements with smaller regional carriers. The disappearance of several major airlines in the early 1990s and the acquisition of their assets by a few major airlines further affected market structure in an unexpected way.[2] While the early 1990s were characterized largely by domestic consolidation and restructuring, toward the end of the decade global consolidation played a major role.

Just when it seemed industry concentration had reached a peak, an even more surprising consolidation and integration became apparent. This included strategic arrangements and mergers between and among major airlines in the domestic market as well as the formation of global alliances among major international airlines. The movement has been toward a few major global networks, each associated with a major US airline. These alliances integrate networks of several major airlines around the globe. They each control a substantial part of the world's aircraft inventory, facilities, and air traffic. They alliances focus primarily on joint marketing (mostly through "code-share" agreements), but they may also include operational covenants as well as joint negotiation, coordination, advertising, and acquisition and supply of maintenance, spare parts, and other inputs, taking advantage of economies of pooling, standardization, density, and scale.[3]

This global consolidation has funneled the vast majority of world traffic into three or four major network coalitions characterized by intrasystem network compatibility and interlining and intersystem rivalry. This phenomenon has become a major target of regulatory bodies worldwide, as they struggle with a developing antitrust perspective and defining the proper responses to a strong tendency to build integrated networks across national borders.

---

[2] Continental, TWA, and America West reorganized, and Eastern, Pan Am, and Midway liquidated under bankruptcy court protection. United, American, and Delta became the emerging industry leaders.

[3] The term "code-share" is used to refer to marketing agreements of diverse characteristics that facilitate travel under one airline code designation.

The consolidation and concentration trend acquired a new dimension during the 1990s, as firms in the input markets—equipment manufacturers and related services—started to engage in merger and acquisition activities and other strategic alliances, generating a parallel consolidation trend in these industries as well. Most notable is the acquisition of McDonnell-Douglas by the Boeing Company.[4] Manufacturers of engines, parts, and components as well as other vendors and service providers have also begun to integrate horizontally or vertically with other manufacturing, maintenance, or support companies.

Certain strategic moves in input markets are surprising in the sense that they create new and complex (horizontal and vertical) market relationships. General Electric, for example, one of the two major US manufacturers of jet engines, has dramatically expanded its activity as an aircraft owner/lessor since the mid 1980s.[5] As the world's largest owner and lessor of aircraft, it directly affects demand for its own engines through ownership and control over aircraft equipped with such engines. GE also acquired several engine overhaul and repair shops, thus becoming a leader in this market, and to a large degree dominates the overhaul and repair of engines, including engines manufactured by its major competitor, Pratt & Whitney. GE can directly influence the price and availability of used Pratt & Whitney engines. In the fall of 2000, GE announced its intention to effect a $45 billion acquisition of Honeywell, one of the dominant players in the avionics market, a move ultimately blocked by European antitrust authorities.

During the first half of the 1980s, the major airlines moved to form strategic complex hub-and-spoke network systems. In the second half of the decade, they fortified their market power at the hub level through various (vertical and horizontal) full or partial integration and cooperation arrangements with other airlines, and increased capacity, frequency, and network size. They used their computer reservation systems, frequent flier programs, commission overrides, and other marketing strategies to tie passengers into particular networks.

The results? The integrated hubs of the major airlines developed into regional bottlenecks with natural monopolistic characteristics.

It is paradoxical that the airlines' post-deregulation strategic behavior shaped the industry into a highly concentrated market of complex networks that resembles in many ways a system that has traditionally justified the public utility concept of regulation. If the mergers and acquisitions proposed by the airlines during 2000 and 2001 had been consummated, the five largest airlines in the US would have accounted for over 80% of the market, representing a significantly higher concentration than ever seen pre-deregulation.[6]

---

[4] Until 1982, three major US manufacturers competed in the commercial jet-aircraft market: Boeing, McDonnell-Douglas (MDC), and Lockheed. The latter shut down its L1011 line in the early 1980s. In 1997 Boeing acquired MDC. The only major non-US competition is the European manufacturer of the Airbus.

[5] The second is Pratt & Whitney.

[6] This includes the American-TWA and United-US Airways proposed mergers, based on revenue passenger miles. Prior to deregulation, the five largest carriers had 68.6% of the domestic market, according to Staff Working Draft, Proposed Bill S.415, March 15, 2001. In June 2001, United announced its withdrawal from the US Airways acquisition agreement. Although it was not

Interestingly, the aviation industry was singled out for the deregulation experiment because it was believed to differ from the standard public utility model. While it had been traditionally assumed that the industry is naturally competitive, after deregulation it shares many similarities with monopolies that are typically regulated according to public utility standards. There have been new and mounting pressures for antitrust enforcement, competition-encouraging intervention policies, and even re-regulation. The post-deregulation industry has evolved from a price-regulated cartel of mostly linear city-pairs and simple hub structures into a concentrated, antitrust-monitored oligopoly of complex networks with market power concentrated at the hub airports' level.

## 2. SOCIAL REGULATION: SAFETY AND NOISE

Government intervention through "social" regulation has become more apparent and more pervasive than ever before. While the government is no longer directly involved in price-setting decisions, it now directly affects almost every aspect of an air carrier's operation through safety and environmental regulation, as well as other intervention instruments, in extremely complex ways. Any aspect of day-to-day ground or air operation, including aspects of corporate structure and culture, detailed financial conditions, and cockpit manners, may be directly or indirectly connected with or related to safety. Thus, through this door, the regulators in fact touch every aspect of airline operation.

Regulation of this sort is manifested through a detailed, complex, and often ambiguous and controversial set of order and command rules. These regulations affect both industry cost structures and expansion patterns. It is noteworthy that although the 1978 Deregulation Act generally deregulated entry of new startup airlines, the government still directly controls certification of new startup airlines for financial fitness—the Department of Transportation (DOT) and safety— the Federal Aviation Administration (FAA).[7] The mechanisms of slot allocation, as well as control over infrastructure (airport and air traffic control), further influence industry expansion patterns. Increased safety and environmental regulation have affected the industry cost structure, as they intensify financial certification requirements and raise other barriers to entry. The regulators' role with regard to safety issues also puts the government into a position to significantly influence the public's perception of airline safety, which directly impacts demand for air travel.

Post-deregulation maintenance and safety rules and regulations have evolved from general guidelines that airlines viewed as minimum standards into extremely detailed manuals of specific mandatory actions, rules, and customs. The FAA is much more involved with safety and maintenance standards than it ever had been. The impact of this involvement is also more complex and controversial. In fact, the post-deregulation FAA prescribes and enforces detailed and specific day-to-day practices and actions.

consummated as planned, this agreement reflects the mega-airlines' tendency to increase market share and concentration.

[7] According to DOT, between 1989 and October 2000, 56 airlines had their operational certificates revoked by the regulator; 42 start-up applications were dismissed; and 2 denied.

Involvement like this should pose some fundamental questions as to the economic efficiency of safety regulation, because of the incentive structure inherent in the structure of safety and maintenance regulatory institutions and related agency problems.

## 2.1 Contestable markets

As we look at the evolution of the industry since deregulation, there is no way to escape the conclusion that the contestable markets doctrine has played a paradoxical role in airline deregulation. The concept came to enjoy celebrity status. It was then twisted and turned, used and abused by legislators, regulators, and the industry to advocate for particular agendas long after it had lost its allure in academic circles. This is obviously not the first time both politicians and the public have perceived empirically untested positive hypotheses in terms of general, simplistic, and intuitively attractive stories, detached from the specific underlying assumptions of an analytic model, and completely disregarding important methodological considerations.

Deregulation advocates during the 1970s and 1980s perceived the contestable markets idea as a deregulation theory. It was adopted with related Chicago School *laissez-faire* ideas as a "scientific" justification for airline deregulation by consumer advocates; by conservatives who believed in curtailing the government's role in the market; by the regulator (the CAB); and by the government itself.

No one who did not directly experience this period in aviation history can appreciate the significance of this idea and its powerful influence on what seemed then a major revolution in the interpretation of industry behavior. The adoption of this point of view had overwhelming subsequent policy implications.

The contestable markets concept ultimately became a rationale for avoiding antitrust intervention during most of the post-deregulation 1980s. If potential competition could be expected to restrain airlines from charging super-normal fares, there would be no need to apply standard antitrust criteria regarding industry concentration. In this respect, the model came to justify a generally conservative line of *laissez-faire* policies including a relaxed position toward the horizontal integration that had long been a major traditional antitrust target.

In fact, the contestable markets model was turned virtually on its head in order to justify the imposition of a new type of social regulation in the late 1980s and 1990s. Legislators and regulators argued that since the market is contestable (turning the model's prediction into an assumption, or axiom), imposing costly safety and environmental regulations that increase airline costs and diminish overall production would not impact the competitiveness of the industry.

Completely ignored was that the airlines were never uniform in terms of production technology; that the new type of regulation impacted the industry's overall costs in a non-uniform way; and that it raised sunk costs. These are facts that violate the basic assumptions of the model and therefore changed its prediction. Ironically, while economists were questioning the validity of the model (noticing the non-conforming empirical evidence) and focusing on the possibility that even a small sunk cost might have a significant impact, regulators were using the same model to justify increasing sunk costs, mostly by imposing new safety and noise regulations.

An economist cannot help but note that while the contestable markets idea was embraced by politicians and regulators and made to justify airline deregulation, a far more developed body of theory dealing with the regulation of externalities was paid no serious attention.

## 2.2    Interest Groups

Noise and safety regulations evolved in response to the industry's developing interest group structure and political power. Before the late 1980s, only minor efforts were made to abate noise, despite dramatic increases in aircraft operations, in residents' complaints, and in pressure by environmental groups. The regulator acted largely as a cartel manager. It protected the airlines' interests and used the industry's financial condition and capacity considerations as an excuse for no action on noise regulation. Things changed quite significantly during the middle and late 1980s, as the industry became more diverse with respect to fleet structure, financial condition, and political power. New heterogeneous intraindustry interest structures started to play an increasing role.

Backed by a small group of the largest and most powerful major airlines and the aircraft manufacturers, the regulator in the late 1980s and early 1990s started to launch noise and safety regulations of unprecedented scope. This coalition, in effect, captured the new regulatory process to serve its strategic interests. The result was major regulatory initiatives that often diverge from standard economic efficiency principles.

One of the coalition's major influences was an effort to do away with the used aircraft market, thus raising rival airlines' costs and barriers to entry. The new regulations set detailed standards and mandated means of compliance in an overreaction to concerns about the safety and environmental acceptability of previous-generation aircraft. This eventually imposed proportionally more of a burden on financially weaker airlines and new entrants.

It is noteworthy that the presence of a used aircraft market was an important factor for advocates of deregulation in the late 1970s, as it was believed the availability of such aircraft would significantly reduce the capital threshold of new entries, which would thus not have to acquire new and expensive aircraft.[8] Exacting safety and noise abatement rules have ended up making older aircraft more expensive to acquire and operate and accelerated their retirement, thus directly affecting the ease of entry and the industry's overall fixed cost structure.

## 3.  BUST AND BOOM AND BUST ...

I spent most of my time during 1991 repossessing aircraft due to airline default or bankruptcy, or otherwise negotiating and restructuring aircraft loan and lease

---

[8] See, for example, CAB (1975, p. 110).

agreements. It continued this way for the next three years as well. The airlines I dealt with were mainly financially weak ones (Pan Am, Eastern, TWA, Midway, Continental, and Braniff). The demise of Pan American was particularly sad. Pan Am was the very symbol of aviation pioneering and a proud example of the American spirit and presence throughout the world. Its collapse in 1992 is emblematic of the failure of the archetypal business model of a pre-deregulation airline to adjust to the challenges of free market competition.

By the end of 1991, it had become apparent that the financial crisis had accumulated more steam and was starting to take its toll on the financially strong airlines as well. At one time in the early 1990s, the ability of the strong major airlines to survive was seriously in doubt. Highly leveraged, crippled by high fuel and labor costs, battered by price wars and weakened by a poor economy, the airlines' future looked quite grim, and talks about bust, gloom, and re-regulation were rife.

Signs of an industry rebound became clear only in the middle 1990s. United, American, and Delta Airlines emerged from the crisis as the industry's indisputable major winners, stronger than ever before and best positioned to reap the benefit of improving economic conditions and the subsequent economic boom into the end of the decade.

*3.1    Antitrust*

The industry by then had evolved into two clearly identifiable groups. On one side were the major network airlines, offering complex global reach, including seamless interlining with network members, and making extensive use of price discrimination based on passengers' demand elasticity. On the other side was the low-cost, low-fare group, with only one significant member reflecting a singular market success—Southwest—offering simple fares, mostly point-to-point travel, and making only limited use of price discrimination.

During the second half of the 1990s, it seemed to have become accepted that new entries were doomed to fail, and except for the expansion of Southwest, no meaningful startup or other market entry appeared to threaten the majors' hegemony. The strong market position and power of the leading network airlines appeared unchallenged. By this time, many observers had abandoned any notion that the airline industry is naturally competitive and that actual and potential entry would restrain fares. The hub-and-spoke strategy was often perceived as an inherent impediment to competition.

Major hubs were associated with market power and monopolistic distortions and were viewed as a source of economic inefficiencies. Hubs were called *fortresses,* and a hub strategy was believed to limit access to essential facilities and entry. When the major airlines used fare-discriminating techniques, this was seen as an exercise of their market power. Several empirical studies of fares identified significant and substantial hub premiums charged by the major airlines on flights from and to such hubs. Reduced fares in response to new entry and increased spreads between fares were perceived as examples of predatory pricing. Then, increasing flight frequency and load factors, especially in the late 1990s, put operational pressures on the majors' network systems, resulting in increasing congestion and delays, along with passengers' overall dissatisfaction with service quality.

During the late 1990s the government and public representatives initiated unprecedented multiple antitrust and regulatory actions against the major airlines. There was an increasing conviction that free market competition had failed to restrain fares and encourage service quality and a conclusion that the government must intervene or the majors would continue to increase market power.

Responding to this opinion, the government initiated regulatory efforts to specify what would count as fair and acceptable competitive conduct by the airlines, to define and protect passenger rights, and to encourage new entry and competition. The government assumed a strong stance against domestic and international code-sharing and other integration and cooperation attempts initiated by the majors. In addition, the Department of Justice launched an ambitious suit against American Airlines for alleged predatory behavior toward several startup airlines.

Antitrust authorities argued that these efforts were necessary in order to protect consumers and assure competition. Antitrust opponents, however, emphasized the economic benefits of large compatible airline networks and claimed that these efforts were protecting *competitors* and not encouraging *free competition,* and were in fact undesirable attempts to re-regulate the industry using antitrust action rather than *economic regulation* tools.

## 3.2    Competition

The 1990s opened with serious concerns regarding the long-term viability of the airlines industry and calls for government intervention to prevent its collapse. They ended with different serious concerns: that the major airlines had become monopolists, and government intervention would be needed in order to control their market power. Antitrust proponents saw the major airlines' behavior of the late 1990s as the epitome of monopolistic evil; they were charging monopolistic fares on hub routes, using predatory fares to ward off new entry, and becoming uninterested in service quality. They believed that the industry exemplified a traditional static monopoly, and put pressures on the government to increase antitrust enforcement.

But looking more closely and beyond the traditional structural industry statistics, revealed a different picture. Undoubtedly there were only a few winning airlines, and they were very big, and dominated markets, and used discriminatory fare techniques. And undoubtedly there were also no meaningful new entries to challenge the majors, except for Southwest. Yet the industry's earnings trend—while showing a few good years—was anything but super-normal even during the booming last half of the decade.

If any airline were able to generate constantly positive returns, it was Southwest, which flew mostly linear, non-hub, routes and charged simpler and lower fares. Southwest became the only significant free market response to the major networks' dominance. It managed to force them to reduce fares on competing markets, and it became a favorite of the regulator and of proponents of the free market concept. At the same time, it also developed into a very big major airline, dominating most of its routes, and becoming the only airline to consistently earn super-normal profits. In terms of traditional economics it seemed puzzling that the free market response to the majors' dominance was . . . an airline with monopolistic characteristics.

At this time, all the major airlines were very concerned with actual and potential competition, constantly experimenting with changes and innovations, and pushing to further increase consolidation and integration with rival networks. This picture does not match the traditional notion of static monopolistic power or the traditional concepts of naturally competitive markets. If the leading major airlines were so powerful and could block entry and charge monopolistic fares, as antitrust proponents argued, why couldn't they maintain super-normal profits or even normal profits over time? Why did they attempt further consolidation and integration with rival airline networks? Moreover, the use of price discrimination techniques did indeed widen the spread between high and low fares, but average real fares declined and the industry's profit margins could not sustain even normal rates over time.

During the second half of the year 2000—before the events of September 11, 2001, and while antitrust authorities were focusing on the major airlines' monopolistic power and predatory pricing practices—the majors began to realize that they were losing altitude, and largely because of their pricing strategies. Business and other high-fare paying passengers, who for several years had generated a disproportionately large part of the majors' total revenue, disappeared. The reason was the economic downturn and worldwide recession, but also passenger frustration with price discrimination and a perception that this pricing strategy was unfair. The network pricing strategy, which had attracted much antitrust attention, invited new entry and in fact became a critical element in explaining the failure of the major airlines' business model but for reasons of free market dynamics and not antitrust intervention.

If many observers thought at the end of the 1990s that the major network airlines had become too strong and were using their power to limit competition and extract super-normal profits, they thought in the early 2000s that the majors might be doomed to go the way of the dinosaur. Calls for government antitrust intervention were replaced with calls for government financial assistance in order to keep the majors flying. Once looked at as invincible, the major hub network airlines were now struggling for survival. For the first time since deregulation, they faced meaningful competition from low-cost mostly point-to-point airlines.

The group of low-fare startups adopted different strategies and responded differently to different market opportunities, but they share several characteristics. Two points are salient in this regard. First, elements of size and scale have played an important role in the new startups. Each one of them has attempted to create the "next big thing" and establish itself as a big winning major airline.

Second, startup members attempted to innovate and offer new alternatives in direct strategic response to the main strategic strongholds of the dominant incumbent airlines. Most of these strongholds had also topped the regulators' antitrust agenda and efforts. For example, the weaknesses of the hub-and-spoke concept—which had been considered the source of the majors' monopolistic power—became the target of the non-stop point-to-point alternative. Price discrimination—considered by many observers a direct manifestation of market power—became a target of low, simple, and "fair" fares. The computerized reservation system and agent commission overrides—which gave the major incumbents a unique advantage—lost a significant part of their power when startups began to use internet booking and ticketing and avoiding agents and their costs. In this environment the effectiveness of fare discrimination and traditional yield management significantly eroded.

Most startup airlines also seized a market opportunity to acquire new aircraft, a move traditionally open only to the financially strong major incumbents. The September 11$^{th}$ and subsequent crisis forced the struggling major incumbents to cut aircraft capacity and largely eliminated them as potential buyers of new aircraft, at least temporarily. The manufacturers, on the other hand, encumbered with enormous fixed costs and downwardly rigid labor and other production capacity constraints, turned to the startup airlines, accommodating them by significantly cutting acquisition costs and providing financial and other support. Surprisingly, the traditional coalition between the manufacturers and the financially strong major incumbents—the coalition that had pushed for regulation to eliminate the market for old aircraft—fell apart. A new ad hoc coalition developed to respond to the new market reality when the manufacturers supported the startup airlines and threatened the market hegemony of the major incumbents.

Will complex hub network airlines follow in the way of the dinosaur? Will point-to-point airlines eventually dominate the market? Is the competition we observe now in fact a battle between two competing standards, linear versus network, for market dominance? Given the current environment and industry history, which of the airlines in the complex network and the point-to-point segments will survive? How will the market structure evolve? Will the startup airlines stick to point-to-point operation as a long-term strategy, or will they adopt hub network operations? Or will we see a combination of both?

## 4. HAS DEREGULATION BEEN SUCCESSFUL?

The two major trends that have affected the aviation industry are first, price and entry deregulation, and second, environmental and safety regulation. Regulators have moved from the first stance—directly setting fares and controlling entry—to the second—directly affecting production processes and costs. Then the increased consolidation and concentration in the industry during the 1990s following deregulation has focused significant antitrust attention on airline conduct.

Deregulation in the airline industry is usually perceived as having been successful in eliminating inefficient government intervention. The reality, though, is that post-deregulation intervention in the form of social regulation is stronger and more pervasive than under traditional regulation, although it is manifested in different and new ways. The public perception that deregulation might have prompted airlines to cut back on safety and environmental protection underlies the public interest rationale for a more complex and still wide-ranging government regulation of the industry. If economic regulation was pushed out one door, social regulation was invited welcomed in at another; one form of regulation has been substituted for another.

The move from economic to social regulation, and the increased public demand for intervention of this nature, has accelerated the adoption of and perhaps the demand for new and more complex regulations. The new focus for regulation is technological and information-related issues that are by their nature ambiguous, fragmented, and contentious—fertile ground for the development of interest group politics and rent-seeking.

And then, a sense of doom and bust in the early 1990s and again in the early 2000s raised concerns regarding the long-run economic viability of the industry, requests from the government for financial aid, and even calls for the re-regulation or nationalization of the industry. The terrorist threats we have become familiar with in the aftermath of the September 11th events generated demand for even more new government security regulation and intervention.

An accurate economic evaluation of deregulation must take into account the simultaneous trends of price and entry deregulation and the combined antitrust, safety, and environmental re-regulation pressures. While some observers continue to celebrate the success of airline deregulation in the old sense of regulation of price and entry, they largely overlook the impact of the second trend: the social re-regulation of the industry.

The court of economic opinion is still out as to whether airline deregulation has proven to be successful. I'd say judging deregulation as a success or failure is largely a pointless exercise. Deregulation is not a controlled experiment. We have no objective yardstick for a standard. While the current airlines industry is better in many ways than before deregulation and it is clear that deregulation have improved on many of the previous regime's failures, we will never know how regulation would have evolved, absent deregulation, or how it would have evolved if different institutions and rules had been adopted to reform it. Neither regulation nor a particular deregulation regime has been efficient by traditional standard yardsticks; deregulation in effect has substituted one imperfect institutional arrangement for another.

PART 1

# ECONOMIC DEREGULATION

# CHAPTER 1

# DEREGULATION

*Consolidation, Concentration, Globalization*

> Service quality and price would be
> highly responsive to demand because
> of the immediate threat of new entry
> even in markets served by a single
> carrier (CAB, 1975, p. 1).

The deregulation of the aviation industry has attracted much academic attention, both before and since the Deregulation Act of 1978. Contributing to this were the direct involvement of prominent economists in the deregulation process, and the existence of a large database relating to the industry's performance, ripe for manipulation in econometric models. There is thus an impressive body of literature dealing with this issue. For economists, the deregulation of the aviation industry became a closely watched real-life experiment.

## 1.  WHAT DID WE EXPECT?

It is generally held that the economic discipline played an important role in developing the conceptual grounds for the deregulation movement and in supporting the political process that led to its implementation. Two related concepts— usually referred to as the *contestable market theory*—played a major role in the deregulation of the aviation industry. The first is embodied in the general Chicago School view. The second lies in the analytical formulation of a contestable markets model by Baumol, Paznar, and Willing (1982). Both concepts were translated into the notion that the industry is naturally competitive, and thus regulation must be eliminated.

### 1.1  *Contestable Markets*

Neither of the two views represents a model of deregulation, nor do they admit aspects of market processes. The Baumol, Paznar, and Willing (1982) formulation is an analytic statement of the properties of possible market equilibrium under certain unique assumptions. The Chicago view has never been developed into a coherent formal model of potential competition at all. Both views play down the traditional notion of barriers to entry, including economies of scale and the advantages of incumbency.

23

One of the major implications of both views is that market concentration should not, by itself, be a determinant of price or necessarily an indication of market failure. In general, these views provide an economic rationale in favor of expanding the *laissez-faire* doctrine to certain monopolistic or oligopolistic industries. Traditional perfect market theory suggests that atomistic markets tend to be efficient since super-normal profits would attract *actual* new entry. According to the new view, the *threat of potential* entry in response to super-normal pricing (and not an actual entry itself) is sufficient to discipline prices if entry and exit are relatively easy. The general metaphor used in this regard is that the threat of potential "hit and run" competition on a "city-pair" market would restrain fares.

For the Chicago School, the contestable markets idea was only one building block within a comprehensive framework that supports curtailing government intervention in markets. Moreover, it tied in neatly with Stigler's *industry capture* concept. Since, it was argued, there are no major obstacles to entry or exit in a typical aviation market, there is no "real" public interest rationale for regulation. Rather, the airlines effectuate the regulatory process in an attempt to eliminate actual and potential entry.

The contestable markets idea was embraced by politicians and regulators during the middle 1970s and early 1980s and raised to iconic status. There was general public frustration with government performance that was translated into a simple political and popular message pushing for the elimination of government regulation, in general, and in the aviation industry in particular. For Democrats, deregulation was perceived as a pro-consumer policy; for Republicans, it implied limiting the government's role in the market.

There was a wide consensus that the airline industry was an ideal candidate for deregulation, that the specific rules and institutions used in regulating the aviation industry had failed, and that a major revision or reform was imminent. Interestingly, even the regulators questioned the wisdom of airline regulation. A Civil Aeronautics Board Special Staff Report published in July 1975 reflected the dominant view at the time, arguing that: "The industry is naturally competitive, not monopolistic. In the absence of economic regulation, it is clear that monopoly abuses would not occur" (CAB, 1975, p. 1).

The only major opponents to deregulation were the major airlines, taking a stance that of course enhanced the notion that interest group politics and industry capture aspects were responsible for regulation to begin with and further justified its elimination.

Economists during this period offered a new political message, shifting from the traditional call for the regulation of industries in the public interest to the deregulation of industry in the public interest—a message that was enthusiastically adopted by the public and by elected officials. The Civil Aeronautics Act of 1938, which had established the ground rules for four decades of economic regulation of the airline industry, was associated with the post-depression political view that government intervention was the remedy for failures of the free market mechanism. The 1978 Deregulation Act reflected the new view that the social cost of the cure may be greater than the costs of the failure. The post-deregulation industry was very closely monitored by economists seeking empirical proof of their hypotheses. In general, the literature may be characterized by somewhat naïve enthusiasm and celebration of the success of deregulation during its first stages and until the middle 1980s. Later came surprise and perhaps some disappointment in light of the generally unexpected outcome of the experiment. Most economists and public officials did not expect the industry to evolve the way it has, despite the consensus that the current outcome is superior to government regulation.

Expectations as to further concentration, along with concerns over increasing fares in the late 1990s, have prompted antitrust initiatives against major airlines for alleged predatory behavior and have encouraged stricter stands against potential increases in major airlines' market power through takeovers and strategic alliances. Political initiatives aimed at protecting passenger rights and improving service have also been launched. The industry has moved from a government-regulated cartel in the late 1970s to an antitrust-monitored oligopoly consisting of a smaller number of larger airlines.

This evolutionary path may suggest that the aviation industry has inherent natural monopoly characteristics, perhaps because of significant fixed costs and other particular network characteristics. Paradoxically, the widely held pre-deregulation view of economists and regulators was the absence of such characteristics in the industry, which is why the aviation industry was viewed as an ideal candidate for deregulation. It is ironic that the structure that has evolved makes the post-deregulation industry closer than ever to the traditional natural monopoly model.

Did pre-deregulation scholars and industry observers misinterpret the inherent characteristics of the industry? Did they misjudge the impact of economy of scale, scope, density, and other advantages of network size? Did they miss the fact that the industry possesses natural monopolistic characteristics? Is the contestable market model irrelevant to the aviation industry, after all, for reasons of the significant impact of sunk costs or incumbents' ability to swiftly and aggressively cut prices in response to entry? Was the potential impact of "small" sunk costs misjudged? In the 1970s and early 1980s the concept of strategic behavior was not as developed in the economic literature as it is now. Did we miss the power of strategic behavior and non-price quantitative competition to alter market structure? The network view attracted attention only in the late 1980s. Did we lose in predictive power by using a city-pair as a market metaphor rather than a complex network metaphor?

I believe the answer to all these questions is yes. Most important, we failed to predict that industry strategic behavior in the post-deregulation era would permit the airlines to innovate and change technology, market structure, and the rules of the game the way they have. In particular, the major airlines moved to transform the industry structure from a relatively simple, mostly linear, city-pair network structure into a complex hub-and-spoke structure. In the new structure fixed costs, sunk costs, and economies of scale, scope, density, and size play a major role, together with other strategic advantages. In such a structure, strategic behavior has been a factor as never before.

*1.2   Route Franchising During Regulation*

It is not that regulation-era airlines did not compete fiercely or behave strategically. On the contrary, tactical and strategic competition was very strong, and at times ruthless. It took place, however, in a very specific and limited number of channels as dictated by the institutions and rules of regulation. While the CAB controlled route franchising, strategic behavior was expressed in the form of exertion of political power and influence over the CAB and the administration in an attempt to obtain desirable route authorities.

A good example was evident during the congressional hearings that led to the Deregulation Act of 1978. Among the stories were: illegal contributions by American Airlines and Braniff to President Nixon's reelection fund; allegations of conspiracy, abuse of power, and illegal funneling of unreported ticket revenues to secret accounts; the suicide of a CAB enforcement officer who was engaged in investigating an airline's conduct, and so on. If scandals and allegations of conspiracy regarding the allocation of route authority to airlines by the Postmaster General motivated the Airline Regulation Act of 1938, scandals and allegations of conspiracy with regard to the CAB and the administration also accompanied the Deregulation Act of 1978.

Under regulation, route authorities were allocated to airlines through a regulatory, bureaucratic process. In an ideal world, one could conceive of the regulator (CAB) as a central (benevolent) planner designing an efficient integrated route system. Planning under regulation like this could take advantage of positive network effects from both supply and demand sides and balance aspects of cost efficiency with market power. In fact, the dominant pattern of pre-deregulation wisdom was to largely ignore network effects and the related advantages to scale, scope, and size. It was believed that the industry lacks increasing return characteristics. The role of the CAB was mostly defined as protection of the airlines against "destructive competition" by limiting price competition and entry. It also forced extension of airline service into small communities that otherwise could not attract flights, while cross-subsidizing these flights by fixing higher fares on other routes. The CAB effectively acted as a cartel manager and was mostly concerned with eliminating any possible entry and price competition, particularly in relation to routes that cross-subsidized small community markets.

For example, according to the 1938 Act, non-scheduled carriers were excluded from regulation as were cargo charter carriers and local service airlines (intrastate). Much of the regulatory energy was focused on reducing the competitive pressures of these groups against the major trunk airlines. The CAB fought any attempt by non-regulated airlines to threaten the hegemony of the cartel members. Proponents of deregulation related several anecdotes to portray the absurdity of regulation. One popular story is the CAB's legal battle against fare cuts offered by the (non-regulated) local service airlines operating on the Los Angeles–San Francisco route. This story featured prominently in the Congressional hearings preceding deregulation. The Chicago School used the story to illustrate the failure of government regulation.[9] It seemed as if the poster child of an industry-captured regulator was protecting its cartel members and using the judicial system to force lower-cost firms to charge consumers higher prices in order to protect the less efficient members of the cartel.

The CAB's route allocation policy was arguably inconsistent and lacked clear and coherent network planning. This is usually explained by its attempts to fight fires while it responded to interest group pressure. In hindsight, however, we can identify a failure to perceive the market in terms of an integrated network system as it is perceived today. To the CAB the industry was merely a simple aggregation of linear, point-to-point (origin to destination) city-pairs. Now we can see that many of the CAB policies were in conflict with the wisdom of the network view of the industry that gained in popularity starting the late 1980s. Regulation-era markets were, in general, more integrated across major airlines than the current structure. At the same time, however, no serious attempts were made to create an efficient system of coordinated networks with easy access, easy switching, and integrated scheduling.

In fact, the CAB usually licensed two or three trunk airlines in most major city-pair routes. This policy accommodated some pressure by several airlines to obtain a route authority, but it encouraged duplication of resources on the same routes as well as non-price competition. When an airline was forced to fly a non-desirable small community service, the CAB cross-subsidized the airline by providing a monopolistic position in another desirable route. Consequently, the regulated market evolved mostly as a system, that could often be better explained by interest group politics rather than overall network efficiency considerations. Interestingly, the smaller, non-regulated local service airlines developed local hub networks and operated at significant lower cost than trunk airlines despite their relative shorter hauls.

*1.3    Free Markets*

Deregulation was intended to do away with the regulatory process of route franchising. It was expected that the free market mechanism would allocate routes better than regulation had. It was expected, in particular, that the threat of new entry would be sufficiently strong to discipline fares. Alfred Kahn, Chairman of the CAB, argued, for example, that:

> A realistic threat of entry (by new and existing carriers) on the initiative of management alone is the essential element of competition. Without it, market regulation is ineffective. It is only this threat that makes it possible to leave to management a wider measure of discretion over pricing: The threat of entry will hold excessive price increase in check.[10]

---

[9] See, for example, Freedman (1990).

[10] Cited in Senate Committee on Commerce, Science and Transportation, S. 2493 dated Feb. 6, 1978, p. 59. Note, however, that a minority view in the same document predicted a different outcome: "The five major carriers will inevitably acquire most of the traffic ... at the expense of the smaller carriers which would become progressively less effective competitors. The ultimate result would be monopoly

The Deregulation Act provided for a transition period when the airlines were supposed to adjust to the new environment. In fact, aggressive competition by the airlines and an inconsistent (but mostly hands-off) CAB policy brought about deregulation before its intended formal date.

The most noticeable and most profound post-deregulation change saw the industry shift from a largely linear or otherwise simple hub network system into a complex, highly concentrated, system with dominant hubs. American Airlines' strategic move in this direction (1981) symbolizes the beginning of this trend. During the early 1980s the airlines moved to set up or take over hub-and-spoke systems. They used a host of other strategic moves to "fortify" their hubs and further increase their dominance. The major strategic moves included mergers and takeovers of other airlines, strategic use of computerized reservation systems, bonus commissions to travel agents, frequent flier plans, and code-sharing and other strategic alliances with regional commuter airlines.

Digital technology allows extremely sophisticated planning and management of fares, scheduling, and capacity, and represents an asset in use of these factors as tactical or strategic variables. Both long-term overall capacity (fleet) planning and capacity offered on a specific single city-pair route have an important strategic impact on competition. Excess capacity at a hub level, for example, signals a credible threat that may deter potential entry. If a competitor is not impressed with such implicit strength, or otherwise decides to actually operate a route into another airline's major hub, it may face a "capacity dumping" response.

In the following I examine in more detail the evolution of the industry from its pre-deregulation, mostly simple, linear structure, to its current complex and global network structure. The first two sections focus on the immediate post-deregulation period and the airlines' strategic move to create dominant hub networks. The next three sections focus on the network consolidation, concentration, and globalization trends, that have characterized the industry since the early 1980s. The last section touches upon the debate regarding the economic efficiency of the unfolding structure.

## 2. THE BIRTH OF THE MAJOR INTEGRATED HUB

The intuition behind the contestable markets idea, as applied to the aviation market, seemed convincing during the early 1980s. The airline market was perceived as an amalgam of simple linear routes connecting city-pairs. The product (a seat on an aircraft serving a city-pair market) was assumed homogeneous. The major airlines were assumed to use similar production technologies and to have homogeneous cost structures. An airplane was perceived as the main component of fixed entry cost. An airplane is mobile and not specific to a certain city-pair market; therefore, it could be moved to other markets in response to above-normal fares.

---

or oligopoly ... simply because there would be no restraint on the growth of the large carriers" (p. 220).

The major reason the air travel market seemed to fit the contestable markets metaphor stems from the notion that fixed-cost aircraft are not market-specific. They could therefore be moved across markets with negligible sunk costs in "hit and run" competition. Aircraft were perceived as *capital investments on wheels,* and under these conditions the threat of potential competition was expected to play a major role in curtailing airline market power.

As is typical in application of equilibrium models of this nature, analysts paid no attention to the dynamic transition process that was expected to reshape a regulated cartel—with given initial conditions and history—into a competitive industry with sustainable levels of price and output as suggested by the theory. There is nothing in the contestable markets theory to suggest that the airlines industry would necessarily follow a path that would bring it to a quasi-competitive equilibrium as predicted by the model. In fact, this has not happened.

Failure of the contestable markets model to predict the evolution of the industry is usually explained by two major lines of reasoning. First, even small sunk costs may have a significant impact. Second, the speed of an incumbent's price reaction to entry may play an important role.

There are several points worth emphasizing in this connection. First, the industry in the late 1970s was, in fact, not homogeneous in terms of production technology and cost structure. This is a violation of one of the model's basic assumptions. In many respects, this one fact has had a major impact on the movement of the industry away from the model's predictions. The established airlines' circumstances fit a standard neoclassical long-run adjustment to *actual* lower-cost competition rather than adjustment to pricing in the face of *potential* competition. The major incumbent airlines faced *actual* competition from more cost-efficient airlines, and the question was how to survive this competition.

Second, the abstract view of an airplane as a non-sunk cost connecting a city-pair diverted attention from the fact that an aircraft must take off and land, and for this purpose it needs airports. Furthermore, passengers must be attracted into the aircraft cabins, and maintenance and other ground activity must be provided. The costs that are related to operating and maintaining these components of the market are location-specific and sunk.

Third, facing relatively rigid and high fixed costs, the major incumbents turned to strategic action that would allow them to survive despite initial differential cost structures. One such major action was the creation of a complex network of routes with major hubs.

The move to create hub-and-spoke systems made location-specific fixed sunk costs extremely significant in the overall cost structure and created barriers to entry far beyond anyone's expectations. In this respect, even if one were to be convinced that sunk costs and other barriers to entry were negligible before and immediately after deregulation, incumbent strategic behavior made them quite significant thereafter. Strategic actions of incumbents and the reshaping of the industry gave a clear advantage to the surviving major incumbents over new competitors in a manner that was inconceivable before deregulation.

## 2.1 Opening Conditions

In October 1978, Congress passed the Deregulation Act, catching airlines generally unprepared. On the eve of deregulation the industry had exhibited heterogeneity in cost characteristics across major (trunk) and non-major groups of airlines and among airlines within each group. Airlines overall differed in their fleet structures and labor contracts, two of the major elements that determine an airline's cost structure. They also differed in the structure of their route systems. Four decades of price regulation had accommodated high aircraft capacity and continually increasing labor costs by fare hikes. Route franchising policies had created somewhat unbalanced route systems. United, on the one hand, had the best-integrated and most efficient domestic system. Pan Am, on the other hand, had a monopolistic position in international markets but almost no domestic base. High fuel prices made the first generation aircraft, especially the 707s and the DC8s that were designed prior to the fuel crisis of the mid-1970s, relatively expensive to operate. These four-engine aircraft consumed more fuel and required more passengers in order to break even and were hard hit by surging oil prices, as well as by the recessionary impact on load factors.

The new aircraft delivery cycle of the early 1970s provided the major airlines with a relatively high number of more efficient, high-capacity, widebody jumbo jets. These aircraft, however, required high-density, long-range markets in order to break even and therefore could be operated economically only in a few high-density markets that remained strong despite the recession.

In general, the financially weaker airlines operated more of the less fuel-efficient aircraft. They faced a competitive disadvantage in operating costs, as well as financial constraints to entering fleet restructuring programs with new and more expensive aircraft. Lenders were reluctant to finance aggressive fleet restructuring programs, and the public debt market assigned highly speculative investment grades to airline debt. Economic slow down and world recession during the late 1970s and early 1980s reduced load factors, fleet utilization, and revenues, putting the acquisition of new aircraft farther out of reach. Withdrawing service of less profitable routes, retiring older-generation aircraft, initiating labor layoffs, and renegotiating of labor contracts were the only major policy choices available to airlines at the time.

The industry challenge was to adjust to a new market regime in face of a revenue collapse due to severe recession and doubled fuel prices. For most airlines, these steps implied contraction in an attempt to reduce costs.

It is important to understand the specific economic conditions of that period and to appreciate their impact on the industry and by extension their implications for deregulation. The advent of deregulation coincided with a worldwide recession and an industry economic crisis. The 1973 oil crisis and recession dramatically impacted the industry. In fact, after more than a decade of an average annual world industry growth of 14%, the industry, for the first time in the jet age, fell to approximately 3% average growth during the years 1973 to 1975 (Boeing, 1991).

Besides significant reductions in the demand for air travel due to recession, oil prices, which constitute a major operational cost component, dramatically affected the supply side. In 1979, airline operational growth (revenue passenger mile - RPM) fell for the first time in aviation history toward 0%.

It was under these specific economic conditions that the industry entered deregulation, and this circumstance has many important implications. Two of them are important for the development of my argument.

First, the economic conditions during early deregulation made major incumbent airlines different in terms of costs. In general terms, one can distinguish between two major production technologies available for airlines (or combinations of them): the first, capital-intensive (purchase of new aircraft) and the second, fuel and maintenance-intensive (operation of "old" aircraft). The financially stronger airlines operated more new aircraft in their fleets, and had relatively higher fixed costs (the acquisition cost of more expensive new aircraft) and lower operating costs (new aircraft in general involve lower fuel and maintenance costs). The economic difference between these two major groups and the subsequent impact on the airlines' cost structure became more significant as fuel prices increased and as new fuel-efficient aircraft were introduced into the market. The oil crisis starting in 1973 generated great cost heterogeneity within the major incumbent airlines, depending on the composition of their fleets and their particular route structures.

The second important happening is that the particular economic conditions in the late 1970s and early 1980s encouraged both the entry of new low-cost startup airlines and the expansion of small incumbents. Entry of new airlines into the market is usually constrained particularly by physical factors, the most obvious of which is the availability of aircraft and airport space. Entry is also constrained by the fixed availability of air and ground crews. That is, if input markets are in equilibrium or all available stock of aircraft and or airport space is employed, new entry is constrained.

The worldwide economic conditions of the late 1970s and early 1980s created a worldwide overcapacity of aircraft at low market rates. In addition, unemployed crews and other airline personnel and gates and airport space were available and could be hired or acquired by new startup airlines for very attractive prices. These airlines were free from contracts with labor unions, and airport authorities and other pre-deregulation commitments that implied high overhead costs and structural rigidities to incumbent airlines. Unemployed crews, mechanics, and other airline personnel could be hired at cheaper rates. This economic environment lured a new group of airlines that enjoyed a different cost structure and an operational freedom not easily available to the major incumbents. New entrants, for example, could use maintenance outsourcing while incumbents were tied to high-cost agreements for in-house maintenance. New entrants could also hire non-unionized labor.

Entry of new, discount "no frills" airlines into the market further contributed to the evolving industry heterogeneity. In this respect, a major incumbent airline faced both real and potential competition from 1) members of its own group; 2) incumbent airlines from a smaller regional group of airlines that enjoyed cost advantages (such as Southwest Airlines), and 3) previously non-regulated niche airlines (such as

World Airlines), and 4) new startups that took advantage of favorable input market conditions (like People's Express).

United Airlines was the largest carrier at the time of deregulation. It was also perhaps the best-positioned major airline to take the role of the post-deregulation industry leader with its more efficient fleet mix, better-structured route network, and superior cash position. Its initial policy responses to deregulation included increasing capacity and price competition on high-density routes, abandoning low-density less profitable routes, and attempting to cut in labor costs. These were the initial choices for all major airlines, but they had little effect.

Fierce competition on high-density routes did not generate enough revenues and resulted in significant losses. The high-density, linear, city-pair routes that were targeted by all were quite vulnerable to competition (including competition by lower-cost entrants). Negotiations with labor did not produce desirable cost cuts either. United Airlines' attempts to renegotiate its labor contracts in 1979 resulted in a two-month mechanics strike that cost the airline dearly. The impact of this strike on the industry was significant, as it transmitted very clearly the difficulty of labor cost adjustments for major incumbents. Not surprisingly, labor unions strongly opposed deregulation and exhibited strong opposition to post-deregulation contract renegotiations.

## 2.2    American Airlines' Strategic Move

American Airlines was the second-largest major airline with the highest cost structure in its group. Most of American's aircraft were first-generation fuel-inefficient 707 and 727-100 aircraft. American's labor was unionized and very highly paid. Judging only by its cost structure and applying the wisdom of industrial organization models of the time, American might have been thought to have an extremely low chance of surviving deregulation as a major airline. Yet American is traditionally credited as the industry leader in making the strategic move to the hub-and-spoke structure, which ended up positioning it as one of the three largest airlines of the post-deregulation era.

All the economic models of the period emphasized the competitive importance of cost structure. Whether in response to the threat of incumbent airlines, and/or new entrants and/or potential competition, American, as a high-cost airline, felt the competition pressure perhaps more than any other major airline because of its cost structure. American seriously considered cutting costs by shrinking its size, selling aircraft, withdrawing service from less profitable routes, or even selling off part of the airline. It also thought about reformulating the airline as a non-union, low-cost airline. American achieved a certain degree of cost reduction by the pre-deregulation move of its headquarters to Dallas, the retiring of 707 aircraft, and the renegotiations of labor contracts. But these steps were not enough to combat the lower-cost competitors.

Other incumbent airlines faced similar problems. Pragmatically, cutting labor costs, withdrawing from less profitable markets, and retiring aircraft were the major immediate cost-reduction policies open to the incumbents. The airlines were caught between the threat of the new, lower-cost, non-unionized entrants and the all-too-fresh memories of the United Airlines labor strike.

American realized that conventional steps of cost-cutting were not sufficient to promise long-term survivability as a major airline, especially when an economic slowdown squeezed revenues as well. Constrained by its contracts and rigid structure, yet driven by its refusal to accept the idea of surviving deregulation as a small, non-distinct, "efficient" airline, it was understood by American that: " we had to do big, dramatic things or we were going to be out of business very soon" (Read, 1993, p. 175).

At this juncture, American took a significant leadership step, which symbolizes the change in the post-deregulation industry structure in the most critical way: It adopted a major hub strategy. In February 1981, American announced its plan to accelerate the number of flights into and out of its Dallas/Fort Worth new hub. In June, eleven new cities were added. By the end of 1981, the number of flights in and out of the Dallas hub had more than tripled to an unprecedented number of over 300 flights a day.

This event symbolizes the first major incumbent airlines' strategic move to a new complex hub-and-spoke system strategy. The move dramatically increased production, while enabling a different deployment of labor and other fixed inputs. It affected average costs and revenues but accommodated rigid labor and other fixed cost structures.

### 2.3    Hub Dominance

Hub-and-spoke structures were not new to the deregulated industry. Prior to deregulation, Delta and Eastern had developed hubs in Atlanta. United had one in Chicago, American in Dallas, and Allegheny (US Air) in Pittsburgh. It is conceivable that the industry would have evolved toward a more complex hub-and-spoke network system even had deregulation not occurred. Yet, route franchising policies of the CAB and the strict limitations on market entry, exit, and pricing kept the industry's structure rigid and limited the strategic role of the hubs in airline competition. Deregulation caused complex hub-and-spoke networks to explode almost overnight. They became a major element in airlines' strategic behavior and in the evolution of the post-deregulation industry.

About a year after American established its Dallas hub it established the Chicago O'Hare hub. United Airlines' announcement of the "High On Denver Plan" in 1982 established its strategic intention to conquer Denver as a hub. United succeeded in shutting Frontier down in 1986 and pushing Continental out in 1994, and, it then became the dominant airline in Denver. The competition between Delta and Eastern over the Atlanta hub ended with the demise of Eastern in 1991, and Delta became the dominant carrier in Atlanta.

Hub dominance was also established by merging or by entering strategic alliance agreements with other airlines. Several local service airlines entered deregulation with smaller but quite developed hubs and reacted to deregulation by expanding and strengthening their regional dominance (Western in Salt Lake City, Republic in

Detroit and Minneapolis, US Air in Pittsburgh, Piedmont in Charlotte, and Ozark in St. Louis). These airlines were acquired by major airlines (or merged) in the quest for extending networks and increasing hub power (Western was acquired by Delta, Republic by Northwest, and Ozark by TWA. PSA, Piedmont, and US Air merged).

Such mergers also eliminated low-cost competition (if you can't gobble them up, buy them!) and in certain cases, averaged down the acquiring major airline's cost. The high-profile mergers of TWA and Ozark and Northwest and Republic involved the merger of the only two hub carriers at St. Louis and Minneapolis, respectively. These mergers provided TWA and Northwest a dominant position in these hubs.[11]

Several startup airlines that understood the power of hubs in the new evolving markets attempted to establish a hub as an entry strategy. The most notable in this category is People's Express, which established a hub in Newark, New Jersey, became the success story of early deregulation, and ended up being acquired by the Texas Air Corp. and operated by Continental. Presidential Airlines was a smaller-scale attempt by People's Express veterans to duplicate the hub strategy at Dulles Airport, Washington. Presidential was swallowed up by United.

The market structure that has evolved has typical complex network characteristics. It provides airlines with new strategic behavior possibilities never before available. These include using composite products (city-pair combination, interlining, bundling), strategic locations, monopolistic bottlenecks (hubs), intra- and inter-network gateway connections, compatibility and exclusion (by scheduling and pricing, for example), price discrimination and other sophisticated pricing (yield management), horizontal and vertical mergers and foreclosures, joint ventures (strategic alliance, feeding, code-sharing), and tying (clubs, frequent flier bonus).

Deregulation has changed industry production functions, demand, and the general rules of the game so that size, scale, scope, and density in production and consumption play an important role. Small airlines and medium-sized airlines have disappeared, and size appears to provide strategic advantage. Major incumbent airlines occupy strategic market positions. Major hubs have become strategic fortresses for airlines. Their investments in such hubs signal credible commitments to fight new entrants by reducing prices or otherwise. Major airlines have maintained physical control over essential facilities through their investments in hub capacity and complex network systems. They have captured limited airport ground and air space.

Investment in overcapacity at a major hub means an airline can deter entrance and exclude competitors. American Airlines scheduled more than 700 flights every day out of Dallas/Fort Worth in the late 1990s. In this hub, only (American) eagles dare to land!

Commencing in the early 1980s, the major incumbents raced to conquer and enhance their hub power. Hub airlines provided bonus commissions and other booking incentives to local travel agents and manipulated the computerized reservation systems (CRS) in order to attract more passengers, to tie agents into their system, to exclude rivals, and to increase rivals' costs. They instituted frequent flier

---

[11] In these cases the Department of Justice opposed approval of the merger on antitrust grounds but was overruled by the Department of Transportation.

programs and established a non-linear price schedule that creates, among other things, costs of switching to another network system and increases the competitive advantage of an airline with a larger network. Participation in community politics and activities has been aimed at creating passenger loyalty and tying passengers to local hub carriers. Hub airlines have developed regional "presence" and loyalty in an attempt to capture and increase market share.

In this race to capture market base, the advantage often went to those that were first in a location and first to establish a hub or a spoke. Incumbent airlines clearly had an advantage over startups. Whenever new entrants or smaller incumbent airlines were successful in establishing a hub, they were acquired or merged into a larger incumbent airline system.

## 2.4    A Note About Strategy and Theory

American Airlines' strategic response to the new competitive threats of deregulation is emblematic of some of the major shortfalls of the traditional economic paradigm as well as the challenges of predicting market behavior in a deregulated airlines industry. According to the traditional view, a firm that cannot operate at the cost level of the most efficient firm must exit the market. This view ignores the importance of strategic behavior in real markets. In fact, American Airlines, the most vulnerable post-deregulation major incumbent, made the most dramatic move and survived as an industry leader in spite of the odds.

The traditional view portrays firms largely as passive price-takers for which technology and demand are exogenously given, and they are therefore assumed to have almost no freedom in their decision-making. The contestable markets model considers aspects of strategic behavior by incorporating a potential rival's response into a firm's pricing decision, but it focuses on pricing as the firm's only strategic variable and adopts unique assumptions about the power of easy entry and exit to discipline prices. Under full contestability assumptions, an airline is forced to price its product subject to a persistent credible threat of hit-and-run competition at a quasi-competitive level, and therefore the market is assumed to force the firm to stick to a unique equilibrium price level.

The airlines were quite aware of these economic views, which were much analyzed during the deregulation hearing process as well as behind closed doors during strategic management forums. The major incumbents realized that whether aircraft are indeed "marginal cost on wings" or "capital investment on wheels" major strategic moves must be taken in order to survive, especially in the face of threats from lower-cost competitors. During the early stages of deregulation, the major incumbents realized that costs are rigid and that highly dense linear routes are vulnerable to competition. Their problem was to survive despite these initial conditions, and, in fact, many of the major airlines' strategic moves after deregulation can be interpreted as attempts to survive despite actual or potential competition by lower-cost airlines.

The strategic moves that were available to the incumbent airlines were far more diverse than pricing alone. The major incumbents understood quite well the trends predicted by the economic models of the time and realized that in order to survive they must introduce strategic changes and innovation in demand, technology and the industry structure, or otherwise change the rules of the game. Price was by no means a single or even a major decision variable for the incumbent airlines. Reshaping the market into complex integrated hub-and-spoke systems with regional monopolistic bottlenecks, was.

The theoretical problem, however, is that the set of possible strategic actions and related competition response is often quite large and far from obvious. Moreover, dynamic strategic moves depend on specific and irreversible institutions and history, and thus it is doubtful that the abstract economic models or even the airlines themselves could provide a unique prediction of such moves and their long-term consequences prior to deregulation.[12]

## 3. FRANCHISE BIDDING

Franchise bidding was an attractive idea advanced by the Chicago School as a possible alternative to regulation. The basis for the argument is that even if production efficiency suggests a monopolistic market structure, it is often the case that many firms may be ready to bid on franchise rights ex-ante. According to this view, customers can auction off the right to sell a franchise using the state as an instrument to conduct the auction. The bidder who offers to supply the product (electricity or cable television, for example) at the lowest rates would win the franchise. This mechanism can substitute for the traditional natural monopoly regulation.

Williamson (1985, 1996) took issue with this idea, suggesting that its applicability is contingent on the attributes of the particular product. That is, if providing particular goods or services involves investment in *transaction-specific* assets, free market contracts may be subject to dynamic inconsistencies, renegotiations, holdups, and other market breakdowns. Under these conditions, contract administration and an enforcement apparatus may be quite complex and, in fact, similar in many respects to traditional regulation.

Williamson does agree, however, that franchise bidding may be an appropriate mechanism in industries that lack asset specificity. The airline industry seemed an ideal example for this idea,

> The deregulation of trucking and airlines arguably benefited from the viewpoint advanced in the franchise bidding literature. The investments in question here really are "assets on wheels," hence lack specificity (1985, p. 328).

Looking at the issue from a different perspective, both the contestable markets proponents and Williamson concluded that the aviation industry was an ideal candidate for deregulation. The contestable markets theory assumes negligible sunk

---

[12] It is interesting to note that retired American Airlines chairman Robert Crandall said in an industry forum in the early 2000 that American's move to build a complex hub system was in retrospect a mistake, and instead a high-frequency linear system of the kind operated by Southwest could have done a better job.

cost; Williamson assumes negligible investment in specific assets. These somewhat related assumptions reflect perhaps one of the major misconceptions of the aviation industry. Airlines' investments in location-specific and non-transferable assets in airports (terminals, gates, slots, hangars, maintenance facilities, computer systems) and airport communities (advertising, promotion, public relation, sales facilities, personnel training) in fact are substantial and sunk.

In hindsight, we can identify two major misapprehensions of airline deregulation. Both of them are related to the fact that the market was perceived universally in terms of a simple city-pair metaphor, which ignores networks' location-specific aspects. The first is the notion that the importance of sunk cost was underplayed. This has been extensively dealt with in the economic literature.

The second misapprehension is in some respects ironic and relates to transactions between airlines and local authorities concerning airports and their facilities.

## 3.1   Airports

Airports are vital for airlines, as airport facilities and aircraft are complementary components that an airline combines to provide service. Unlike the monopolistic air traffic control system, which is owned and operated by the federal government, most commercial airports are controlled directly or indirectly by local authorities such as airport authority enterprises or states, cities, or counties.[13] Airports are regulated to some extent by the federal government, but otherwise are controlled by the local authorities, which have considerable discretion with respect to franchising airport services.

The air travel market is constrained by the physical availability of airports in general and by groundside capacity (roads, parking lots, terminals, and hangars) and airside (runways, taxiways, gates, and slots) capacity of a specific airport. There is also a related time dimension. Takeoffs and landings must be spread over no more than 24 hours a day and are further constrained by a fixed number of desirable peak hours. Only a certain maximum number of landings or takeoffs can be squeezed into a unit of time and space for operational and safety reasons, given a certain level of groundside and airside capacity. Local government authorities control the allocation and franchising of airports' groundside and airside capacity. The way this capacity is franchised directly affects market structure.

An airline building location-specific facilities pursuant to a franchise agreement with an airport authority has high fixed costs. It thus may become a natural monopolist at that airport location. Clearly an airline that acquires long-term exclusive rights to operate all (or most) of an airport's facilities acquires a dominant position at that location.

An airline must have access to groundside and airside space in order to fly a route. An airport gate, for example, is one of the major (but not the only) location-specific assets that an airline must access in order to operate a flight. The number of

---

[13] A few states (Alaska, Hawaii, and Maryland) own airports. The federal government owns two major airports in Washington and has leased them to a public managing entity.

gates and other necessary facilities in an airport is fixed at any time, and the relevant local authority controls their franchising. The distribution of gates and other airport facilities across airlines, in fact, is analogous to route franchising. An airline may serve a city-pair only if it has access to gates and other airport facilities in both cities. The threat of "hit and run" competition is credible only if a competing airline has equal access to gates in the same pair of cities. Since, for example, markets are differentiated by departing and arriving times, this will also require access to parallel gates at the same times.

Economic wisdom suggests that under such conditions it is advisable to auction the franchise rights to airlines, as suggested by the Chicago School. The alternative is to regulate the industry. In reality, airlines entered long-term exclusive contracts with local authorities and acquired (regional) monopolistic or otherwise dominant positions in major airports parallel to price and entry deregulation. The franchises were not auctioned, but rather acquired in private bilateral agreements between airlines and local authorities, away from federal government or public attention. The resulting contractual agreements are complex long-term contracts that gave airlines significant market power at the airport level.

The local airport authorities enjoy federal development grants and tax-exempt financing and are authorized to impose passenger facility charges. They must comply with certain federal policies in order to qualify for these financing instruments. In addition, they are subject to general federal guidelines with respect to landing fee rates chargeable to airlines. They enjoy almost complete freedom to negotiate and enter lease contracts with airlines regarding the use of airport facilities. Such agreements suffer from all the well-known potential transaction costs and difficulties of dynamic inconsistency emphasized by Williamson. As it happens, airlines and airport authorities have typically entered very long-term and complex contracts that stretch a franchise as much as possible toward almost complete possession and control by one major airline over an airport's facilities.

Airport authorities finance airport development projects mostly with long-term tax-exempt bonds that are secured by airport revenues. They are motivated to enter long-term lease agreements with financially credible airlines for matching duration. A major incumbent airline clearly constitutes a more attractive financial party to a local authority than smaller or startup airlines. Airport use contracts often run twenty years or more and consist of complex covenants relating to the use of gates and covering airline investment in airport facilities. In certain cases airlines have approached less-developed or secondary airports that were interested in attracting new investment and economic activity at the specific local level. In many cases, major airlines' investment in airport facilities has been significant.

In exchange for investment in airports, airlines demanded contractual provisions to protect them against holdups and other problems of dynamic inconsistencies. Provisions like these tended to deter airport authorities from arbitrarily increasing lease rates, for example. Contracts have also included complex risk-sharing schemes, in which airlines bear the financial risks of unallocated costs of running airports, as well as majority-in-interest and other clauses that give a tenant airline the rights to block or effect airport development and expansion.[14] It is obvious that when it controls all or most of an airport's facilities, an airline surely excludes rivals from access to an essential resource.

One of the characteristics of these contracts is that they include exclusive-use-rights of airport facilities by a major airline tenant. They also grant airlines almost complete control and possession over gates, including sublease and assignment rights. These provisions are not surprising under such agreements. They protect airlines' investment in transaction-specific assets, but they also inevitably provide airlines with a dominant or even a full monopolistic position in an airport.

Landing or taking off at an airport requires ground facilities and gates. Exclusive-use agreements give airlines control over entry into a market. An airline that controls a gate or other facilities may refuse to sublease it to a competing airline, or may lease it for a high cost, or may lease it only during less desirable off-peak times. Primary lessors of gates often require that the sublessees hire their own personnel to service the subleasing airline as well as other maintenance and ground services at extravagant rates.

A 1990 survey by the General Accounting Office (GAO) claims that:

> Our survey of the 66 largest US airports … revealed that 85% of their gates were leased to established incumbent airlines under long-term, exclusive-use leases. At some airports, every gate was under an exclusive-use lease (1996, p. 9)

Under these circumstances, it is extremely difficult, if even possible, for "hit and run" or any new entry to occur or otherwise challenge many of the dominant hub airlines.

## 3.2    Slots

Barriers to entry relating to airport access have evolved in a unique manner at four large airports: in New York (JFK and LaGuardia), Washington (National/Reagan), and Chicago (O'Hare). Federal limits on takeoff and landing slots and perimeter rules (applicable to LaGuardia and National airports) created additional barriers to entry that together with exclusive-use leases directly benefited established incumbents.[15]

The slot control story started in 1969, when the FAA set limits and allocated the number of takeoffs and landings at these airports among airlines, attempting to reduce congestion. In practical terms, an airline that does not hold a right to use slots couldn't take off or land at any one of these airports. Controlling gates grants an airline physical access to its aircraft; controlling slots allows an airline to take off or land at a particular time. Gates are controlled and allocated to airlines by local governments; slots are controlled and allocated to airlines by the federal

---

[14] In general, there are residual or compensatory methods of computing fees or several combinations and variants of these methods. In the first case, airlines pay for the residual cost net of non-airline revenue. In the second, fees are related to actual airport facilities used.

[15] The perimeter rules limit the landings to flights originated inside the perimeter's area. These rules imply that flights originating from major incumbents' hubs can, almost exclusively, land at these two airports.

government. An airline at these four airports must have both gates and slots to be able to operate. The theoretical Chicago School rationale for auctioning slots is, in general, analogous to the argument related to gates and other airport facilities.

In 1985, the DOT amended its rules and in the spirit of deregulation permitted airlines to freely trade slots. Yet incumbent slot holders of record as of December 1985 were grandfathered and could continue holding the slots. Obviously, the grandfathered rights benefited the major incumbent airlines, which could continue holding dominant positions at the four airports.

DOT retained about 5% of the slots and distributed them in a lottery to airlines with few or no slots at these airports. With the increased industry consolidation and concentration, however, many of the lottery winners subsequently went out of business or otherwise merged with or were acquired by other major airlines. Most of the slots are held today by the major incumbent airlines, and only a small fraction are held by post-deregulation entrants. Major airlines claimed that holding the slots grants long-term protection of their significant investment in developing airports.

According to the GAO:

> By the early 1990s, we found that a few carriers had increased their control of slots to such an extent that they could limit access to routes beginning or ending at any of the slot controlled airports—airports that are crucial to establishing new service in the heavily traveled eastern and midwestern markets (GAO, 1996, p. 4).

### 3.3 A Note About Theory

During the 1980s, when economists and regulators perceived the market in terms of a simple linear, city-pair metaphor, the major airlines emphasized a complex hub network view. While the industry, observers, and regulators expected a "hit and run" competition by "assets on wheels" or otherwise by "marginal costs on wings" the industry developed integrated hub-and-spoke networks that made this move in many cases almost impossible. Capturing a dominant position at the major hub level became a major strategic objective for an airline.

As observers celebrated the significant expansion of the industry and plummeting airfares during the first stages of deregulation, the major incumbent airlines negotiated long-term exclusive-use contracts that gave them, in many cases, simple old-fashioned monopolistic power in hub airports. And as the CAB and the federal government largely withdrew from route franchising, airlines and local governments entered agreements for route franchising that raised significant barriers to new entry. While Chicago School economists and other deregulation enthusiasts celebrated the success of deregulation, monopolistic franchises were captured and negotiated at a regional level, usually in a bilateral setup and not through franchise bidding.

By the time analysts and regulators caught up with the new structure, the major incumbents had already established a complex network system including major hubs and radiating spokes with regional monopolistic bottlenecks. Antitrust analysis of the industry in the 1990s looks much like that related to the breakup (or regulating) of the communications and utility industries' regional bottlenecks. The basic structure of the telecommunications industry involves serving cities by single local-exchange networks. Major hub airports evolved during the 1980s as regional monopolists and share many things in common.

Even if franchise bidding had been imposed, however, it is doubtful that the resulting market structure would be significantly different from or more "efficient" than the one that in fact evolved. Contractual arrangements between airlines and airports involve significant uncertainties and investment in specific assets, they are, thus prone to breakdown, and require complex contingencies, payoff schedules, and enforcement schemes. Traditional regulation, antitrust monitoring, or contractual provisions with similar attributes seem to be necessary under any plausible market structure. Each one of these institutional arrangements is flawed, and one can only speculate as to which one is least imperfect.

It is also important to remember that history matters when it comes to the real-life evolution of an industry. When deregulation commenced, incumbent airlines already controlled airport facility gates and slots subject to binding contractual agreements. Franchise bidding in the manner envisaged by economists ignored to a large degree non-reversible constraints of institutional arrangements and history. Therefore, even if one ignores transaction costs, it is doubtful whether the franchise bidding idea could ever have been implemented in reality.

## 4. NETWORKS

A new economic view of networks gives us some insight into various economic and strategic aspects of the major airlines' move to create hub-and-spoke network systems.

### 4.1    Hub-and-spoke Networks

The network view suggests interpreting the air travel market as a two-way network.[16] In such networks, components are complementary to each other and create a composite product (for example, Origin A-Hub B-Destination C creates composite A to C and C to A routes in addition to the non-stop ones).[17] In an n-component network, there are $n(n - 1)$ potential goods. The addition of a new component adds $2n$ potential new goods through the provision of complementary links. The positive reinforcing benefit of adding spokes to the network system is usually referred to as a direct network effect.

This description assumes full compatibility of the system's components so that a full range of composite goods can be generated. Scheduling, for example, is one of the important variables that affect compatibility in air travel markets. An inbound passenger must arrive at the hub in time to catch a connection. One of the general ideas of an integrated major hub is that flights should be coordinated in "waves" (banks), in order to connect as many inbound and outbound combinations of origins

---

[16] See, for example, Economides and White (1994).

[17] Two-way networks refer to the fact that an A-HUB-B combination is different from a B-HUB-A one. .

and destinations through the hub airport. Ideally, there is a wave of all incoming flights arriving at the hub at about the same time. All transit passengers get on their connecting flights and take off to their destinations in an outbound wave.

## 4.2    Advantages of Hub Networks

The network models emphasize demand-side (consumption) related network effects. Hub-and-spoke systems also provide traditional production and cost-related effects. First, the hub-and-spoke structure requires fewer flights to connect the same number of nodes. Second, it creates advantages of density and scope. It increases average load factors (over a non-hub route) and therefore provides better utilization of existing capacity. It is noteworthy that most of the operational elements of an airline network system involve fixed costs or otherwise indivisibility. Aircraft, gates, ground equipment, terminals, marketing and sales, advertising and management and coordination involve fixed costs, and are indivisible.

The advantage of scope and density reduces the average cost of operation. In an integrated hub–and–spoke network, traffic from (or to) a hub includes passengers from other origins who connect at the hub as well as passengers originating at (or flying to) the hub. Connecting passengers are added to what otherwise would be a linear origin destination market from or to the hub. The hub-and-spoke system integrates several markets into one flight cabin.

Third, the hub structure may reduce the average (fixed) cost of creating a new route or market, compared to a linear origin destination market, since the cost of adding a new spoke is averaged over many other spokes. Many origins and destinations through a hub can generally be connected with fewer aircraft than under a strict linear system.

Fourth, geographic concentration of certain activities (such as management, coordination, advertising, and maintenance) may reduce fixed average costs as well. For example, there is a significant cost advantage to run one major maintenance base at the hub location. Maintenance force concentrated at the hub can very efficiently maintain aircraft during overnight layovers, for example.

Fifth, increased density, scope, and flight frequency, as well as the characteristics of the network structure, allow hub airlines to "optimize" over aircraft type, using mainly "hub aircraft" in the short- to medium-range category. Scheduled airlines produce indivisible aircraft flights but sell separate seats on such flights. An aircraft is physically indivisible into seats and may sometimes take off with only a few passengers on board or at other times take off with full capacity sold and potential passengers left on the ground. Average load factors and break-even costs of a flight are directly affected by the size of the aircraft.

The move to a hub network increased density on many short routes and encouraged hub airlines to integrate flights previously performed mostly by small turboprop (commuter) aircraft into larger, more efficient (per seat-mile) jet aircraft. In addition, many long routes require high-capacity (mostly widebody) aircraft that break-even only on highly dense markets that provide high load factors. When demand did not justify the operation of a large aircraft, routes were broken into shorter segments. In such cases, a city-pair market could be served, for example, as a combination of two shorter flights with a hub connection. In general, the same number of passengers flown in a smaller aircraft implies a higher load factor and therefore more efficient economics than a non-stop linear flight of a high-capacity aircraft with a low load factor (all else equal).

To see this, assume a simple linear route structure with a daily flight from A to B and from B to C, performed by one aircraft (ignore the return flight for now) as depicted in Figure 1. Under a typical point-to-point structure, the airline operates in two major markets (AB and BC). The number of passengers boarding will include only A and B originating passengers wishing to arrive at B or C, respectively. By using B, for example, as a hub, passengers originating at A are able also to connect to C. Therefore, the airline expands its activity to the AC market. There will be more passengers on the BC flight than before, and this will include passengers originating at A wishing to arrive at B or C (analogously, the CA market is added on the BA flight when return flights are considered).

Using B as an integrated hub eliminates the need for a flight between A and C and increases the number of passengers the airline carries on each flight in comparison to the linear system alternative. The hub functions as a switch. If the flights are compatible (for example, the AB flight arrives on time to connect to BC), then the airline in fact combines two separate components (AB, BC) to create a compound new service (AC).

Hub systems in general increase the average number of passengers boarding hub-and-spoke flights compared to a simple linear structure and generate economies of scope and density. Adding a new spoke has a systemwide positive impact on the number of passengers; it also benefits passengers who can connect to more destinations.

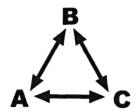

*Figure 1. Simple Hub Network*

The major cost component of operating the routes is fixed cost, which is independent of the number of passengers carried. The incremental cost of adding a passenger to an otherwise scheduled flight is small compared to the fixed cost component (sometimes this is referred to as the peanut cost). In our simple example, the added passengers on the BC leg originating at A would increase the airline's revenues with a negligible or small cost increase. In fact, the cost of operating two linear routes with or without connection is generally the same, so any additional BC passenger gained by making a connection would mostly reduce this average cost.

This simple illustration also demonstrates the interconnected nature of a network system. An increased demand for travel from A to C will increase density and reduce average production cost in the AB and BC markets, for example. Similarly, an increased demand in the BC market will reduce average cost for a combined ABC service. Adding a spoke D to the system will increase demand and density in AB and CB markets (for passengers originating at A and C traveling to D).

## 4.3   Hub-and-Spoke Networks and Competition

The benefits of network size from both supply and demand sides may be quite significant and reduce average production costs and fare levels. At the same time, this factor may negatively impact entry and market contestability.

### 4.3.1   The Competitive Advantage of Scope and Density

For purposes of illustration, assume that an incumbent airline operates from B as a hub to and from A and C. Assume also that a competitor enters the market with non-stop flights between C and B. The hub airline has an advantage of higher density since its flights between C and B also integrate passengers from or to A. An entrant on the CB city-pair must have a significant cost advantage to compensate for the incumbent's density disadvantage, or else an ability to differentiate its product, or must otherwise be able to duplicate a similar hub advantage.

If the C market is relatively small and there is no other hub in the region, or if an alternative hub exists but is also dominated by the same incumbent, entry may never occur. In this case, only a hub airline may be able to attract enough density to justify serving the route, and linear competition is eliminated.

This story was the major rationale behind the (unsuccessful) objection of the US Department of Justice (DOJ) to the TWA/Ozark and the Northwest/Republic mergers in the late 1980s. The DOJ argued that only hub airlines are expected to have sufficient density to serve certain small city connections with the hubs (Bismarck, North Dakota, or Cedar Rapids, Iowa) and therefore the merging hub airlines might charge monopolistic fares with no threat of entry.

Note, however, that if the AC market is big enough and passengers assign a higher value to non-stop flights, the entrant could target the AC market and charge a premium over the one-stop flight, or otherwise attract enough passengers to increase its density and yield compared to the hub airline. Moreover, a non-stop AC flight costs less to operate than the same flight with a stop at the hub.[18]

As a general observation (focusing only on a simple network structure and ignoring other strategic elements), a hub airline is expected to be more vulnerable to competition that targets or combines spoke markets, compared to flights from or to its hub. This general conclusion is not necessarily dependent on whether the hub airline is a monopolist in its hub, and this is why linear competitors may prefer to

---

[18] Assuming AC is a longer flight (and everything else equal), the higher cost of takeoff and landing is spread over a longer cruise time.

target spoke markets and not hub markets. Higher competitive pressures on spoke markets are one of the reasons suggested for hub airlines' tendency to price ABC flights (with hub connection) lower than just the AB or BC legs sold separately.

The incumbent's advantage over a competitor is expected to increase with the relative size of its network. In a standard n-component star network with a central hub, there are n(n - 1) combinations of products. Any direct flight from or to the hub will integrate passengers from many destinations and will enjoy benefits of a higher load factor. In general, the larger the network, the higher the airline's average load factor and density and scope advantage (everything else equal). As the number of spokes radiating from the hub increases, so too does the number of daily takeoffs and landings serving such spokes from and to the hub. In addition, airlines accommodate passengers' preferences for high frequency by increasing the number of landing and takeoffs. It is usually assumed that airlines are encouraged to increase frequency due to the non-linear positive impact of frequency on load factors (the so-called S-curve phenomenon).

### 4.3.2    *Control of Essential Facility*

Network compatibility requires that takeoffs and landings be scheduled in "waves." Since passenger daily demand is cyclical, takeoffs and landings are usually concentrated during peak demand hours. This pattern brings about several important effects.

First, a major integrated hub is prone to congestion, which is one of the major cost elements of increasing network size, considering the systemwide impact of delays. Second, by integrating high-frequency flights to and from many spokes at the hub location, the hub airline captures a dominant portion of the limited amount of groundside and airside capacity available at the hub location.

The integrated hub-and-spoke structure is by its nature exclusionary in the sense that essential capacity is captured by the hub airline's operations and therefore cannot be freely accessed by a competitor, especially in peak demand hours. In fact, congestion and groundside and airside capacity constraints may even limit the hub airline's access to its own facilities during peak demand hours and limit its own flight frequencies.

Exclusive airport use contracts allow a hub airline to control essential facilities and space that are necessary to operate a high-frequency, integrated hub-and-spoke network system. A hub airline's ability to offer compatible, composite service requires control over access to groundside and airside capacity. Exploiting the advantages of scale, density, and scope inherent in the hub concept, and providing passengers with a high-frequency, wide and diverse range of compatible composite service, creates and requires a regional monopolistic or dominant market position at the hub level.

This story confirms well-established principles: Responding to economies of scale, scope and density, and transaction cost may increase market integration and concentration and therefore market power, but provide positive production and consumption effects.

We can interpret the capture of a monopolistic position at a hub level as a major airline's attempt to monopolize the market in an attempt to extract super-normal profits. In addition, investing in overcapacity at the hub level sends a strong deterring signal to potential competitors while it also captures physical access to and excludes potential entrants from essential capacity-limited facilities. Yet capturing a dominant position in a hub location is also the inevitable consequence of an airline's quest for improved network connections, coordination, and efficiency. It is doubtful whether a complex hub-and-spoke system could have emerged without the creation of monopolistic bottlenecks.

Creation of potential market power at the hub level is an inseparable consequence of exploiting the efficiencies embodied in a network structure. An entrant that ventures to compete directly with a major hub airline may need a significant cost advantage and or an ability to differentiate its product. Otherwise, it may have to duplicate the advantages of a hub-and-spoke network in some way, or obtain other advantages in order to compete.

Even if a competitor enjoys a clear cost advantage, whether through specialization in a different aircraft type or different market, it may not have access to the groundside or airside capacity that is necessary to compete on any route to or from the hub. The pattern of geographic distribution of airports, as well as the distribution of market power of major airlines over potentially competing hub airports, may preclude entry or be enough to ward off significant threats by competitors against the dominant hub.

It is difficult to isolate the direct impact of the hub network architecture per se on entry conditions, since it is only one element in a complex set of interwoven airline strategic policies. Marketing devices like computerized reservation systems, agent commission overrides, frequent flier programs, and other techniques that major hub airlines use in connection with their complex network system may raise barriers to entry and enhance the hub airlines' market power as well.[19]

## 5. THE INTEGRATION OF MAJOR AND REGIONAL AIRLINES

A more complex market structure would combine two local star-shaped networks, each with a different major hub and radiating spokes, through a hub-to-hub connecting "gateway" (see Figure 2). The gateway connection allows passengers at any spoke radiating from one of the hubs to connect to the second hub and to any of its spokes. (The two networks may use the same airport as a hub.) Connection of the two (or more) networks dramatically increases the number of origin and destination combinations, creating positive effects (as well as congestion and other costs).

Assume that the two networks in this illustration do not compete on any city-pair combination and therefore have a clear-cut vertical (complementary) relationship. In this case, integration is considered socially desirable. The merging of two such

---

[19] Frequent flier programs tie passengers into a network and create advantages to larger networks.

networks would be expected to improve coordination (compatibility) and efficiency (by eliminating double marginalization).

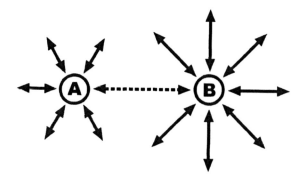

*Figure 2. A Two-Star Network*

## 5.1 Vertical Integration

Suppose, for example, the vertical integration of a major airline at a hub with a regional commuter (feeding) airline. The two airlines specialize in different technologies and operate largely in different markets. The commuter airline may operate smaller turboprop aircraft and on shorter routes; therefore, it can in general be viewed as complementary to and non-competing with the major airline's network. Integration of two such networks makes many new compound products possible. Obviously, the airlines must coordinate their operations in order to make the networks compatible and interconnected; this would include joint scheduling, marketing, pricing, ticketing, and more. The airlines may share gates, counter space, personnel, and other activities or facilities at the hub. Such coordination is often achieved by mergers, joint ventures, or other types of strategic marketing arrangements usually referred to as *code-sharing*.

Vertical integration that is similar to that can be traced to the pioneering code-sharing agreement between Allegheny Airlines and Hagerstown Commuter in the middle 1960s. Allegheny established a comprehensive code-sharing arrangement that assigned the commuter routes it could fly more efficiently with smaller aircraft under Allegheny's code designation. Allegheny provided marketing, sales, full ground services, and access to ground facilities, as well as financial assistance in acquiring new aircraft. The commuter agreed to adhere to Allegheny's standards, configuration, and required schedules. A federally mandated joint fare arrangement made the price of a combined flight on both systems lower than the sum of its components. This mainly vertical integration story included some horizontal elements as well, due to the consolidation of some previously competing routes that the commuter could operate at a lower cost, thus improving production efficiency as well as providing positive network effects.

The Allegheny integration was unusual compared to most of the other feeder arrangements of the pre-deregulation era, because in most other cases the smaller commuter or regional airlines served as "common feeders," interlining to all airlines located at their destinations. During the regulation era, regional and commuter airlines had relatively easy access to and connection into major airlines' networks, and a mandatory joint fare agreement (which expired in 1983) forced the major airlines to offer a comparable fare to all feeding airlines.

Vertical arrangements of the post-deregulation period seem far less benign, more complex, inconsistent, and many times ambiguous as to their welfare implications. In many cases, vertical integration evolved as a part of a complex scheme of strategic behavior that varied according to each airline's objectives and policies.

### 5.1.1 The General Antitrust Challenge

Economists and antitrust authorities often sanction vertical integration of this nature. This view has its origin in Cournot's *complementary duopoly* model, which shows that the integration of the two firms might reduce price for the benefit of consumers. In reality, vertical integration or joint operations are part of a complex interactive network system with real-time strategic actions and not always obvious dynamics.

One of the major problems is that it is quite difficult, even if possible, to force a complex market reality into a simplistic binary "good or bad" framework. Yet the traditional fundamentals of normative economics and antitrust thinking are dichotomistic in nature—we try to say whether a certain vertical merger, for example, has, in aggregate, a "good" or "bad" impact on society. Does accepting a small cost of horizontal integration, while internalizing a greater positive vertical externality, add up to an overall gain to society? In fact, we cannot see the dynamic impact of accepting a small cost or externality in the context of a non-linear, interactive, dynamic network system. In such systems, even a small deviation may result in a significant future impact. We might, arguably, in all good faith accept a small reduction in horizontal competitiveness in an otherwise mainly vertical integration case and trigger the evolution of a monopoly in the future.

The analysis of these issues becomes even more problematical and uncertain if one assumes that airline production technology as well as demand exhibits non-linear dynamics. In reality, while both vertical and horizontal integration (whether full or partial) involve advantages of average cost reductions on the supply side and network extension on the demand side, they often have some potential anticompetitive effects. Can all these conflicting effects add up to support a straightforward policy conclusion?

### 5.1.2 The Regulator's Position

During most of the 1980s, airlines were largely left free to merge and to enter horizontal and vertical mergers and strategic alliances with minimal regulatory intervention. Starting in 1989, antitrust challenges of inter-airline transactions were transferred from the Department of Transportation to the Department of Justice, which adopted a stricter position as officials saw increasing concerns with airlines charging hub premiums. The DOJ adopted the general (static) notion that vertical integration is acceptable as opposed to horizontal integration and that positive (vertical) and negative (horizontal) aspects can be aggregated to suggest a policy direction. A merger, for example, that includes mainly complementary routes and no significant direct substitute routes was in general considered acceptable. This policy characterized reviews of integration and strategic alliances between major and commuter airlines.

A quotation can summarize the DOJ position toward the major industry trend of vertical integration between major hub and smaller regional airlines:

> Examples in the US of domestic code-sharing agreements that tend not to raise significant horizontal issues are those between commuter and jet carriers. Our investigations over the years have shown that, because they operate different types of aircraft, jet and commuter airlines seldom serve the same city-pair markets and are not likely to enter very many of the same markets (Binyamin, 1996, p. 6).

The DOJ's position largely overlooks the fact that vertical integration between major and regional (commuter) airlines has enhanced hub dominance by major airlines and created horizontal foreclosures and consolidation among the regional airlines. In this respect, the DOJ's tolerance of vertical integration is directly related to the establishment of hub dominance and its potential anticompetitive impact.

## 5.2    Horizontal Foreclosure and Increased Hub Dominance

Figure 3 is used in the network literature to show the possible negative consequences of end-to-end vertical integration and can illustrate the commuter airlines' consolidation trend.[20] Assume that B is a major airline's hub (such as the American hub in Dallas or Delta's in Atlanta). AB or BA represents any route from or to the hub. BC or CB represents a regional route that is served by two regional airlines. Traffic in this simplistic structure can be regional (BC) or long distance (ABC). Airline 1 is a monopolist at the B hub. Connecting to BC requires an aircraft change at B. B is an "essential facility" that is controlled by airline 1.

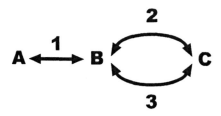

*Figure 3. End-to-End Vertical Integration*

---

[20] See, for example, Economides and White (1994).

In general, airline 1 has a few strategic options. It may offer both airlines interlining with its network under uniform terms; it may vertically integrate with one of the regionals or with both; it can integrate with one and foreclose (deny access) or otherwise charge the second airline a higher segment fare.

While, regulatory experts generally emphasize the positive impact of vertical (complementary) integration as discussed above, they have often voiced concerns as to the possibility that a vertical integration of firms 1 and 2 may end up foreclosing access to firm 3 or creating price discrimination against it. In fact, this is the reason for the introduction of the *joint fare agreement* by the CAB during the regulation era. With expiration of the agreement and the regulatory tolerance of vertical mergers and cooperation arrangements, these theoretical concerns indeed materialized.

In typical cases of strategic vertical cooperation, the regional airline may benefit from lower costs of ground handling, marketing (through a major computerized reservation system, for example), ticketing, and terminal and counter facilities provided by the major airline. Usually, the major airline transfers to the regional the benefit of a discounted bulk fuel price as well as participation in frequent flier programs that attract regional passengers into an integrated system. Such integration provides increased density and scope on both networks as well as reduction of average costs.

Under such arrangements, it is often inevitable that the non-integrated regional airline 3 will pull out of the BC/CB route in favor of the integrated one, since it will not be able to obtain the advantages of the integrated system. The negative impact of integration on airline 3 may make it a target for a takeover by the integrated airline. In either case, a regional (horizontal) monopoly may be created. Airline 3 may survive if it can align with another major airline. Yet with the geographic location and the dominant positions of major airlines at the hub level, such an alternative competitor is not often available.

The expiration of the *joint fare agreement* in 1983 and the regulator's forgiving attitude toward vertical integration opened the door for an aggressive move by major airlines to integrate with local or regional airlines. The major airlines' move to strategically align themselves with the regional airlines was motivated by attempts to expand their market base.

A hub serves as an important gate into the integrated network system, attracts origin, destination, or connecting passengers, and provides intranetwork and sometimes internetwork gateway connections. The move to increase hub traffic has included efforts to tie the local origin passengers residing in the hub location into the major hub airline's network. It is often the case that by dominating the hub traffic an airline obtains a dominant position with respect to passengers residing within a certain ground transportation distance from the hub location. Using full vertical integration or a variety of strategic alliance agreements with the smaller regional airlines, the majors can expand their market bases to include residents of more distant communities. Controlling the regional airlines implies direct and exclusive feeding of the passengers into the major hub airline's network. Compatibility of regional and major airlines' flights requires coordination and schedule integration, which, in turn, increases the capacity utilization of groundside and airside capacity in the hub airport and limits competition's entry into the hub.

Although integration of major and regional airlines has been viewed as basically vertical (or complementary) in nature, it often includes horizontal integration as well. In many cases, the integration has eliminated competition between airlines on certain parallel routes. The elimination of such competition, although anti-competitive, has allowed operation that is more efficient due to the reduced cost of using a smaller (or larger) airplane or the ability to take advantage of lower input costs.

As a consequence of this strategic vertical integration move, the regional airlines underwent a consolidation trend, ending up with the creation of only a few coalitions of networks, each characterized by exclusive affiliation with one major airline. The regional airlines restructured and consolidated parallel to the major airlines and created integrated networks with intranetwork compatibility and interlining and, in most cases, internetwork exclusion. In the new structure, internetwork interlining is almost impossible.

Two groups of regional airlines have been formed. The first group, consisting of the vast majority of the regional airlines, merged or entered strategic integration arrangements with a major airline. The second smaller group, accounting for fewer than 5% of the total regional airlines' traffic, stayed independent and concentrated on small niche markets. Most airlines in the first group interconnect exclusively with one major airline, usually through its major hub. There are a wide range of agreements between the major and the regional airlines, including full ownership, equity participation, and a variety of joint marketing agreements. Joint marketing agreements usually assign the code designation of the major airline to the regional, so that one ticket bundles service by two airlines under the brand name of the major airline.

## 5.3    Was This Integration Move Efficient?

The integration of major and regional/commuter airlines has produced mixed and complex welfare results. Overall, it seems to have yielded reduced production costs and increased positive network benefits. The integrated system improves operational efficiency and compatibility and provides passengers with a large and diverse connectivity into a large major airline's network system. These benefits, however, have come at the cost of increasing major airline dominance and have produced other anticompetitive results.

The integrated airlines have used exclusionary mixed bundling and foreclosure that has created horizontal consolidation and integration at the smaller, regional airlines level, which also enhances the major airlines' market dominance at the (horizontal) hub level, increasing their market base, density, and control over limited hub capacity. What seemed initially to be a simple, complementary, downstream (vertical) integration has turned out to have potential strong horizontal anticompetitive aspects at least at two levels over time.

The overall impact of these effects has become even more ambiguous in a dynamic world of innovation and changes in technology that often result in surprising complex strategic interaction and long-term industry evolution.

For example, one of the DOJ arguments is that the regional airlines operate different types of aircraft and in different markets from the majors so mergers are complementary. In fact, the composition of the commuter airline fleets has changed quite dramatically in response to the integration with the majors.

In particular, the nine- to fifteen-seat turboprop aircraft (once the backbone of the commuter fleet) have almost completely disappeared, and higher-capacity (50- to 100-seat), longer-range jet aircraft have entered service in large numbers since 1990. The new technology has advantages of increased speed, capacity, and safety. At the same time, this trend may increase potential hub power and have the effect of diminishing service to smaller communities traditionally served by smaller commuter airlines that can no longer compete on this playing field.

It is doubtful whether this fleet change trend could have been predicted when the DOJ was reviewing many of the vertical integration transactions. Moreover, it is questionable whether this trend would even have emerged without the evolution of integrated hubs and the consolidation of the commuter airlines. The larger aircraft accommodate the denser traffic that is created by the hub-and-spoke networks system, and it is doubtful if this technology would have evolved absent such integration. There is also no clear-cut conclusion as to the long-term dynamic impact of this trend. For example, retirement of small and medium turboprop aircraft by the integrated commuter airlines may facilitate the entry of new small commuter airlines into niche markets. Also, the impressive success of the manufacturers of the regional jet aircraft (in particular Bombardier and Embraer) has put new competitive pressures on Boeing and Airbus.

## 6. CONSOLIDATION, CONCENTRATION, AND GLOBALIZATION

The unfolding industry structure may be characterized by several major trends. First, there has been a dramatic overall network expansion, including more origins and destinations (and combinations) served and more passengers and miles flown.

Second, there has been a trend of increased consolidation through a host of arrangements, including mergers, equity participation, and diverse forms of marketing and other strategic alliances of various degrees of collaboration and integration.[21] This second trend has created a relatively small number of network coalitions, each characterized by intra-coalition interlining and largely inter-coalition exclusion and rivalry.

Third, the new network structure raises barriers to entry by tying up resources and access to markets and increasing scale and scope requirements as well as exit costs.

---

[21] I use increased consolidation to describe the overall reduction in the number of airlines in the industry and increased concentration to the reduction in the number of airlines competing on a route/market. There are various ways to measure these trends and not always consensus regarding the results. There is no consensus that concentration indeed increased.

Fourth, average real fares (although becoming quite complex and involving increased variability and non-obvious non-linear aspects) seem to be falling constantly.

This picture is somewhat puzzling if we look at it in the traditional context, as the increased anticompetitive aspects of the new structure have not resulted in either obvious overall price increases or super-normal profits.

The historical evolution of this consolidation and concentration trend may be broken into three major waves. The first characterizes the second half of the 1980s, the second, the early 1990s, and the third the late 1990s and early 2000s.[22]

### 6.1    The First Wave

Regulation originally forced the industry into a rigid structure of three major airline categories: major (trunk), national (local service), and regional (commuter). Each category specialized in different markets, and airlines belonging to each category interlined vertically and horizontally, across and within these categories. For example, a commuter airline could feed passengers into a national airline that fed passengers into major airlines. In addition, horizontal interlining was available by combining flights on two major airlines.

The first wave of industry consolidation during the 1980s included complex vertical (complementary) and horizontal (substitute) mergers. Pre-deregulation major airlines merged with national airlines (for example, American with Air Cal, Northwest with Republic, and TWA with Ozark). Several national airlines (Allegheny, Piedmont, and PSA) merged to form US Air as a major airline, taking advantage of their pre-deregulation hub structure. Major airlines merged and integrated with other majors (for example, Delta merged with Western, and Texas International merged with two pre-deregulation majors, Eastern and Continental). The major post-deregulation entrants were People's Express, and New York Air. In addition, all major airlines merged or integrated with regional commuter airlines to provide exclusive feeding into their hubs. Most mergers were aimed at, or otherwise resulted in, increased airlines' overall network size and enhanced dominance at major hubs.

During most of the 1980s, the regulator tolerated airline mergers and integration of vertical and horizontal characteristics. Horizontal integration—unlike vertical integration—is perceived as anti-competitive. During the 1980s, however, regulators relied on the contestable markets notion to dismiss horizontal integration concerns. It was argued that the total number of airlines competing nationwide is immaterial since the threat of potential entry would discipline fares. Taking this view, the government has not challenged the first post-deregulation wave of industry consolidation, although hub dominance has been created.

The mergers of TWA and Ozark and of Northwest and Republic have been analyzed thoroughly in antitrust literature. These cases became quite famous not only for the specific issues involved but perhaps also because of the different

---

[22] The post September 11th trends are discussed in Chapter 8.

opinions argued by DOJ and DOT. The debates regarding these mergers reflect a growing awareness of the evolving integrated hub system as well as increased skepticism about the power of market contestability to discipline fares in such a framework.

## 6.2 The Second Wave

The second major wave of consolidation emerged during the severe industry crisis of the early 1990s, most notably the demise of Pan Am, Eastern, and Midway, as well as the bankruptcy and reorganization of TWA, Continental, and America West. Defunct airlines sold a significant portion of their assets to the financially strong airlines in attempts to generate cash, or otherwise as part of their liquidation process. This process progressed toward further industry integration (both horizontal and vertical) and consolidation, as American, Delta, and United gained in network size and dominance.

One interesting effect here is that the traditional domestic airlines (American, Delta, and United) acquired international routes from defunct airlines that had dominated these routes for several decades (Pan Am, Eastern, and TWA). In this process, traditional northeast gateways to destinations over the Atlantic moved west to provide extensive global connections, eliminating the need for interlining with the once traditional international airlines and pushing their complex integrated hub networks globally. Delta was a major winner as the demise of Eastern Airlines and Pan Am granted it dominance over its Atlanta hub, as well as international routes across the Atlantic.

The accelerated consolidation wave of the early 1990s faced somewhat more government watchfulness, as the authority for antitrust challenge was transferred from the DOT to the DOJ. Basing its position on the *horizontal merger guidelines*; the DOJ focused its attention on potential horizontal anticompetitive aspects of inter-airline transactions while it largely tolerated moves toward vertical integration.

For example, in 1989, the DOJ opposed Eastern's proposed sale of eight gates in Philadelphia to USAir, a competing hub carrier, due to concerns that USAir would dominate the Philadelphia hub. In 1991, the DOJ opposed Eastern's proposed sale of 67 slots at Washington National Airport to United Airlines. The DOJ argued that since United operated a significant hub at nearby Dulles Airport, such a sale would combine horizontally competing (substitute) hubs.

These two cases emphasize two different categories of horizontal concerns. The first focuses on intrahub competition, the second on interhub competition. The DOJ adopted a more tolerant attitude toward intra-hub horizontal integration if there were an interhub (or over hubs) competitive challenge.

It is important to remember, however, that with the severe industry crisis of the early 1990s, accelerated integration was imminent and the DOJ had a limited impact on the industry's overall consolidation trend. In this respect, transferring the job of challenging airline mergers and integration from the DOT to the DOJ in the late 1980s may have affected the details, but it certainly did not stem the tide of the general trend. The DOJ's position notwithstanding, the drive toward increasing concentration, network extension and hub dominance continued unabated during the early 1990s.

The dramatic industry consolidation of the early 1990s was perceived as inevitable. It is perhaps not unexpected that industry consolidation and restructuring will follow an economic downturn of such magnitude and characteristics. Toward the middle 1990s, however, it seemed that further consolidation of major airlines had stopped and new, low-cost, startup airlines were gaining market momentum as the economy in general and the industry in particular, robustly expanded.[23] The general perception was that further consolidation, if it occurred, would be case-specific and not part of a general trend. There was speculation, for example, on whether the ailing TWA would make it.

*6.3    The Third Wave*

The third wave of accelerated integration and strategic alliances by major airlines during the second half of the 1990s was thus quite surprising. This trend included domestic and global integration attempts of an unprecedented nature, consisting mostly of vertical alliances of major US airlines with major foreign airlines to create cross-border network coalitions.[24] In addition, the six largest major US airlines announced in early 1998 their intention of forming three major domestic alliances with significant horizontal implications.

These two moves are usually viewed as two separate strategic choices. As one is perceived as mostly of a vertical nature and the second entails significant horizontal aspects, the first has been generally blessed, while the second raises regulatory concerns. In fact, these two types of alliances, as well as integration at the regional level, affect each other and must be viewed and analyzed together.

This formation of global network alliances is as yet unfolding, and it is still too early to predict its direction. Several alliances are still subject to cross-border regulatory reviews, and their results are not clear at the time of this writing. It seems, however, that the frameworks of three or four possible major global alliances have been formed. In some respects moves like this, at least during their initial stages, are contagious, as each alliance attempts to enlist an increasing number of members in order to create the largest network.

At the foundation of each such alliance there is a code-sharing agreement among a major US airline, a major European airline, and a major Far Eastern airline. The largest global network is Oneworld, headed by American Airlines, with British Airways as a major European partner and Qantas and Cathay as Far Eastern partners. The second-largest is the Star alliance, headed by United Airlines, with Lufthansa and SAS as major European partners, Thai and Singapore airlines as Far Eastern partners, plus Air Canada. The third alliance is Sky Team headed by Delta as a US partner. It started with Swissair and Sabena as major European partners and

---

[23] Value Jet is the most celebrated example. West Pacific, Kiwi, Vanguard, and Sun Jet are others.

[24] The major direct horizontal effect of such alliances is the potential reduction of competition on the hub-to-hub connections.

later joined by Air France and Alitalia as well as the pioneering members of international alliances—Northwest and Continental.

Each of these coalitions of alliances includes collaborative arrangements of various degrees of integration with numerous airlines across the globe. These alliances are interpreted as mostly vertical (complementary) in nature, although they present a similar repetitive horizontal integration issue with respect to gateway-to-gateway connections. For example, a consolidation (through code-share) of British Airways and American would create a dominant position for the alliance with respect to direct US–London Heathrow flights. Similarly, Northwest and KLM already dominate the US–Amsterdam route. The US regulatory position with respect to these alliances is largely supportive due to their complementary nature, with concerns regarding the gate-to-gate aspects that are typical to each alliance.

In the domestic arena, the six largest US airlines, which account for nearly 70% of domestic traffic, announced in 1998 their intention to form three major alliances. The most integrated alliance was to be the one between Continental and Northwest (possibly in order to preempt a takeover attempt by Delta), which includes an equity stake, code-sharing, and integrated network systems. The United–Delta alliance proposed to include code-sharing as well, but this was scaled back to include mainly reciprocal frequent flier programs and access to airport lounges. A similar scope of alliance was entered between American and US Airways. The latter two alliances primarily focused on attracting and tying passengers into the combined airline networks.

The strong position taken by the DOJ seems to have played at least some role in scaling back and revising the initial proposed alliances. After these alliances were announced, numerous reports appeared in the media about possible expansions of these alliances and possible further consolidation and mergers in different combinations among the major airlines. In the spring of 2000, United Airlines (the largest airline in the world) and US Airways (the sixth-largest in the US) announced their intended merger under the United name in a transaction valued at $11.6 billion.[25] The airlines agreed to spin off and sell the US Airways position in Washington, DC, to a new airline (DC Air) in order to avoid a major antitrust issue concerning the possible elimination of competition between the Reagan and Dulles hubs. Subsequent to this merger announcement, it was reported that other major airlines were discussing possible mergers in response and that the six largest major airlines might consolidate into only three. In early 2001, American Airlines announced its intention to acquire TWA in a pre-packaged bankruptcy transaction along with certain assets from United GAO (2001). Consummating these mergers was expected to give the two airlines a combined 50% share of the market and the largest three over 80% of the market.

---

[25] United walked away from the deal in the summer of 2001.

*6.4    What Next for the Major Network Airlines?*

The tendency of the major US hub airlines to further integrate their systems, together with the move to form global alliances suggests, perhaps, the general direction of the evolution of the major hub network airlines into three or four major global network coalitions. Each such coalition is characterized by intra-coalition compatibility and collaboration and inter-coalition rivalry. Each coalition is bound by mutual interests, yet is inherently fragile due to internal conflicts among coalition members.

In addition, we may see coexistence of a complex mix of rivalry and collaboration of a strategic and tactical nature among competing coalitions of networks. For example, interconnecting two rival networks may sometimes work for the benefit of both coalitions, so rivalry is often, but not necessarily, manifested by inter-coalition exclusion of networks.

An example is the agreement reached in December 1999 by the two largest airlines in Canada, Air Canada (a member of the Star alliance) and Canadian Airlines (a member of the Oneworld alliance), to merge. The immediate solution reached involved the merged airlines keeping both pre-merger global alliances. This solution works for the benefit of the merged airlines, since it allows interconnection with the two largest global network coalitions. It is in American Airlines' interest to align with the merged airline, since otherwise it would lose its position in the Canadian market. Although it is too early to speculate on the evolution of this case, it is quite possible that the merged major Canadian airline would become a switching point between the two global coalitions. Certain major foreign airlines have elected not to join one alliance exclusively, but rather to stay independent and have the advantage of connecting to more than one global network. Japan Airlines is one example.

There is no doubt that the evolution of domestic and global alliances will attract attention in the future. It is too early today to predict clear-cut directions for their long-run evolution, as this new pattern of competition is still an experiment. It seems now, however, that the initial collaboration steps that have been established so far focus primarily on interconnecting network systems by intra-coalition interlining through code-sharing, mostly for marketing purposes.

It will be interesting to observe the development of possible collaboration in other areas such as pooling of spare parts and joint negotiations and acquisition of aircraft, fuel, and other inputs that may reduce production costs. A major global coalition of such size would be expected to benefit from lower costs on bulk purchases of its inputs. Consolidation of marketing efforts and elimination of duplicate facilities and other activities may reduce costs as well. It will also be interesting to see if airlines will use intra-coalition relationships to coordinate capacity. This issue usually becomes important during economic downturns as falling demand for air travel and excess capacity ignite price wars.

## 7.  IS THE COMPLEX NETWORK STRUCTURE EFFICIENT?

The pre-deregulation industry consisted of a rigid structure of three vertical categories of airlines: major (trunk), national (local service), and regional (commuter), where several major airlines specialized in domestic markets (such as Delta, United, American) and several mostly in international markets (such as Pan Am, TWA). Distinctly separate airlines existed in each category, differing in their fleet composition, size, and markets served. Passengers in general could interline vertically and horizontally over the domestic system, and the basic unit of competition was the airline firm.

The post-deregulation industry has shifted its orientation from the individual airline firm level to a higher level of a multi-firm, network coalition, that divides the world markets along vertical lines, each offering a large variety of local, regional, national, and international connections across continents. In general, the industry is evolving into three or four major global network alliances, each supported by integrated dominating hubs with domestic and foreign monopolistic bottlenecks. The pre-deregulation patterns of airline specialization and competition have been replaced by a few rival network coalitions, each offering full service along vertical and horizontal global lines (one-stop shopping). In the new framework, firms are more likely to lose their individual identity as complex composite products are offered by more than one airline.

The rules of the game and the unfolding structure of the post-deregulation industry are complex and the models that economists, courts, antitrust specialists and other observers are using to interpret them are incomplete and somewhat slow to catch up. Viewed from a traditional perspective, however, the evolving industry characteristics are quite alarming.

Economies of scale density and scope, increased concentration, network effects and sunk costs—which are typical of integrated hub-and-spoke network systems— suggest the presence of potential undesirable anticompetitive aspects. In addition, strategic alliances by their nature entail aspects of coordinating capacity and pricing, activities that are traditionally attacked by antitrust authorities. Moreover, computerized reservation systems make price coordination remarkably easy, even between rival networks, since airline officials don't have to meet secretly in order to rig prices. They can just observe (or signal) price policies on their computer screens in real time.

According to the traditional view, the new industry structure is prone to super-normal pricing and social inefficiencies—a view that has been adopted by the government entities that regulate the industry. The regulator emphasizes hub market power as the source of social "evil" and argues that since major hub airlines usually don't compete at the hub level, startup entries must challenge prices. Hub strategy, however, makes entry almost impossible, and indeed most post-deregulation startup airlines have disappeared.

The major hub airlines and several economists, however, suggest that the efficiency distortion of the hub-and-spoke system is negligible or otherwise outweighed by the social benefit provided in terms of reduced overall fares, increased network size, and greater flight frequency. In fact, there are industry observers who argue that the industry is still "over-hubbed," and that further consolidation would increase efficiency without impairing competition.

## 7.1    Empirical Studies

Most empirical studies related to this debate target the dominant hub as a potential monopolistic bottleneck and examine whether hub (price) premiums exist. The conventional wisdom is that such a premium does exist, but its magnitude and social impact is a subject of debate. The gap between the various estimated premiums perhaps best reflects the extent of the debate. On the one hand, a widely quoted study by the GAO (1993) suggests a premium as high as 33.4%. On the other hand, an equally well-known study by Morrison and Winston (1995) suggests a dramatically lower rate of only 5.2%.

How should we go about empirically measuring a monopolistic distortion of a hub network system? Usually, economists construct an ideal *first-best* standard against which to contrast a distortion; a perfectly competitive equilibrium is compared to a monopolistic production level in order to estimate deadweight loss, for example. In the case of airlines, most empirical studies focus on estimating a "hub premium" as a measure of monopolistic price distortion.

A premium is a relative measure; what should a hub's fares be compared to in order to estimate a premium? In analytic models, we compare an imaginary ideal competitive price with a monopolistic price of the same (homogeneous) product. In practice, related empirical studies often compare average yields (fare per mile) on a group of hub routes with the average yields of a control group of non-hub routes.

This approach, while empirically convenient, suffers several problems. Perhaps the most critical is that the finding that a higher average fare characterizes a group of (hub) routes by itself is not sufficient to substantiate either a price premium or a net social welfare distortion. The most popular criticism relates to the argument that hub and non-hub routes do not represent homogeneous markets. In addition, hub traffic may include more business passengers who prefer flying during peak demand periods and who may be ready to pay more (before tax) than other passengers for increased frequency.[26]

The hub premium may reflect the heterogeneity of passengers based on demand elasticity. Berry, Carnall, and Spiller (1997), for example, distinguish between elastic and non-elastic demand groups and argue that higher fares and lower costs due to economies of scope are not mutually exclusive. They find price premiums of 20% and 5% for low, and high-elastic demand passengers, respectively, but according to their interpretation this premium need not have negative welfare consequences.

It is noteworthy that the theoretical and empirical arguments are often based on the notion that airlines maximize profits in relation to homogeneous city-pair

---

[26] Business trips are usually recognized as expenses for tax purposes, so the effective fare for business travel is considerably lower than the published one. Tax deductions in fact subsidize hub flights and may be associated with a significant part of the measured premium.

service, while airlines' behavior perhaps is better described in terms of maximizing market share or revenues in a multi-product network setting. Moreover, airlines may maximize revenues or profits on a system or subsystem basis and not necessarily on a city-pair basis. Yield management often involves computerized dynamic learning programs that can differentiate demand on the basis of a group of seats on the same flight.[27] Hub premiums may thus "cross-subsidize" other routes, markets, or seats that airlines may keep operating sometimes even at below average cost due to high fixed costs, exit (sunk) costs, or other strategic reasons

We might extend this argument and suggest that it is not necessarily that certain hub fares are too high, but rather that some of the non-hub fares are too low. Should we compare fares across routes, or perhaps look at a measure of an overall industry or an airline average fare, or profits? Usually we estimate yield; is this the right statistic? Should costs be considered?

Morrison and Winston (1995) incorporate the impact of several trip attributes including stage length (which affects average cost, among other things) as an explanatory variable in obtaining their dramatic reduction in the premium level. It is also worth emphasizing that with non-obvious pricing (frequent fliers, for example) and an ever wider range of restrictions and fare variability, it is quite difficult to characterize the "real" average fare for a trip.

Questions like this are typical of the challenges that economists face in empirical studies. While we might be able to address them and to provide better estimates, the main question remains. Even if we can come up with an ideal econometric model and confirm that a hub premium does exist, it remains to be shown that there is an overall net cost (or benefit) to the system from a social welfare perspective. This is a difficult challenge in and of itself, and it is particularly challenging in a complex, evolving, dynamic industry with real-time strategic interactions and subject to continuing technological changes and uncertainties.

If a significant hub premium does exist, does the benefit of a complex hub-and-spoke network outweigh the hub premium? The evolving concentrated network coalition structure delivers increased network benefits and production cost reduction advantages as well as increased anticompetitive aspects and other costs (congestion, more connecting flights). Traditional methodology suggests that these costs and benefits have to somehow be added up and then compared to some alternative benchmark in order to assess social benefit or cost.

Morrison and Winston (1995) claim that the hub premium is negligible in relation to deregulation's benefits of fare reduction by comparing their estimated hub premium to an artificial fare calculated according to a pre-deregulation CAB formula. Their conclusion is widely quoted in celebrating the success of deregulation. There is no doubt that this argument is interesting—but is it meaningful? One must be hard pressed to believe that the CAB would have kept its regulation policy and pricing formula unchanged for more than twenty years absent deregulation. Nor do we know how the industry would have evolved in the absence of deregulation. Moreover, it is doubtful that the current system and related technology and other innovations would have emerged under regulation.

---

[27]Yield management and pricing are discussed in more detail in Chapter 7.

The Morrison and Winston argument can be countered, for example, by suggesting that we compare fares charged by major hub airlines to fares charged by Southwest and small low-cost airlines that use mostly linear network systems as a competing technology, representing an ideal theoretical structure. Such a comparison might indicate a high social cost of the hub-and-spoke system compared to a mostly linear one and turn Morrison and Winston's conclusion on its head.

The problem is that we do not have a control group and that ideal benchmarks don't exist as real-life alternatives. Southwest adopted a unique strategy of selecting specific niche airports that are dense enough to support linear traffic yet often not extensively served by the major airlines, and it obtained operational efficiency by using one family of (short-range) aircraft (737s) that can serve such a niche. Such operations serve only certain selected markets and cannot substitute for a basic air travel network system that provides high-frequency operation to a large and diverse number of markets with diverse aircraft types and passenger tastes. In addition, numerous attempts by startup airlines to duplicate Southwest's strategy since deregulation have failed, and its success is often viewed as a unique case. In a way, Southwest's strategy may be described as capturing markets that are "leftover" by the major hub airlines, and it is therefore doubtful that such a general strategy could be successful without the dominant hub network systems that created such leftovers. It is also important to note that Southwest has dominated the low-fare segment of the market, and its advantages of scale might preclude entry by new low-fare airlines. In fact, while Southwest sets lower fares than the hub airlines, one might argue that it earns super-normal fares relative to its own cost and demand conditions, and it is not facing enough competition by airlines in its specific market segment.

## 7.2    Policy Implications

Perhaps the most difficult question is related to the pragmatic policy implications of these findings and debates. During the late 1990s, antitrust authorities were confident that a hub premium exists, saying that hub-dominant power has been perhaps the most significant public policy issue in the deregulated market and that it must be battled. A study by the GAO (2001) compares fare levels at major hubs where there is competition by low-cost airlines to those where there is no such competition, and finds a significant premium (41%). These and similar findings are often titled the "Southwest effect," since it is argued that major airlines set significantly lower fares in hubs that serve flights by Southwest (as well as few other low-cost airlines).

The government position is that major incumbent airlines tend not to compete with each other and use aggressive predatory practices against small low-cost entry into dominant hubs. What can the government do?[28] Sue the hub airlines for exclusionary practices or monopolizing the market? Break the hub-and-spoke system? Compel entry of low-cost competitors into major hubs? Subsidize startup

---

[28] The DOJ and the DOT have wide authority to regulate airlines' competitive practices: the DOJ pursuant to the Sherman and Clayton Antitrust Acts and the Hart-Scott-Rodino Act, and the DOT pursuant to 49 USC 41712.

airlines? Would taking a strong position against the major airlines help discipline pricing and other strategic behavior with anticompetitive aspects? Should the government block proposed mergers of major incumbents?[29]

It is no coincidence that TWA and US Airways were targeted for takeover during the year 2000. These were the two least efficient and most financially troubled airlines within the majors. It is important to note that these takeover trends reflect not only the leading airlines' tendency to increase market share but also the struggle of the less efficient ones to survive or else exit the market in the most efficient manner, given overall industry attempts to adjust capacity to a bumpy business cycle.[30]

Government attempts to issue enforcement guidelines for fair competition or to otherwise interfere in a significant way with major hub airlines' acquisition of market power have thus far largely failed due to institutional and political constraints as well as the complexity and ambiguity of the issues involved. A major antitrust lawsuit alleging predatory pricing against American Airlines was decided in spring 2001 in favor of the airline. The judge in this case used the traditional view of average variable cost as a measurement against which to compare fares in order to determine predatory behavior and found that American priced its fares consistently above this measure.

This case joins a long history of court reluctance to take strong positions against aggressive competition in the absence of an alternative non-ambiguous and widely agreed upon litmus test that could help in determining when a response to new entry becomes illegitimate. Attempts by the Antitrust Division in this case to introduce new post-Chicago School economic theory largely failed and the court, in fact, legitimized future aggressive competitive response by major incumbents.

A new legislative initiative in 2001, the Aviation Competition Restoration Act, S415, focused attention on the exclusionary impact of gate and slot control by major incumbent airlines. One of the main ideas was to open some access to airports through reallocation of gates and slots as well as to emphasize gates and slots concentration as a major consideration in merger and acquisition scrutiny by the regulator. It is noteworthy that while forcing such competition is perhaps the only pragmatic policy available to the regulator (given the antitrust court's position and the absence of price regulation), it is not clear that such a policy would reduce systemwide prices in the long run or whether it is justified from a theoretical efficiency perspective.[31]

---

[29] These and other policy issues are discussed throughout the book and are summarized in Chapter 9.

[30] Eastern Airlines and Pan Am were the least efficient airlines in the previous economic cycle and exited the market in the early 1990s.

[31] The general theoretical approach to this issue assumes competition over a homogeneous product between equally efficient firms or else firms with access to the same technology and markets. The general antitrust wisdom is to stop an inefficient incumbent from driving efficient competitors out of the market. Low-cost airlines, however, use a different technology and offer a differentiated product that only partly competes with the set of products offered by the major incumbent. Analytically, one should perhaps adopt a model that emphasizes the multi-product and the system nature of the competition between such networks and investigate the welfare implications of forcing competition into hubs, given various possible strategic responses by the major airlines. Under certain conditions it is possible that the incumbent will accommodate entry and that prices may eventually go up rather

The new industry crisis, beginning in the early 2000s, and the September 11 events forced certain airlines into bankruptcy and may further increase the consolidation of the major hub network airlines.[32] The new reality made many of the antitrust arguments of the late 1990s irrelevant. Can the government object to further network integration and consolidation moves of an industry struggling to survive? Such further consolidation and concentration of the major network airlines may be necessary in order to reduce average cost and face the challenge of the new low-cost airlines.

The major concern of the regulators is that the increased market power embedded in the dominant hub network system has resulted or ultimately will result in super-normal fares and profits. Yet, the average long-term real-fare trend seems to be declining, profits have not been super-normal, and there are consistent concerns with the industry's long-term ability to finance itself. Moreover, it seems that the public during the late 1990s complained more about poorer product quality and service and less about high fares. While political initiatives to protect passengers' rights seem to have gained some public support, initiatives aimed at fighting airlines' exclusionary strategic behavior and unfair competition have not attracted much public attention. In addition, during the late 1990s the industry faced overcapacity (relative to infrastructure constraints), which translates into congestion and delays, especially at major hub cities—a condition that could have required increasing fares in order to reduce traffic.

As for economists, it seems that while the view that the industry has natural oligopolistic characteristics with potential anticompetitive effects has gained in popularity, it is still debatable whether the social cost of the free market failure justifies the cost of the government's cure.

---

then down. Also, an incumbent may reduce or match prices in response to entry but will increase fares on other routes. It may also respond by increasing capacity or offer new connection combinations or adjust frequent flier benefits and agent commissions.

[32] The impact of the September 11th events and the early 2000s trends are discussed in Chapter 8.

# CHAPTER 2

# AIRCRAFT

> [The airline business]... has historically run
> as an extremely elaborate version of a model
> railroad, that is one in which you try to make
> enough money to buy more equipment.[33]

An economic recession, high oil prices, and an air traffic controllers' strike made the airlines' transition into deregulation in the early 1980s a bumpy ride. Aggressive competition over high-density linear routes resulted in industrywide losses. With an oversupply of equipment, airlines resorted to grounding mostly older-generation aircraft, and labor forces were severely pared down. Yet, as is often the case in a highly cyclical industry, boom follows gloom, and an impressive economic recovery accelerated demand for air travel during most of the 1980s. The deregulated industry responded with a spectacular network expansion on the one hand, and an increased consolidation on the other.

The year 1988 was one of the best years for the United States and the world airline industry, as revenue passenger miles and operating profits reached new peaks. When economic growth rates slowed toward the end of the eighties, so did revenue passenger miles and airlines' profits. It became apparent that the booming eighties were fading away. Then, in a move that largely ignored the business cycle and the industry's financial condition, the airlines placed the highest number ever of orders for new aircraft with manufacturers. These enormous financial commitments for new aircraft with the economic downturn of the early 1990s eliminated possible industry profits for the next several years.

This chapter examines aspects of strategic behavior with respect to aircraft as input in the air travel market. Strategic considerations played an important role both in post-deregulation interest group politics concerning safety and environmental regulation and in the airlines' motivation toward the end of the 1980s to order an unprecedented number of new aircraft.

The typical dilemma for an aircraft manufacturer is that it competes with itself; that is, it must replace an established and earlier version of a product it has sold. Older aircraft have turned out to be durable and efficient, and they thus constituted a significant part of the market. Older aircraft are extremely tough competitors for new models. The manufacturers actually became the victims of their own success, and adopted a strategy of fighting the market for the old aircraft in an attempt to promote demand for new aircraft.

---

[33] Levin (1996, p. 46).

Aircraft acquisition policies also played a strategic role in the developing competition among airlines in the air travel market. Fleet composition (in terms of newer- and older-generation aircraft) became an important strategic variable in airline competition as new generations of aircraft became available. This in turn affected airlines' production technology and cost. Post-deregulation diversity in fleet composition went hand-in-hand with acceleration of intraindustry heterogeneity in cost structure. It is traditionally the case that startups and small or less financially strong airlines, and charters and cargo airlines operate proportional older aircraft. The major financially stronger airlines operate more new aircraft. This heterogeneous fleet composition is associated with a heterogeneous industry structure and interest group structure.

The financially strong airlines, as a group, used this heterogeneity strategically by supporting government intervention and regulation that imposed a higher burden on the other airlines. Such a strategy raises the rival group's cost and poses additional barriers to new entry. The major airlines with the newer aircraft lobbied for a surtax based on fuel consumption, for example, because such a tax favors the newer, more fuel-efficient aircraft. Similarly, the major airlines operating the newer equipment supported safety and environmental regulations that were harder for older aircraft operators to meet.

Also, aircraft age emerged as a marketing tool. Airlines operating newer aircraft attempted to differentiate their product, suggesting that a seat on a newer airplane is better than a seat on an older one, safer and more comfortable. Actions like this played an important role in the post-deregulation airlines' strategic behavior.

Aircraft manufacturers and the major financially strong airlines (operating newer aircraft) came together to form an ad hoc coalition with a mutual interest of disparaging the older aircraft. During the last quarter of the 1980s, the industry embarked on an unprecedented regulatory effort directed at old aircraft. The cost of compliance often amounted to the market value of the aircraft at the time the regulation became effective.

At the same time, a great number of new aircraft orders were placed, while it must have been clear to the industry that economic growth was slowing down, that profits were declining, and that such a volume of new orders could not be justified unless there were a massive retirement of old aircraft. It was also clear that the old aircraft were still efficient in operation and not less safe than the new ones.

In a further turn of events, the new aircraft were not delivered until the early 1990s, when the industry was struggling with a major economic crisis, which ended with the demise or bankruptcy of several major airlines and further industry consolidation.

In this chapter I suggest that oligopolistic competition among manufacturers over market share in aircraft markets and among airlines over market share in air travel markets caused aircraft ordered during the late 1980s to be completely out of step with standard considerations of economic cycles or the demand for air travel. I focus more attention later on the specific environmental and safety regulation initiatives that targeted the older aircraft.

# 1. AIRCRAFT GENEALOGY

The introduction of US-built commercial jet aircraft in the late 1950s not surprisingly had a devastating economic impact on the previous generation of aircraft. The new jet engine-powered aircraft had longer ranges, higher speeds, greater seat/cargo capacities, and significantly lower costs per seat mile. But— they required many more passengers to break even. The surviving propeller-driven aircraft technology maintained only a marginal market niche in serving low-density short-haul markets, where they retained economic superiority over jet-powered aircraft.

## 1.1 First Generation

The first four-engine Boeing 707/720 aircraft were delivered in 1958, followed by the Douglas DC8s in 1959. In 1963, Boeing introduced the 727-100, a three-engine aircraft that was able to carry up to 129 passengers over short- to medium-range routes. In 1967, a stretched version of this aircraft, the 727-200, capable of carrying 170 passengers, was delivered, and in 1972, the first heavier version with an improved wing, called the B727-200 Advanced, came to market. The 727 was in fact a family of aircraft that could cover short to medium ranges with diverse engine intermix capabilities (Pratt & Whitney JT8D-7, -9, -15, -17), diverse weights, and possible modification with addition of extra fuel tanks that could extend its range.

In 1965 and 1967, Douglas and Boeing introduced (respectively) their DC9-10 and 737-100 twin-jet, short-range aircraft in the 100-seat category. These aircraft as well were subsequently stretched, to develop into a family of aircraft with more seat capacity and longer ranges. In the early 1970s, a new widebody technology was introduced, as the jumbo jet aircraft (Boeing 747-100/200, DC-10, and L-1011) were offered as replacements for the B707 and DC8 aircraft. Increased engine power, range, and seat-capacity made these aircraft suitable mostly for high-density coast-to-coast and international markets.

All these aircraft represent the general fleet in use when the airlines made their transition to deregulation. I refer to these airplanes loosely as either first-generation or "old" or "older" aircraft. I should also distinguish between the short- and medium-range single-aisle aircraft, which I call "small" or "narrowbody" aircraft (727s, 737s, and DC9s) and the long-range "large" or "widebody" aircraft (747s, DC-10s, and L-1011s).

## 1.2 Aircraft Age

Old and new are relative descriptors that have different meanings in different contexts. There is no avoiding metaphorical significance. For aircraft, people usually associate "old" with slowness, fragility, tendency to break down, high operating costs, high noise levels, and lower levels of safety. A commentator on a television talk show I watched was shocked by the fact that aircraft that are 15 years old are still flying. "I don't feel safe driving a 10-year-old car," she said. "Why would I want to fly in a 15-year-old aircraft?" To the uninformed, this conclusion may seem reasonable, but is the comparison correct? Maybe we should compare aircraft structure to the life of a bridge; after all, there are certain similarities in the design and maintenance of aircraft and bridge structures (by this standard, a 15-year-old aircraft is an infant in comparison with the London Bridge).

The first commercial jet aircraft, the British Comet, suffered several fatal crashes that were attributed to metal fatigue—this when the aircraft was barely one year into operation. The supersonic transport Concorde, on the other hand, was the oldest aircraft crossing the Atlantic (over 30 years old) before it ceased operation in 2004, yet perceived by both public and passengers as a technological marvel. When does an aircraft become too old for commercial use?

The industry's perception of age has all along been different from the public's. In fact, the industry has held that a properly maintained aircraft can fly forever. The industry's view says:

> there is no limit to the service life of Boeing damage-tolerant-design airplane structure, provided necessary inspections are carried out along with timely repair and or replacement of damaged structure or with preventive modification (Goranson and Miller 1989, p. 1).

The public, though, thinks that aircraft age directly and significantly affects safety. I would propose that no real effort has ever been put into educating the public or changing the perception that older aircraft are less safe, because it has supported the strategic interest of the largest major airlines and the manufacturers to disparage the old aircraft.

Aircraft age is typically measured by the number of total flight hours and cycles flown (one cycle is equal to one takeoff and landing). The number of cycles flown is usually a more critical measure than calendar age, because it reflects wear and tear and stress that are related to landings and takeoffs and cabin compression and decompression. Age measured in terms of calendar years only is less informative because it does not reflect an aircraft's actual use patterns.

When is an airplane old enough to be retired and replaced? The industry has adopted a two-dimensional framework for this question. One dimension is *mechanical life*, focusing mainly on maintenance and safety requirements. The second is *economic life*, focusing on the cost of maintenance.

### 1.2.1  Mechanical Life

With respect to the mechanical issue, the industry has adopted (and the government has formalized by regulation) the notion that design and production requirements together with continued and systematic maintenance, monitoring, and modification of aircraft in operation must produce an infinitely safe mechanical product. Regulation requires manufacturers to comply with quite strict requirements of "fail-safe" and "damage-tolerance" standards in designing and building aircraft. These standards require structural and system redundancy (including system multiplicity and backups), significantly enhancing an aircraft's ability to recover in case of failure.

Extensive testing of structures and systems is required prior to certification by the FAA for commercial use, and mandatory maintenance requirements are imposed on an aircraft in commercial use. It is the airline's responsibility to obtain the FAA's approval for both its specific maintenance program and the manuals that it develops based on the aircraft manufacturer's recommendations. Continual monitoring and review by the regulator, the operator, and the manufacturer are required once the aircraft enters service.

Defects and problems that occur during normal operation or that are revealed in incidents and accidents are evaluated by the industry. Usually they trigger a recommendation by the manufacturer, typically in the form of a Service Bulletin (SB). When such recommendations have airworthiness implications, they are issued as mandatory regulations, usually as Airworthiness Directives (ADs) or Federal Aviation Regulations (FARs). If an aircraft type exhibits recurrent problems that may be associated with faulty design, specific mandatory modification of the aircraft is triggered. Problems can trigger the grounding of an entire fleet or class of aircraft, or even a Special Certification Review (SCR) by the FAA.

Ongoing maintenance is usually conducted by the airlines on a routine scheduled basis, as well as a non-routine basis. Non-routine maintenance addresses specific discrepancies if any, before during, or after scheduled maintenance. Maintenance checks of aircraft are performed at mandatory scheduled intervals. During scheduled and recurrent structural checks, the fuselage is inspected and repaired, and parts of the structure may be replaced. Critical parts and components of airframes and engines are limited by hour or by cycle of utilization and/or calendar time, and must be overhauled or replaced at mandatory intervals.

Avionics and other equipment are continually updated and upgraded according to mandatory FAA requirements and an airline's own configuration standards. For example, all commercial aircraft of any age must comply with current requirements for ground proximity warning system (GPWS); traffic and collision alert system (TCAS), windshear alert systems, and flight data and voice recording systems (FDR and FVR). Many airlines have installed new global positioning satellite (GPS) navigation systems as they have become available.

An airplane might be 20 years old, but many of its systems have been updated, upgraded, and routinely overhauled or modified. An engine goes through a similar process. All its critical life-limited parts are replaced at mandatory intervals with new and/or overhauled parts. Hot-section parts are replaced periodically, and other parts and components are overhauled or replaced during scheduled maintenance. It is conceivable that the only original part in an old JT8D engine, for example, is the identifying placard (showing the serial number) attached to the gearbox, because all other parts and components have been replaced during years of maintenance. How would we define the age of such an engine?

Any aircraft and engine maintenance work must be performed by FAA-regulated and certified personnel and entities, whether by airlines or by outside vendors. Similarly, all parts, components, and repair and testing tools and equipment, as well as manufacturing, inspection, and repair procedures, must be certified and subject to FAA regulation. In general, the FAA must certify a repair shop (whether an airline's or an independent firm's), and the airlines must audit and monitor the performance of the shop according to established standards. The FAA monitors and enforces performance of both the shop and the airline.

### 1.2.2 Economic Life

The second dimension of aircraft age is its "economic life." An aircraft becomes obsolete if its operating cost exceeds the cost of a newer competing aircraft. This could happen if a superior new technology is introduced. As we have noted, the introduction of jet engine technology made most propeller-powered aircraft in the 1960s uneconomic for operation almost overnight. The introduction of the second generation of jet aircraft during the 1980s was expected to cause retirement of many first-generation aircraft because of the newer aircraft's lower fuel consumption. Or, an aircraft may become obsolete if the maintenance costs necessary to keep it airworthy rise above a certain level.

One of the major cost disadvantages of an older aircraft is generally higher maintenance costs. Older airframes are more susceptible to metal fatigue and cracks because of stress and corrosion. They thus require more inspection, more repairs, and more aircraft down time for maintenance. All things equal, an older aircraft is more expensive to maintain, and the cost increases with increased use (age) of the aircraft.

### 1.3 Second Generation

The second generation of narrowbody aircraft was introduced to the market during the first half of the 1980s, starting with the MD80—a stretch version of the DC9 with new and more powerful engines. In 1982, a new, longer-range, higher-capacity (one-aisle) aircraft—the 757—was delivered, and in 1984, Boeing ceased production of the 727 and started to deliver a new family of 737 aircraft (designated B737-300, -400, and -500). The new Boeing 737 and 757 aircraft covered the markets previously served by the 737s and 727s. Among the larger aircraft produced in 1982 was a smaller twin-engine (double-aisle) model 767 that could carry over 250 passengers between 3,100 miles in its shorter-range version to over 6,000 miles in its later extended-range version.

The second-generation aircraft were designed following the oil crisis of the 1970s. Reducing fuel consumption was a major design challenge. It was achieved primarily by developing a new generation of high bypass engines, producing higher thrust at lower fuel burn levels. In addition, new digital technology and increased automation reduced pilots' workload and required only two cockpit crew members instead of three. The expectation was that the savings due to lower fuel consumption, smaller flight crews, and reduced maintenance expense would justify retirement of first-generation aircraft and the acquisition of new second-generation aircraft.

The 727 had been the best-selling Boeing airplane, with 1,832 units produced. Its production line was closed with the delivery of the new 737-300/400 aircraft in late 1984. The three-engine, three-person cockpit, 727 was expected to be the main economic casualty of the newer more efficient family of 737 aircraft. Boeing adopted the 737 designation for the new generation of its aircraft, and abandoned the designator 727, the most popular of its aircraft. The company expected that an accelerated retirement of the fuel guzzling 727 aircraft would create significant demand for its new family of 737 and 757 aircraft.

The new 737 airframe was a descendant of the first generation 737-200 aircraft. Its fuselage was extended to accommodate up to 149 passengers, and new and more fuel-efficient (CFM56-3) engines were installed.[34] For passengers, the new 737 aircraft had a look and performance (in terms of speed and range) very similar to the previous generation of narrowbody aircraft. Its ability to effect significant retirement of older-generation aircraft was thus critically dependent on the market behavior of oil prices.

*1.4    Oil Prices*

The pendulum swing of oil prices during the 1970s and 1980s is important for our understanding of the story. In ten years, oil prices increased over tenfold, from under $3 per barrel at the end of 1972 to $34 in 1981 (jet fuel increased from 11 cents to $1.14 per gallon) Boeing (1991, p. 14). The operation of first-generation aircraft, designed in the 1960s before oil became such a major issue, suffered significantly in the 1970s from oil price behavior. Reducing fuel consumption constituted the major design challenge for the new-generation aircraft designed in the late 1970s (the MD80s and 757s) and the early 1980s (the new 737), when oil prices reached their peak. Then, starting in 1981, the oil price trend reversed itself through most of that decade (see Figure 4).[35] In fact, jet fuel prices dropped by almost one-half (in real terms) between the peak level in 1981 and the average level during the second half of the 1980s.

Newer, expensive aircraft, designed with the objective of cutting fuel costs, were introduced into a falling fuel price world that dissipated most of their economic advantage.

Demand for the old narrowbody aircraft increased significantly starting in the early 1980s and throughout the decade. This occurred not only because of the general boom in demand for domestic air travel and falling oil prices, but also because of structural market changes. One reason was the development of hub-and-spoke networks. Longer routes came to be served by a combination of shorter ones connected at a hub. Economies of density and scope at local hubs required greater seat capacity and replacement of smaller commuter aircraft with larger jet aircraft in this category. (The DC9 and B737, for example, were ideal hub aircraft in the 100-130-seat category.) More destinations served from hubs, as well as a significant increase in frequencies of flights, required more aircraft.

[34] Produced by a joint venture between GE and the French company, Snecma.
[35] Jet-fuel cost per gallon, 1972 price = 100. Source: American Transport Association.

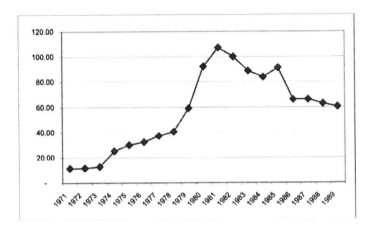

*Figure 4. US Airlines Fuel Price Index*

In addition, older, narrowbody aircraft were in demand by the new startup airlines that attempted entry into the market during the 1980s. A fascinating phenomenon was the almost overnight explosion of a new market for small packages and overnight mail service, led by Federal Express. This market used a hub system with relatively more demand for short- and medium-range aircraft, and absorbed a large quantity of older aircraft, mostly 727s, which happened to have a relatively high volumetric efficiency for this specific cargo.

With declining fuel prices, the durability and reliability of the older-generation aircraft and the dramatic expansion of the deregulated market kept demand high for these aircraft throughout the 1990s. During the recession period of the early 1980s, approximately 800 older-generation aircraft were retired. Most of them were disassembled for parts that were used to support operation of the surviving first-generation aircraft.

## 2. AIRCRAFT ECONOMICS

Declining oil prices were a major factor in maintaining high demand and prices for the old narrowbody aircraft. In fact, prices of certain old narrowbody aircraft more than doubled between 1981 and the middle 1980s. The difference between the acquisition costs of the old 737-200 or 727 aircraft and the new 737-300/400/500 or 757 aircraft, however, did not justify accelerated retirement of older planes. With the relatively low oil prices, the difference in operating cost was not enough to justify the difference in ownership cost. This experience was much like the one for automobiles during the early 1980s; the incremental acquisition cost of a fuel-efficient Japanese car did not justify the dollar value of the gas savings compared to a less-efficient American car.

## 2.1 First- vs. Second-Generation Aircraft

Table 1 reflects comparative operating data of first-generation versus second-generation narrowbody aircraft for the quarter ending December 31, 1989, extracted from an industry publication.[36] It breaks down operating costs per hour of aircraft utilization by standard industry cost categories.

*Table 1. Operating Data 1st Versus 2nd Generation Aircraft*

|  | DC9-30 | 737-200 | 727-200 | 737-300 | 757-200 |
|---|---|---|---|---|---|
| **Flying:** |  |  |  |  |  |
| Crew | 405.00 | 380.02 | 493.56 | 371.77 | 481.83 |
| Fuel | 545.00 | 539.54 | 854.93 | 507.90 | 667.41 |
| Insurance | 4.00 | 4.41 | 3.96 | 6.48 | 11.61 |
| Other | 2.00 | 0.75 | 2.11 | 0.08 | 0.01 |
| Total **Maintenance:** | 956.00 | 924.72 | 1,354.56 | 886.23 | 1,160.86 |
| Direct | 285.00 | 259.51 | 322.25 | 219.24 | 267.15 |
| Burden | 159.00 | 120.14 | 212.81 | 93.35 | 84.51 |
| Total | 444.00 | 379.65 | 535.06 | 312.59 | 351.66 |
| **Total** | 1,401.00 | 1,304.37 | 1,889.62 | 1,198.82 | 1,512.52 |
| Dep/Rent | 280.00 | 329.13 | 263.00 | 499.57 | 590.93 |
| **TOTAL** | 1,681.00 | 1,633.50 | 2,152.62 | 1,698.39 | 2,103.45 |
| Load Factor % | 57.39 | 57.90 | 58.61 | 58.84 | 60.25 |
| ASM | 102.60 | 110.00 | 147.90 | 130.50 | 186.90 |
| Cost S/H | 16.48 | 16.78 | 14.56 | 13.01 | 11.26 |
| Use (Hr) | 6.70 | 7.30 | 7.50 | 8.60 | 9.10 |
| Flight Length | 415.00 | 432.00 | 669.00 | 586.00 | 652.00 |

According to the publication's calculations, total direct operating cost of the second-generation aircraft analyzed was 8% lower than the cost of the older-generation aircraft. This difference is explained mostly by lower fuel consumption. The ownership cost component (depreciation and rent), however, is significantly higher for the newer-generation aircraft, making up nearly 28% of the total direct

---

[36] Source: *Air Transport World*, "Aircraft Opearating Data" October 1990, p. 150.

operating cost for the new generation, compared to only 14% for the older-generation aircraft. [37]

A comparison of cost per seat mile across the aircraft shows that the new 737 and 757 aircraft are more efficient than the older-generation aircraft. The 757, for example, consumed approximately 250 gallons less in fuel per hour compared to the 727 (representing a savings of approximately $188 at 1989 fuel prices). The new digital ("glass") two-person cockpit saves an additional almost $12 per hour over the 727. These savings reflect the major advantage of the new aircraft technology over the old one. The 757 is equipped with two engines that generate more thrust at less cost than the three old JT8D engines installed on a 727. In addition, the 757 can carry more passengers on longer-range routes.

Cost differences are highly dependent on jet fuel prices, however. Table 1 reflects airlines' accounting for the last quarter of 1989, when jet fuel prices were slightly above 60 cents per gallon. Obviously an increase or a decrease in cost per gallon can change the picture either way.

The data in Table 1 are average accounting (historical) data. Accounting ownership costs depend on somewhat arbitrary depreciation assumptions. They do not reflect cash flow and cannot tell much regarding the cost of adding the next (marginal) aircraft to a fleet.

For purposes of illustration, assume that an airline contemplates adding an aircraft to its fleet.[38] Table 2 reflects average market values and monthly rents for various aircraft types in December 1989.[39]

*Table 2. Aircraft Market Value and Rental Rates*

| A/C | DC9-30 | 737-200A | 727-200A | 737-300 | 757-200 |
|---|---|---|---|---|---|
| Value | 6,500,000.00 | 6,750,000.00 | 6,000,000.00 | 20,000,000.00 | 30,000,000.00 |
| Rent | 100,000.00 | 100,000.00 | 110,000.00 | 250,000.00 | 375,000.00 |
| Monthly Hr | 201.00 | 219.00 | 225.00 | 258.00 | 273.00 |
| Rent per Hr | 498.00 | 456.62 | 488.89 | 968.99 | 1,373.63 |
| Total Cost | 1,401.00 | 1,304.37 | 1,889.62 | 1,198.80 | 1,512.52 |
| TC + Rent | 1,898.00 | 1,760.99 | 2,378.51 | 2,167.81 | 2,886.15 |

---

[37] The publication includes in its 14% rate other aircraft that are not included in Table 1.

[38] While general industry statistics are quite useful for illustrating these points, they are far from accurate. For example, the airlines are viewed as a coherent industry, and airline-specific aspects are ignored. They show reported costs, given a certain route allocation. 757 routes, for example, are longer, and therefore expected to cost less per hour. Also, aircraft are assigned to different routes with different levels of demand and load factors. A specific comparison analysis requires specific route analysis.

[39] Compiled from industry publications.

The monthly rent is divided by the actual average flight-hour utilization for the respective aircraft from Table 1 in order to normalize the rent per hour. The resulting hourly rent cost is substituted for the hourly depreciation/rent cost in Table 2, in order to indicate the expected market cost of operating an additional aircraft (as opposed to historic rent or accounting depreciation). Table 2 shows that when market rents are considered, the new-generation aircraft lose their attractiveness.

Another important issue is evident from the operating statistics. The second-generation 737-300 and the 757-200 aircraft average operation costs reflected in Table 1 are based on significantly higher average monthly utilization. 757 and 737-300 aircraft are operated roughly 20% more (hours) than 727s and 737-200s. The 757 and 737-300 are far more expensive, and lose much of their economic attractiveness if they are operated at lower average utilization rates. At an average utilization of 200 monthly hours, which is the traditional average utilization of most non-major hub airlines, they may not break even with current average load factors. When a high level of utilization is required in order for the economics of the new aircraft to work, only high-frequency scheduled airlines can justify acquiring them. Moreover, the cost statistics show that the load factors of the 737-300 and the 757 are higher than load factors for the old aircraft.

The industry in fact assigned the new-generation aircraft to higher-frequency, higher-density, operations. High utilization and load factors would be required to reduce the high fixed ownership cost of the new aircraft. Such an operational profile could be achieved only in a major hub operation or in an otherwise high-use high-density linear route network. The economic rationale behind this observation is the increasing return to scale and density. A significant part of aircraft operation cost is its fixed acquisition cost. In fact, if one considers the rental cost of an aircraft on the margin (Table 2), this is the greatest cost component. For old aircraft, the fixed acquisition cost is small relative to the variable operating costs, so lower utilization levels are sufficient to amortize the cost. The operational principle of new expensive aircraft is straightforward: They must spend most of the day in the air serving high-density routes in order to amortize their high ownership cost.

## 2.2    Second Generation Aircraft and Hub Operation

The importance of utilization rates are not always understood, particularly by observers who may not be directly involved with these issues. It was conventional wisdom at the time that the new aircraft are more efficient to operate than the old ones. In fact this is a myth. The conclusion is true only if the new aircraft are operated at high levels of use on routes that can support relatively high load factors.

I have been approached several times by non-major hub operators interested in acquiring new aircraft, encouraged by general industry statistics and manufacturer presentations suggesting that the new aircraft would be more profitable than the older ones. The operators were disappointed to find out that this perception is not borne out when they plug their actual cost and market data into specific route plans. As a general observation, the operations profile necessary to justify purchase of the new expensive aircraft could be achieved only by a major airline in a major hub where high frequency and economics of density and scope reduce the average ownership cost. Southwest Airlines is an exception, because of its unique ability to achieve very high levels of aircraft utilization (the industry's highest) with high load factors on its linear routes.

Major hub airlines can generally offer high flight frequency and density out of their hubs. Hub operations facilitate increased aircraft utilization and load factors. The uniqueness of Southwest's strategy is that it targets niche markets that are less congested but have sufficient demand to justify high-utilization, high-load factor, linear route systems, while eliminating aircraft ground time and improving aircraft utilization. With high operational efficiency of ground and aircrew systems, Southwest has achieved remarkable economic success by producing the highest production rates from its fixed-cost production capacity.

The requirement for relatively higher utilization rates and load factors makes the new aircraft more susceptible to cyclical downturns. First, load factors traditionally decline during recessions. In addition, reduced utilization due to falling demand does not change airlines' commitments to pay rent or make loan payments for the acquisition of the new aircraft. Older aircraft are more expensive to operate (while less expensive to own) so reducing utilization rates during a recession reduces the major cash outlay of operating an old aircraft. The major cost component of a new aircraft is the ownership cost, however, which must be incurred irrespective of the economic cycle.

This background is important for an understanding of the ad hoc coalition that developed in the late 1980s between the manufacturers and the major airlines.[40] Expensive new aircraft could be acquired and operated most profitably mainly by major hub airlines. Small, cargo, charter, and startup airlines, as well as low-frequency linear or other non-hub major airlines came to be largely excluded from the market for new aircraft. It was in the manufacturers' interest to instead support major airlines with highly concentrated hub systems and high-frequency, high-density operations, in order to sell new aircraft. The hub-and-spoke network systems were a necessary condition; they provided a combination of high utilization (frequency) and high load factors that could justify the high acquisition cost of new technology aircraft.

This essential connection between expensive new aircraft and hub technology is often overlooked by industry observers and is worth emphasizing. Buying new aircraft mandates a high fixed cost.[41] Yet the savings of the new technology were not sufficient to justify large-scale retirement of older aircraft or to otherwise significantly reduce average operating cost. Under regulation, increases in new aircraft prices and capacity were met by increased airfares. Following deregulation, increases in new aircraft prices along with high labor costs and falling airfares required increased aircraft utilization and load factors, and these were delivered

---

[40] The situation changed in the early 2000s. The manufacturers cut prices of new aircraft, and a new coalition was formed with startup airlines. See Chapter 8.

[41] A new 737 aircraft, for example, in the late 1980s cost an average of $30 million; a new 747-400 cost in the $130 million range. Once an aircraft is acquired, its rent or ownership cost is unavoidable.

mainly by complex hub-and-spoke systems that supported high flight frequencies and generated benefits of increased scale, scope, and density.

The conundrum is that the integrated hub-and-spoke systems involved high fixed costs in infrastructure and other assets mostly of a high sunk cost nature (besides aircraft). Attempts to reduce average cost encouraged an increasing production scale; more aircraft acquired and operated as well as more flight-hours used and more spokes served, which further heightened density and scope. These are important relationships to be recognized between new aircraft technologies and hub networks. These dynamic relationships contribute to the airline industry's tendency to consolidate and concentrate while expanding networks.

A somewhat analogous tendency characterizes the aircraft manufacturing industry. Aircraft design and building involves increasing-return technology due to steep learning effects, high fixed costs in design and development of new technology, and economies of scale and scope. A major portion of the cost in aircraft production is the fixed cost associated with developing and building a prototype, particularly when a new type of aircraft is developed (a 747, or a 777, for example), but also when derivatives in a class are developed (the 737-300/400/500, for example). The increasing-return nature of aircraft production encourages manufacturers to accelerate sales and increase their market share. In general, the cost of aircraft development and design (in proportion to actual production cost) has risen with the introduction of new aircraft technology, and it has become necessary to sell more units in order to amortize this cost and reduce its average level. The extent of aircraft sales, however, is constrained by the overall size of the market and the competition's share in it. Given then-expected market growth rates and the increased competition from Airbus, accelerating the retirement of previous-generation aircraft played an increasingly important role in manufacturers' strategies starting in the late 1980s.

One implication is that a smaller market for new aircraft or a stagnant one, in the face of growing development costs of new technology, tends to increase concentration in the aircraft manufacturer industry. We see an example in the debate concerning the economic viability of designing and building a new "super jumbo" aircraft. Analysts believe there is room for 500 such aircraft in the international market. Airbus officials estimated the development cost at about $12 billion, and projected 250 units would need to be sold over nine to ten years in order to break even. Boeing officials estimated the development costs at up to $20 billion, which would require almost 500 units to be sold in order to break even. It is quite clear that there is no room for more than one manufacturer in this market. If Airbus ventures into such a project (as it eventually did), it faces the risk that Boeing would develop a 747 derivative at a lower development cost and/or reduce significantly the price of its 747-400, which would make the potential market smaller for Airbus. A joint venture between Airbus and Boeing is a possible solution to this dilemma. Consider still that airlines that would buy such aircraft at an estimated cost of $230 million per unit would need considerable market share and a feeder network system that would allow the necessary load factors and utilization levels to justify such high fixed cost.

## 3. AIRCRAFT ORDERS

Falling oil prices and the high mechanical reliability of the first-generation aircraft caused retirement rates of those airplanes to be very low, significantly lower than the manufacturers' predictions. The first new 737-300 aircraft were delivered only at the end of 1984, and the 737-400 in the summer of 1986. The old aircraft flew during the first part of the unprecedented market growth of the 1980s before the new 737s were available. MDC delivered its MD80 in 1980, and by the time the new 737-300 was delivered, approximately 200 MD80 were in operation in the industry.

Competitive pressures were also exerted by Airbus. The European consortium penetrated the US market in 1977 with its A300 model aircraft, originally designed for high-density, short- to medium-range markets. Over 30 aircraft had been delivered to US airlines (particularly to Eastern Airlines) by the time the first new 737-300s were delivered at the end of 1984. Airbus took aggressive marketing steps in an attempt to penetrate the world market in general as well as the US market.[42] The first versions of the A300 were intended to provide the attractive economics of high-capacity (widebody) aircraft on short/medium routes, but this contradicted in some respects the strategic move to hub systems, which required high-frequency operations. Subsequent versions of the A300 extended its range and made it more suitable to longer linear routes. At the beginning of 1984, Airbus started designing the A320 aircraft, in direct competition with the new 737 family. This move together with an increasing market share for Airbus aircraft mostly in foreign markets made the Airbus threat more serious.[43]

In 1986, orders for new aircraft dropped significantly for the first time since the early years of the decade, mostly with respect to new narrowbody 737 and 757 aircraft. In 1986, orders for 737s fell from 253 in the previous year to 199 and in 1987 to 170, while the number of orders for 757s fell from 45 in 1985 to 13 in 1986. At the same time, the average retirement rates of older aircraft dropped to approximately 40 aircraft per year, the lowest since the mid-1970s.

With the last quarter of the 1980s, it became clear that the long economic boom and the unprecedented industry expansion of the 1980s were both coming to a halt, as the economy and airline traffic growth rates together started to decline. Orders for new aircraft declined as well. Figure 5 plots the total number of aircraft orders (per year).[44] The number of yearly orders for new jet aircraft more than tripled in 1986 compared to 1983. In 1987, orders fell from that peak. It was clear to the industry at the time that market expansion by itself would not create enough of a demand for new aircraft orders. The manufacturers realized that accelerating the retirement rates of older aircraft would be necessary in order to generate orders for new aircraft. Stubbornly, the older aircraft exhibited strong market resiliency. It is at that point that the manufacturers adopted an aggressive marketing policy of killing the market for the old-generation aircraft. They took aggressive marketing steps to persuade airlines to order new aircraft, and they encouraged the retirement of older equipment

---

[42] Airbus delivered aircraft to EAL and waived rent payments for several months of operation.

[43] Braniff placed the first US order for 110 A320 aircraft with Airbus during 1986.

[44] Source: *World Jet Airplane Inventory Year End 1990*, Boeing Commercial Airplane Group.

by pushing for additional safety and noise regulation aimed specifically at those aircraft.

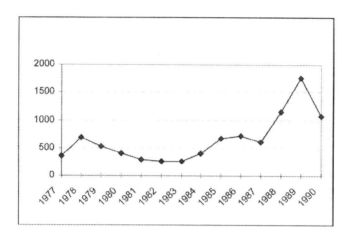

*Figure 5. New Aircraft Orders*

In a move that impacted the aircraft market in a dramatic way, the industry in 1989 placed an unprecedented number of orders for new aircraft. The number of aircraft orders placed in 1989 was almost three times the number in 1987, amounting to 1760 units. Altogether, the number of aircraft orders placed with the manufacturers during the last three years of the decade represented over 40% of the total aircraft inventory in commercial use in 1989. In dollar terms, orders of $54 billion were placed in 1988, of $96 billion in 1989 (a 78% increase over the record level of the previous year), and of $81 billion in 1990 (current dollars, according to Boeing Outlook, 1991). In 1990, Boeing reached its all-time high volume of orders: $51 billion. This enormous volume of orders was placed despite a significant drop in the world air travel growth rate (measured in revenue passenger miles, RPMs) from about 10% in 1987 to about 5% in 1989, and despite a similar expected trend in world GDP growth rates and in airline profits.

## 3.1    The Manufacturers' Problem

In the standard model of a market, products are assumed to be perishable. The completion of production, sale, and consumption of a product is an instantaneous event; the product is sold, and disappears forever (aircraft seats on a specific flight are a good example). The picture is different, however, for the firm that manufactures a durable good. Once the product is delivered to the market, it competes with demand for a new version of the product. A manufacturer of a durable good may have to fight for market share against its own product that it has sold previously. This fight is harder, the better and the more durable the old good is. The manufacturer's strategic and tactical decisions today affect both the current market for used versions of the previously delivered product and the future market for a new generation of the durable good the manufacturer expects to sell in the future.

Introduction of a new edition by a book publisher is an example of such intertemporal relationships. In general, the more significant the additions to and the modifications of the new edition, the higher the demand for this edition is expected to be. Pricing, advertising, product characteristics, and other strategic decisions made by the manufacturer in one period may conflict with its objectives in the second.

Ronald Coase has generated a theoretical debate regarding such intertemporal aspects of pricing by a durable-good monopolist. Coase's major insight is that durability might reduce monopolistic power. Since maximization of revenues implies that only a part of the product stock is sold every period (Coase uses land as an example), the monopolist incentive is to cut prices every period. Yet, since consumers are aware of such behavior, they may refrain from purchasing until the price comes down.

Coase's idea that durability erodes monopolistic power is based on his perception of buyers' strategic understanding of and response to the monopolist's behavior. A monopolist's systematic policy of intertemporal price discrimination is transparent to buyers, and they will not facilitate it (assuming there are no costs or any other consequences to waiting for the price to drop). Lease, buy-back, tie-in, trade-in, and other contractual arrangements that reflect credible commitments to maintain prices may enhance monopolist power. But even this is not for sure, transmitting credible commitments to buyers regarding high pricing may encourage entry and competition by other manufacturers. Similarly, the manufacturer's decisions regarding the durability of the product may affect its market power in the next period.

Will monopolistic manufacturers systematically build in lower durability for their product than for competitors' products? Will they overinvest in R&D in order to destroy the used version of the durable? Will competitive producers behave differently from a monopolist? Will they support regulation to reduce the value of the used versions of their product?

It is instructive to focus on three major questions: First, can an aircraft manufacturer affect the durability of its product in a significant way, given the stringent durability and safety standards imposed by the regulator? Second, is killing the market for used aircraft by, for example, promoting regulation necessarily in the manufacturer's best interest? Third, if we answer yes to the first two questions, what would the buyers, the airlines, do? It is highly unlikely that airlines would not see through such a strategy. How would they react?

*3.1.1    Can an Aircraft Manufacturer Affect Its Durability?*

Manufacturers can affect the market value of an old version of their product in several key ways: first, by developing and offering a new product or technology that changes the market for the old version; second, by strategic pricing; and third, by directly affecting the value of the old version of a durable through after-sale support contracts, maintenance and repairs, warranties, and so on. Support of regulation initiatives that are expected to impact the economic life of the old version of the durable can directly influence its market value as well.

Aircraft manufacturers are uniquely positioned to impact the economic durability of used versions of their aircraft through their important role in directing the operation and after-sale support of used aircraft.[45] All operational, maintenance, modification, and repair activity related to aircraft (or engines or any part or component) is directly controlled by the manufacturers. In most cases, manufacturers' recommendations set the required standards for operation and maintenance of aircraft. Changes in aircraft configuration or modification by airlines require the manufacturer's approval and the purchase of proper documentation. The manufacturer also controls spare parts support. Manufacturers continue research, testing, and development of techniques, procedures, improvements, and modifications of aircraft long after their delivery, in parallel with the marketing of new generations of aircraft. They participate in the investigation of accidents and the development of safety procedures and actions to guard against accidents. Safety-related service bulletins issued by manufacturers are usually enforced by the FAA as legally binding regulations in the form of Airworthiness Directives (ADs), Federal Aviation Regulations (FARs), or otherwise. Issuance of a safety-related Service Bulletins (SB) triggers an immediate regulatory response, and in most cases is translated almost automatically into a mandatory AD. Some airlines or civil aviation authorities require compliance with certain SBs even if they are not adopted as mandatory ADs by the FAA.

Manufacturers may initiate new regulation, or respond to demands for new regulation initiatives by other players. They are an integral part of the regulatory process. Indeed, the institutional core of the regulatory process is the manufacturers, the airlines, and the FAA, each player with its particular interests, information, and political power.

Aircraft manufacturers' power in the regulatory process stems to a large degree from their specialized information regarding aircraft design and production in general and in particular regarding their own product. Their expertise is in developing and researching aircraft structures, for example, and they have extensive budgets, engineering capabilities, and other resources to deal with these issues, more than many other players in the regulatory process.

It is, for example, highly unlikely that an airline or a consumer organization would invest resources in wind tunnel testing in order to study the long-term structural integrity of an aircraft. This is the kind of activity that a manufacturer would engage in.

[45] This is in addition to other strategic policies such as advertising, R&D, or pricing of new products..

Additionally, in most cases the manufacturer is the only provider of the after-sale technical and engineering support to an aircraft, including, for example, the parts and documentation that are necessary in order to comply with an SB issued by the same manufacturer. The manufacturer by and large enjoys a perfectly monopolistic position in this market as the sole source of these services.

### 3.1.2    Is Killing the Market for Used Aircraft in the Manufacturer's Best interest?

Do producers of durable goods in general benefit from supporting legislation and regulation restricting the market for used versions of their durable product? Do aircraft manufacturers benefit from killing the market for old aircraft? Economic theory deals with such issues quite extensively, but no clear-cut results have been suggested.

The traditional line of reasoning, which can be traced back to the decision in United States v. Aluminum Co. of America, is that new and used versions of a good are substitutes. Used versions of a product capture a portion of the market and stand in the way of sales of new product. The manufacturer competes with the used versions of its product as a substitute product; everything else equal, its incentive to limit the used product market is positively related to the elasticity of substitution.

The first- and the second-generation jet aircraft are close substitutes, and there is no doubt that first-generation aircraft captured (and still capture) a part of the market that otherwise could be served by new aircraft. On this basis, it would not be unexpected that the manufacturers would attempt to kill the market for old aircraft. The manufacturer's policy, however, is known or otherwise understood by the market. A move by manufacturers to limit the use of an older version of the aircraft or otherwise impose additional costs through regulation will be evident to the airlines and will be incorporated in the market price.

Economists call this the "present value effect." The market value of a durable reflects the present value of the stream of income it is expected to generate, including its future resale or scrap value. A general manufacturer policy to diminish the future value of used aircraft must therefore be reflected in the demand for and the market price of the new aircraft. The present value impact acts in an opposite direction from the substitution impact, and the manufacturer's ability to benefit from such a policy depends on these as well as the location of the supply curve.

A move by a manufacturer to undermine the market for used aircraft will also affect the industry supply curve and therefore its size and concentration. Because new and old aircraft are substitute factors of production, increasing the cost of operating older aircraft would be expected to change the industry fleet mix, production function, and supply curve. Costs imposed by such regulation can be interpreted as a tax on old aircraft. Regulation can increase the fixed cost of operating old aircraft and/or the operating variable costs.[46]

---

[46] For example, stage III noise regulation of a 727-200 aircraft required a one-time modification cost of almost $3 million. In contrast, part of the Corrosion Prevention (CPCP) and Supplemental Structural Inspection Document (SSID) regulations require recurrent inspection and modification overtime often as a function of aircraft flight time/cycles.

New aircraft are more expensive to acquire and less expensive to operate than older ones, so imposing regulation on old aircraft is expected to increase both their cost and the demand for new aircraft, causing the industry's fixed cost to move up (everything else equal). Assuming a negatively sloped demand curve for air travel, regulation is expected to dampen industry production. Increasing the cost of old aircraft also raises the financial barriers to entry by new airlines. Traditionally, new entrants acquire older, less expensive aircraft. Increasing the cost of older aircraft makes entry more expensive.

One of the arguments in favor of deregulation in the middle 1970s was that the *capital threshold of entry* into the industry was relatively low due to the availability of used aircraft that could be acquired or leased for significantly less than new aircraft. In its analysis of the industry the CAB argued:

> The potential entrant can reduce the capital threshold in a given market through the purchase of used aircraft, at a cost some 10 to 40 percent or more below that of comparable new equipment (CAB, 1975, p. 110).

Indeed, the availability of highly reliable old technology aircraft at significantly lower prices did make the entry threshold relatively low during the 1980s. Imposing aging and noise regulations directly affected the acquisition cost of old aircraft and raised the threshold costs of entry.

Is increased industry concentration in a manufacturer's best interest? There is no clear-cut answer to this question either. The smaller, financially weak, cargo and startup airlines are expected to be proportionally more affected, and because these airlines usually don't acquire new expensive aircraft, it is arguable that an industry contraction may not affect current new aircraft sales. Yet increased industry concentration may reduce the demand for new aircraft in the future, and may enhance the surviving major airlines' bargaining power with the manufacturers with respect to new aircraft acquisition in the future.

One other important element makes the decision to kill the old aircraft even more complex. The after-sale support of aircraft is a source of revenue for manufacturers, and therefore regulation aimed at modifying and fixing old aircraft creates an opportunity for additional revenues. It is not generally clear, and it is quite difficult to predict, which of these conflicting effects is the stronger, and what their overall long-term impact is.

Boeing, for example, which was best positioned to develop noise abatement technology for its aircraft, elected not to take part in this activity. Therefore, an aircraft modification that is normally treated as a manufacturer SB was left to other market players to develop and sell. Federal Express, a major operator of 727 aircraft, for example, developed noise abatement kits for installation on its fleet of aircraft and sold them to the market as well. It enjoyed a monopolistic position in this market for almost ten years while Boeing conceded a significant source of revenues in the after-sale market. Unlike Boeing, MDC elected to support its DC9 aircraft; it offered, among other things, a life extension program that included structural enhancement and engine upgrades, and it participated in the design and sales of noise abatement kits. Similarly, Boeing did not take a competitive position in the market for converting 727 aircraft into cargo configurations, and thus other companies entered the market.

It is interesting to note that, in general, Boeing adopted a more aggressive position toward killing its old aircraft than MDC. It provided the minimum required support for the after-sale market, and not much more. To the extent that Boeing's policy did encourage the sales of new aircraft, sales would have come at the cost of giving up potential additional income from the support of older-generation aircraft.

Competition among aircraft manufacturers plays an important role as well and is worth further emphasis. The hegemony of the United States in the commercial jet aircraft market started with introduction of the Boeing 707 in the late 1950s. In 1974 Airbus delivered the first four A300s, and in 1977 it penetrated the US market and delivered the first A300s to Eastern Airlines. In 1983, the A310 series was introduced, and in 1985, the first four aircraft were delivered to a US operator. The first A320s were delivered in 1988 and during the next year the first aircraft deliveries were made to the US market.

Toward the end of the 1980s, the European threat became serious. Airbus's share of the US market was small but not negligible, and grew slowly during the 1980s with over 100 aircraft deliveries by the end of 1990. Airbus could only benefit from the destruction of the old aircraft, since none of its aircraft fell into that category. It was obvious that killing the old aircraft would affect mainly US manufactured aircraft, and Airbus targeted this segment of the market.

The European public views aircraft noise as a major environmental issue, and European governments responded to demands by high-profile environmental movements by pushing for aggressive noise reduction that targeted old US manufactured aircraft. Europe in fact became the political leader in pushing for stricter noise regulations. It is also noteworthy that during the second half of the1980s new Airbus aircraft sustained above-normal accident rates, a fact that raised questions regarding the safety of the new technology incorporated in the aircraft. It was obviously expedient for Airbus and the European governments that own and control the consortium to focus attention on (US manufactured) old aircraft as a major safety and environmental hazard.

It is not a priori clear whether the decision of a manufacturer to kill the old version of a durable in general, or old aircraft in particular, is beneficial on a theoretical or practical basis. A critical element in the decision for aircraft manufacturers in reality was perhaps the importance manufacturers assigned to revenues generated by selling new aircraft compared to the expected costs of such a strategy. The investment in development of old aircraft was already amortized. The pressure at the time was to generate immediate sales of new aircraft in order to capture market share and drive down the average fixed costs of developing and building the new aircraft. Possible long-run costs of such a policy were discounted at a higher rate than the immediate impact of generating new aircraft sales.

It is also important to recall the specific conditions under which this policy decision was made during the last third part of the 1980s. The country's rate of economic growth had started to slow; the absolute number of orders for new aircraft fell in 1987 for the first time since the beginning of the economic recovery in 1983; and the price differential between new and old aircraft did not justify significant retirement of old aircraft. The major objective of the US manufacturers was to generate immediate sales of new aircraft and to increase market share by accelerating retirement of the previous-generation aircraft.

## 3.2    The Airlines' Problem

Theory gives us a way to understand the so-called present value effect, which captures the market response to a manufacturer's strategy. This effect corresponds to Coase's idea of the buyer's response to the monopolist's intertemporal pricing strategy.

In our story, the airlines' response to the manufacturers' strategy is crucial for an understanding of the overall market result. In the air transportation industry, aircraft transactions largely represent a bilateral-monopoly arrangement between a manufacturer and a major airline. It is hard to credit that the manufacturers' strategy not be transparent to the airlines—that airlines would fall blindly into the manufacturers' trap. What should the airlines' strategic response be? Should airlines attempt to circumvent efforts by the manufacturer to kill the market for old aircraft, or should they accommodate the manufacturer's strategy? In our story, the airlines effectively colluded with the manufacturers, and responded by placing an unprecedented number of orders for new aircraft at increasing prices. Why?

The airlines' conduct can be interpreted in the context of strategic behavior models. The previous chapter discussed the strategic importance of investments in hub-and-spoke networks. Investment in a hub system, while directly impacting the hub airline's production and cost functions, also strategically affects the competition's position. A partial explanation of the major airlines' move to place such a volume of aircraft orders can be related to strategic investment in overcapacity directed at deterring entry. Credible threats to deter or preempt market entry require actual investment in durable, transaction-specific assets. The major airlines made a significant specific (sunk) investment in hub-and-spoke network systems. Contrary to the contestable markets argument that aircraft are not specific to a route, and are therefore not a sunk cost, in fact aircraft are an *integral part* of a network system. An airline cannot have a route system without the aircraft to operate it. Nor is investment in a complex network system credible without acquisition of the aircraft to operate the system. A network system including the aircraft is specific and requires meaningful sunk costs. The major airlines' strategic move both to create such network systems and to order a significant number of new aircraft represented a credible threat to new entry, and had a direct exclusionary impact on competitors. The major airlines had captured ground and airside limited space by high-frequency aircraft operations.

## 3.2.1    Raising Rivals' Costs of Acquiring Aircraft

The strategic nature of hub-and-spoke networks has long since been widely recognized. I'd like to focus on a related aspect of strategic behavior that has gained acceptance in economic theory in general, not with particular respect to the airline industry. The group of major (financially strong) airlines embarked on a policy aimed at doing away with the old aircraft in an attempt to raise the costs of rival airlines that specialized in operating such aircraft. Raising rivals' cost (RRC) is a familiar exclusionary strategy in industrial organization as well as in antitrust cases. An example is a celebrated 1985 study by the Department of Justice, which concluded that American Airlines through control over its computerized reservation system raised booking service prices for a group of new entrants (Air Florida, NY Air, and Midway). In this case, there was a direct strategic impact on the rivals' cost, and through a practice implemented at a negligible cost to the incumbent.

The move of certain airlines to affected old aircraft in an attempt to increase rivals' cost falls into a somewhat more complex category of RRC. Adopting such a policy would require strategic investment by the group of airlines that adopted it, and the policy moreover would subsequently be expected to increase costs for all airlines, not just new entrants. Yet the heterogeneous structure of the industry made it likely that the group of airlines that specialized in and depended on older aircraft technology would suffer rather more than the group that specialized in new aircraft technology. A landmark antitrust case that illustrates this strategic behavior is the Pennington case (Williamson, 1968). In this case, it was alleged that capital-intensive coal producers conspired with the labor union to raise wages. This strategy was expected to more severely affect labor-intensive rival producers.

It is instructive to look at the strategic problem for the airlines using a simple formulation of a two-stage game of an oligopolistic setting. We assume for simplicity that airlines can be divided into two groups: one using proportionally more new-generation aircraft and the second proportionally more old-generation aircraft. The first group makes (in stage one) a strategic investment in lobbying for regulation to kill the old aircraft. Such an investment affects both groups' costs in the second period. The standard theoretic solution requires that equilibrium in the second stage will depend upon the strategic investing in the first stage and the impact of a marginal (ex-ante) investment on profit (ex-post).

The first group's strategic move increases the cost of operating old aircraft and the cost associated with acquiring new aircraft for both the first and the second group of airlines. The general analytical characteristics of the equilibrium suggest that such a strategic move has offsetting effects of increasing the first group's cost as well as the rivals' cost, and the result depends on both groups' optimizing responses. The analytical model shows that the profitability of such a strategy for the first group cannot be taken for granted. It depends on the specific formulation and the parameters of the game, since the reaction functions move in opposite directions.

One of the problems in analyzing such strategic games is that their complexity often makes it impossible to ascertain winners and losers, if any. This is particularly evident in making antitrust arguments, because simplified analytical models may shed light on some of the underlying forces but are often partial and tentative, and depend on specific assumptions. Real-life situations, on the other hand, are often too complex and uncertain to provide the degree of analytical specification required for a clear-cut solution. Analytically and intuitively, however, it is clear that for the new-old aircraft strategy to make sense, the cost effect on the rival airlines must be significant in order to compensate for the increased strategic investment and its impact on the major airlines' cost. The difference in production (and cost) between the two groups of airlines (the extent of heterogeneity) is significant in the overall solution.

### 3.2.2   Industry Heterogeneity

Increased industry heterogeneity was in fact one of the important effects of deregulation and free competition. The gap between the financial position of the strong airlines and the weak ones had widened toward the end of the 1980s. Figure 6 reflects the distribution of operational margins of the major airlines in July 1989.[47] EAL, PAA USA, and TWA experienced negative margins, the remaining airlines positive margins. Heterogeneity had also evolved with respect to fleet composition. As the second generation of aircraft became available, airlines faced a wider choice of aircraft in their fleet composition decisions.

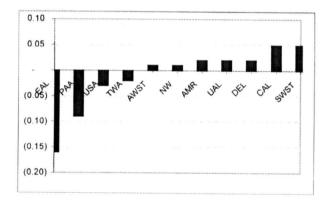

*Figure 6. Profit Margins*

Figure 7 reflects the distribution of first- and second-generation aircraft across airlines in 1989. The financially stronger hub airlines specialized in newer aircraft technology. American Airlines, United, and Delta, the three largest airlines, which controlled close to 60% of the market, operated more second-generation aircraft than the rest of the airlines, and also were better positioned than other airlines to acquire new aircraft. On the other side of the pole, Pan American, Eastern Airlines, TWA, US Air, and Northwest had the highest proportion of first-generation aircraft (65% and more), so imposing regulation on first-generation airlines would have a disproportionate effect on this group. These airlines were also financially weaker than the other group, which made an accelerated retirement of older aircraft and acquisition of new aircraft very difficult, if possible at all.

---

[47] Source: Air Transport Association, six-month period ending June 1990.

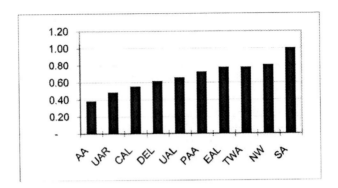

*Figure 7. Stage II Aircraft—Ratio by Airline—Year-End 1989[48]*

The acquisition of new aircraft required taking on significant amounts of debt in capital markets. The industry's long history of low profitability made the use of public debt problematic. Prior to deregulation, a few of the major airlines had issued public debt in spite of the industry's relatively low profitability. The fact that the industry was regulated helped a few of the major airlines gain low ("speculative") investment grades from Moody's and Standard & Poor's. Shortly after deregulation, almost all major airlines entered the public debt market. They received mostly non-investment-grade ratings of BB+ or lower from S&P. During the second half of the 1980s, things changed somewhat, and the three major airlines (American, United, and Delta) as well as Southwest obtained investment-grade ratings. The other airlines were forced to borrow at high junk bond rates

Such borrowing in the middle and the second half of the 1980s increased the leverage ratios of the second-tier airlines and exposed them to high interest costs. For example, Eastern Airlines, Continental, and TWA raised a significant amount of so called "junk" debt during this period through the then-popular Wall Street underwriter, Drexel, Burnham as part of leveraged buyouts or otherwise. This borrowing largely depleted their borrowing power. One of the junk bond issues of the time was nicknamed the "light bulb indenture," referring to the pledging of all the airline's unencumbered assets (including the light bulbs) as collateral. Borrowing under these conditions further weakened the future borrowing ability of the less stable airlines in the late 1980s, making their prospects for modifying old aircraft or acquiring new ones highly questionable.

Regulation that increases the cost of older-generation aircraft was indeed expected to affect the industry as a whole, although it was supposed to have more of an impact on the least financially strong airlines. American had the lowest percentage of old aircraft, and was the strongest proponent for noise regulation that affected older-generation aircraft. For the weaker airlines, complying with new noise regulation required diversion of needed resources from the creation and extension of

[48] Source: Calculated from data provided in *World Jet Airplane Inventory*, Boeing Commercial Airplane Group, 1990.

hubs and new markets, and for certain airlines actually threatened their ability to survive. These new regulations also directly raised financial barriers for new entrants into the market.

For these major reasons, the financially stronger airlines joined the manufacturers in pushing for new regulation that focused on first-generation aircraft. The regulations included age-related maintenance schedules as well as noise abatement requirements of unprecedented scope. At the same time, the airlines placed a record-breaking number of orders for new aircraft at increasing acquisition prices. Figure 8 shows the changes in the cost per seat-mile spent by the airline industry for aircraft acquisition during the 1980s. The rate of growth in the cost reached its lowest point of over 3% in 1986 but then more than tripled to over 10% in 1989.[49]

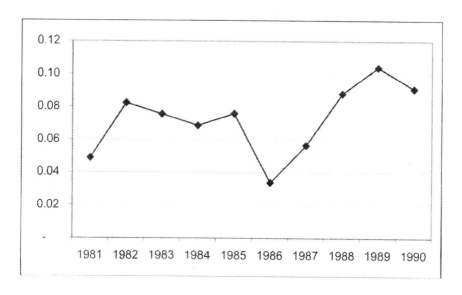

*Figure 8. Rate of Change in Aircraft Acquisition Cost*

## 4. ON ESTIMATING DEMAND FOR NEW AIRCRAFT

I have routinely watched the behavior of orders and prices of new aircraft. I was particularly intrigued with the data during the last several years of the 1980s, sensing that a change was afoot, but I could not figure out exactly what. Even today, with a better understanding of what I believe happened, I am still puzzled. What makes an industry's orders book take off in such a manner? A review of a time series of

---

[49] Calculated from data in *Air Transport World*, December 1999, p. 7.

aircraft orders and deliveries against economic (and/or industry) cycles since the advent of the jet age reveals that new aircraft orders usually increase at the end of an economic cycle. Then actual deliveries reach the market later, when airlines may already be struggling with recession and the aircraft are needed the least.

## 4.1    New Aircraft Orders

With the advantage of hindsight, we know that new aircraft orders overshoot and are not synchronized with the market cycle. Several reasons have been suggested for this phenomenon. Airlines are too optimistic in their predictions; they traditionally err in predicting recessions; orders follow capacity shortage at the peak of a cycle; capacity adjustments are never smooth; airlines place orders in strategic response to other airlines placing orders; airlines are ego- and prestige-driven and sometimes they just like new toys, and so on. In 1990, we experienced the Gulf War, which provided a standard justification for creating a large surplus capacity of aircraft. The standard explanation became the "Gulf War surprise." In fact, who could blame the industry for not being able to predict the Gulf War?

There may be some truth in explanations of what happened, but they disguise the non-obvious side of the story. In fact, forces other than expected demand drove orders for new aircraft up. The manufacturers took aggressive steps to boost aircraft orders and adopted a policy of undercutting the older aircraft in an attempt to increase the new aircraft user base. The larger airlines joined the manufacturers in an attempt to raise rivals' costs and increase their market share. I was sceptical at the time that either the manufacturers or the airlines would gain long-term profits from such a move. The manufacturers should have known that even if the airlines accommodated their strategy, payback time would arrive—in the workings of the present value effect.

The manufacturers' strategy was transparent to the airlines, which were expected to negotiate lower prices in the current or the next round of aircraft orders. In addition, the manufacturers' commitments to finance a portion of the new aircraft acquisitions made them vulnerable to an airline's default. The manufacturers fueled this order frenzy by providing financing and assuming the risks of airline defaults, all to create demand for their own aircraft.

A growing industry of "operating lessors" participated in this aircraft order spree as well. The two major leasing companies, GPA and ILFC, encouraged by the manufacturers, placed a large number of orders and bought options for new aircraft deliveries, in many cases without identifying a particular end-user. These leasing companies shared some of the airlines' and manufacturers' risk, and provided an additional source of financing in the face of a general shortage of traditional credit sources, but their competition for dominance in the operating lessors' market further increased the number of orders compared to the industry's needs. As the number of orders increased, so did the manufacturers' contingent liabilities and negative exposure with respect to their production and financing offers. It was clear that the manufacturers would have to absorb a major portion of the cost of airlines defaulting on their commitments.

I was also skeptical as to whether the deterring entrance and increasing rivals' costs strategies would eventually benefit the major airlines to an extent that would cover the cost of acquiring and operating the new aircraft. At the end of the day, airline revenues must cover the acquisition cost of aircraft—and the problem is that the overall cost of operating the new aircraft including rent or ownership costs was high. Even a senior official in American Airlines, one of the leaders of this strategy admitted that: "[ the] new aircraft don't give very good operating cost economies. New planes are better but don't totally offset the ownership costs."[50]

From the beginning, it was highly questionable whether the industry would be able to generate enough revenues to cover the cost of acquiring and operating the new aircraft, especially since new aircraft make economic sense only with high levels of utilization and load factors—yet demand was falling.

The picture became even more puzzling in 1990. More and more observers were predicting economic slowdown, and there were increased fears of inflation and uncertainty regarding oil prices even before the Gulf War commenced. The industry activity measured in revenue passenger miles for 1988 and 1989 fell. During the last quarter of the 1980s, airlines' costs increased and revenues lagged. The airlines faced a significant reduction in the traditional revenue-generating business travelers, due both to the economic cycle and the exploding popularity of new communications technology in the form of fax and teleconferencing.

Starting in 1988, jet fuel prices increased proportionally more than crude oil prices, disadvantaging the industry; meanwhile, labor negotiations concluded, and increased costs as well. Airlines responded to the diminishing growth rate of demand in 1989 with fare cuts, and revenues fell in 1989. Mergers and leveraged buyouts and takeovers increased the industry's overall interest expense and leverage ratios. The financial markets were reluctant to lend to finance aviation transactions in the late 1980s, due to deteriorating balance sheets, even before the beginning of the Gulf crisis. The Far East was the only market that was still growing strongly and could mitigate to some extent the impact of the approaching economic downturn on demand for new aircraft.

It was clear to many observers that placing such a large number of aircraft orders was out of line, not to say extremely risky, since there was no need for such capacity, nor was it clear how the industry could finance and pay back such an expense. Even later in 1990, after the Gulf crisis erupted, manufacturers continued their aggressive marketing efforts, and airlines responded by placing orders for even more new aircraft backed by manufacturers' financing commitments.[51]

### 4.2    Market Outlook

One of the rituals of the airlines industry is publication of the manufacturers' market outlook at the beginning of every year. The early 1990 forecasts attracted much

---

[50] Donald J. Carty, quoted *in Commercial Aviation Report* (1990, December, p. 10).

[51] For example, Boeing and P&W participated as lenders to UAL (*Commercial Aviation Report*, October 15, 1990, p. 3). Boeing provided a "backstop" commitment to finance Continental's acquisition of 757s (*Commercial Aviation Report*, November 1, 1990, p. 8).

attention. Boeing's was the most optimistic forecast, predicting that world airline market activity would grow at 5.9% per year throughout the decade (Airbus predicted 5.6% until 1998). Even with respect to the US market—where recessionary pressures had started to emerge along with concerns that market maturity might alter historical growth rates— Boeing predicted a 5.2% growth rate per year (Airbus predicted 4%). The forecasted growth rates were translated into expected aircraft orders on the basis of some obscure combination of a simple regression analysis not always disclosed and not obvious judgment.

Generally, it had been assumed that the industry's activity (measured in RPM) would grow at two to two and a half times the economic growth rate. This coefficient was based on the unprecedented economic boom of the 1980s and the accelerated post-deregulation industry growth

It struck me as odd that Boeing predicted that by year-end 2005, the industry would need an additional 10,000 new aircraft at a total value of $626 billion. I did not see how the market could absorb so many aircraft, or how the industry could finance their acquisition while generating enough revenue to repay the debt and provide reasonable return to shareholders. I was not alone in pointing out this anomaly. Almost everyone saw it, yet orders for new aircraft kept coming. By the end of 1990, Boeing's orders for new aircraft broke the record, and reached their highest point.

I eagerly waited to review the Boeing Current Market Outlook published in February 1991, more than six months after the Gulf crisis started and more than a month after Eastern Airlines, the first major casualty of the industry crisis, was shut down. The airlines recognized that they faced a major crisis. The editorial section of the October 1990 *Air Transport World* opened with the following:

> There is a chill in the air. A traffic downturn for the airlines, a drop in orders for manufacturers and an overall business recession seem to be the likely result of Iraq's attempt to grab the riches of its neighbors. For some struggling US carriers, this development may be the final straw (*Air Transport World*, October, 1990, p. 2).

A detailed article in the same issue underlined the problem of increased capacity. A review of industry statistics for the first seven months of 1990 indicated that capacity had grown more than traffic. This trend was stronger in the domestic market, where available seat miles (ASM) rose 6.3%, twice as fast as traffic (RPM).

To my surprise, Boeing largely ignored the Gulf War's impact on the industry as well as the deteriorating general economic and industry conditions. When I read the February 1991 Market Outlook, I was already fully involved in liquidating Eastern Airlines' assets. In a complex (and unhappy) logistical operation of a magnitude that was never seen before, we flew a large number of aircraft to be parked and stored in the Mojave Desert. Quickly thereafter, this became almost a routine practice, as more aircraft were mothballed in the desert. Boeing, however, suggested in its forecast that the industry would bounce back quickly. Air travel is projected to return to its position on the demand curve, "which has usually been the outcome when unexpected disruptions have occurred" Boeing (1991, p. 3).

This published statement referred to a chart showing two standard textbook demand curves, one to the left of the other, with an arbitrary equilibrium point P1 indicated on the right curve. It stated that the curve "shifted [left] due to income." A new equilibrium point P2 representing a higher level of airfares and a lower number of passengers was identified on the second demand curve, with the note: "Near-term influences could cause a move from P1 toward P2. Upon resolution of problems, recovery back to P1 should occur" Boeing (1991, p. iii).

Boeing decided to ignore the nature of the crisis, suggesting that the industry focus on its average long-term growth trend *and continue ordering new aircraft*. Boeing also did not change its last year's predictions and claimed that:

> The substantial growth in forecast incremental travel volume combined with the replacement of retired airplanes provides a forecast market for the manufacturers of $617 billion (1991 dollars). This is approximately the same amount as forecast in last year's Current Market Outlook (Boeing, 1991, p. iii).

Not only did Boeing not change its general market outlook in 1991, relative to the previous year, but in fact it also locked into its overly optimistic predictions, thus encouraging the airlines to place more aircraft orders.

Most of my time during 1991 was spent repossessing aircraft due to airline default or bankruptcy, or otherwise negotiating and restructuring aircraft loan and lease agreements. It continued this way for the next three years as well. The airlines I dealt with were mainly financially weak ones (Pan Am, Eastern, TWA, Midway, Continental, and Braniff). By 1991, it had become apparent that the crisis had accumulated more steam and was starting to take its toll on the financially strong airlines as well.

At the beginning of 1991, US airlines had an estimated total of $165.2 billion in aircraft on order: $45 billion by United, $23 billion by American, $26 billion by Delta, and $21 billion by Northwest. (*Commercial Aviation Report*, 1991). Concerns mounted as to how this amount could be financed and how the debt could be paid back. There were rumors for several months that American Airlines planned to significantly cut its capital spending. In a sequence of announcements and speeches, starting September 1991, Robert Crandall, American's CEO, confirmed the airline's intention to reduce its capital and aircraft spending. In November, it became public that American was planning to trim up to $4 billion over the next five years. During the inauguration of American's new Seattle-Tokyo service, "Crandall dropped a bigger bomb. The company was negotiating to defer aircraft deliveries." The CEO said American had presented Boeing with a proposed rescheduling of aircraft deliveries. According to an industry publication distributed in November 1991, US Department of Transportation Secretary Sam Skinner had: "growing concern about the ability of the US airline industry to pay for the billions of dollars' worth of aircraft on order." (*Commercial Aviation Report*, 1991, p. 1). According to the same publication, Skinner discussed this issue with Boeing's chairman in September.

In March 1992, Boeing's Current Market Outlook was published. Again, the document largely ignored the industry crisis, suggesting instead a focus on the long-run industry growth trend as it had been forecasted on the basis of a simple econometric model and subjective judgments regarding explanatory variables. On the first page of the document, Boeing stated, "there are no cycles in the forecast." The word "cycle" was footnoted as follows:

94

Cycles, by definition, mean regularly sequenced phenomena. The Boeing view is that unique circumstances caused the major adverse change in the historical market and that such events are random and, therefore, not predictable (e.g., energy crises, wars). Even economic growth is hardly cyclical. Good monetary and fiscal policies can prevent major economic disruptions. Only two major world recessions have occurred in the jet era, and they were begun by energy crisis (Boeing, 1992, p. 1.1).

The product delivery section almost repeated the language of the previous year:

The substantial growth in forecast incremental travel volume combined with the replacement of retired airplanes provides a forecast market for the manufacturers of $857 billion (1992 dollars) through 2010. This is nearly equivalent to the forecast in last year's Current Market Outlook (Boeing, 1992, p. 1. 8).

## 4.3 Aircraft Deliveries

The Gulf war, recession, and other market changes brought about a major crisis in the aviation industry during the early 1990s. A cyclical economic downturn was not unexpected after a long expansionary trend that had lasted almost eight years, but a dramatic (although relatively short) oil shock was a surprise. Accelerated by this shock and aggravated by a great overcapacity of aircraft, the recession had a devastating impact on the industry. The impact of the recession was particularly destructive because so many new aircraft ended up being delivered to an industry that needed them not at all.

In 1989, oil prices averaged $17.37 per barrel. Affected by a cold winter, prices averaged $19 per barrel in the first quarter of 1990, before settling back to about $15 in the second quarter. In August, Iraq invaded Kuwait. The subsequent embargo and fear of war sent oil prices to over $40 a barrel. By year-end, prices had dropped back to $25 (Boeing, 1992).

The supply and demand shocks affecting the air travel market, together with the overall recession and the industry's overcapacity, brought about far-reaching changes in the industry's structure. In the fall of 1990 it was already clear that:

Things are likely to get worse before they get better, because with 500 new jet transports scheduled to be delivered in 1990-91—80% of them narrowbodies for domestic service—capacity growth is likely to accelerate for the remainder of this year and next, unless some airlines begin retiring older jets...but no one wants to be the first to cut capacity, because that could translate into loss of market share (Air Transport World, October 1990, p. 62).

The unfolding crisis became more severe and lasted longer than even the most pessimistic observers would have predicted. In February 1992, Bob Crandall claimed:

The airline business lost $5 billion last year and if [it doesn't] stop losing money then there won't be an airline business in the future. The airline business is going broke, and better times are not near (Air Transport World, February 1992, p. 62).

In some respects, the major airlines reaped even more than they had hoped for in their wildest strategic dreams. The cost, however, was very high. By the end of 1992, before the new aircraft age and noise regulation had a chance to impact the market, Eastern Airlines, Pan American, and Midway went out of business, and

TWA, Continental, and America West filed for bankruptcy protection. The wave of bankruptcies and airline shutdowns spread all over the world, but the deregulated US industry was the hardest hit. The major airlines acquired the failing airlines' assets, gaining additional market share and becoming even larger and more powerful. After the demise of Eastern, Delta became the dominant carrier in the Atlanta hub. It also acquired Pan Am's international routes to become a major player on the Atlantic routes. American acquired Eastern's and TWA's international routes, and expanded to capture a dominant position in the Latin American market.

During 1991 and 1992, a record-breaking number of new aircraft were delivered into an otherwise devastated industry. More than 10% of the industry's aircraft fleet was estimated to be grounded; aircraft utilization levels had been reduced; and West coast and Midwest deserts quickly became aircraft storage places or graveyards. First-generation aircraft were disassembled or "cannibalized" for parts, as spare part values often exceeded the market value of a complete aircraft. As new aircraft utilization and load factors fell, orders for additional aircraft were cancelled or deferred. In some cases new ("white tail") aircraft simply rolled off the manufacturing line and into storage in the desert.

Figure 9 plots the number of new aircraft deliveries to the world airlines market. It shows very clearly the significant increase in aircraft deliveries during the period 1990-1993.[52]

The unprecedented number of aircraft orders of the last quarter of the 1980s materialized into an unprecedented number of deliveries during the first quarter of the 1990s. And then 1991 turned out to be one of the worst years in aviation history, as the growth in world airline traffic became negative (down 2.3%) for the first time since the advent of the jet age. Even during the two previous major recessions, in 1973–1975 and 1979–1982, average growth in world traffic had been positive.[53] The industry total losses during 1991–1993 wiped out the cumulative profits of the industry since the beginning of the jet age.

---

[52] Source: Boeing, *World Jet Airplane Inventory*, 1994.
[53] 4.1% and 1.9%, respectively (*Boeing Current Market Outlook*, 1992).

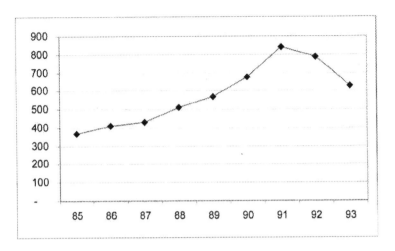

*Figure 9. New Aircraft Deliveries 1985 –1993*

Figure 10 shows the yearly losses of the world industry during this period.[54] The year 1991 was one of the worst years in world airline performance—as well as the year the number of new aircraft deliveries broke all previous records. Close to 850 new aircraft were delivered to the industry during 1991 and close to 800 in 1992. Already plagued with significant overcapacity and fighting for survival, the industry had to start paying the bills for these new aircraft.

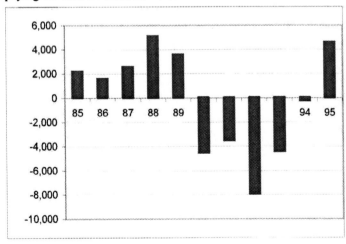

*Figure 10. World Airlines Net Profits 1985–1995*

[54] Source: ICAO data 1996.

There were many losers in this round of the game. Financially weak airlines filed for bankruptcy; Pan Am, Eastern, and Midway went out of business; TWA, Continental, and America West operated under bankruptcy protection. The manufacturers could not deliver all the ordered or optioned aircraft. Orders and deliveries were cancelled, delayed, or restructured, and the manufacturers absorbed significant losses. GPA, the largest operating lessor, became practically insolvent and had to be bailed out by General Electric. Operating lessors of older aircraft filed for bankruptcy or otherwise exited the market. The falling values of old aircraft caused the collateral value of bank and public debt to collapse. Private and institutional investors who had invested in bonds backed by aircraft lost significant portions of their investment.

The diminished used aircraft market values caused market equity that airlines had accumulated to evaporate. The only winners may have been aviation lawyers, as defaults, repossessions, foreclosure sales, bankruptcies, and financial restructuring soared. The major airlines absorbed a significant portion of the defunct airlines' assets, thereby increasing their market share, but at a very high price. Ironically, the majors ended up absorbing the bulk of the noise and safety regulation costs they had hoped to impose on their rivals as much of the competition disappeared from the market.

## 5. RECOVERY

The combination of manufacturers' competition for increasing user base in the aircraft market and the airlines' competition for market share in the air travel market pushed the industry to a point where standard economic reasoning was ignored or else made not applicable. The manufacturers pressed to increase deliveries in an attempt to reduce average fixed production costs. With the expected falling rates of market growth, killing the old aircraft was adopted as a strategy that would encourage demand for new aircraft.

The airlines themselves faced a somewhat similar problem in the air travel market. The high fixed costs of the complex and expensive network systems they had built required increased aircraft operations and market share. Overcapacity at hubs captured limited groundside and airside space, foreclosed rivals' entry, and deterred potential new entry. Killing the old aircraft was for the airlines a strategy aimed at raising rivals' costs.

In the late 1990s, the manufacturers and the airlines were locked into what became a self-destructive strategy, induced by their respective search for increasing market share. The number of aircraft orders surged, which made the impact of the imminent economic downturn even more severe. The unexpected Gulf War and domestic recession, coupled with an unprecedented number of aircraft deliveries during the early 1990s, forced the industry into the longest and most severe depression ever. Ironically, the surviving older aircraft that had not been permanently retired returned to haunt the big airlines and the manufacturers in the next round.

## 5.1    The Revenge of the Old Aircraft

Oil prices stabilized quite quickly after the Gulf War. In fact, their average level during the 1990s was to become even lower than in the 1980s. The old aircraft maintained their operational attractiveness. The events of the early 1990s did not change the basic situation: The relative savings offered by new aircraft technology could not justify their acquisition cost. On top of this, in the early 1990s, the price of older aircraft plummeted.

The 727 were the most affected aircraft. An early 1980 model (the youngest in the old aircraft group) was valued at the $12 million level in the late 1980s. Six such aircraft were sold in an auction by the bankrupt Pan Am for just over $3 million each, in the early 1990s. An older 727-200 advanced aircraft (manufactured during the middle of the 1970s) was sold for $6 million a unit during the late 1980s and for just over $1 million in the early 1990s.

The DC9 was perhaps the second-most affected aircraft. The demise of Eastern and Midway Airlines put a relative high number of DC9 aircraft on the market. Retirement of DC9 fleets by Delta, Turkish Airlines, Alitalia, and others further increased availability and pushed prices down. An average DC9 that had been valued at around $6 million in the late 1980s went for under $1 million in 1992 and 1993. To put this into perspective, one must appreciate that an airline considering acquiring a new fully refurbished DC9 or 727-200 aircraft was expected to pay up to $3 million per aircraft ($4 million for a 737-200). The competing new 737-300/400 aircraft were valued at an average $27 million. At one point in 1992, I was involved in negotiating a possible transaction with a Far Eastern airline that was considering acquiring a fleet of 30 DC9 aircraft for about the same price of *one* new 737-400. The combination of low fuel prices, low acquisition cost, and abundant supply of spare engines and parts made the older aircraft more attractive than ever. The acquisition cost of the old aircraft, even including the cost of compliance with the age-related maintenance and noise regulation that had become effective in the 1990s, was still lower than their late 1980s value. And then oil prices stabilized at a lower level once again.

A large number of old aircraft were acquired for operation during the early 1990s in at least two high-profile cases. The first case was Northwest, which decided to expand its short-haul routes using DC9 aircraft. The second was ValueJet. Northwest adopted a different fleet acquisition policy from the policy of the big three major airlines. It decided to take advantage of the depressed market for old aircraft and acquire a large number of DC9 aircraft. Even later in 1996, when general market conditions had improved quite dramatically, Northwest decided to defer an order for A330 aircraft and acquire DC10s instead (*Air Transport World*, August 1996, p. 46). According to Michael Levin, EVP of Northwest, the airline decided to base its aircraft acquisition decision on the standard business criteria of return on capital. Therefore, the fleet was expanded with old aircraft.

Table 3 indicates statistics regarding aircraft operation in 1994.[55] The first row shows the average operational statistics of the DC9 aircraft acquired by Northwest,

---

[55] Source: *Aviation & Aerospace Almanac*, McGraw Hill, 1996.

and the other statistics reflect industry averages. It is apparent from the Table that Northwest's operating costs per seat mile for DC9 aircraft were significantly lower than the respective industry average operating costs for DC9s. The F100, a newer aircraft with a similar operational profile, was more expensive to operate. 737-300s and 737-500s were less expensive to operate, but required significantly higher utilization and load factors and ranges—and a new 737 aircraft at the time cost almost ten times more than a DC9.

*Table 3. Selected Aircraft Operating Costs 1994*

| Aircraft | Flight Hours | Av. Seats Flight | Av. Stage Length (miles) | Operating Cost ASM (cents) |
|---|---|---|---|---|
| DC9-30 (NWA) | 6.6 | 100 | 498 | 4.37 |
| DC9-30 | 6.5 | 100 | 423 | 5.32 |
| F100 | 6.7 | 97 | 466 | 5.58 |
| 737-500 | 8.5 | 111 | 570 | 4.12 |
| 737-300 | 8.7 | 130 | 572 | 4.19 |

ValueJet, like Northwest, decided to use a DC9 fleet. According to its Vice-Chairman:

> If the company had opted for new aircraft, the depreciation and rental category unit cost would have been four to five times the ownership cost of used aircraft. One could argue that ValueJet would have the benefit of the lower fuel burn and maintenance costs to offset the higher ownership. However, airlines feel compelled to schedule high-cost aircraft for maximum utilization to lower their unit cost of ownership. This is an appropriate tactic if traffic warrants (Gallagher, 1995, p. 37).

Table 4 shows a comparison of domestic cost (in cents) per available seat mile (ASM) in 1994 according to ValueJet Gallagher (1995). It should be obvious from the Table that the increased fuel and maintenance costs are offset by the lower aircraft acquisition cost. It is noteworthy that ValueJet acquired most of its aircraft at the lowest point in the market for DC9 aircraft.

*Table 4. Selected Airlines Operating Costs*

| | Delta | USAir | Southwest | Industry | ValueJet |
|---|---|---|---|---|---|
| Labor | 3.90 | 4.90 | 2.66 | 3.66 | 1.60 |
| Fuel | 1.05 | 1.04 | 0.98 | 1.05 | 1.47 |
| Dep & Rent | 1.41 | 1.70 | 1.02 | 1.43 | 0.26 |
| Maintenance | 0.40 | 0.63 | 0.63 | 0.45 | 0.88 |
| Other | 2.99 | 3.25 | 1.93 | 2.74 | 2.59 |
| Total Exp. | 9.75 | 11.52 | 7.22 | 9.33 | 6.80 |

## 5.2    Third Generation

During the second half of the 1990s, the industry embarked on a new aircraft acquisition cycle. New aircraft technology had became available as the Boeing 777 joined the widebody long-range aircraft category, and a family of new-generation Boeing 737s (600, 700, 800, 900) and a smaller 717 aircraft were introduced into the shorter-range (mostly hub aircraft) family, as well as a higher-capacity 757-300. Airbus expanded its production into the Boeing dominant long-range "jumbo" market with its A340. The smaller narrowbody Airbus A320/321 version accumulated significant market share and conquered previously US captured markets, and the new and smaller Airbus A319 and A318 were offered in competition with the B737/B717.

The new aircraft in general have more advanced cockpits, airframes, and engines, and are more fuel-efficient. The new technology, however, has in most cases translated into only a relatively small increment of operational economic advantages over the previous generation aircraft at the traditional high price level of new aircraft offered for sale during the second half of the 1990s. Much as was the case for the second-generation aircraft, the third generation—although it represents an impressive technological advance—did not deliver an economic knockout punch to the second-generation aircraft. For the traveling passenger and the airlines, the sometimes increased speed, more advanced wing design, and the more advanced avionics and controls, which are expensive to develop, are typically not much apparent, so the manufacturers could not price the new aircraft at much more than a respective previous-generation piece of equipment. And in fact, list prices of new-generation aircraft during the late 1990s in many cases were similar to or even lower than comparable previous-generation aircraft delivered at about the same time.

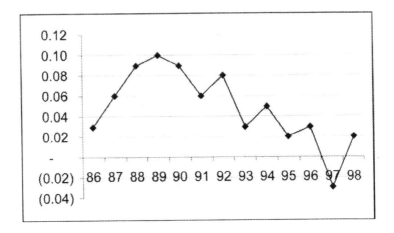

*Figure 11. US Airlines Aircraft Cost Index 1986-1988*

Figure 11 reflects the behavior of average aircraft cost (rate of change normalized per seat) between the years 1986 and 1998.[56] During the later 1990s and in spite of the increase in orders for new aircraft, cost growth rates were

---

[56] Source: Air Transport Association.

substantially lower than during the late 1980s (and even negative in 1997). This is an important phenomenon; while during the late 1980s increased aircraft demand and orders occurred together with increased aircraft cost, in the late 1990s demand and orders occurred together with a reduction in cost. A major factor in this trend is the increased competition between Boeing and Airbus over market share.

It is important to note that while the takeover of MDC by Boeing in the middle 1990s resulted in the creation of a duopoly market structure (Boeing–Airbus), competition between manufacturers became stronger than ever before, and the combined post-merger Boeing seems to have lost its clear market dominance. One reason is that during the 1990s Airbus expanded its product line so that it could offer an aircraft to compete against Boeing in every aircraft category (except for the 747-400 where Boeing still had a monopoly). Until the early 1990s, prior to the Boeing and MDC merger, Boeing had been the only manufacturer to offer aircraft in every category. With the introduction of the 319, 318, 320, 321, 330, and 340 aircraft, airlines could in most cases select between competing Boeing and Airbus model aircraft.

The competition over market share by the two manufacturers pushed new aircraft prices and airline costs of acquisition down for the first time in the jet age. In these new circumstances, the price of old first-generation (mostly narrowbody) aircraft was very low and therefore they still maintained their economic attractiveness for certain airlines. Increased industry consolidation and relatively high oil prices in the early 2000s, however, accelerated their retirement. The relatively lower acquisition costs of new-generation aircraft and the increased regulatory burden for older aircraft made newer models–for the first time since deregulation–more attractive for startup airlines as well.[57]

It is no surprise that additional new regulatory efforts focusing on aircraft age, noise, and other negative environmental damages have developed, with an even wider target: killing the first- *and* second-generation aircraft that continued to exhibit very strong market resilience.[58]

[57] ValueJet (Airtran) and JetBlue reflect two new aircraft entry models. ValueJet started up with low-cost DC9s, which significantly reduced its entry cost. Due to the negative post-accident public perception of its old fleet, after gaining a large enough market share that could justify expensive new aircraft and obtaining an attractive deal from Boeing, it gradually moved to operate factory-new Boeing 717 aircraft. Equipped with a significant level of working capital provided by investors to cover the (mostly sunk) cost necessary to capture a break-even market share and obtaining an attractive deal from Airbus, JetBlue started up with factory-new aircraft. These issues are discussed further in Chapter 8.

[58] Noise regulation is discussed in Chapter 5. The September 11th events retarded stage IV regulation efforts somewhat.

# CHAPTER 3

# DESTRUCTIVE COMPETITION

> I talked about the possibility that there might be really
> destructive competition, but I tended to dismiss it and
> that certainly has been one of the unpleasant surprises of
> deregulation.[59]

Justification for airline regulation evolved as a tale of two extremes: at one end the "public utility" story, at the other the "elimination of destructive competition." One extreme emphasizes consumer concerns about a marketplace with no competition the other concerns a marketplace with too much competition. The first story dominated political and economic thought for several decades, while the second gained some political attention but captured only a marginal place in economic thinking compared to the orthodox "public utility" story.

## 1. THE ECONOMIC CONCEPT OF DESTRUCTIVE COMPETITION

In a classic article on regulation, Noll summarizes the dominant view as follows:

> Destructive competition is the circumstance in which an industry is not a natural
> monopoly, nonetheless lacks a stable competitive equilibrium. It was used to support the
> argument for regulation of truck and airline transportation in the 1930s, but
> subsequently has been almost unanimously rejected in economic research. (1989, p.
> 1257).

Noll's "destructive competition" was dismissed by the mainstream orthodoxy since it could not be interpreted within the standard perfect markets paradigm. Indeed, the classical and neoclassical theories (and the associated political doctrine of *laissez-faire*) and the destructive competition idea represent an oxymoron.

The foundation of *laissez-faire* economics is that competitive markets have a natural tendency toward stable equilibrium, as built-in economic mechanisms of local negative feedback will cause prices to clear markets at a long-run minimum average-cost level. Marginal cost pricing is expected, in the long run, to drive non-efficient firms out of the market. Obviously, firms that are forced to exit the market are expected to complain about destructive competition, and perhaps even plead for government help.

According to this point of view, what seems destructive competition to a non-efficient firm is, in fact, constructive from a social welfare perspective, reflecting the private cost of moving toward the social optimum. Destructive competition that

---

[59] Alfred Kahn, Quoted in Dempsey (1995, p. 194).

causes the market system to break down or industries to crash and collapse, however, seems impossible under the standard conception of the natural competitive market system.

Empirical studies performed by respected economists at least since the early 1960s have indicated that the air transportation industry is naturally competitive. Therefore, airlines' complaints about destructive competition were interpreted as a temporary phenomenon, or a political argument intending to camouflage industry's attempts to sidetrack the regulation process. It was thus easy to largely dismiss a long history of airlines' concerns with destructive competition.

Economists do recognize destructive competition in the presence of high fixed and sunk costs and increasing-return-to-scale technology. Perelman (1994) reminds us of the view of the prominent economists who founded the American Economic Association at the turn of the 20th century, challenging for a short time the prevailing *laissez-faire* view. Impressed by overinvestment in railroads' fixed-cost capacity, strong competition, and frequent bankruptcies, they questioned the merit of free competition under these specific circumstances. Their concern was that marginal cost pricing might have a disastrous impact on the railroad industry.

This is the other side of the standard monopoly story: high fixed costs and overcapacity in the railroad system induced price cuts below average cost and drove railroads into bankruptcy. According to H. C. Adams, the railroad system was overbuilt, because "the private individuals who constructed the railroads" expected the market to support "all the roads that could be built."[60]

In the railroad industry, there were too many cars chasing too few passengers and freight, in an attempt to increase market share as demand fell due to recession. Under these conditions, any cash flow to an operator would seem better than no cash flow at all, and prices tumbled. Marginal pricing that under perfect competition stabilizes a system may be obtained at a level that cannot sustain industry long-run cost, and, in the absence of government intervention, increased consolidation and concentration toward a monopolistic structure may be inevitable. In the 1890s this took the form of the establishment of trusts.

The destructive competition that Adams and his colleagues describe is different from the one suggested by Noll. Adams tied destructive competition to an industry that is naturally monopolistic. The fundamental law of railroad economics is that

> the cost of movement is in direct inverse ratio to the amount moved. [The] cheapest possible transportation [is achievable by] directing the largest possible volume of movement through the fewest possible channels. [Therefore] competition and the cheapest possible transportation are wholly incompatible.[61]

Adams's view may be interpreted as a dynamic evolutionary perspective on the railroad industry, looking at how a natural monopolistic industry evolved. Railroads were competing to survive as the natural monopolist firm in their respective market niche. Both investor oversubscription in railroads on the supply side and recession on the demand side promoted pricing below average fixed cost, leading to an

---

[60] Adams (1877, p. 118), quoted in Perelman (1994, p. 191).

[61] Quoted in McCraw (1984, pp. 9,10).

industry-wide crisis, bankruptcies, and increasing industry concentration. In the standard monopoly story, the industry charges too much, and produces too little at the prevailing demand levels. Government intervention, therefore, is expected to set price ceilings. On the other side of the story, demand is not sufficient to sustain the current production capacity; the industry produces too much compared to prevailing demand, and charges too little to survive.

Adams's colleague, Arthur Hadley, emphasized what economists of our generation call "asset-specificity." It involves:

> a large permanent investment, which can be used for one narrowly defined purpose, and for no other. The capital, once invested must remain. It is worth little for any other purpose.[62]

Capital is specific and sunk, so firms stay in the market and fight for survival by cutting prices to a level that cannot sustain the industry's long-term survival. Government intervention in this case is expected to put a bottom on the price floor.

The similarity between what happened in the aviation industry in the early 1990s and in the railroad industry at the turn of the century is striking.

Within the aviation industry, the notion of destructive competition has been a real concern for decades. It is only during times of crisis, however, that this view is strongly voiced and gains some attention by industry observers. The industry has waved the red flag of destructive competition in three high-profile public debates: in the 1930s when it asked for government regulation, in the 1970s when it attempted to hang on to regulation, and in the early 1990s when it faced an unprecedented industry collapse.

The concept of destructive competition was largely dismissed by mainstream economists with respect to the first two occasions, but it gained somewhat more support in the third (if only for a short time). As the industry's financial condition improved during the second half of the 1990s and as calls for government help in the face of destructive competition subsided, so did political and scholarly attention to this issue.

## 2. 1930s – REGULATION

Economists and historians inquiring into the origin of airline regulation, especially during the 1970s and 1980s, were puzzled by the specific institutional arrangement established by the 1938 Civil Aeronautics Act. There was an apparent contradiction between the Senate view that the industry at the time lacked natural monopolistic characteristics and adoption of the standard public utility model of regulation, as if the industry did possess natural monopolistic characteristics.

McCraw (1984), for example, suggested that:

> the [House] committee regarded airlines, like railroads or electric utilities, as a natural monopoly industry. Thus, a mistaken economic assumption seems to have formed the foundation of the bill. The Senate report [said] that "competition among air carriers is being carried to an extreme." In this judgment the House report agreed. (p. 262).

[62] Hadley (1903), quoted in Perelman (1994, p. 40).

McCraw's comments reflect the dominant interpretation of the origin of airline regulation: an assumption that the industry is naturally competitive and that the destructive competition argument is not sufficient to justify regulation in the public interest. The major airlines, however, continued to complain about destructive competition, and called for regulation of the type applied to public utilities.

The president of the Air Transport Association, an industry trade group, for example, told the House Committee that $120 million of private investment had been poured into the industry and that half of the investment had been lost. He called for the adoption of legislation in order "to protect [it] from cutthroat competition."[63] A Federal Aviation Commission report suggested: "We consider that it will still require controls as a public utility, and one which in some cases must take on a monopoly character."[64]

The airlines' position was largely dismissed by most researchers since under the dominant model the industry was naturally competitive, and therefore destructive competition could not exist. Instead fierce competition and mounting losses were often associated with the economic crisis of the 1930s, which gave the impression that excess competition was a sort of a market failure.

Interpreting the industry's evolution from an oligopolistic competition perspective may turn many of the traditional conventions on their head. For instance, it is arguable that the economic assumptions of the bill might not have been mistaken, as was suggested by McCraw (1984) and others, and that the industry in the 1930s had natural monopolistic (or oligopolistic) characteristics, so overcapacity and destructive competition were indeed major problems.

Increasing-return characteristics during the 1930s included: high fixed costs and steep learning effects in aircraft development and design; learning by doing in aircraft operations;[65] competing standards in aircraft technology; network effects in route structuring; and significant sunk costs relative to low air travel demand. A major problem in the aviation industry since its inception had been that there was no independent economic justification for its existence. Aircraft were too small, too slow, and too risky, and passengers were not at all eager to fly. Despite the impressive rate of growth in traffic, the market remained relatively small.[66] Nor could the advantage of airmail justify its cost compared to surface mail through most of the 1920s and 1930s.

The new technology may have been very exciting, but it could not be supported by the free market. Survival of the industry was tied in general to the industrial policy of the government and in particular to the subsidy distributed through the US postal service system. There was no way the industry could cover its costs without this government support; mail pay was set at a level that kept the air transportation industry going, whatever the cost of alternative mail carriers. The government

---

[63] See, for example, McCraw (1984, p. 263).

[64] Report of the Federal Aviation Commission, 1935, cited in (CAB, 1975, p. 25).

[65] The fact that the Army pilots who took over flying of the mail in 1934 were unable to perform the job suggests that the airlines accumulated valuable operational knowledge and expertise during years of learning by doing.

[66] It grew from 6,000 passangers in 1926 to 418,000 in 1930 to 2,900,000 in 1940.

directly subsidized increasing-return technology during a period when the market could not.

Looking at the events of the 1930s from this perspective, and assuming in fact a natural monopoly can cast a different light on the evolution of the industry during this period. The scandalous policy adopted by Postmaster General Walter Folger Brown in the Spoils Conference, for example, may make economic sense from this perspective. Brown's "industrial policy" was to subsidize the large airlines. On the demand side, he hoped to attain a more efficient and more integrated route network, since the larger airlines used larger fleets of longer-range, higher-capacity, aircraft than the small airlines. On the input side, the government intended to subsidize the development of an infant industry with increasing-returns aircraft design and building technology. Only the large and financially stronger airlines could afford acquiring the new (high-cost) aircraft technology, so creating and subsidizing large airlines meant subsidizing the new aircraft manufacturers and related technology.

The connection between the airlines and aircraft technology is an important point that has often escaped researchers. Since the government generated most of the demand for airline transportation, government became key to creating demand for new commercial aircraft. Government subsidies became especially important for manufacturers during the late 1920s and beginning of the 1930s with the reduced demand for military aircraft. Subsidies affected derived demand for aircraft; therefore, government policy toward the airlines was directly related to its policy toward the manufacturers.

During the 1930s aircraft technology made significant progress. Many believed it was the most innovative period in aviation history. By 1931, the first all-metal stressed-skin airplane had been built, making an aircraft's internal structure stronger and lighter. More powerful and more reliable air-cooled engines were developed. New avionics significantly improved navigation. In 1932, radio beacons first became operational. Significant steps were made toward high-altitude flying. One of the major breakthroughs in technology was the idea of aircraft compression, starting with Boeing's design of the B17 in the middle 1930s, and emerging later in the Stratoliner.

In 1933, the first modern airliner, the Boeing 247, was unveiled. It incorporated a revolutionary design, including a lighter fuselage, retractable landing gear, low wings, and ten passenger seats. The new aircraft allowed higher capacity, higher speed, and greater range using only two radial pistons Wasp engines, a remarkable achievement if we look at the previous generation of Trimotor aircraft.

United, a large major airline at the time, ordered the first 60 aircraft, tying up production lines for the next two years. TWA, another major, contracted with Douglas for the DC2 aircraft, and started a competing aircraft rolling off production lines after ordering 20 in September 1933. American Airlines, a potential customer for the DC2, suggested that Douglas develop a sleeper version to facilitate the 16- to 18-hour long transcontinental flights, and the DC3 was born. American ordered 8 DST aircraft and 12 DC3s in 1935.[67] By 1936, the first DC3 aircraft had been delivered, changing the nature of commercial aircraft for a long time to come.

---

[67] See, for example, Davies (1964, p. 133).

These remarkable technological achievements coincided with a tumultuous and volatile economic and political period for the airlines. The so-called Waters Act, in 1930, gave Postmaster General Brown the power to restructure the industry. He had in his mind a notion that in many respects resembled Adams's view of the railroad industry, and he tried to accelerate the industry's evolution into a regulated monopoly.

Brown's view is reflected in a quotation from his presentation before the Congress in 1932:

> Monopoly in public service under definite regulation is my idea, and I think that is what will come here ultimately. We will have air systems knit together giving a competitive service . . . These big organizations with spare equipment—passenger and mail planes—are much better able to do the job than a fellow with two or three planes and no money, with the sheriff just one leap behind him all the time.[68]

In the famous 1930 Spoils Conference, the postal service awarded the transcontinental mail contracts to the large airlines. In response, the airlines contracted with the manufacturers for the new-technology aircraft.

Brown was interested in helping the big airlines acquire the new technology, and by subsidizing them he in effect subsidized the new technology. The competition between the small and the large airlines was also a competition between "old" and "new" technology standards. Brown's promises to the large airlines in the Spoils Conferences justified ordering new aircraft technology, and they proceeded with such orders on the expectation of mail revenues.

In 1932, Franklin Delano Roosevelt was elected president in a landslide. Representatives of the small airlines that felt betrayed by Brown's policy started a political snowball rolling, resulting in the Airmail Act of 1934, which changed the rules of the game until it was replaced by the 1938 Civil Aeronautics Act. The 1934 Act cut the subsidy level significantly, making bidding more competitive. A significant part of the airlines' traditional demand disappeared overnight, and the existing passenger demand was not sufficient to cover the cost of the then-current capacity. Obtaining mail contracts at any price (and even for no price) was required in order to keep flying even at rates below average cost.[69]

The airlines in the mid-1930s pleaded for government regulation. Their major story was: There is nothing to prevent the entire air carrier system from crashing to earth under the impact of cutthroat and destructive practices. Interestingly, the structure that was eventually established by the 1938 legislation was quite similar to the one envisioned by Postmaster General Brown. In fact, the major airlines that participated in the Spoils Conference became the major airlines of the regulated cartel, and even differences in political views, fierce criticism of Brown, and high-profile scandals could not change the direction the industry was heading.

Another aspect of the 1930s industry often escapes observers interested in this issue. The aviation industry during the early 1930s was highly integrated. Aircraft design, building, and commercial flight operations were concentrated in the hands of a small number of holding companies. United Aircraft & Transportation, which

---

[68] Quoted in Van der Linden (1995, p. 252).
[69] Braniff's bid was $0.00.

dominated the commercial market at the time with its B247 aircraft, included aircraft design and building (Boeing Airplane Company), commercial airline operations (Boeing Transport), and engine manufacturing (Pratt & Whitney). A somewhat similar structure characterized the competing Aviation Corporation and North American Aviation holding companies. Brown's "industrial policy" as exemplified in the decisions of the Spoils Conference implied enhancement and support of this vertically integrated structure of major manufacturers and affiliated operators. The major airlines were seen as a vertically integrated structure that included the manufacturing side and had naturally monopolistic characteristics.

Business structures of this type, however, were a major target for political attacks by opponents, who mounted the familiar criticism of business combinations, monopoly, corruption, and government abuse of power. Responding to such arguments, the 1934 Act forced the break-up of the integrated structures of the holding companies and the separation of aircraft design and building activities from their commercial use, resulting in a structural collapse of the industry.

While rent-seeking and interest group politics played an undeniable role in early aviation, the vertically integrated structures of the holding companies also served an important economic purpose. The development and design of aircraft involved uncertainty and significant investment in non-trivial specific assets, and thus was prone to dynamic inconsistencies and other free market transaction inefficiencies. Moreover, manufacturers were required to make major investments in developing aircraft technology that could be recovered only by a large number of future aircraft sales. For example, Douglas's attempt to compete with the B247 by developing its DC2 model required the sale of over 75 aircraft (a large number of aircraft relative to the market size and more than the B247s sold by Boeing) at $65,000 each (in 1930s' dollars) in order to break even (Lynn, 1997, p. 46). Manufacturers tried to tie airlines into aircraft acquisition commitments before venturing into a project in order to reduce their investment risks. Such contracts involved specific investments and (ex-ante) uncertainties and information imperfections regarding the (ex-post) performance of the new technology.

One can see the rationale behind the industry's tendency to vertically integrate and the evolution of the holding company structure. The 1934 Act can be interpreted as an unsuccessful attempt to impose free market competition on an industry that indeed has high specific investment, production and marketing uncertainties, and natural monopolistic characteristics. The 1938 Civil Aeronautics Act, then, imposed government regulation as an alternative to the vertically integrated structure, which facilitated investment in specific assets, but indirectly subsidized increasing-return technology as the traditional mail subsidies became less meaningful with increases in passenger operations.

### 3. 1970s—DEREGULATION

The second major round of airline complaints regarding destructive competition came up in the public debate, legislative hearings, and other political action that led to deregulation in the 1970s. The airlines and the economists who were proponents of deregulation spoke in different voices, and the airlines believed that the economists misunderstood the industry. The airlines argued that deregulation would bring destructive competition and increased concentration; the economists argued that it would bring constructive competition.

American Airlines' Bob Crandall, for example, is quoted as suggesting: "You academic pinhead! You don't know [anything]. You can't deregulate this industry; you are going to wreck it. You don't know a goddamn thing!" Peterson & Glab, (1994, p. 49). Delta's chairman suggested, that: "under the banner of 'free enterprise and less government regulation' the [deregulation] movement actually promised more regulation and perhaps eventual nationalization" McCraw (1984, p. 269).

The strong opposition of the airlines was often interpreted in the context of Stigler's *industry capture* idea, which would see it as obvious that an industry would refuse to give up any benefits of regulation. The dominant economic perspective was rigid and saw only two extremes: Markets could be either naturally competitive or naturally monopolistic, and "destructive competition would be inconceivable except for the presence of market imperfections Kahn (1998, p. 175). [in particular] fixed or sunk costs that bulk large as a percentage of total cost; and long-sustained and recurrent periods of excess capacity " Kahn (1998, p. 173).

Among economists, there was an overwhelming consensus that the industry was naturally competitive, a view that was supported by empirical studies conducted by prominent researchers. The government's position as reflected in a CAB (1975) report confirmed this view: "The industry is naturally competitive, not monopolistic," so destructive competition was ruled out as impossible in what was believed to be a naturally competitive market (p. 1).

The proponents of deregulation based their view on the conclusions of various economic models and concepts that generally supported the desirability of free market competition. The first line of rationalization was the traditional *laissez-faire* notion of the neoclassical theory. Alfred Kahn was often quoted as suggesting that "aircraft are marginal costs with wings."

The possibility that there would be increasing returns to scale was dismissed out of hand: "Every study we have ever made seems to show that there are no economies of scale."[70] Concerns about "cut-throat" price competition, for example, were usually interpreted within the concept of predatory pricing in which the "big [airlines] will eat the little," and industry concentration would increase. Kahn adopted the general Chicago School's view on this issue, arguing that:

> We don't find in American industry generally when you have a few relatively large carriers competing with one another that they engage in bitter and extended price wars.[71]

Concerns about increased industry concentration were dismissed on the basis of the contestable markets idea, suggesting that even if an airline were a monopoly in a certain market,

[70] Quoted in Dempsey & Hardaway (1992, p .457).
[71] Quoted in Dempsey & Hardaway (1992, p. 457).

the ease of potential entry into the individual markets and the constant threat of its materializing could well suffice to prevent monopolistic exploitation.[72]

The pro-deregulation economists and politicians in fact did not have a coherent model of deregulation. Nor did they portray a clear and uniform picture of how they believed the industry structure would evolve. They accepted a general notion that any emerging post-deregulation market structure would be fine; whether in an atomistic market structure, a monopoly, or anything in between, it was believed that both real and potential competition would discipline prices. Supporters of deregulation were concerned mostly with airline overpricing and dismissed underpricing. They believed in the power of potential "hit and run competition" to eliminate monopolistic exploitation, and thus underestimated the possibility of actual and destructive competition.

The airlines' claims turned out to be more complex than the economists perceived. Industry concerns could be viewed from both the destructive and constructive competition paradigms and more. Moreover, the industry's voice was not monolithic.

On the eve of deregulation, airlines were heterogeneous with respect to their financial condition, fleet composition, network structure, and labor contracts. Less efficient airlines were concerned that they might be forced to exit the industry. This notion conformed to the traditional economic paradigm; if you don't fit, you must quit! The airlines did not dismiss the risk of fare wars and increased concentration. They could predict the possibility of takeovers or ongoing rivals' attempts to gain dominance in specific markets.

Frank Lorenzo, at the time chairman of Texas International, argued, for example, that:

> We will, over a period of years, end up with a couple of very large airlines. There will be many small airlines that will start up here and there, but they will never amount to a very significant amount of the transportation market.[73]

Airlines also experienced chronic overcapacity. On the eve of deregulation, aircraft flew almost half-empty, and the industry average load factor was 55%. Airline executives were concerned with destructive competition as seen in the railroad industry in the 19th century. Even before deregulation, some airlines were operating hub networks, and airlines had come to appreciate the benefits of network economies before this issue gained significant theoretical interest.

It was obvious to the airlines, for example, that United Airlines had the most efficient and most integrated domestic network system (including established routes and suitable aircraft), and therefore enjoyed an advantage over most of the airlines. On the other side, Pan American enjoyed a monopolistic position in mostly linear international markets, but lacked any significant network benefits or a domestic feeder system. Pan Am's failure to acquire or develop an efficient network structure is often suggested as one of the major reasons for its demise after deregulation.

---

[72] Quoted in Dempsey & Hardaway (1992, p. 457).
[73] Congressional testimony, cited in Vietor (1991, p. 34).

Airline competition under regulation focused on increasing market share and not on maximizing profits. In fact, the airlines practiced a brand of destructive competition even then. Since market prices were fixed, the major decision variables were cost-related, including capacity, flight frequency, and quality of service. In the preregulated railroad story, firms cut prices below average cost. In the regulated aviation industry, competition drove airlines to increase average cost above the regulated price, even though the regulator increased prices periodically, approved bilateral or multilateral capacity coordination by competing airlines, distributed route licenses, or otherwise took steps to maintain a rigid cartel structure. The industry could not provide normal returns on capital even with the benefit of regulation.

A new cycle of aircraft orders and deliveries started in the second half of 1975. Then, the number of new aircraft orders placed by US airlines in 1976 was over four times higher than the year before at 126 units. The number increased to 151 in 1977 and peaked at 323 in 1978, including newly designed Boeing 757s and 767s that were ordered for the first time. These new aircraft were more efficient to operate, but involved significant fixed costs.

## 4. EARLY 1990s—AN INDUSTRY IN CRISIS

In August 1990, the Persian Gulf crisis erupted with Iraq's invasion of Kuwait. The industry ended that year facing increasing costs, falling demand, and excess capacity. Capacity and fixed costs are rigid, and slow to adjust, so price is the major immediately available policy variable. A cohesive industry or a cartel might be envisioned to carefully analyze demand elasticity and the overall impact of increasing fares on revenues, weighing the trade-offs of a price increase aimed at covering higher fuel cost and its negative effect on demand. And in similar crises during the regulation era, the CAB had increased fares and limited capacity.

In the deregulated industry

> within days of the Iraqi invasion, a number of airlines proposed fare increases. But within a week, unity has collapsed: while some airlines attempted to impose a 5.3% fare increase, others—including Pan Am, Eastern and TWA—announced fare reductions. The inability of the industry to take a common stand reflects the division between strong and weak airlines, needing every bit of cash flow to stay ahead of creditors.[74]

This pattern was but a prelude to the events that followed. A year later, Robert Crandall stated that:

> most of our problems can be attributed to managements who seem to believe their mission in life is to put every living human being on an aircraft—at any price—and who have failed to do their economic homework on subjects such as price elasticity.[75]

The press was full of tales of destructive competition during the early 1990s. There were stories about the weak airlines hurting the strong. Most notable were

[74] *Air Transport World*, October 1990, p. 62.
[75] *Airfinance Journal*, October 1991, p. 6.

American Airlines' attacks against the bankrupt airlines. Crandall led a vigorous campaign asserting that:

> airlines operated under chapter 11 bankruptcy leave massive debt and liabilities behind them and are pricing tickets just to cover basic operating costs.[76]... Failing airlines struggle on, often resorting to extreme tactics—such as initiating "fare wars" to bring in cash to cover only direct operating costs—which contribute to the poor economic performance of the industry as a whole.[77]

Crandall promoted new legislation that would shorten the time during which an airline could reorganize under protection of the Bankruptcy Code. He was backed by Delta's Wolf, who questioned

> whether an industry can remain viable if substantial amounts of excess capacity are artificially permitted to remain in the system for years, while bankrupt carriers attempt to reorganize.[78]

And then there were the stories about the strong airlines hurting the weak:

> While American complains about bankrupt carriers filling too many seats at too-low prices, the real culprit is American itself, followed by Delta and United.[79]

US Air's chairman

> placed the blame for much of the airline industry's trouble on excess capacity—particularly that of United, American and Delta. According to US Air calculations, those three airlines increased their total capacity by 35% during the past three years despite the recessionary economy.[80]

Others claimed that

> the Big Three do not want to reduce capacity. They invested in short-term losses to operate unneeded capacity in order to achieve long-term dominance.[81]

Referring to "fare wars" during the summer of 1992, US Senator John McCain (R., Ariz.) suggested that this

> is not simply a new round of fare wars, but a determined and thinly disguised effort to bring about the final round of concentration in the industry.[82]

Continental sued American for practicing illegal predatory behavior. America West's CEO (whose airline was also operating under Chapter 11 protection), referring to American's price competition against his airline as well as against TWA, called American "a predator on the loose."[83]

American tried to assume a price leadership role, suggesting simplifying fares. Its attempt was not popular among all the airlines; "outside the big three." the

[76] *Flight International*, February 1992, p. 14.

[77] *Flight International*, February 1992, p. 6.

[78] *Aviation Week*, February 22, 1993, p. 29.

[79] *Air Transport World*, December 1992, p. 55.

[80] *Aviation Week*, February 22, 1993.

[81] *Air Transport World*, May 1992, p. 75.

[82] *Aviation Week*, June 15, 1992, p. 40.

[83] *Aviation Week*, June 15, 1992, p. 40.

industry did not follow "American's marching orders." Northwest's introduction of the "child-plus-adult twofer" was met by 50% discount response by American. Northwest claimed that American's fare response was triggered by information it developed from the American-controlled SABRE Computerized Reservation System. Northwest claimed that it offered summer fare discounts in order to stimulate demand and projected the discounts would generate $20 million in profits. Instead, the airline faced estimated losses of $40 million when it was forced to match the American rate. Price strategies like this were blamed for devastating the industry's potential profits during the summer of 1992.

If people thought fare wars were a summer activity, they were in for a surprise in the winter. In January 1993, Northwest introduced a "Take Along" fare: 20% discounts for a group of two, 30% for three, and 40% for four, mainly on flights to or from its major hubs. Delta's response was to apply a deeper discount in markets where it competed with Northwest. Immediately thereafter, American matched the fares, "setting up the possibility of a low-fare bonanza through May."[84]

Finally, there were stories about the use of predatory behavior to drive competition out of specific markets in an attempt to achieve monopolistic power. It was alleged that

> United's self-proclaimed "aggressive plan for expansion" in Denver, launched in 1992 with another massive increase in capacity and flight frequency at Denver, succeeded in eliminating Continental as a hub competitor in Denver by 1994 (Dempsey, 1997).

Allegations that major airlines were practicing predatory pricing against new startup airlines started to surface. An excess supply of aircraft, mechanics, and crews made it quite attractive for small discount fare airlines to enter the market in the early 1990s. Several small startup airlines even attempted to fly into major hub airports, seemingly posing a very small challenge—yet apparently still a challenge—to the big airlines in certain markets. This was a dream come true for the free market economists, as the invisible hand encouraged startup airlines and new entries to compete and discipline prices.

ValueJet is a celebrated case. It started out as a remarkable success story but ended up in disaster. There were also others: the new Frontier, Western Pacific, Vanguard, Sun Jet, Reno, Spirit, Kiwi, and more. Although comparatively very small, these airlines were apparently perceived as a potential threat by the majors. It was alleged that United targeted Frontier and Western Pacific (the latter ceased operation); American targeted Vanguard and Sun Jet International (the latter ceased operation); Delta targeted ValueJet (which reemerged as a smaller airline under the name Airtran); and Northwest targeted Reno (ultimately acquired by American) and Spirit.

Each of these stories is somewhat different. Most of them, however, have a major theme in common—the airlines cut prices below the level necessary to keep the industry running in the long run, given then-current capacity and market size. Together they describe a long period of substantial and persistent losses to the industry as a whole, representing the very paradigm of destructive competition.

---

[84] *Aviation Week*, January 18, 1993, p. 33.

Cutting fares below average cost (maximizing revenues) may seem rational behavior for an individual airline that is facing overcapacity and high fixed costs during a cyclical downturn—it may even be the only available choice for an airline to survive. It may also be a natural tendency of an oligopolistic network or industry in which firms compete over market share.

What might seem rational or natural to an individual firm, however, may hurt an industry as a whole. According to traditional economics, such behavior is not desirable from a society's viewpoint. In such a game, the desired cooperative solution may not represent a stable equilibrium, and each player might pursue an individual policy, causing overall societal cost. This is the essence of the destructive competition story that Adams suggested in the case of the emerging railroad industry.

In theory, an ideal regulator would figure out what the cooperative solution might be and then impose it on the various players for the sake of the public interest. A government can enforce contracts that other cartel managers cannot. According to this view, destructive competition is a result of increasing return to scale, high fixed costs, and excess capacity. It represents a form of market failure, which traditionally has been used to justify regulation.

In fact, during the early 1990s the idea of re-regulating the airlines industry surfaced to gain some momentum. Proponents of re-regulation observed that the industry had survived severe crises during the regulation regime, avoiding catastrophic failures and bankruptcies. They also noted that the deregulated US industry had been hit significantly harder than the *regulated* foreign airlines.

An editorial in *Air Transport World* commented as follows:

> The public-utility concept is being discussed more. Pena [then Transportation Secretary] told Congress that US airlines need help and there should be more of a partnership between the industry and government, similar to what exists at some of the foreign airlines. Domestically, a limited form of regulation toward the public-utility idea not only would stifle the industry's urge to eat itself but it also would restore some of the franchise that airlines lost when the Civil Aeronautics Board died, making them a more attractive investment.[85]

This new call was for a more limited type of regulation than the one practiced before, responding to the notion that the established instruments of government intervention (mainly antitrust legislation and decisions) seemed to be inadequate to deal with the problem. The antitrust perspective is to target industry monopolistic pricing or exclusionary strategies aimed at creating market power in order to charge monopolistic prices. This framework, however, was no longer appropriate; nor was it adequate for dealing with the problems that had emerged in the airlines industry. Antitrust actions may address the concerns of monopolistic power, but they do not help with regard to the presence of destructive competition and general industry crisis. Fare wars and below-average cost pricing, in many cases, were not predatory by the legal antitrust definition, but the practices all the same led to increased concentration and the possibility of creating future monopolistic power.

---

[85] *Air Transport World*, March 1993, p. 5.

While society had provided institutional tools and procedures to deal with one set of the deregulated industry's problems (monopolistic exploitation), it left another set unaddressed. During similar crises in the late 1940s, late 1950s, and early 1960s, and in the 1970s, the CAB responded as a cartel manager by raising fares, limiting entry, and limiting capacity competition. Many of the calls for "re-regulating" the industry focused on remedying this deficiency. One suggestion was to

> [inject] modest governmental oversight now to provide some measure of stability to pricing and allow a rationalization of capacity (Dempsey, 1995, p. 194).

This voice could gain no political momentum, as industry conditions gradually improved. The dominant view remained against re-regulating the industry, as there was no serious political resolution to push for a significant institutional change in any direction. After all, the public enjoyed low fares, and the strong major airlines enjoyed increasing market shares.

## 5.  IS THE INDUSTRY INDEED NATURALLY COMPETITIVE?

It started as a response to an unpredictable short oil shock in the summer of 1990 and evolved into an almost four-year-long crisis. Fifteen months in, the crisis had already eradicated all traces of accumulated profit earned in the 67-year history of scheduled airline service. This was the Gulf War in 1991.

Certain market players and observers attributed the industry crisis mostly to the Gulf War. Others downplayed the role of the war, and instead emphasized inherent structural characteristics that made the industry's ability to function in an unregulated environment doubtful. An *Air Transport World* editorial suggested:

> If anything has been learned during the 15 years since the US embarked on its noble deregulation experiment, it is that traditional airlines do not thrive in this environment.[86]

While it is clear that the Gulf War affected the industry quite dramatically, several points are worth emphasizing: 1) in 1990 oil prices were lower than the levels they had reached during the previous oil crisis; 2) the industry was better equipped than ever before with fuel-efficient aircraft; 3) this was a relatively short-lived oil crisis as prices stabilized quite quickly at a relatively low level; and nevertheless, 4) the crisis was more devastating to the industry than anything seen before.

Overemphasizing the Gulf War's impact obscures some major chronic problems in the industry. Perhaps a prime symptom of the inherent characteristic of the problem was that the industry's average profit margins throughout the 1980s and before the Gulf War became an issue. Airline profit margins were only 1% compared to the average profit margin for other sectors of the American industry of 5%.[87] In fact, even during the era of regulation, profit margins only rarely approached "normal" rates.

---

[86] *Air Transport World*, March 1993, p. 5.
[87] *Aviation Week*, April 6, 1992, p. 36.

It should go without saying that different observers interpreting the industry's behavior from different perspectives will reach different conclusions regarding its evolution and the related policy implications. The essence of the debate from a theoretical perspective, however, boils down to whether one assumes the industry has natural competitive characteristics or natural monopolistic characteristics. In the former case, actual and potential competition is expected to discipline fares. In the latter, increasing returns to scale and scope and other network characteristics might amplify concentration and market power.

If you adopt the first view, the rest of the story falls into place for you almost automatically. The industry came into deregulation as a government-controlled cartel. Deregulation permitted free entry and exit, and price competition. Average fares declined. Inefficient airlines became extinct, and the surviving firms have been moving toward a long-run equilibrium at a competitive (or quasi-competitive) level.

This was the general expectation of deregulation enthusiasts, a view that seemed to prevail among many economists during the 1980s and 1990s and was not changed despite the events of the early 1990s. A detailed empirical study by Morrison and Clifford (1995) that covers the events of the early 1990s reaffirmed this tradition. It became an overnight classic with deregulation enthusiasts, and its major conclusions have been widely cited in praise of deregulation.

Now, one might be different and see the airline industry as a public utility, more like a railroad. This would be the traditional natural monopoly model. High fixed costs and increasing returns to scale at the relevant demand range induce airlines to overcharge when demand is high (relative to capacity) and to undercharge when demand is low. In the latter case, overcapacity might induce firms to set fares below average cost; bankruptcy and further concentration would be the natural consequences.

More up-to-date views might resort to more complex metaphors of dynamic (increasing-return) network firms competing over market share, using a variety of strategic variables in a winner-take-all (almost) game. One possible theoretical solution to such a problem is the eventual emergence of a monopoly, or else a trajectory of increased consolidation and concentration in particular niches. According to this view, the downward trend in average fares may indicate that firms are competing over market dominance and not moving toward a long-run stable competitive equilibrium.

According to the naturally competitive view, increased concentration and airline size are negligible issues, due to the threat of potential competition. According to the naturally monopolistic view, network size may have a positive impact on production and consumption efficiencies, but might also increase concentration and create market power. In the latter case, potential hit and run competition cannot be trusted to discipline prices.

It is interesting that the academicians who played a major role in deregulation of the industry in the 1970s came around to agree that the post-deregulation industry had evolved differently from what they expected. Airlines' concerns with destructive competition thus have gained somewhat more legitimacy.

Alfred Kahn, for one, has stated:

I talked about the possibility that there might be really destructive competition, but I tended to dismiss it. And that certainly has been one of the unpleasant surprises of deregulation.[88]

As for pricing and entry, he said:

We didn't dream of the way airlines could manipulate fares with such great sophistication.... We were a little naive about what "freedom of entry" means in the airline business.[89]

Commenting on contestability, he notes:

Contestability is not a sufficient protection, in my opinion, and anybody who looks at the airline industry certainly knows that the likelihood and opportunity of entry, particularly by new carriers—low cost, price-cutting carriers—has greatly diminished in recent years and is likely to remain much lower than before.[90]

Michael Levine, who played an important role in the deregulation process and later became a Northwest official, said:

what we have learned was that there were substantial economies of scale and scope on the revenue side. Because once airlines discovered the network in a serious way and really started developing hub-and-spoke systems, hub-and-spoke systems exhibited fairly dramatic economics of scope.[91]

## 6. OVER CAPACITY

Observers who believe the airlines industry has natural monopolistic characteristics focus, on the one hand, on a tendency to build overcapacity and as a result to set low fares, and, on the other hand, on the accumulation of market power at the major hub level. These two characteristics are somewhat difficult to explain in the context of a naturally competitive model.

Morrison and Winston (1995) explain the overcapacity phenomenon as follows:

Given that overcapacity is widely considered a problem in the airline industry, it is likely that forecast errors are a major source of the problem. (p.96) "The primary source of carriers' losses appears to be their failure, because of poor forecasts, to adapt efficiently to changes in the business cycle and to disruptions of the Persian Gulf War and its impact on air travel and fuel prices (p. 116).

There is no doubt that overcapacity can be explained as a forecast error. The airlines industry is sensitive both to the business cycle and to fuel prices, and the latter constitutes a significant cost component. The major industry crises of the last three decades have involved oil shocks, downward business cycles, and certain elements of surprise.

A persistent tendency of an industry to err in forecasting, however, causes one to wonder about the possible structural reasons for such reoccurrences. A long history

---

[88] Quoted in Dempsey (1995, p. 194).
[89] Quoted in Dempsey & Hardaway (1992, p. 459).
[90] Quoted in Dempsey & Hardaway (1992, p. 460).
[91] Quoted in, *Air Transport World*, March 1998, p. 32

of building overcapacity should not be viewed as an exogenous random event. I have suggested before we look at industry capacity decisions through a strategic behavior lens to help identify the reasons why overcapacity has developed. Several other reasons will be described in what follows.

For the "naturally competitive" school, airlines plan capacity ahead of time to accommodate expected demand. In this context, overcapacity (or undercapacity) can mainly be explained by a failure to predict or to otherwise directly follow actual demand fluctuations. But this is only one part of the story. In reality, capacity is a strategic variable that airlines often use to affect cost and demand, so capacity decisions are driven by factors other than the business cycle.

On top of this, the overall market outcome in the airlines industry is a result of oligopolistic competition in two major segments of the market: the manufacturer, and the air travel market. In both markets, aspects of increasing return and network economies are quite strong. Manufacturers (using dynamic increasing-return technology) compete for market dominance in the aircraft market; they strive to increase their user base and to set the industry standard. Airlines (taking advantage of network effects from the cost and demand sides) compete for market dominance in their particular market niches. These strategic interactions combined have resulted in capacity overshooting.

This is not a simple story. It is complex, and perhaps not reducible to an elegant regression analysis of the type suggested by Morrison and Winston. It does suggest, however, a useful perspective that allows us to interpret an extremely important phenomenon.

American's Robert Crandall has been one of the major proponents of the natural oligopolistic view, arguing that

> Because of the huge capital costs, airlines have an incentive to sell excess seats for virtually any price that will cover incremental costs. The problem is that these prices do not necessarily cover the fixed costs. Because of this history, it is likely that an over-populated airline system, with large amounts of excess capacity, will be perpetually unprofitable.[92]

A similar view has been suggested by Paul Dempsey, who represents the opposite voice, that of the small airlines in their struggle against the big ones. According to Dempsey:

> the airline industry exhibits a relentless tendency, both to produce excess capacity and to price its product below fully allocated costs (1995, p. 188).

Crandall (1995) identifies several reasons for this tendency. First, in the aviation market, quantity supplied (flight frequency) is also the product *quality* (consumers prefer more frequent scheduled flights). This creates a powerful incentive for airlines to add flights, especially in a complex hub-and-spoke system where the impact of adding flight frequencies has a network-wide density effect.

Second, the industry faces cyclical, seasonal, daily, weekly, and other reasons for fluctuating demand. Capacity planning involves multiple peak and off-peak

---

[92] *Commercial Aviation Report*, September 1992, p. 6.

considerations. It is the very nature of the industry that there is overcapacity during off-peak periods.

Third, the airline industry by its nature involves an amalgam of high fixed costs with a very low marginal cost (the incremental cost of seating an additional passenger on an aircraft).[93] A seat on an airplane is a perishable product; once the airplane doors are closed, all unsold seats perish. One can see how this attribute may encourage airlines to sell empty seats at almost any price.

Capacity is affected by two major factors: the number of aircraft in an airline's fleet, and the extent of their use (flight frequency, or the number of aircraft cycles). An airline's fixed cost includes the cost of the aircraft, certain maintenance items, marketing (advertising), and sales, as well as other costs of maintaining and operating an integrated network system, including a substantial groundside infrastructure. The industry's fixed costs are estimated to represent between 80% to 90% of its total cost (Dempsey, 1995). Cost reductions can be achieved mainly by adding to the number of aircraft an airline operates and by more frequent use. The expensive, mostly fixed-cost, integrated hub-and-spoke network system encourages increasing the number of aircraft and increasing their use.

In addition, the acquisition of new aircraft involves complex bilateral agreements between the manufacturers and an airline, including training, spare parts support, participation in advertising, financing, trade-ins of old equipment, and more. There is an advantage in negotiating a large aircraft package for a lower average unit price, which may be another incentive for airlines to order more aircraft. I have noted other incentives for excess capacity that are related to strategic behavior, including deterring entry, excluding rivals by capturing limited airside and groundside capacity, and increasing rivals' costs.

Moreover, since traditionally customers prefer new aircraft rather than old, airlines are encouraged to refurbish their fleets and to acquire new (more expensive fixed-cost) aircraft versions as they become available. In fact, airlines often compete to be the first to offer new aircraft technology.

Being the first to place an order and becoming a launching airline for new technology has several major benefits. First, a launching airline is in a better bargaining position with the manufacturer with regard to aircraft acquisition cost, specifications, and related support. Second, new airplanes attract passengers, and airlines compete in offering the newest technology. Third, a launching airline placing a large number of aircraft may use up production capacity, and thereby slow the acquisition of the new technology by its competitors.

Design and production of new aircraft technology requires a substantial and irreversible, sunk investment by a manufacturer. Before investing in building an aircraft, manufacturers attempt to make airlines commit to order enough aircraft that will let the manufacturer at least break even on its investment.

There are clear examples of these patterns. United's order of B247 aircraft in the 1930s tied up Boeing's production line for two years, motivating TWA and other airlines to look for competing technology with Douglas. In the 1950s, when jet technology was introduced, Pan Am monopolized both Boeing's and Douglas's

---

[93] A scheduled flight must take off even if not all seats are sold, and the cost of the flight is mostly fixed.

production lines, with 25 aircraft each. United and American followed Pan Am's lead, and in only a few months the industry ordered $1.4 billion worth of new equipment (Vietor, 1991).

In the 1970s, with the introduction of jumbo jets, Pan Am was the first to order Boeing 747 aircraft (25). Domestic carriers followed by placing orders for 747 or smaller three-engine DC10s and L1011s. This significant capacity jump affected the industry dramatically during the oil crisis of the 1970s, and triggered government intervention in controlling competition.

The placement of a large number of aircraft orders in the late 1980s is by no means unique. "Capacity competition" is one of the major arguments deregulation proponents raised in support of scrapping regulation. Starting in the 1930s, through the post-war introduction of higher-capacity, four-engine aircraft, through the introduction of jet aircraft in the late 1950s, through the jumbo jet orders in the 1970s, and continuing with the fuel-efficient aircraft of the 1980s, the industry has repeated the same patterns: ordering a large number of new aircraft without regard for fluctuations in the economic cycle and in the demand for air travel.

Crandall (1995) also emphasizes the high exit costs that further motivate financially weak airlines to stay in the market and under price their seats. According to him

> The network nature of airline companies—which are worth the present value of the future stream of cash flows generated by the integrated use of airplanes, people and facilities—means that an airline cannot efficiently liquidate its assets piecemeal, as many companies do (p. 7).

This applies to any airline that might consider abandoning a market or adjusting capacity, and it would explain some airlines' reluctance to pull out of non-profitable markets.

These circumstances contradict the major premise of the contestable markets idea. In the contestable markets story, an aircraft is the major fixed cost component in a city-pair market. It is assumed to be not specific to a route or a network, so it can be moved from one market to another with negligible sunk cost. In fact, the aircraft is but one component of a complex integrated network system that includes other significant fixed costs that are location- and market-specific.

In reality, entering and exiting markets involves costs that cannot be recovered once a market is abandoned. The value of an aircraft and the value of an operating aircraft in a current and functioning market system are different. When an airline decides to abandon a market, it is the aircraft value that constitutes most of the recoverable portion of its exit cost. Most other costs are sunk.

During periods of recession and overcapacity, aircraft resale values drop significantly as well, and it may be difficult to dispose of them even at fire-sale values. During the early 1990s, for example, it was almost impossible to dispose of excess aircraft because of overall market excess capacity; many aircraft were parked or otherwise operated at below-normal rates, while rent and loan payments either continued to be paid or accrued. The result was that airlines were inclined to stay in markets and continue operation as long as they covered their direct operational costs, or else as long as their working cash balances allowed them to survive despite losses.

The bankruptcy laws moreover provide institutional support for a financially weak airline to defer, restructure, renegotiate, or eliminate debt, labor costs, rent, and other fixed or variable costs. Under bankruptcy protection, an airline may endure a long reorganization period by covering only operating costs—while enjoying significantly lower costs than other airlines that are meeting their obligations.

While we might debate whether bankruptcy laws and procedures are socially efficient, there is no question that they permit a relatively long period of below-average-cost pricing by airlines that, according to traditional economic theory, would otherwise be expected to exit the market. With or without bankruptcy code protection, the sunk cost of abandoning an integrated market system encourages airlines to keep operating in a market, even at below average-cost levels.

## 7. LATE 1990s – THE BEGINNING OF A NEW CRISIS

The events of the early 1990s and the political attention they attracted forced industry observers and politicians to look into the evolution of the airlines industry, to debate the merit of deregulation, and to suggest policy implications. A Presidential Committee established in 1993 for this purpose promised much but delivered almost no practical solutions, it did become a forum for various views and opinions to be presented and discussed. All the same, the various groups continued to interpret events according to their particular industry interests and political views.

On the one hand, deregulation enthusiasts celebrated the success of deregulation. They defended the natural competitive nature of the industry, blamed the government for many of the problems, and called for further deregulation. On the other side, there were calls for re-regulation or more aggressive antitrust policy. In between the two camps, there were calls for increased government regulatory involvement in controlling competition. These are the same generic policies that were debated in the 1930s before regulation was adopted and again in the 1970s before deregulation was launched. More than fifteen years of deregulation in practice had changed the details but assuredly not the scope and the nature of the policy debate. Once again, as the memories of the early 1990s crisis faded, so did the feeling of urgency, the heated level of the debate, and the idea that destructive competition was an issue to be immediately addressed.

During the second half of the 1990s, demand for air traffic grew, and a better balance was achieved between capacity and demand as the industry slowly emerged from the crisis. Along the way, new concerns over increasing market power, predatory pricing, and deteriorating levels of service quality substituted for the earlier concerns over destructive competition. The regulators attempted to deal with these concerns by proposing new guidelines for airline competition, by launching lawsuits alleging predatory behavior and other antitrust issues, and by initiating political and legislative efforts to enforce service quality and passengers' rights. After almost twenty years of hands-off oversight and only limited antitrust enforcement, the government has slowly moved to increase its involvement with airline competition, using the available tools (mostly antitrust actions) and ignoring altogether the issue of overcapacity and destructive competition.

It is useful at this time to revisit the history of orders and deliveries for new aircraft by the world airlines since the beginning of the jet age (Figure 12).[94] The peak of the first cycle of aircraft orders occurred in 1965, and deliveries on this cycle materialized during the recession associated with the 1967 oil crisis. The peak of the second cycle of aircraft orders occurred almost twenty years later, in 1973, and these orders materialized during the recession and industry and oil crisis of 1973-1975. The third peak occurred only a short time later, in 1978, when the deliveries were made during the 1979-1982 recession and industry crisis. The fourth order peak was in 1988, and the deliveries were made during the 1990-1993 recession and industry crisis.

Each industry crisis is associated with a downturn in the business cycle, with Middle East unrest and high oil prices, and amid flying security concerns and significant overcapacity. In every case, orders for new aircraft peaked at around the highest stage of the economic cycle, but the associated deliveries were made during the succeeding recession, and contributed further to the industry crisis.

In the late 1990s, out of the political limelight, far from the public eye, a new potential capacity problem began to develop. While barely recovered from the crisis of the first half of the 1990s, the industry embarked on a new aircraft acquisition cycle. New aircraft technology was offered by Boeing (the 777, the "new generation" Boeing 737, and the 717)[95] and by Airbus, which had expanded its production into the previously Boeing-dominant long-range jumbo market with its A340, and into the narrowbody market (A320/321 and A319/A318). In addition, orders for a very large number of new regional jets, in the 50- to 100-seat category were placed with the manufacturers. These aircraft were planned to enhance the short-range hub feeding systems, replacing turboprop aircraft traditionally operated in this niche market.

Toward the end of the century airlines' orders for new-generation aircraft were skyrocketing, raising once again the question of excess capacity. Already in January 1999, *Aviation Week*, a leading industry publication, had suggested:

> The 10 US airlines are adding capacity at a rate that will boost competition to new heights this year, which could lead to a renewal of fare wars or a reshaping of the industry. Major carriers are planning to add 275 new aircraft of 50 seats or more in 1999. This expansion, even considering scheduled retirements, will increase seating capacity by 4% over 1998.... This seating boost is expected to be nearly double the increase of last year.... The results of the heightened competition could renew fare wars, at least in selected markets. At worst, it could mean the loss of a major carrier in a shakeout of the majors' lineup that has been threatened for years.[96]

It is important to note that this observation was made in 1999, long before the post-September 11, 2001, dramatic drop in demand.

---

[94] Source: *World Jet Airplane Inventory Year – End 1990*, Boeing Commercial Airplane Group.
[95] The 717 was started as the MD95 before Boeing took over MDC.
[96] *Aviation Week*, January 18, 1999.

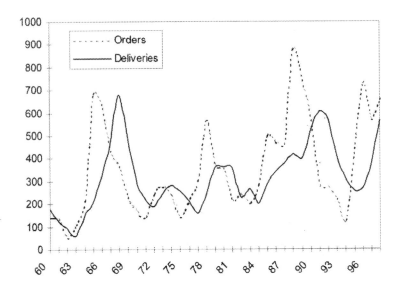

*Figure 12. New Aircraft Orders and Deliveries 1960-1998*

By the end of 1999, Boeing and Airbus had a backlog of over 2,950 aircraft orders totaling more than $211 billion.[97] During the first half of the year 2000, almost 200 additional orders were placed. And again, in what is referred to by some observers as an industry revolution, a large number of orders were placed by regional airlines for the new smaller 50- to 100-seat regional jet aircraft that have been expected to both replace and expand routes previously served mostly by turboprop aircraft.

In early 2001, cumulative backlogs approached new heights, and signs of economic slowdown started to materialize. A series of airline failures commenced, beginning with the smaller startup, charter, and local airlines (such as Legend, Trans Meridian, Sun Pacific, Fine Air), and spreading into the more national carriers (Tower Air, Kitty Hawk, Midway, Amerijet). In the major airlines category, US Airways and TWA, the two most financially troubled major airlines became takeover targets by United and American Airlines, respectively. Atlas and Polar—two major widebody cargo airlines—merged in the face of shrinking markets.

As financial statistics for the first and second quarters of the year 2001 were published, it became evident that high oil prices, slowing demand, and capacity overshooting were—once again—pushing the industry into yet another cyclical

[97] Compiled from industry publications. See, for example, *Airline Business*, September 2000, p. 103.

crisis. In August 1990, the Gulf War had pushed an otherwise struggling industry over the brink. In September 2001, the World Trade Center in New York City was destroyed.

# PART 2

# NOISE AND SAFETY REGULATION

# CHAPTER 4

# SOCIAL REGULATION

> The equilibrium or the outcome of the game
> of policy will typically not maximize
> anything.[98]

According to traditional economic thinking, perfect regulation should (or would) fix market failures related to environmental and safety externalities. In reality, regulation is an imperfect tool, an institutional arrangement that responds to information problems, interest group power, technology, and other transaction and institutional costs.

This and the next two chapters examine aspects of environmental and safety regulation as they have been practiced in the aviation industry. The first discuses major economic concepts of social regulation and its real-life practice. The next chapters examine the evolution of noise and safety regulation in more details. These regulations had an important impact on production costs and market structure during the 1990s.

## 1. IMPERFECT REGULATION

The deregulated airline industry, much to some people's surprise, evolved into a concentrated oligopoly, while its major input market (the aircraft manufacturers) evolved into a duopoly. At the same time, a new form of social regulation has evolved, focusing mainly on noise abatement and safety. The new regulation has different characteristics, involving complex and specialized technical areas that require the oversight of highly trained government personnel and substantial amounts of information and resources.

Regulators no longer focus on the traditional price- and market-related issues (monopoly) but rather on production function and cost-related issues. The new objects of regulation are information-intensive and complex, and involve many uncertainties and ambiguities.

### 1.1 Imperfect Information

Information imperfections play an important role in the regulatory process of safety and environmental issues. Information is costly to acquire and incompletely

---

[98]Dixit (1997, p. 2).

available. The players specialize in different activities and are constrained to various degrees by their budgets, and therefore a diverse and asymmetric information structure prevails.

For example, aircraft manufacturers build aircraft. They concentrate on different aspects of information from the airlines that operate the aircraft, from the airport authorities that run airports, and from consumer groups and so on. The uncertain and incomplete nature of information and in particular its asymmetric distribution among the various groups—the manufacturers, the airlines, the airport authorities—creates opportunities to extract rents. Players are motivated to invest resources in obtaining information and manipulating it in order to enhance their positions in the regulatory process.

The public largely relies on information provided by one or another player in the industry. It is thus easily misinformed or manipulated by interest groups seeking to turn public opinion to their advantage. Complex institutions have evolved to mitigate some of these information problems. Even these, however, have involved complex multi-agency relationships with information and incentive problems of their own.

## 1.2    *Interest Groups*

The traditional postulate of interest group politics is that a small well-organized group is expected to have a larger stake in a regulatory initiative in comparison to the general public and that such a small group may therefore benefit the most from inefficient regulation. In its pure form, the *industry capture theory* identifies the airlines as the high-stake interest group, rather than consumers; therefore the airlines would be expected to capture most of regulation's benefits. This perspective would envision a bilateral game between the public and a coherent and better-informed industry (cartel) that is motivated by a unified interest in capturing monopolistic rents by restricting entry. According to this view, the government would be the cartel manager, which conspires with the airlines to hide information from the public and to issue and enforce inefficient regulations.

More recent interpretations suggest a slower dynamic process (with many interconnected sub processes), evolving under uncertain and changing conditions and constrained at any time by current rules and institutions that are at least partially made up and amended by the players as they go along (Dixit, 1997). This process may be separated into two major phases (connected and repeating). The first phase ends with the enactment of certain formal rules or regulations, which can be interpreted as an incomplete long-term contract. The second involves the actual implementation and enforcement of the regulation over time in a manner not always consistent with the formally enacted regulation. Each phase involves different players, uneven and changing bargaining powers, and asymmetric information problems.

According to this view, a published regulation is the outcome of a political bargaining process in which many diverse interest groups interact to generate rules and orders that are directly imposed on the industry as mandatory legally binding requirements.

The uncertainty and controversial nature of the issues create opportunities for diverse interest groups to participate in a complex political scenario of rent-seeking and bargaining. The outcome usually has a great deal to do with the basic information structure and the specific balance of political power of the various interest groups and not necessarily much to do with the best interests of consumers or of any one specific interest group. Diversity of interests operating within the power structure creates complex solutions that often cross industry lines. A group of airlines, for example, may join an airframe manufacturer, a certain segment of the public, a labor union, and a local airport operator in an ad hoc coalition advocating the imposition of a certain regulation, which would be overseen by several federal and local government agencies. Figuring out the winners or losers (if any) in such circumstances is quite challenging.

## 2. WHO BENEFITED FROM ECONOMIC REGULATION?

Did the civil aviation authority under regulation indeed act as a manager of a cartel and set price to maximize airlines' profits—as suggested by the *industry capture* view, or did it maximize consumer surplus—as suggested by *the public interest* view? Most empirical studies on this issue conclude that pre-deregulation consumers did not benefit from regulation. They also indicate, however, that the airlines did not benefit from regulation either. Perhaps the most puzzling fact is that, despite high regulated airfares, the industry's profitability was anything but impressive throughout the regulation era.

So who did benefit from regulation of the airline industry? Two general conclusions are suggested. First, the distribution of gains changed over time in response to changing market and political conditions.[99] Second, aircraft manufacturers—which were largely excluded from the formulation of the *industry capture* argument—extracted significant gains from regulation at least during the sixties and early seventies.[100] By setting regulated airfares higher than the maximum profit level, the regulator, in fact, supported aircraft overcapacity (Olson and Trapani, 1981).

In 1975, the Council of Economic Advisers portrayed the consequences of regulation as follows:

> the airlines tend to compete on the basis of scheduling over which the Board does not exercise direct control. The result is "excess capacity" and efforts to raise the regulated fares in order to assure a return on investment greater than the industry's perceived cost of capital serve only to set the stage for further capacity augmentation. Carriers as a

[99] Olson and Trapani (1981), for example, show that regulation changed from favoring aircraft manufacturers in 1971 to favoring the airlines in 1976 and 1977.

[100] During these periods, new aircraft technologies were introduced, starting with the pioneering class of narrowbody four-engine jet aircraft (707s and DC8s) in the early sixties, followed by a new class of short- and medium-range aircraft (727s, 737s, and DC9s), and then in the early seventies by new widebody jumbo jets (747s, DC10s, and L1011s).

group have consequently tended to earn neither excess profits nor losses, but the traveling public has paid higher fares because of the regulation-induced excess capacity (CAB, 1975, pp. 10-11).

The report also suggests that the regulated fares tended "to maximize seat capacity as opposed to maximizing total passenger traffic" (CAB, 1975, p. 11).

The CAB's regulatory policy did not merely encourage overcapacity. It also provided airlines with direct incentives to fill this capacity with new aircraft, as they became available. Regulated rates were calculated on the basis of major airlines operating new aircraft. Operators of older aircraft were not allowed to differentiate their product by offering lower rates in order to protect their market share. This policy:

> involves society in the necessity for bringing a larger number of these new planes into service and scrapping more of the older ones, than would have been the case had passengers been presented with a choice between the two at prices reflecting their respective attractiveness (Kahn, 1998, p. 214).

Deregulation proponents in the 1970s and 1980s argued that regulation encouraged airlines to operate too many (mostly new) aircraft, at low load factors (just over 50%) and at increasingly higher fares, thereby imposing an overall high social cost compared to an ideal "perfect markets" benchmark. This popular portrayal of regulation, however, did not take account of the positive impact of excess capacity on the aircraft manufacturing industry.[101]

Design and development of new aircraft technology involves an enormous fixed cost, at times at higher levels than the manufacturer's overall equity value. In fact, manufacturers risked their companies' ability to survive on the design of new aircraft types and airlines and their continued operation on the cost of acquiring them. The regulated environment facilitated the taking of such risks, promising the industry that airfares would be set at levels sustaining the necessary production volume and that entry would be restricted so that the airlines could maintain adequate market share to justify the high fixed cost of acquiring the new aircraft.

For example, there is no doubt that regulation encouraged Boeing to venture into the design and building of the revolutionary 747 jumbo jet technology, with its unprecedented cost and potential impact on air travel in the 1960s. According to a CAB official before the inaugural flight:

> The potential impact of the 747 upon the future of mankind is so great that it is difficult to identify another incident with which it may be compared in the entire history of transportation (Petzinger, 1995, p. 18).

This project, however, was launched only after Pan Am placed an order that was described at the time as the largest acquisition ever made by a non-government-owned corporation ($550 million in 1965 dollars). With a monopolistic position protected by the CAB, Pan Am based its decision on the regulatory mechanisms that promised to shift the added costs to passengers through increased fares.

Other major airlines followed suit and ordered a large number of widebody aircraft, which turned out to have a devastating impact on the industry's capacity in

---

[101] Another major beneficiary of regulation was labor, which earned above-normal wages.

the early 1970s. Subsequent CAB policies of fare-setting, elimination of entry, and exit and capacity coordination, however, maintained the industry structure in spite of the 1973 economic downturn and the severe industry crisis.

When we consider this story in the context of new views of regulation, it is arguable that regulation played a far more pervasive role than is suggested by the traditional perspective. It served to subsidize increasing-return technology that had an economy-wide positive spillover in a product category that came to be a major export component in the US balance of trade. Regulation essentially provided an institutional structure that facilitated investment in non-trivial and uncertain technologies and in specific assets and transactions (between manufacturers and airlines and between airlines and passengers) that would otherwise be prone to dynamic inconsistencies and market breakdown. Regulation created and protected a highly concentrated industry structure, providing major trunk airlines with high market shares that justified the acquisition of expensive, high fixed-cost, new aircraft technology.

It is arguable that by its indirect subsidy of the industry the government also corrected what would otherwise be an industry tendency to be smaller than socially desirable due to network externalities.

When we look at regulation this way, the question of who benefited from airline regulation has a far more complex and non-obvious answer. We come to question the simple dichotomy of a zero-sum game between the public and the airlines. Perhaps, after all, economic regulation had other social benefits that economists downplayed during the 1970s and 1980s.

## 3. NOISE AND SAFETY REGULATION

The politics of environmental regulation during the 1960s and 1970s developed along the general lines of economic regulation. Aircraft noise emerged as an important issue on the national agenda starting in the sixties, as the first-generation jet aircraft were delivered to the industry in increasing numbers.

Although jet airplanes had been used by the military since the fifties and their noise was anything but surprising to the manufacturers and the regulator, the impact of noise was not one of the design and certification considerations. The FAA refrained from introducing noise-related regulation in the design of the first generation of commercial jet aircraft. Despite increased environmental concerns during the sixties and seventies, which resulted in the 1968 and 1973 amendments to the FAA Act to directly address the noise issues, these amendments did not result in any serious noise abatement. Available aircraft technology at the time and aircraft production and operation costs dictated the level of aircraft noise, and the federal government's reaction was to protect the industry and largely dismiss concerns of airport neighboring communities.

During the regulation era, the industry was perceived as a coherent interest group, with the uniform interest of fixing high fares and limiting entry. Intraindustry conflicts existed mainly with respect to the distribution of route franchises to airlines, reflecting intraindustry allocation of the benefit of regulation. How did things change after deregulation?

The changes in the industry's structure after deregulation and the shift of regulation to production- and technology-related issues created a new and more complex interest group structure. New entrance and price competition clustered the industry into heterogeneous interest groups. New generations of aircraft were introduced into the market by the manufacturers, and fleet mix gradually changed, with the stronger major airlines specializing in new aircraft technology and the smaller, financially weaker and startup new entries, in older aircraft technology. Under the new conditions, the airlines lost their coherent interest structure vis-à-vis the public and the regulator, and the stronger airlines encouraged regulation that penalized old aircraft and their operators.

This time around, increasing political pressures by airport neighboring communities and an impressive increase in aircraft operations (and noise) met an interest group structure that facilitated ambitious noise abatement efforts. Similarly, public demand for increasing safety and the general perception that new technology is safer resulted in unprecedented safety regulations focusing on old aircraft and airlines that operate them as a major safety threat.

As the new social regulation evolved, so did the industry recognition of its potential opportunities and threats and its use as an instrument in the strategic competition of air carriers, manufacturers, and other market participants. They invested resources in connection with this regulatory process in order to generate information and power to influence the process and obtain regulatory favors. The interest in influencing regulation has been active and/or reactive. Players have tried both to initiate or influence regulation initiatives in order to enhance their specific competitive market position and to block or shape proposed regulations that seen to operate against their interest.

Aircraft manufacturers in general have consistently encouraged regulation that imposes expensive maintenance and noise requirement on previous-generation aircraft in an attempt to enhance demand for new generation aircraft. Also, major incumbent airlines often encouraged regulation that increased sunk costs and entry barriers or that put a relatively higher financial burden on rival airlines that operate a different mix of aircraft in their fleets. Manufacturers and other players focused on regulatory opportunities to develop and offer technical modifications ("hush kits") or new equipment that meet the regulation requirement.

Starting in the late 1980s, the global implications of aircraft noise became more apparent. The delicate balance obtained between the local characteristics of noise damages and the local (state) versus federal regulatory powers became even more complex due to the globalization of the noise standards. This globalization introduced new and more complex interest group politics into the problem. One of the new aspects of this reality was that noise regulation became a strategic competition issue in international trade between the US and Europe. By adopting stricter (*non-addition*) noise restrictions in the early nineties, for example, the European authorities in fact reduced the importation of older US manufactured aircraft into the European market, a step that discriminated against US interests and was expected to positively affect the market share for Airbus aircraft. Similarly, attempts by the European Community (EC) to ban older aircraft that were modified to comply with the Stage IIII noise regulation in the late nineties in fact singled out US manufactured aircraft and US airlines that used them.

The noise abatement and safety regulations can be interpreted as a tax imposed on old aircraft. On the one hand, they increase the cost of old aircraft and accelerate their retirement, and on the other hand they increase demand for new aircraft. The result of these general trends is similar to the new-aircraft-support policy that characterized the CAB economic regulation policies during the 1970s.

In addition, the post-deregulation safety policy has been pushed by the public's perception that old aircraft and startup airlines that traditionally operate such aircraft are accident-prone, a perception that directly influences safety regulation. Two high-profile accidents—Aloa Airlines in 1987 and ValueJet in 1996—became major milestones in the evolution of safety regulation. The first one made old aircraft a major regulatory target and imposed new expensive modifications and maintenance requirement on this group of aircraft. The second one made the startup airlines that usually operate such aircraft a major target. In the aftermath of the ValueJet accident and related public criticism of the regulator, the FAA intensified its safety requirements and scrutiny, in fact targeting new entry as a major threat.

Facing higher regulatory hurdles and mounting public concerns with old aircraft, market entry became more difficult then ever before. First, most of the post-deregulation new entries disappeared, in several cases citing FAA safety scrutiny or grounding as a reason. Second, traditional entry with an old aircraft fleet became significantly more complicated due to new regulatory policies and the higher expense of acquiring and maintaining old aircraft. Third, new entry had to overcome an increasingly suspicious public perception that such airlines were highly risky. Fourth, overcoming these hurdles by acquiring new aircraft imposes a significant financing threshold for entry, requiring high-density and an aircraft utilization level that is usually difficult for a startup to gain in the short run and increases sunk cost. These are the reasons that startup airlines traditionally selected older and less expensive aircraft for operation, yet the new regulation made such entry very difficult.

In the next two chapters I will deal in more detail with the evolution of noise and safety regulation at the end of the 20$^{th}$ century. My major argument is that a post-deregulation interest group structure caused these two regulatory efforts to deviate from traditional (static) economic efficiency standards. In cases, manufacturers and the group of financially strong major airlines created ad hoc coalitions that "conspired" with the regulator to extract rent. Assigning marginal importance or otherwise ignoring aspects of traditional cost benefit analysis, noise and safety regulation have been translated into a struggle between "old" versus "new" aircraft standards. Since the new aircraft technology—although quite impressive—could not always justify its cost, noise and safety regulations were seized on by the manufacturers and a group of major airlines in order to accelerate the retirement of old aircraft that otherwise were efficient to operate due to their lower ownership cost.

It is noteworthy that while this interpretation suggests that noise and safety regulation have been inefficient based on traditional static standards, it is possible that by creating *a new-technology bias* it has accelerated the development and design of increasing-return technology with substantial economy-wide learning effects and spill-over with overall net (dynamic) social gains. The empirical answer to this question is still to come.

# CHAPTER 5

# NOISE REGULATION

> Sound ... may be perceived as beautiful, desirable, or
> unwanted. It is this unwanted sound which people
> normally refer to as noise.[102]

Economists and economic theory have played an important role in the deregulation of the aviation industry. A large body of economic thinking and a coherent view of the nature of pollution and related policy implications, however, were largely ignored in the environmental regulation of the industry.

This chapter reviews the major economic concepts of environmental regulation and examines the evolution of aircraft noise regulation.

## 1.   ECONOMIC PRINCIPLES AND NOISE REGULATION

Aircraft noise is a standard textbook case of negative production externalities. Aircraft takeoffs and landings generate noise that bothers residents of communities that neighbor airports. Since there is no functioning market for noise, airlines' production is expected to exceed the social optimum. To fix this problem, the industry must be induced to internalize the full social cost of its activity at the margin. The normative role of the regulator is to provide the industry with the proper incentives in the absence of a free market signal.

### 1.1   Cost-Benefit Analysis

In the early 1980s, economists scored a limited although important success in introducing systematic cost-benefit considerations into environmental regulation. This idea is perhaps the most important conceptual contribution of economists to environmental regulation.[103]

Economists don't doubt that pollution is an inevitable negative consequence of modern life, but they argue that it is in society's best interests to accept a certain level of pollution (an "optimum" level) and, in any case, not to spend on pollution abatement efforts more than the expected benefit of such efforts. Economists argue not for a clean environment "at any cost" but rather at "a balanced (social) cost."

---

[102] FAA (1985), *Aviation Noise Effects*, Washington, DC March ADA-154319 NTIS

[103] Other attractive theoretical ideas of incentive regulation or attempts to relate pollution emission or abatement efforts to market signals were largely ignored.

This standard argument, although it may seem obvious, has been only partially and inconsistently implemented in environmental regulation. There are two major practical difficulties with it that are worth noting at the outset. The first is a political one; environmentalists object to viewing pollution as just another cost item on the national agenda and believe that applying cost-benefit constraints may serve to legitimize pollution emission.

The second difficulty has to do with imperfect information and uncertainties that make the identification and measurement of the net benefit of most environmental regulation quite problematic. Noise is a prime example of nuisances or annoyances that are difficult to quantify. Furthermore, although there are numerous claims of negative health effects of noise, both the degree of such effects and the transmission mechanism are not widely recognized and are subject to debate.

*1.2    First-Best Solutions*

A traditional textbook fix to environmental externalities would involve the levy of a Pigouvian tax (reflecting the social damage) directly on the polluting activity (in our case on a unit of noise emitted). According to this concept, once the polluting agent internalizes the social cost of its activity, those who suffer from the activity are expected to freely select their own level of defensive activity, and there is no compensation from polluters to victims.

An alternative fix with equivalent theoretical efficiency implications is regulator issuance of marketable emission permits (or quotas) at the aggregate efficient quantity and allowing bidding for them. Although this policy instrument seems more market-oriented, it has similar information requirements as a Pigouvian tax for specifying a first-best solution. Extension of this idea to conditions of uncertainty suggests using a combination of price and quantity instruments to achieve social efficiency.

There are several theoretical and practical challenges to this concept. First, imposing a Pigouvian tax on a monopolist industry may end up actually diminishing social welfare. Second, in the presence of externalities the second-order condition for optimization may break down, and a first-best solution may not be determinable. Third, imperfect information and measurement problems raise a critical obstacle for designing and implementing first-best regulation in the real world.

*1.3    Second-Best Solutions*

It is widely accepted that the traditional solution of first-best environmental regulation can be implemented only in economic theory. Yet the theory conveys a strong and practical general message, in its emphasis of *incentives* as a cost-effective mechanism of achieving environmental goals. The general idea is that once society determines a certain set of environmental goals, setting up a regulatory system of economic price (effluent tax) and/or quantity incentives (tradable permits) would work better than *command and control* rules in reaching such goals.[104]

Incentive regulation imposes less demanding information requirements on the regulator. It provides firms with more freedom to pursue cost-minimizing techniques to achieve environmental standards. The incentive regulation idea has been quite slow to gain attention in the political process and has so far achieved only a limited (but growing) recognition in the US and Europe, despite its considerable theoretical attractiveness.

## 1.4 Property Rights

Ronald Coase (1960) and his followers have mounted one of the major intellectual attacks on the traditional approach to regulating externalities. Coase argues that in the absence of transaction costs and strategic behavior, voluntary transactions between polluting agents and victims would resolve the problem. In order for this to happen, however, there must be a well-defined transferable and enforceable set of property rights. Although this idea has attracted much theoretical attention, it has not been seen as a serious fix to the social cost of environmental externalities.

A few problems with Coase's proposal are noteworthy. First, on a theoretical level, it involves transactions between polluting agents and victims. Defensive actions by victims may be altered, and the analytical market solution would deviate from a first-best optimum. Second, transaction costs may be considerable, especially because in many cases a large number of polluting agents and victims are involved in case-specific and diverse circumstances. Three, the same information and uncertainty problems that inhibit implementation of first-best regulation are expected to pose obstacles to definition and enforcement of property rights and to limit the scope of voluntary transactions.

Although decentralized bargaining and transactions between polluting agents and victims may diminish the information demands on the regulator, markets are expected to fail for the same reasons that make first-best regulation non-trivial. In the case of the aviation industry, airplane noise damage and related property and liability rights are difficult or very costly to define, negotiate, and enforce, either by economic agents, the court system, or the regulator.

## 1.5 Legal Liability

A related view suggests that enforcement of legal liability by the judicial system may elevate the negative social impact of noise externalities and accomplish what regulation is intended to do.[105] Economists are partial to the *strict liability* theory, since conceptually it seems a possible way to internalize environmental externalities.

---

[104] In general, *command and control* regulation specifies a desirable standard and mandates specific means of compliance.

[105] A major difference between the property right and the legal liability theories is that under the first, transactions are negotiated before the polluting action is taken, and under the second after the damage occurs.

Under the strict liability theory, a polluting agent must compensate a victim without regard to whether its actions were at fault or not. This principle could apply to aircraft noise, since noise damage is inflicted on neighbors of airports as a result of normal aircraft operations within acceptable operating standards and not as a result of negligence or fault.

In practice, however, legal liability adjudication is expected to differ from economic efficiency principles for several reasons: 1) there are costs entailed in prosecution; 2) damages awarded may differ from economic costs and may be higher or lower than desirable; 3) there are constraints in our current legal system (like bankruptcy, or statutes of limitation); 4) there are information constraints (definition and measurement of noise damage, uncertainty over causation).

Moreover, aircraft noise is an ongoing problem that has cumulative impacts, and not a one-time event, while damage awards usually deal with inflicted damages in the past and not with expected damages in the future. This problem also affects transaction costs in voluntary transactions of the sort Coase envisions, since those transactions may involve long-term dynamic contracts subject to measurement and enforcement issues as well as unknown changes in future aircraft technology and operation and other related market phenomena.

## 1.6    The Problem with Noise

According to the traditional economic view, environmental regulation is expected to respond to incomplete markets by providing market-like signals that will maximize social welfare or otherwise help in attaining a desirable standard at the most effective cost. Consensus among economists notwithstanding, most environmental and safety regulation involves detailed rules that specify standards and mandate compliance by specific equipment type and related operational procedures, rather than incentive regulation. Moreover, incentive instruments that have evolved in real life differ in many respects from the theoretical ones.

A major challenge in dealing with aircraft noise relates to the difficulties of defining and measuring noise damage. In this regard, a standards-based-rule, which focuses on the source of the noise (the aircraft), avoids the need to deal with specific noise damage and therefore is easier to define and enforce.

"Noise" is unwanted sound; for sound to be interpreted as noise, it must be both heard and found to be offensive or undesirable. Noise consists of generation (transmission) and reception (recognition, interpretation, reaction) of a signal (sound). To the human listener, the signal, its reception and processing, and the reaction it triggers are inseparable. The processing of sound signals and reactions to it (annoyance, fear, irritation) are subjective. Reactions are affected by, among other things: time (day, night, season), location (distance from noise source), area listener is located in (industrial, residential, recreational), activity listener is engaged in (rest, study, sleep), listener's age and sex (found to be related to sleep response), and other physical variables like atmospheric conditions, or topography, or weather. Therefore, noise impact is subjective and extremely difficult to quantify and measure.

Noise impact is not always predictable. A slightly amplified signal or a pitch change, or a change in sound pressure, or an unexpected sound may be interpreted as significantly more annoying. Noise impact depends on how often a noise occurs (the number of landings/takeoffs per hour). It has a cumulative impact ("after several aircraft took off, I could not stand the noise any more!"). It may impact productivity (reduced concentration, fatigue); it may be associated with accidents (workplace, traffic); it is claimed to have hearing, speech, cardiovascular, and a long list of other negative health effects; and it may negatively affect farm animals and wildlife, real estate values, and more.

In theoretical models, a perfectly informed benevolent dictator would be able to figure out the "efficient" level of noise pollution and enforce a discipline on society by promulgating standards or implementing incentive schemes. Or, a benevolent dictator might define property and liability rights in order to facilitate transactions in such rights or otherwise enable judicial enforcement of liability rules to internalize environmental externalities to some extent.

In the real world, however, noise damage is a complex and ambiguous phenomenon that society can address with only a limited range of voluntary market transactions, political and judicial actions, and regulation. Such complex institutional arrangements are different from the traditional normative or positive theoretical models, but include aspects of all of them.

The core of the problem is that the uncertainty, the information imperfections, and the transaction costs that cause free market mechanisms to fail cause regulatory, judicial, and political mechanisms to fail as well. Under this circumstance and in a manner that is quite contrary to economists' prescription, noise regulations in the airlines industry emerged as a negotiated set of rules rather than an incentive-based instrument that aimed at internalizing the social cost of noise.

## 1.7    *Interest Groups*

Industry capture theories that can be traced to the Virginia School (Buchanan and Bullock, 1975) suggest that a well-organized industry group would influence the process of selecting a standards-based rule system, with the intention of raising barriers to entry and increasing industry profits. There is no doubt that rent-seeking and interest group politics play an important role in lobbying for regulatory instruments, but real-life strategic interest group impacts are far more complex and directly related to information and uncertainty problems.

Noise regulation has been shaped by a complex interest group structure that includes: 1) environmental protection organizations, 2) airport neighboring residents and communities, 3) local, state, federal, and foreign government authorities, 4) elements of the aviation industry (such airlines, manufacturers, labor unions) and 5) consumer and other public interest groups. At any particular time, these groups are constrained by the current political, administrative, market, and regulatory institutions and rules, information, transaction costs, technology, and the established political power structure. The various players have interacted, mostly through political and judicial institutions, to slowly shape noise regulation in the manner it has developed.

The particular form of noise regulation that emerged arguably increases barriers to entry and poses additional social cost. However, such standard-based rules and commands may be less costly to specify, negotiate, and enforce than to incentive-based regulation. They are also more responsive to the political power structure of the various groups and to technology constraints.

## 1.8    Technology

Technology constraints have played an important role in selecting the regulatory instrument. At the time the two major noise regulation initiatives were enacted, the available technology enabled new-generation aircraft to produce significantly less noise. A major consequence of these initiatives was an accelerated retirement of older aircraft and acquisition of new ones; this action was expected to reduce noise across the board without regard to location- or market-specific aspects.

With today's technology, we may have reached the point of diminishing returns with respect to noise reduction. There are increased development costs to reduce noise further, and future regulation may be forced to put less emphasis on the airplane as the source of noise. In this case, noise regulation might focus more attention on the ground impact of noise, and incentives would play an important role in internalizing certain negative aspects of noise impact.[106]

Current noise regulations give the industry a certain range of discretion to select compliance techniques. Safety regulations, however, dictate that any noise reduction solution that affects the aircraft or its operation must go through a long and expensive review and certification process before it can be implemented. The FAA oversees an extremely complex, technical, and controversial regulation that both sets noise standards and mandate how the industry is to comply with such standards.

The FAA is charged with testing, inspecting, analyzing, developing, approving, and certifying (or rejecting) technology, new products, modification of current equipment and aircraft operating procedures, and voluminous related manuals and documents that specify the actual compliance means and the related operational techniques.

Noise regulation is the most aggressive piece of regulation in the aviation industry after the economic deregulation act. It has required, in addition to setting noise levels for the development and certification of new aircraft, retrofit or retirement of previous-generation aircraft at mandatory deadlines. A complex noise monitoring system was built at airports in order to measure and detect deviations from the standard and enforce compliance on a single aircraft landing and takeoff at the airport level.

---

[106] Higher landing fees might be levied according to landing time, frequency, proximity of airport to residential areas, and so on.

## 2. PRIOR TO 1968—DEFINING PROPERTY RIGHTS

The aviation industry evolved into the late 1960s with no direct federal regulatory involvement in aircraft noise, despite its dramatic expansion and a shift into jet propulsion technology. The noise issue was nowhere directly addressed in the extensive aviation legislation and regulations, and neither the regulator nor the legislator assumed an active role in dealing with it.

Section 307(c) of the FAA Act of 1958 empowered the FAA to prescribe regulations for the protection of persons and property on the ground. In this regard, however, the FAA followed a narrow interpretation that did not include noise aspects in its certification considerations. The CAA/CAB focused on fare and entry regulation and did not see noise impact as a relevant consideration in route franchising. Issues related to individual or community noise damages were largely left to the judicial system. In this arena, claimants had only very limited success in obtaining injunctions or compensatory relief. Into the early seventies, environmental constraints were largely missing from the equation as aircraft technology and the industry evolved.

Then, as aircraft operations expanded and as their noise impact became less bearable, so too grew the number of legal cases filed. The judicial system began to search for an adequate legal theory for this unfolding new phenomenon. The established concepts that had evolved in the early nineteenth century in response to surface transportation systems were adopted for adaptation to the new technology. The ability to fly, however, meant we had to redefine property rights to include a brand-new, never experienced before, vertical dimension.

Perhaps the first question that comes to mind in this respect is who should hold property rights with respect to airspace. A corollary is how much of the airspace above a property is owned by the landowner. The Air Commerce Act of 1926 (amended in 1938 and 1958) was the first major piece of legislation to define the basic rules allocating these rights. The basic ingredients of the statute are that: 1) the government has complete and exclusive national sovereignty in the air space over the country; 2) "navigable airspace," a new term, was defined as: airspace above the minimum safe altitudes of flight prescribed by the Civil Aeronautics Authority;[107] and 3) such navigable airspace shall be subject to public rights of freedom of interstate and foreign air navigation.

This statute and related regulations eliminated both possible claims by landowners and attempts by state or local authorities to charge over flight fees and to a large degree ultimately preempted local and state government attempts to interfere with or influence aircraft operation in any way that might reduce noise. Yet, since the impact of noise—and any other related environmental effects—was missing in the statute, the question of who should bear the cost of noise was largely left for the judicial system to determine.

Most aircraft noise-related litigation has involved claims for relief of property owners who neighbor airports. Their excessive noise complaints are based on legal

---

[107] Navigable airspace was amended to include airspace required for safe landing and takeoff after Causby 328 US 256 (1946).

theories of trespass, nuisance, or inverse condemnation. While claims under the first two theories rarely succeeded, a variant of inverse condemnation that includes aspects of trespass and legalized nuisance became the prevailing legal theory in cases where relief was granted.

It is instructive to generalize the basic rules developed by the judicial system during this period. In most cases, the judicial system: 1) denied injunctive relief; 2) denied compensatory relief except in a relatively small number of cases where property owners could show that they suffered more than the "ordinary incidents of life near an airport"; and 3) made airport proprietors (and not the airlines or the government) liable for damages in cases where compensation was ordered.

## 2.1  Peculiar Private Burden

The judicial concept adopted to tackle aircraft noise was quite similar in its principles to the models that evolved in response to the negative environmental impact of railroads and national highways. The basis is usually traced to Richards v. Washington Terminal Co., 233 U.S 546 (1914).

Landowner Richards sought to be compensated for the operation of a railroad track and a tunnel near his property. As trains passed by, they emitted noise, smoke, and vibration. In addition, the nearby tunnel had an exhaust system that directly polluted Richards' property. The presence in this case of two clearly separable pollution sources allowed the court to distinguish between public nuisance, borne by all owners of property adjoining a railroad as trains pass by, and a disproportional nuisance that was particular to landowner Richards and was related to the tunnel's exhaust system. The court found the first damage to be "legalized nuisance" and barred recovery, absent negligence. It found the second type of damage to be a specific burden that was not shared by other similarly situated landowners and on this basis granted compensation.

The judicial system in Richards' and succeeding cases viewed the noise and pollution problem as an inevitable inconvenience of modern life, and attempted to strike a balance between the general public's interest in a national transportation system and the burden of noise on affected individuals. The balancing rule adopted is that "normal" incidental inconveniences of aircraft or other public transportation systems are not compensable. For pollution damage to be compensable, a property owner must be seen to bear a disproportionate peculiar burden relative to other owners whose properties lie within a similar range of inconvenience. This general principle has largely been preserved by the court system until today.

## 2.2  US v. Causby

The case of US v. Causby, 328 US 256 (1946) has served as the dominant model of dealing with aircraft noise pollution for more than 50 years. The Causbys had owned 2.8 acres near an airport outside Greensboro, North Carolina, since 1938, where they had their house and several buildings that they used to raise chickens. In 1942, the US government entered into a contract with the Municipal Airport Authority to operate bombers, transport planes, and fighters that used a glide path directly over the Causbys' property.

According to the Causbys, the aircraft "come close enough at times to appear barely to miss the top of the trees as to blow old leaves off." At night the glare from the planes lit up the place. The Causbys were frequently deprived of their sleep and became "nervous and frightened." Their chicken raising business was destroyed as well; as many as six to ten of their chickens were killed in one day by flying into the walls from fright. Total chickens lost in that manner amounted to about 150. Production also fell off.

The Supreme Court was presented with the problem as to whether the Causby property had been *taken* within the meaning of the Constitution, or, as argued by the government, that absent physical invasion or negligence, there was neither a taking of property nor a compensable damage.

The first major question the Court tackled was a landowner's rights in the air above his property. The Court redefined and assigned to a landowner the property rights only with respect to the land's *superadjacent airspace*—"as much of the space above the ground as he can occupy or use in connection with the land." By this decision, the Court in fact rejected the then-prevailing concept of a landowner's property rights, in accommodation of the new aviation phenomenon. "It is ancient doctrine that a common law ownership of the land extended to the periphery of the universe. But that doctrine has no place in the modern world. The air is a public highway."

Upon determining the general property rights issue, the Court found that the flights were "so low and so frequent" that they therefore constituted in fact a *direct and immediate interference* with enjoyment of the land. The government was held to have used the super-adjacent airspace and thereby to have limited the utility of the land and directly caused a diminution in its value. The *"frequent and low altitude"* nature of the flights in this case was found to constitute an appropriation of the use of the land in a manner equivalent to a physical invasion.

This case, although different in its details, relies on the same general principle established in Richards more than 30 years before. The unique location of the Causbys' property directly under the glide path singled them out to bear a particular burden not shared by their neighbors. One of the major implications of the way Causby was subsequently applied is that only a relatively small number of property owners located close to a runway and directly under the glide path have been compensated for noise damages.[108]

## 2.3    Griggs v. County of Allegheny, Pennsylvania

The next landmark story started quite similarly to the Causbys' but ended with a switch. The case was Griggs v. County of Allegheny, Pennsylvania, 369 US 84 (1962). Aircraft flying above Griggs's property created noise that was "comparable to a riveting machine or steam hammer" when taking off and "to that of a noisy

---

[108] Depending on state law. Later on, a somewhat broader interpretation was made.

factory" on landing approach. Frequent and low-altitude flights made Griggs and occupants of his property "nervous and distraught," "unable to sleep even with ear plugs and sleeping pills," as they would "frequently be awakened" by the flights; windows of their house "would rattle" and "at time plaster fell down from the walls and ceilings"; and their health was impaired.

The court held in Griggs that there was a taking that required just compensation. The question then was who is liable: the airlines, the federal regulator (the United States), or the local airport authority? Traditional economics suggests that the polluting agent should bear the cost of the externality it creates.

Due to the peculiarities of the judicial process, the airlines' potential exposure was removed, as only a government entity can take a private property for public use and therefore be liable for just compensation. The remaining issue, therefore, was whether the federal government or Allegheny County was liable for the taking.

The court decided that the county acting as the airport operator was liable:

> The Federal Government takes nothing; it is the local authority, which decides to build an airport and where it is to be located. We see no difference between its responsibility for the air easements necessary for operating of the airport and its responsibility for the land on which the runways were built.

In Griggs, the Supreme Court reaffirmed the rights of a very small class of landowners, those who face a peculiar noise impact, to be entitled to just compensation, and it assigned aircraft noise liability in this case to the local airport proprietor. With this decision began a long line of complex lawsuits dealing with the balancing of a local proprietor's liability and its freedom to take defensive regulatory action to abate noise.

## 2.4   Economic Implications of the Noise Litigation

Causby and Griggs became the dominant cases in the definition and enforcement of noise-related property rights of airport neighboring residents. The institutional solution unfolded in a different manner from the solution that would be prescribed by most economists. There are some noteworthy principles.

First, except in narrowly defined circumstances, the society did not ascribe to property owners the rights to "a noise-free" environment. The courts therefore eliminated market bargaining solutions of the type Coase would recommend.

Second, except in a very few cases, the judicial system did not levy compensation for noise damages; it therefore eliminated strict liability impacts or other possible impacts on polluting agents. In fact, the airlines were granted the right to make noise, and most residents were denied the right to a noise-free environment.

Third, the legal theory of a *constitutional taking* and the standards of proof regarding property value diminution are difficult and expensive to litigate. Also, the "peculiar damage" view and the case-specific nature of noise-related damages largely foreclosed class actions (which arguably could reduce individual legal costs).

Fourth, the taking theory in general focused on the reduction of property value as the compensation rule, while most of the complaints regarding the negative impact of noise fall into the annoyance category. Courts have traditionally been reluctant to allow damages for annoyance, and claims as to bodily injury or the health and hearing damages of noise were not generally established and proven. For uncertainty and measurement reasons, among other things, the negative economic impact of noise was in general not addressed by the judicial system.

It is arguable that reduction in property value may capture related annoyance aspects, and therefore it may not be necessary to directly measure the noise impact. Yet measuring the impact of noise on property values is no easy concept either, and it may not be possible to separate the noise impact from other factors. For example, airport expansion (which increases noise) may also raise neighboring land values for commercial use.

Finally, in cases where compensation was ordered, it did not directly affect the noise-generating agent (the airlines) or their activity. Once the Supreme Court held that the airport proprietor is liable for the taking, the proprietor could not directly cross-claim against the airlines. Although proprietor damages may affect landing fees or rent of facilities, no additional charges were directly imposed on the airlines, particularly no charges related to noise emission.

To sum it up, the political and judicial systems have held overall that the benefit to society from a national air transportation system far outweighs the cost inflicted on airport neighbors (except for a few) and did not contribute to the internalization of noise externalities into the market system.

### 3. 1968–1977

Noise-related issues during the 1960s and 1970s came to the courts in two major ways. The first related to the landowner rights issue, where the judicial system reconfirmed with some small adjustments—based on specific circumstances and state laws—the Causby precedent. The second evolved in response to state and local attempts to initiate noise regulation.

In the second line of litigation, the system searched for answers to whether and how a state or local authority may regulate aircraft noise. These questions are related to federalism and to society's ongoing search for a balance between individual and local rights versus the national interests. In this case, the issue played out as seeking a desirable balance between the role of the states and the local authorities in regulating noise and the role of the federal regulator. These questions are typical of an aviation transportation system: that it is a public good with nationwide benefits, while at the same time it creates pockets of noise damage that are a public nuisance, with mostly local impact.

In 1968, for the first time, a federal noise regulatory system gained some momentum in response to judicial and political pressures. The status quo was preserved until the late 1970s, however, and regulation had only a negligible impact on noise. Airline financial condition and then-current technology constraints continued to govern noise standards.

## 3.1 Local and State versus Federal Regulation

The Civil Aeronautics Act of 1938, as amended, left no doubt that the federal government intended to fully control the industry by extensive legislation and regulation and through actual management of air traffic. Aviation was seen as an interstate commerce system of unprecedented national importance, requiring centralized and uniform procedures for safety and commercial purposes and special professional expertise and competence regulation.

The Supreme Court in Causby reaffirmed this view. It is interesting to note that dissenting Justice Hugo Black argued that federal control of the navigable airspace precludes any conclusion that there has been a taking. According to Justice Black, complete control of the airspace necessary for aircraft operation is entrusted to Congress, and therefore no flight should constitute a compensable taking, even if it were to impose a particular damage of the type suffered by Causby.

When we read Causby today, we should remember that the decision that became the dominant model in noise litigation was made immediately after the war, and dealt mostly with damage in the form of noise emitted by military aircraft. The significance of military air power in the nation's security and the interstate and international economic potential of commercial aircraft became clear only during the war and undoubtedly affected the direction of the Court decision.

The Court in Griggs, however, made the local airport proprietor liable for noise damages and not the federal government. By doing so, it implied that the local airport operator must also have a certain degree of regulatory power to defend itself against liability. The court therefore imputed to airport operators preemption rights that one could infer that the Supreme Court had assigned to the federal government in Causby. This decision opened the door to a long legal debate as to the power of local interests to regulate noise.

Justice Hugo Black dissented in Griggs as well, arguing that this decision was wrong even according to the Causby precedent. According to Justice Black, extensive federal regulation and control of the aviation industry—and its national characteristics—dictated that the federal government must be liable for the taking and not a local operator.

The airspace is

> so much under the control of the Federal Government that every takeoff and every landing at airports such as the Greater Pittsburgh Airport is made under the direct signal and supervisory control of some federal agency.

The county as the local airport operator acted under the supervision of and subject to the approval of the government. With this very limited discretion, it therefore must not be responsible for a taking liability. In addition

> it would be unfair to make Allegheny County bear expenses wholly out of proportion to the advantage it can receive from the national transportation system.

## 3.2    Federal Preemption

City of Burbank v. Lockheed Air Terminal, 411 US 624 (1973), is an important case dealing with federal preemption in general and with noise regulation in particular. In two previous cases (Allegheny Airlines, Inc., v. Village of Cedarhurst and American Airlines v. Town of Hempstead), the court established that a local government is prohibited from enforcing altitude regulations, noise limits, or other laws that interfere with aircraft operation or use of the navigable airspace. In Burbank, the City had tested a different regulatory instrument—a curfew on jet flights between 11 P.M. and 7 A.M. Much as in the previous cases, the court decided that the federal government trumped the police power of the state, and it held the curfew ordinance to be unconstitutional. Although the federal regulations did not expressly provide for preemption, the Court held that "it is the pervasive nature of the scheme of federal regulation of aircraft noise that led us to conclude that there is pre-emption. " Ironically, what makes this decision so important in noise litigation history is not so much what the Court found, but what it left out. The Court recognized that there is a difference between a local and state government exercising police power or acting as an airport proprietor, but it stopped short of dealing with this issue. A famous footnote (number 14) states, "we do not consider here what limits if any apply to municipality as a proprietor." This case as well as subsequent related litigation established the general rule that state and local attempts to regulate aircraft noise are unenforceable because of federal preemption according to the supremacy clause or the commerce clause of the US Constitution.

## 3.3    Airport Proprietors

The main implication of Griggs was that the airport proprietor became the major liable party for noise damages. The FAA regulation, the 1972 EPA noise regulations, and subsequent judicial decisions reconfirmed this interpretation. This made the proprietor a likely defendant in lawsuits by airport neighboring communities and other local entities, a plaintiff in suits launched to enjoin attempts by local and state authorities to regulate noise, and always a major target for political pressure by local groups. The proprietor represented (and to some extent was potentially liable for) federal interests and actions vis-à-vis local interest groups, yet its hands were tied to a large degree in taking regulatory action by an extremely highly regulated federal system. Moreover, its regulatory powers were vaguely defined by federal government rules and regulations, not to mention subject to continued litigation and conflicting court decisions.

After the Supreme Court held in Burbank that noise regulation is preempted by federal regulation, it was expected that the federal government would assume liability for noise damage along with its regulatory control. In fact, neither the judicial system nor the regulation evolved in this direction. In the 1973 case of Aaron v. City of Los Angeles, 419 US 1122 (1975), for example, the City used the federal preemption argument as a defense against an inverse condemnation claim.

The Supreme Court held that federal preemption is not complete and the City acting as proprietor had the power to regulate noise.

In another important case, ATA v. Crotti, the Federal District Court reviewed a state law implementing noise regulation in California. The state had contemplated enforcing two noise level restrictions. The first, Community Noise Equivalent Levels (CNEL), was supposed to establish maximum noise levels around residential communities; the second, Single Event Noise Exposure Level (SENEL), was supposed to do the same with respect to an individual aircraft in flight. The court found that while a state proprietor may apply the first type of the regulation, the second is preempted by federal authority.

The legislature did not resolve the situation but left it to the judicial system to struggle with defining the powers of a local proprietor to regulate noise. The federal government could completely preempt the field and assume the full associated liability, but it left the local proprietor liable for the burden of noise litigation and the related costs and compensation of residents for a constitutional taking. When it adopted FAR, Part 36, noise regulation, the government specifically stated that the regulation was not intended to change the local responsibilities borne by an airport proprietor (whether a state or local government or not) as defined by the Supreme Court in Griggs.

In fact, in its legal strategy, the government was careful not to cause a reversal of the Griggs decision. A good example is the position taken by the regulator in connection with the high-profile case of British Airways v. Port Authority of NY and NJ in 1977, regarding the banning of Concorde operations into Kennedy Airport. In this case, the proprietor forbade Concorde experimental operations into Kennedy Airport, in direct contravention of a federal government order. The government, however, did not try to preempt the proprietor's right to regulate noise, so as not to reverse Griggs on the issue of federal liability. In fact, the federal government reaffirmed the Griggs decision in its regulation and made the local proprietor potentially liable for a constitutional taking or other noise damages that might be imposed by the judicial system. But the federal government also elected not to specifically define the proprietor's role.

The regulator vacillated between the need to maintain full federal control over the aviation system and the legal requirement to cede some regulatory powers to airport proprietors in order to protect itself against liability. Its answer to this dilemma was to avoid clear direction and specific definition of a proprietor's powers. Airport proprietors were implicitly forced to assume the liability of noise at the local level. They were thus required to themselves balance local political pressure, somewhat ambiguous federal rules, and the need to appease the powerful regulator that provided them with grants and financing.

Since the government did not take the lead in defining airport proprietors' power, this issue ended up being mainly determined by the judicial system on a case-by-case basis, resulting in non-uniform regulation across different jurisdictions.

## 3.4    Regulatory Awakening

Noise issues appeared on the national political agenda in the second half of the 1960s as jet aircraft operation expanded and as did awareness of environmental issues. Public pressure by environmentalists, airport neighboring communities, and local and state governments, together with a growing number of noise-related lawsuits, caused the legislature and the regulatory agencies to address the issue.

In 1968, Congress passed an amendment to the 1958 FAA Act (49 USC.) that granted explicit statutory power to the FAA to include noise considerations in certification of aircraft, in addition to safety considerations. It directed the FAA to develop both standards for measuring aircraft noise that focused on the aircraft as the source of the noise and noise abatement rules that are technically practicable, consistent with the highest degree of safety, and economically reasonable. One year later, on November 3, 1969, the FAA issued FAR 36, which established operational noise limits for new aircraft seeking to obtain certification, in effect exempting the operating aircraft fleet as well as aircraft in production from compliance with new noise standards.

Section 7 of the Noise Control Act of 1972—the first comprehensive federal government venture into the field of noise abatement—amended Section 611 of the FAA Act to give the EPA a role in aircraft noise regulation. In practice, however, the FAA retained the full power and authority to direct noise regulation and did not implement many of the EPA's recommendations. In 1973, the FAA amended the regulation to include all new aircraft leaving the factory, irrespective of their type certification date in FAR 36 standards.

### 3.4.1 Noise Metrics and Measurement Points

The early noise regulation adopted a workable metric of a single-event noise scale for measuring noise and defining standards, out of a diverse set of possible alternatives. The scale was defined as *effective perceived noise level* (EPNL), measured in decibels (dB) units of EPNdB.

Sound is usually interpreted as energy that can be described by two basic physical characteristics: intensity (pressure) and frequency; these physical attributes can be measured and represented as a "spectrum of sound." The human reaction to sound is affected among other things by the specific combination of intensity, frequency, and duration.

Human hearing is more sensitive in the middle and high frequencies; everything else equal, a higher-frequency sound (within the audible range) is usually perceived as louder than low-frequency sounds of the same level of intensity. To reflect this phenomenon, the standard dB scale is "frequency filtered" to reduce the effect of the low-frequency noise and to compensate for the annoyance of the higher frequencies.[109] Ratings of noisiness by this measure were defined as *perceived noise level* (PNL) expressed in dB.

The PNL is considered a good estimate for perceived noisiness of broadband, similar-time duration sounds without a strong discrete frequency component. Aircraft noise, however, does not fall into this category, for a large part of it is made up of distinctly different sounds created by the various engine components (fan, compressor, turbine, and jet exhaust). The high-pitched whine—which is associated with an engine inlet—and the rumble—which is associated with the high-velocity jet plume—for example, have different sound characteristics. Different aircraft moreover produce different spectrum sounds and therefore different annoyance impacts.

To correct for this, the EPNL adjusts the noise scale to account for the presence of discrete frequencies and pronounced irregularities in the spectrum, as well as different time durations.[110] The EPNL corrects for discrete noise sources in an engine and provides a scale for comparing different aircraft with different noise spectrums.

Another important principle in early noise regulation was establishment of three ground measurement points to reflect noise: during takeoff (3.5 nautical miles from the start of the roll on the extended centerline of the runway); at the sidelines (0.25 and 0.35 nautical miles from the extended center line of the runway, for three- and four-engine aircraft, respectively); and during approach (1.0 nautical mile from the threshold on the extended centerline of the runway).[111]

### 3.4.2 Noise Levels

Once the scale and the measurement points were defined, the regulator defined the maximum allowed noise levels. For takeoff noise, the maximum was 108 EPN dB for aircraft that weigh 600,000 pounds or more, dropping to 93 EPN dB for a maximum weight of 75,000 pounds. For approach and sideline noise, the maximum was 108 EPN dB for aircraft that weigh 600,000 pounds or more and 102 EPN dB for maximum weights of 75,000 pounds.

These noise limits did not reflect a desirable or target standard toward which the industry would aim, but rather were tailored to a large extent around the actual noise levels of the then-current aircraft fleet. A major advance in engine technology during the seventies was introduction of high bypass engines and a shift from so-called turbojet to turbofan engines. With a new (and larger) fan design, these engines were able to increase thrust with less fuel consumption; they also produced less noise per unit of thrust than the old technology. These new-technology engines powered the new generation of widebody aircraft (747s, L1011s, and DC10s).

---

[109] In a logarithmic conversion of sound pressure, the "quietest" sound (the reference pressure) is assigned 0 dB, while the loudest sound we can hear without pain is usually 120 dB.

[110] The Port of New York in 1959 made a pioneering attempt to set 112 PN dB as a single-event noise limit.

[111] In 1978 the point locations were slightly amended.

The noise regulation of 1969, grouped the aircraft fleet into two classes of aircraft according to their engine technology in terms of limiting levels of EPNL. As complex as the 1969 FAR Part 36 noise limits may have seemed, they in fact said something quite simple: All new aircraft applying for type certification must use the new turbofan technology. This regulation required the obvious, since no airline intended to use the less efficient technology for new aircraft anyway.

With continuing noise concerns, the manufacturers during the early seventies applied acoustic technology to reduce somewhat the "perceived annoyance" factor of the old turbojet engines as well. This included mainly relatively minor acoustical treatments of the nose-cowls and thrust-reversers in a manner that changed the composition of the noise frequencies the engines produced.

The 1973 amendment to the noise regulation mandated that all aircraft leaving the factory starting December 1, 1973, would be either turbofan widebody aircraft or narrowbody 727s, 737s, or DC9s that were acoustically treated by the manufacturers. The 1973 regulation exempted all narrowbody aircraft as well as a relatively small number of first-generation 747 aircraft that had been manufactured and delivered prior to December 1, 1973, which in fact represented most of the industry fleet in operation at the time. This regulation thus had a negligible effect on noise reduction, a fact that did not escape the notice of environmentalists in the political debate.

## 3.5   Increasing Political Pressures

By the middle 1970s the regulator was facing increased pressure from several interest groups. Both the airlines and related interest groups complained about increasing regulatory pressures by local authorities—which resulted in a lack of standardization - and demanded federal intervention in order to preempt or at least standardize local rules. Buffeted by the oil crisis and experiencing significant financial troubles, the airlines pushed the regulator to preserve the status quo and not to impose stricter noise regulation. It was hoped that the new widebody aircraft with their lower noise levels might improve the situation in the future with no need for further noise regulation.

Industry support groups argued that the noise problem was affecting only a relatively small number of people and that the cost of further noise abatement outweighed the benefit. Environmentalists and airport neighbors took the opposite position, complaining about the inadequacy of the regulatory efforts and blaming the FAA for foot dragging. A more general public awareness of environmental pollution issues and increasing demands for government regulation coincided with increased public and media attention to aircraft noise issues. The EPA suggested more aggressive and stricter noise regulations, but the FAA rejected them and refused to adopt alternative rules.

In 1976, several states filed lawsuits against the federal government for failure to implement the EPA recommendations.[112] In Congress, Representative Norman

---

[112] Illinois, Massachusetts, and New York filed suit in US Court for the District of Columbia.

Mineta of California proposed on May 13, 1976, a bill imposing stricter noise regulation, directly accusing the FAA for not moving ahead on this issue. One of the major issues considered was how to pay for noise abatement, since in its current financial condition the industry could not support the costs involved. Among the proposals put forward was imposition of taxes on airline passengers or on noisy aircraft, but these were rejected.

In the fall of 1976, the Department of Transportation and the FAA, pushed by President Gerald Ford, issued an Aviation Abatement Policy document outlining for the first time the government's position with respect to aircraft noise regulation and calling for establishment of a schedule for aircraft compliance with the FAR 36 standards. In October 1976, President Ford advised that he accepted the DOT and FAA position and instructed them to promulgate new regulations by January 1977. The new regulation ordered that all aircraft in operation would meet the FAR 36 standards by January 1985.

President Ford blamed Congress for not acting promptly on reforming price and entry regulation, and he blamed the airlines' inability to finance noise abatement on the failure of the CAA regulation. Senate Aviation Subcommittee Chairman Howard Cannon, one of the major opponents of these regulatory efforts, blamed the administration for pushing this "highly controversial and poorly thought out" policy to solve "not a pressing environmental problem" just before a new administration was about to take office (with election of President Jimmy Carter). Objections notwithstanding, the noise regulation became effective.

### 3.6    Impact of the Regulation

The regulatory efforts of the seventies had only a limited direct impact on noise abatement throughout the decade. Yet they set the basic ground rules and the initial conditions that were to dominate the way noise regulation evolved into the 21st century. The efforts have some interesting aspects.

First, note that the federal regulator completely captured the issue. It preempted any and all aspects related to aircraft noise at the source, and in fact retained full control over all related aircraft and engine technology and operations issues.

Second, in a way that is not necessarily unique to aviation, the regulations set the noise discussion in terms of complex scientific measures and parameters. Attention was focused on specialized aspects of acoustical theory and technology, thus contributing to the creation of information asymmetries among the participants in the debate, as well as leaving ample room for rent-seeking behavior. When it came to generating scientific information, including research and interpretation of noise and a focus on the aircraft and the engines as the source of the noise, the industry, the manufacturers, and the regulator all had better resources and information than the affected residents or the general public. This one factor put the industry and the regulator in a favorable position to control noise regulation and protect the industry's interests.

The regulator focused on developing acoustic metrics and scales to represent energy levels and spectrum analysis of sound. The non-linear and "filtered" scales to reflect elements of noise annoyance made it difficult especially for the untrained public to compare approaches. Moreover, the use of different approaches—single (peak) noise metrics in FAR Part 36 and cumulative (average) DNL for on-the-ground exposure in FAR Part 150—further confused and frustrated affected airport neighboring residents.[113] Confining attention to these issues also meant that the regulation avoided the economic nature of noise damage, which is the essence of the problem.

Although the noise parameters of the FAR were labeled "perceived levels," they did not really address either the subjective nature of the problem or its economic impact. From an economic point of view, government intervention is required to internalize the damage (costs) suffered by airport neighbors into the market process, so regulation must focus on the way noise impacts affected communities. The evaluation of a noise regulation initiative cannot be based on improvements in noise abatement at the aircraft level from a scientific point of view, but rather on the perceptions of the people affected and the resulting economic damage suffered. In fact, costly noise abatement—as this regulatory effort eventually became—might not justify the benefit as perceived by affected individuals.

One of the sorts of questions economists like to ask is whether airport neighboring communities could be paid to stop their noise-related claims and complaints for a total dollar amount that is lower than the cost of the regulation. This question has never been answered.

Third, one of the major characteristics of the noise limit definition was that heavier aircraft were allowed to make more noise. But obviously, noise is perceived in absolute terms; affected residents are not likely to assign less economic value to the noise abatement or restrictions of heavier aircraft.

Fourth, the federal government focused most of its regulatory attention on the aircraft as the source of noise. Other abatement methods (including land management, acoustic treatment of buildings, and construction standards) were largely delegated to local authorities. By focusing on noise reduction at the source, the federal regulator generally removed itself from direct involvement in developing and implementing other useful and perhaps less expensive noise abatement methods. The FAA developed its noise regulatory strategy as an independent solution without regard to possibly more economically efficient methods of abating noise and reducing its impact on the ground.

Although ground abatement was paid lip service in the regulatory process, and some positive steps in this direction were made in the Aviation Safety and Noise Abatement Act of 1979, it was largely beyond the major thrust of FAA regulation. One implication for future regulatory initiatives is that alternative solutions to the noise problem were not considered in the cost-benefit analysis of noise regulation at the federal level, an issue that gained more prominence when noise regulation became more expensive.

Finally, the regulator during the sixties and seventies viewed the noise issue as something of a marginal problem that was overwhelmingly outweighed by the benefit of the aviation system. Regulatory steps were taken only when political and

---

[113] The regulator adopted DNL greater than 65dB as the most critical exposure limit.

judicial pressures made the issue impossible to be ignored. Even then, the regulator did not consider noise abatement as much as protection of the industry from the burden of abating noise and preemption of state government attempts to police noise at the local level. In this respect, a regulatory initiative that the public might perceive as environmental improvement-oriented was to a large extent an attempt by the regulator to capture the process and to protect the industry from political and legal pressures.

A citation from the FAA Adoption of Amendment 36-7 perhaps best describes the FAA position:

> as a result of the impact of aircraft noise on airport neighbors, serious pressures have developed that could threaten the continued growth of a healthy air transport system. These pressures include restrictions on airport usage such as curfews, restrictions on the use of certain aircraft, opposition to airport development and serious liability exposure for existing airports. For example, over the past five years, airport proprietors have paid out over $25 million in legal judgments and settlements in noise related suits and have spent over $3 million in legal fees and other defense costs. This is in addition to the moneys being spent by airport proprietors in acquiring land adjacent to their airports and surrounding affected buildings such as schools, residences and public buildings. The critical conclusion coming out of the many years of FAA review of this problem is that . . . Federal action is required to provide effective aircraft noise reduction at its source (p. 58).

## 4.  1978–1990

The year 1978 was an exciting years for the aviation industry. Alfred Kahn, as new chairman of the CAB, started experimenting with liberalized entry and price restrictions. In October 1978, when the Airline Deregulation Act was passed, the industry became free to compete. Diminishing oil prices, higher economic growth rates, and aircraft capacity adjustments improved airline profits (if only for a short period), and the negative impact of the early 1970s oil crisis and world recession that had hit them hard seemed to dissipate.

All these factors likely made airlines somewhat more receptive to noise regulation. In February 1977, the FAA issued rules requiring the retirement of the first-generation aircraft, or their modification to comply with the noise limits, by a given deadline. The rules were amended in 1978 and then again in 1979, extending compliance deadlines in order to accommodate new airlines' financial concerns.[114]

The regulation initiatives of the late seventies largely framed the arguments for aircraft noise abatement into the end of the eighties. Aircraft were grouped into three categories according to the noise limits defined in EPNL (Stage I, Stage II and Stage III). The most noisy first-generation aircraft in the Stage I category were required to be retired or retrofitted to comply with the Stage II limits (the 1969 FAR Part 36 limit) by a certain deadline. All new applicants for type certificates were required to comply with the Stage III limits. The overall reduction in noise levels (in EPNL terms) from Stage II to Stage III standards was less than the reduction from Stage I to Stage II and was significant mainly with respect to the smaller two- and three-engine aircraft.

This regulation initiative directly affected aircraft that were already in commercial operation. Its effect was to require investment by the airlines to either retrofit aircraft or accelerate retirement and acquisition of replacement capacity. After several years of battling such a provision, using as an excuse the industry's weak financial condition and its inability to shoulder the burden required, the airlines and the regulators gave up on this issue and accepted this provision.

To understand the implication of this noise regulation initiative, it is important to look once again at the aircraft fleet (rather than the acoustical measurements of aircraft noise). Stage I aircraft comprised two major groups of aircraft equipped with turbojet engines: the first-generation, long-range, high-capacity, narrowbody, four-engine aircraft (mostly 707s and DC8s), and the smaller two- and three-engine, short- to medium-range aircraft (mostly DC9s, 737s, and 727s). At the time the regulation was enacted in 1977–1979, the first group was no longer in production, having been replaced by widebody aircraft equipped with turbofan engines.

The second group was still in production (the DC9 and the 727 until the early 1980s and the 737 until the late 1980s), but all aircraft delivered after December 1973 had already complied with Stage II limits, according to the 1973 amendment of the FAR 36 rules. Thus only aircraft that had been delivered prior to 1973 were

---

[114] The 1979 amendments also include new provisions for community noise measurement and aspects of land management.

<

affected by the regulation, and the technology that the manufacturers had used to comply with the 1973 regulation was readily available to retrofit these aircraft.

This was not the case for the first group, which required development, design, testing, and subsequent certification of acoustic treatments in order to comply with the Stage II standards. Also, the age of these aircraft, not to mention the competition with widebody technology, made the cost of retrofitting significantly higher relative to the aircraft market value than was the case for the second group.

The noise regulation introduced in 1977 was the last major initiative prior to the deregulation of fares and entry. The major airlines generally took a unified stance with respect to new aircraft order strategies. New aircraft were usually introduced by the major airlines at the same time, and development of new types of aircraft usually was a response to a specific airline's specifications and orders. The FAR Part 36 limits were set together with the manufacturers to be tailored to the current technology. Manufacturers, as we have said, had superior information regarding aircraft noise abatement at the source and in fact dominated and dictated the noise limits of the regulation as those "technically practicable."

The manufacturers' main interest was in selling new aircraft; not surprisingly, they encouraged the major airlines to order new aircraft and to retire the older versions. This was particularly relevant to the Stage I, four-engine aircraft (DC8s and 707s) and the older three-engine 727-100 aircraft. With the development of third-world aviation markets with less sensitivity to noise and smaller budgets for the leasing and operation of used Stage I aircraft, the major US airlines decided to retire most of theirs independent of the noise regulation. Facing improved economic prospects, the airlines started a new cycle of aircraft orders during the second half of the seventies. Orders included narrowbody 727-200As, 737-200s, and DC9s; widebody 747s, DC10s, and L1011s; and the newly designed 757s, 767s, and A300s.

Once again the noise regulation thus hardly seemed a bump on the road in what otherwise was the general major airlines' aircraft acquisition and retirement strategy, except for the cost imposed for the retrofit of pre-1973 aircraft that would stay in service. The compliance deadline for these aircraft was set by the regulation for the middle eighties, and the general consensus was that a significant proportion of these aircraft would be retired and the rest retrofitted.[115] The FAA stated its position in this respect that the regulation was intended to encourage the introduction of the newest-generation airplane as soon as practical and to provide a compliance schedule to maximize the incentive to replace rather than retrofit older aircraft.[116]

Yet, as is often the case, reality turned out to be different from what was anticipated by the industry and the regulator when the noise regulation was developed. First, a new oil crisis and world recession dramatically changed the industry's financial condition. Second, deregulation affected the industry structure and strategy in an unexpected manner. During the early 1980s, the industry suffered one of its severe cyclical crises. As a result, aircraft retirements were accelerated,

---

[115] In response to the next cycle downturn, the deadline was extended once again with respect to two- and three- engine aircraft, and in certain cases exemptions were granted.

[116] FAA Amendment 36-7, p. 57.

and orders for new aircraft fell. Approximately 800 aircraft, most of them of the older Stage I group, were retired during the industry crisis of the early 1980s. Then, the subsequent economic boom and the unprecedented industry growth found the industry substantially short of capacity.

The economic expansion together with opening of the aviation market to free competition generated a boom in demand for air travel into the late 1980s, far beyond the expectations of the 1970s. World air travel (revenue passenger miles) grew at a rate in excess of 7% per year, and shortages in aircraft capacity developed. The decline in oil prices, the favoring of less expensive older-generation aircraft by newer startups in the deregulated market, and the increased demand for smaller narrowbody aircraft for hub-and-spoke and for overnight cargo operations made many of these aircraft more desirable and no longer candidates for retirement.

Consequently, aircraft modification for noise abatement became attractive, particularly for the two- and three-engine aircraft but also for some of the older 707s and DC8s that found new life, mostly for cargo operation.

## 5. THE AIRPORT NOISE AND CAPACITY ACT OF NOV 5, 1990

The Airport Noise and Capacity Act (ANCA) is considered one of the most significant pieces of legislation since the Deregulation Act of 1978. For many in the aviation industry, however, the ANCA and the subsequent FAA noise regulation came as something of a surprise. It was enacted at what would have seemed to be the least expected time: the waning hours of the congressional session, wrapped in with some other unrelated legislative loose ends and desk cleaning matters, and pushed by the Bush administration and by the financially strongest major airlines that had traditionally objected to noise regulation. Even more startling was that only about three months before enactment of the Act, Iraq had invaded Kuwait, with dramatic jumps in oil prices and industry losses that raised concerns regarding industry health.

The regulation seemed particularly striking, given that for over two decades the industry and the FAA had objected to imposition of noise regulation on the basis of industry condition and the burden of financing. At the beginning of 1991, US airlines reported a loss of approximately $4 billion for the last quarter of 1990 and were expecting another $2 billion loss for the first quarter of 1991. In December 1990, Continental Airlines filed for bankruptcy; in January 1991, the Gulf War started, Pan American filed for bankruptcy, and Eastern Airlines ceased operation after flying for two years under the protection of the bankruptcy court.

In the midst of all of this, in February 28, 1991, the FAA, traditionally criticized for regulatory stalling, filed a detailed and extensive proposed regulation document (NPRM) outlining the reduction in the number of Stage II aircraft until their complete elimination by year-end 1999. Mounting financial difficulties and strong objections by the weaker airlines notwithstanding, the regulation was enacted with only minor amendments, and the stronger airlines headed by American Airlines and the manufacturers argued in favor of the regulation.

## 5.1 Major Provisions of ANCA

The 1990 regulation included two major provisions: the "non-addition" and "phased transition" rules. The first banned the addition to the US registry of Stage II aircraft that were not owned by US entities prior to the effective date of the legislation. By this initial step, the regulator intended to freeze the number of Stage II aircraft allowed to enter the US.

The second rule defined the progress toward the complete elimination of Stage II aircraft operations by December 31, 1999. Two options were provided: the first required the phase-out by December 1994 of 25% of the Stage II aircraft (relative to an initial baseline) and an additional 25% every two years until the complete elimination of all Stage II aircraft by the deadline. The second option allowed the phase-in of 55% Stage III aircraft by December 1994, 65% by December 1996, 75% by December 1998, and 100% by the deadline date.

The "baseline"—representing the number of Stage II aircraft on the effective date—was calculated by the FAA as including 2,247 domestic aircraft, constituting over 55% of the domestic fleet.[117] These aircraft were expected to be either retrofitted or retired by the end of the century. Most of the Stage II aircraft that were targeted by this regulation were the 727s, 737s, and DC9s that had served as the workhorses of the industry. The number included as well fewer than 200 four-engine aircraft that were manufactured as Stage I airplanes but had been retrofitted to Stage II in the previous round of regulation.

The regulation required airlines either to acquire new aircraft, or to modify older aircraft in their fleets by either installing "hush kits" or replacing the engines with new higher bypass engines.

## 5.2 High Bypass Engine Technology

A brief discussion of noise abatement technology and "hush kitting" is perhaps warranted. Aircraft noise is the sum of all the noise produced by aircraft major components. The engines generate most of the noise and thus attract most of the abatement efforts. Airframe noise is more difficult to reduce and because in current production airplanes there are only a few decibels difference between engine and airframe noise, it may not be feasible to reduce airframe noise significantly once the engine noise approaches the airframe noise level.

Engines developed after the noise regulation of the early seventies include integral noise abatement technology built into the engine design. The mechanisms include primarily an increased bypass ratio and acoustically designed nacelles. The major element in the industry's impressive success at reducing aircraft noise is incidental to progress in high bypass technology.

The high bypass principle rests on the fact that it is more efficient to develop thrust by moderately accelerating a large air mass through the fan than a greater acceleration of a smaller mass. This efficiency is achieved by designing a larger fan

---

[117] An additional 834 aircraft of foreign airlines were affected by the US regulation.

that accelerates significantly more air mass than the mass that moves through the engine core. In the early JT3D turbojet engines that powered the 707, all air passed through the engine core, producing a bypass ratio of one. The JT8D engines that powered the 727, 737, and DC9 had a bypass ratio of close to two. Development of high bypass engine technology produced a ratio of almost five for engines powering the 747-400 and MD11 aircraft. The GE90—powering the Boeing 777—has a bypass ratio of 9.

Although future-generation engines may have even larger bypass ratios, further noise reduction becomes more difficult.

The high bypass technology provides a better-balanced composition of engine component noise with a noticeable trade-off between the jet noise and the fan and compressor noise. While jet noise dominates low-bypass engines, fan noise dominates high-bypass engines. Jet noise is reduced by significantly increasing the fan size and its noise. The resulting fan noise is reduced by addressing the size, angle, number, and spacing of the fan blades and by acoustically treating and increasing the length of the inlet and fan duct. Engine noise is also reduced by acoustically treating the engine nacelle (usually considered a part of the airframe) and adding noise-absorbing lining.

## 5.3   Hush Kits

Once the first-generation low bypass engines (mostly JT8D and JT3D) were manufactured, their noise was a given. The challenge of the regulation was to reduce it within the constraints of the existing design and particularly the bypass ratio limits. Noise has been reduced by adjusting the inlet guide vanes and the first-stage blades, installing internal gas mixers, and modifying the nose cowl, tail pipe, exhaust nozzle, and thrust reverse. Modifications that incorporate some or all of these methods are usually referred to as "hush kits."

Modifications like this, together with noise-oriented operational profiles (flap setting, for example) were able to qualify Stage I and II aircraft for Stage III compliance. The Stage II noise criterion was established in 1969 (overall limit 93–108 EPNdB), subject to then-current technology. It contemplated mostly acoustical treatment by the manufacturers of aircraft equipped with low bypass engines in production after December 1973 and acceptance of the existing noise limits of aircraft equipped with higher-bypass engines.[118] The regulations of the late seventies established Stage III limits (overall 89–106 EPNdB) for newly produced engines. They assumed that most of the noise reduction would be achieved by new higher bypass engines planned to power the new generation of narrowbody aircraft. Thus, noise reduction for the highest-weight aircraft was quite small relative to the lower-weight aircraft (2 EPNdB for the heavier aircraft).[119]

---

[118] This means acoustical treatment of mostly 727s, 737s, and DC9s equipped with first-generation JT8D and acceptance as is of mostly 747s equipped with JT9Ds, DC10s with CF6s, and L1011s with RB211s.

[119] It usually takes 4 to 5 dB for a sound to be perceived by the human ear

Since none of the Stage II aircraft were in production when the 1990 regulation was enacted, the manufacturers were not required to develop hush kits as they did in the previous round for JT8D powered aircraft, for example. The manufacturers therefore decided not to directly develop or encourage modification, but rather to push the sales of new generation aircraft.[120]

The aircraft manufacturers' strategy provided an opportunity for independent companies to develop and sell hush kits. Federal Express was a pioneer in this development. Operating a large fleet of three-engine 727 freighter aircraft and facing pressure from local airport authorities (most small package flights occur at night), FedEx started developing 727 hush kits in the early eighties. FedEx developed kits for all 727-type aircraft, and for close to ten years it was in a monopoly position in selling such kits. Only in the late 1990s were two competing kits certified (Raisback and Dugan Air), which reduced the cost of hush kitting 727s quite dramatically. ABS similarly developed hush kits for DC9 aircraft and enjoyed a monopoly with respect to this type of aircraft throughout most of the transition period until a competing alternative was offered in early 2000 for a considerably lower cost. Two kits are available for 737 aircraft (Nordam and AvAero).

The cost of hush kitting Stage II aircraft equipped with the JT8D family of engines (cost of the kit plus direct costs of installation and modification of engines and airframe when required) throughout most of the transition period ranged from $2 to $3 million per aircraft.[121] In some cases, this cost dropped by more than half when competing alternatives became available in the late 1990s and the original vendors lost their monopolies. Yet during almost the entire transition period (1990 through 1999), original vendors enjoyed monopolies, and prices were high.

In September 1996, when the phase-out rule required 75% Stage III compliance, Pratt & Whitney announced that more than 40% of its 3,100 aircraft powered with these engines (over 11,000 engines) were being hush kitted as more than 1,200 kits had been ordered.[122]

## 5.4    Buy a new Aircraft or Hush Kit an Old One?

The Stage III limit was defined in the late seventies based mainly on then-current technology in new aircraft. The same limit was imposed as a mandatory (minimum) target in 1990 to be fully achieved in 1999. Major questions for the industry were how much it would cost to bring the Stage II aircraft into Stage III compliance, and whether this cost would justify hush kitting (or retirement) of specific aircraft, given the cost of alternative aircraft and air travel demand. A relatively large proportion of Stage II aircraft were modified even though in many cases the cost of hush kitting amounted to almost 50% of the modified aircraft value.

Due to the high cost of replacement with Stage III aircraft and the lack of competition in the hush kit market, the modification costs were not related to the

---

[120] MDC was more supportive than Boeing and took a more active part in hush kitting DC9's. P&W was supportive as well.

[121] Not including the cost of aircraft downtime.

[122] P&W press release in Farnborough Air Show, September 1996.

economic cost of noise abatement at all. It is also not clear if and to what extent this one-time fixed cost of compliance in fact accelerated the rate of retirement of the Stage II aircraft.

Perhaps the most important question that was never answered is whether the cost of modifying the Stage II aircraft justified the benefit to airport neighboring community. It is quite likely that in many cases residents could not perceive any difference between an originally produced Stage II aircraft with or without modification and a new Stage III aircraft, or that otherwise the difference in noise warranted the costs.

## 6.   INTERNATIONAL ASPECTS

It is generally held that environmental regulations controlled at the federal level help to prevent state or local governments from exporting environmental externalities to other jurisdictions through the exercise of their local regulatory powers. Federal preemption of state policing power as to aircraft noise largely eliminated noise as an issues and focused state and local governments' efforts mostly on land management issues. In addition, the regulatory powers of state and local governments as airport proprietors are to some degree controlled and coordinated by the FAA pursuant to the 1990 ANCA. In this respect, the legislative, judicial, and executive systems have interacted to create institutional rules that maintain certain local and federal rights and powers.

The global nature of aviation raises similar issues regarding the global regulation of aircraft noise and pollution. Since all governments hold full sovereignty and regulatory powers over their skies—including power over foreign aircraft operated within their territories—there is a need for coordination and regulation by an international regulator. The International Civil Aviation Organization (ICAO) is an international organization established after World War II that deals with coordinating international aviation and setting global standards including standards relating to safety and noise. The organization has gained some strategic importance with the globalization of aviation, but its enforcement power, much as is the case for the United Nations, depends on the balance of power and the interaction of its member countries. The world aviation industry adopted the US FAR Part 36 noise limits, as defined in Part II, Chapter 2, Volume 1, of Annex 16 to the Convention of International Civil Aviation. ICAO was slow to respond to noise issues before 1980 and did so only after the US government's pressures to adopt the standards.

### 6.1   Globalization

A full treatment of the international aspects of noise and other environmental issues is beyond the scope of my analysis. I would like, however, to identify several major issues that are typical. The first is an analogue to the federalism issue. Countries differ in their attitudes toward noise for various reasons, including the different locations of airports relative to communities as well as the political power structure of the particular interest groups typically involved in the noise abatement debate. In Western Europe, for example, airports in general are located nearer densely populated areas, and the affected communities and environmentalist group are often more politically powerful than in the US. In many less developed countries, on the other hand, aircraft noise as well as other environmental concerns may not appear on the political agenda at all.

Balancing local, national, and international aspects is quite complex, especially in the absence of an international regulatory agency with enforcement power, so strategic interactions among governments affect the way that global regulation has evolved.

In the late 1980s, European authorities responding to strong political pressure by environmentalists took the lead in launching noise regulation. On December 4, 1989, almost a year before Congress enacted the ANCA, the European Community issued Council Directive 89/629/EEC, imposing a non-addition rule on Stage II aircraft starting November 1, 1990. Subsequently it issued in the summer of 1991 phase-out rules banning the operation of Stage II aircraft not otherwise modified to a Stage III compliance level. The European and US rules were largely similar, although a most notable difference is that the US regulator adopted December 1999 as the deadline for complete banning of Stage II aircraft and the European Community adopted a 2002 deadline.

One of the arguments used by the US regulator in favor of noise regulation imposition in the early 1990s was a need to respond to the EC regulation and block the "dumping" of noisy aircraft into the US. The almost universal result of the EC and US regulation was the exportation of aircraft noise to less developed markets. It is noteworthy that since the imposition of the noise regulation reduced the value of Stage II aircraft, the less developed countries that imported these aircraft were in effect subsidized by the developed world and were able to expand their airline systems with less expensive aircraft.

## 6.2    Interest Groups and Strategic Trade Issues

It is interesting to look at the attempts to impose stricter noise regulation in Europe. The Europeans took the first noise regulation step in the late 1980s and did the same again in early 1999. The second time around, however, the action was far more controversial and triggered a different response by the US government. In legislation that was passed by the European Parliament and was submitted for approval to the EU Transport ministers, it was proposed to adopt more stringent noise regulations in Europe even before the current regulation deadline had been reached.

The new proposals targeted aircraft originally produced as Stage II or I that had obtained their Stage III noise compliance by modification by either hush kitting or reengining. The proposed regulation called for no further addition of such aircraft after April 1, 1999, and a complete ban of their operation by April 2002. [123]

---

[123] The 1999 deadline was postponed due to very strong US objections.

The major European explanation of this move cited different "tastes" for noise in most western European countries. Proponents argued that the noise modifications of the older aircraft to comply with the late 1970s standards were artificial and not sufficient and called for new standards that will relate the noise limits to the bypass ratio of the new-generation aircraft. They also claimed that they must take a leadership role due to the abdication of the ICAO in setting stricter international standards. This position does not sound unreasonable and might be seen as analogous to one state trying to respond to local pressures by issuing stricter rules than the federal ones (California is a good example) except that there are no equivalent checks and balances by similar global judicial or legislative systems.

But there is more to the European move than meets the eye. The number of modified aircraft to have been affected by the new regulation is quite small (only about 10% of the world aircraft in this category fly in Europe), and many European local authorities had penalized these aircraft by imposing higher landing fees even before the new initiative was launched. Moreover, most of the older DC9s and 737s were being phased out by European airlines, and the 727 aircraft was not particularly popular there, except for small package and overnight mail service—and there is no equivalent newer-generation aircraft that would efficiently substitute for it.

The European regulation was supported by an ad hoc coalition of at least four major European groups: governments, environmentalists, the major European airlines, and Airbus. The concern of the major European airlines facing liberalization and deregulation was new entry of discount airlines operating the less expensive, older aircraft. By restricting these aircraft, the majors would raise entry barriers and eliminate to some degree the potential relative advantage of startup entry.

For its part, Airbus (controlled by European governments) supported the initiative since it would accelerate retirement of old aircraft, all of them manufactured by a US manufacturer (Boeing) and encourage new aircraft orders. Moreover, in the late 1990s, a cargo conversion program was developed for Airbus's oldest aircraft A300. Although the A300's operational characteristics and volumetric efficiency do not match the 727 for small package and overnight mail service, the banning of the 727 could force airlines to use the A300 for operations that were traditionally performed by the 727.

The European governments obviously had an interest in supporting Airbus and in responding to a strong political environmentalist movement that made the old American-built aircraft a potential target. At the same time, the governments wanted to capture the regulation process in the domestic as well as the international arena. Yielding completely to environmentalist pressures could result in environmental regulation that would be more restrictive than the industry would wish. The local airport authorities in Europe had adopted non-uniform noise regulations that had already singled out and penalized the older Stage II aircraft; the new regulation initiative could preempt and stop the local authorities from expanding restrictions to cover newer aircraft.

The European attempts to impose stricter noise regulation faced strong objections from the US industry and government and developed into something of a "political football" (*Air Transport World*, 2000, p. 48). To begin with, the US government objected to the EC's unilateral step.[124] It argued that the ICAO must be the global standard setter and the regulator of noise. Obviously, independent EC steps of such a nature impair the hegemony and political power that the US can use through ICAO, where only 15 countries care about noise and "the other 170 don't. Some care a lot more about food." (*Air Transport World*, 2000, p. 51).

The US government also strongly objected to the EC step on the basis that it is discriminatory and violates international trade agreements by singling out aircraft that are manufactured by US companies and operated mostly by US airlines.

On February 10, 1999, a bill was submitted to Congress proposing that Concorde aircraft—symbols of European technological achievement and pride, although of only negligible commercial importance—would be banned from landing in the US if the EU adopted its proposed regulation (H.R. 661). The US airlines in general object to banning the hush kitted or reengined aircraft, since they own and operate most of the population of these aircraft, and such a regulation would impose a heavier burden on them than on their European competitors. Moreover, some US airlines had invested significant amounts of money in aircraft modification to comply with the Stage III rules and if such aircraft were banned they might not be able to amortize their investment. Northwest was the strongest opponent of the proposed EC regulation since it operated the largest proportion of originally Stage II aircraft that were hush kitted during the 1990s to comply with the US regulation.

Obviously the hush kit manufacturers, all of them US-based, would be negatively affected by the EC proposal. Although the US government and the industry as a group presented a unified front against the EC's step, industry members had different interests. For example, P&W, the manufacturer of all the modified engines and of most parts that are installed in the hush kits, was a strong opponent. GE, on the other hand, was in a different position, since none of its engines were affected by this initiative and it could benefit from the elimination of competing engines.

Adoption of stricter noise limits was congruent with Boeing's traditional policy toward accelerated retirement of older aircraft. EU leadership in setting new noise policy, however, might lead to establishment of standards that would be tailored around Airbus's technology as opposed to setting limits that would put US aircraft technology in a preferred position. Moreover, since political maneuvering could postpone but not eliminate the European pressures, the US government was in affect forced to enter into negotiations regarding new Stage IV noise limits in order to regain control over the process and preempt regulation by European authorities that could negatively affect US interests.

## 6.3    A note About International Noise Regulation and Theory

Standard economic theory calls for regulation that would provide proper incentives for airlines to internalize the cost of noise in the absence of free market signals. The *industry capture* concept, on the other hand, views a coherent industry conspiring

---

[124] The EU is not a member of ICAO but an observer. Each of the European nations is a member.

with the government to impose environmental standards that raise barriers to entry and create rent-extracting opportunities. More recent models suggest that the industry and environmentalists may form a coalition with a common interest of pushing for regulations that would restrict production and increase industry's rent (Laffont and Tirole (1994), for example).

In reality, noise regulation has evolved as a complex phenomenon that cannot be explained by any one of these models alone, but includes some aspects of all of them.

Globalization of the industry compounds the complexity even further and makes generalization rather speculative. In this respect, three major points are worth special attention.

First, global standards evolve in response to the diverse levels of acceptance of noise pollution and the political agendas and power structures as well as the national and local preferences of citizens and governments across borders.

Second, aircraft sales play a major role in national balances of trade worldwide, and thus governments tend to support their manufacturers and directly involve themselves in strategic marketing efforts of aircraft on their behalf. The US government, for example, has pressured countries that receive its political support and/or economic aid to reciprocate by ordering Boeing aircraft and not Airbus.[125] Governments also issue national regulations and participate in the international political process of design and enforcement of international standards. Consequently, strategic aspects of international trade policies play a direct role in domestic and international regulation policies.

And finally, the globalization of the airline industry and the creation of global alliances make the interest structure of the airlines far more diverse and indeterminate compared to the traditional "coherent industry" views that are presumed in the *industry capture* concept. And, airlines on one continent may use aircraft manufactured in another (or a mixed fleet), which further complicates the picture.

One thing is clear, however. Standards that are continuously negotiated and variably enforced in practice on a global basis make regulation even less related to the economic cost of noise that economists argue should be internalized into the market system.

---

[125] For example, Saudi Arabia and Israel

# CHAPTER 6

# SAFETY REGULATION

> One of the aviation industry's major safety
> concerns is the flying of perfectly good airplanes
> into the ground—also known as Controlled Flight
> Into Terrain.[126]

According to standard economic principles society should put scarce resources to
work in their most cost-effective uses. This means that the next dollar should be
spent on a regulatory effort that is expected to have the greatest impact on risk
reduction. Contrary to these principles, though, public perception of commercial
flight risks and the industry's strategic behavior have resulted in misallocation of
resources. Subchapter 1 examines this general claim.

Resources are misallocated in two major ways. First, a higher priority is given
to regulating flight risks than is "objectively" justifiable. Second, priorities are
misplaced across prevention targets within aviation risk. In the first place, the
resources used for regulating aviation risk could be used more cost-effectively to
improve safety in other risk categories—automobile accident risks is one example.
In the second place, the resources that society devotes to regulation of aviation risk
could be more effectively used if allocated differently across prevention strategies—
targeting pilot fatigue instead of airplane metal fatigue is a good example.[127]
Subchapter 2 and 3 examine these two claims.

Major airlines—looking to serve their strategic interests during the late 1980s
and 1990s—accommodated public misperception and overreaction to old aircraft as
a major safety threat, while playing down the importance of new aircraft as the real
major threat. This in spite of the industry's prevailing perception that it is the latter
and not the former that constitutes a more alarming threat. Subchapter 4 examines
the old aircraft threat, focusing on the Aloha accident that ignited this regulatory
issue as a case study. Subchapter 5 examines new aircraft technology as a major
safety threat, underlining pilot-automation-interaction as the core of the problem.
Finally, the American Airlines 757 crash in Cali Columbia is analyzed as a model of
a typical accident, combining new aircraft technology, pilot errors, and *control flight
into terrain* (CFIT)—issues identified by the industry as the most important safety
threats, but otherwise flying under the public and political radar.

---

[126] Boeing (1996a, p. 11).

[127] The time a crew is awake (above a median number of 12 to11 hours) is found to be associated with
more procedural and tactical decision errors (NTSB 1994).

## 1. REGULATORY BIAS –AN INTRODUCTION

Safety of a product or service is an attribute that is desirable to consumers but costly to produce. Suppose a perfect world in which many competing small airlines use an auctioneer to announce their flight numbers, departure times, and a menu of possible incidents (engine failure, severe turbulence, landing gear that does not retract), accidents (controlled flight into terrain (CFIT), explosion), and their probabilities. In this world, passengers would bid for tickets according to their risk preferences, and market prices would induce airlines to provide desirable levels of risk. In this ideal world, government regulation is not required.

### 1.1    Why Regulate Aviation Safety?

The problem is that "safety" is uncertain, and information regarding flight risks is incomplete, costly, and asymmetric; the airlines are often better informed regarding aspects of a specific flight's risk than the consumer is. In this case, economists would say that the free market system does not provide airlines with the proper market signals to select the efficient level of risk-reducing efforts, and thus government regulation is advisable.

Certain aspects of this story tie into the two major categories of insurance market failures that economists like to analyze: *moral hazard* and *adverse selection*. In the first case, insurance and other risk-sharing arrangements might motivate an airline to deviate from optimal levels of risk reduction efforts. In the second case, since the safety level of a specific airline or flight is not observable, and ticket prices depend on industry average practices, safer airlines would exit the market, and safety levels would plummet. Government intervention, in such cases, is expected to internalize the otherwise missing market signals, and induce airlines to undertake efficient levels of safety efforts.

It is also costly for an individual passenger to collect information on and deduce a flight's risk for a number of reasons: the highly complex and uncertain nature of such risk, the asymmetric distribution of relevant information, and the specialized knowledge required for its interpretation. The *public-good* nature of such information suggests another market failure justification for regulating risk. Under these conditions, a centralized agency may act as an *information intermediary* for the public. The regulators develop the tools and expertise necessary to collect and analyze safety information and to specify and enforce standards.

The regulatory agency's role can be viewed from two general and sometimes conflicting perspectives. On the one hand, the agency acts pursuant to a general social contract in which it undertakes to develop general safety rules and regulations and enforce them subject to overall economic efficiency considerations. On the other hand, a passenger boarding an airplane is expecting the agency to ensure the full safety of that specific flight. The passenger has no access to information about the airworthiness of the aircraft, its maintenance status, the weather, or the pilots' and other crew members' training and health conditions. The passenger delegates to the regulator the task of ensuring that the flight is safe and views the clearance for takeoff as a signal that the flight is in fact safe.

## 1.2 The Problem with Safety Regulation

The traditional justification for risk regulation assumes a perfect government correcting imperfect markets in the consumer interest. The problem is that regulation is not perfect either, and must cope with the same information problems that cause markets to fail—in addition to complex agency problems, interest group politics, and the related costs that are typical to regulatory institutions.

The major regulatory agencies involved in aviation safety are the Department of Transportation (the DOT), as regarding financial fitness, and the Federal Aviation Administration (the FAA), as regarding safety. The National Transportation Safety Board (NTSB) is an influential accident investigative body that has no direct regulatory power. The FAA is a part of the DOT, and the NTSB is an independent agency directly reporting to the President. Due to the national interest in airline safety, the White House often plays a direct role in accident investigation and uses its influence as well. Airlines and aircraft manufacturers are also involved in the process of regulation. So are labor unions, media, and other interest groups—each with its own specific information, interests, and political power.

It should not be surprising that the interaction of information asymmetries regarding rare and highly uncertain phenomena and diverse interest groups generates complex and often controversial regulation. Information imperfections have resulted in a complex multi-layered, *multi-principal* dynamically evolving *agency* structure. The influence of the public on regulators' actions comes through their elected representatives. Yet neither the public nor the elected representatives have the specialized knowledge and expertise necessary to affect actions in the industry. They depend on information that is provided mostly by the airline industry, the regulators, and the media to form their views concerning safety.

One of the major problems in safety regulation relates to the perceptions of risk by the public. It is recognized by economists that people tend to misperceive risks that are characterized by a low likelihood of a personal catastrophic event. Commercial aircraft accidents in fact occur with a very low probability but at a catastrophic cost if an accident does occur. Cognitive pathology produces an overreaction to aircraft accident risks, causing people to ascribe to them a higher probability than an "objective" observer would. Individuals, moreover, may tend to overreact to risks when they feel unable to control a situation. Aircraft accidents obviously fall into this category as well. Once a passenger boards a flight, he cannot go back, but must completely subject himself to an unknown crew and their actions.

In addition, because airplane accidents involve a relatively large number of people in one occurrence, they are perceived as a national catastrophe. Airline accidents attract mass media coverage and special public attention. Beyond contemporaneous news coverage, real and or recreated aircraft accidents are featured in full-length motion pictures and coffee-table books.[128] The media and entertainment coverage typically causes people to see the catastrophic expected losses of aircraft accidents but not their low frequency of occurrence.

The result is that aircraft safety has been elevated to a major national concern, regardless of the "objective" safety record of the industry compared to other modern risks in society. In a classic book on risk regulation, Stephen Breyer (1993) describes risk regulation failures as a vicious cycle in that public misperception of low-probability risks plays a major role in triggering a systematic regulatory bias.[129] In this cycle, public demand for regulatory response causes Congressional overreaction and the adoption of inefficient policies, including overly strict standards and misplaced priorities within or across risk categories. This is surely true in regulating aviation risks. Both the inherent uncertainty and information problems and the public's perceptions of flight risks bring about public mistrust of the regulator as well as political pressures to react to high-profile accidents or other notions about flight risks.

Accidents are an integral part of aircraft flying, and it is impossible to eliminate them unless we leave all the planes on the ground. When an accident occurs, the public often blames the regulator for not preventing it, and the regulator responds by promising a "zero accident rate." But accidents serve as the major observable measure of the regulator's performance. When the next accident occurs (and there is always a next one), increased pressure is placed on the regulator.

Not surprisingly, there is often not a uniform view of either accident causes or prevention strategies, which we can attribute to the uncertain nature of accidents, to information imperfections, and to diverse interest structures. These conditions further impact public perception of risks and increase mistrust between the public (the "principal") and its agents.

The FAA may have a different position from the NTSB; the airlines may have a different position from the manufacturer, and so on. Media coverage of accidents, tedious and long investigations, and the fact that an accident's probable cause cannot always be determined beyond a reasonable doubt all increase public suspicion, and give rise to speculation and stories regarding conspiracies and cover-ups. The media seem to be more interested in reporting on (and the public is certainly more interested in hearing about) a conspiracy theory (a US Navy missile hit a commercial airliner—in TWA Flight 800, for example) rather than venture into a complex analysis of a mechanical failure (a fuel or electric system failure igniting fuel vapors in an empty fuel tank). The problem is not just that the public and the media like sensational news and therefore a wrong perception may be quickly formed. It is also that in certain cases the absence of clear-cut and persuasive evidence may make either story—the missile or the mechanical cause—speculative and questionable.

---

[128] I was quite surprised to find a full-length movie of the anxiety, pain, and horror of the passengers of Aloha Airline as the structure of their aircraft suffered catastrophic decompression failure, for example. A new York City theatre runs a show that dramatizes the last minutes of six aircraft crews before crashing, based on voice recorder information.

[129] See also Pollak (1995).

As a result, the FAA's role is inherently problematic from a public opinion perspective. The FAA acts as the public's agent regarding the setting, enforcing, and signaling of safety standards in an information-asymmetric world, in which the communication of safety information is distorted by human cognitive problems. People who fly want this agent to fight to eliminate accidents, yet the agent's information and perceptions regarding airline safety are often different. The public perceives attempts by the FAA to communicate this message as the agent's failure to understand the underlying seriousness of the problem, or as the agent's excuse for not preventing accidents.

Furthermore, the regulator's general mandate is to balance promotion of safety and economic considerations. The cost-benefit analysis of risk issues includes valuing human life and prioritizing safety efforts over alternative risk challenges faced by society. These issues require specialized information and knowledge as well as application of personal judgment. Decisions can be very difficult to defend publicly, especially in the face of individual personal catastrophe. Sometimes it seems that the FAA is a target for more post-accident public criticism than the airlines themselves. An accident investigation often ends with more public and political pressure for increased FAA personnel and resources rather than a focus on the risk itself.

### 1.3    The Nature of Accidents and Their Investigations

Both the inherent nature of accidents and their investigation play a major role in risk regulation and deserve a more detailed discussion. Many factors contribute to create an aircraft accident. Investigation of an accident can be viewed as the ex-post analysis of a complex dynamic system involving the occurrence of a specific sequence of events in which human beings, machines, and nature interact.

An accident investigation is an attempt to suggest a hypothesis regarding the probable cause of the accident. The investigator's assignment is to identify not only the complex events and states of nature involved, but also the specific causal relationships among them. Conceptually, there is not one causal factor for an accident, but rather a combination or an accumulation of specific events and circumstances that explain it conjointly.

As aircraft technology progresses and human interaction with computerized systems becomes more common, new types of system failures occur, and they are more difficult to understand and interpret. The new systems involve sophisticated automated computerized systems that are interactively complex, tightly coupled, and involve multiple functional modes. It is thus often impossible to suggest only one interpretation, or to identify a unique reason for what went wrong.

Moreover, the rarity of accidents and the uniqueness and specificity of each accident make statistical inference difficult and unstable. When it tries to prevent future accidents, the regulator mandates certain corrective maintenance or operational actions. But because each accident is unique, and there is no statistical control group, it is usually very difficult to verify (ex-post) the contribution of a certain rule in preventing an accident.

It is not unusual for NTSB accident reports to list about fifty major factors and states that are involved in an accident. They usually distinguish between a "probable cause" that is directly related to the accident and "contributing factors."

Conclusions of NTSB reports are frequently the subject of debate and criticism as to either their merit or general methodology. A major line of criticism relates to the overemphasis of "probable cause" relative to "contributing factors." Some have argued that the NTSB should emphasize the triggering factor or factors that started the chain of events instead. It has also been suggested alternatively to focus on: 1) all the factors as one contingent complex event, or 2) factors whose elimination could have prevented the accident, or 3) missing factors whose introduction could have prevented the accident. It has also been argued that probable causes should not dominate regulatory agendas and that safety regulations should be proactive and systemic rather than reactive and specific.

A story often used to illustrate the limits of the "probable cause" methodology is borrowed from the medical world. A kidney failure of a cancer patient after aggressive chemotherapy treatment caused heart failure and death. The medical examiner identifies heart failure as the "probable" cause of death. There are a few lessons from this analogy. First, the cause of death is the conjoined impact of cancer treatment, kidney failure, and heart failure. Heart failure was the last to occur, but it is not necessarily the most important factor in reducing the risk of death. Cancer prevention, different chemotherapy, or other alternative treatments, for example, might have prevented the death.

Second, a focus on the probable cause may be misleading. For example, focusing on the heart failure as the major cause may lead the profession to encourage exercise and reduction in cholesterol levels, which are irrelevant to our case.

Third, dynamic and interactively complex phenomena have a long history, and may have many non-obvious and preventable causes, and actions or inactions along the way might change the outcome. For example, someone might argue that the cause of death was smoking (which caused the cancer to begin with), or the doctor's decision to treat the patent with chemotherapy rather than surgery or radiation, or the failure of society to find a cure for cancer.

## 1.4    Interest Groups and Rent-Seeking

The inherently complex nature of aviation risks will always give rise to diverse interpretations, emphasis, and speculation regarding accident causes and prevention efforts and thereby information manipulation and interest group rent-seeking behavior. As potential liabilities are also likely involved, an airline may attempt to put the blame on an aircraft or an aircraft component for an accident, while the manufacturer may try to put the blame on the pilots or the regulator, and so on. The regulator, on the other hand, may support a different theory, and it could do this in an attempt to elevate public or other political pressures.

Figuring out an accident cause plays an important role in the regulatory process and creates regulatory rent opportunities. There is a direct regulatory response to each perceived or identified cause, especially in reaction to public demand relating to high-profile accidents. This often results in recruitment of new personnel for the regulatory agency, appropriation of a new budget and other resources, research and development, establishment of committees, development of new equipment, changed maintenance requirements, and much more. For example, the initial speculation that the TWA Flight 800 accident was a result of a terrorist act initiated a substantial regulatory effort in this direction, including a proposed new appropriation and budget reallocations of $1.1 billion for the acquisition of new explosive detection technology and other security enhancement efforts (White House Commission, 1997).

NTSB accident investigations as well as safety initiatives sponsored by the FAA or the industry often result in mandatory requirements for corrective action that are imposed on groups of aircraft or components. In many cases the compliance cost is significant. Starting in the late 1980s, for example, the FAA instituted several major safety programs, including: structural modification of 747 class aircraft (Section 41) estimated at that time at $2.5 million per aircraft; aging and corrosion inspection (CPCP) on 727 and 737 aircraft estimated at $1 million per aircraft; and traffic and collision avoidance (TCAS) and wind shear alert systems estimated at $250,000 per aircraft. Responses to regulation that require modifying or developing new parts, components, and procedures provide manufacturers opportunities to extract rent.

Imposition of such regulation raises operating costs, reduces the market value of non-modified aircraft, and increases the cost of entry into the market. The combined cost of safety and noise regulation that became effective in the early 1990s in fact more than doubled the cost of some older narrowbody aircraft traditionally used by startup airlines.

Stephen Breyer (1993) suggests that the interaction of public misperception and congressional reaction to public regulatory demands results in *random agenda selection* rather than an objective systematic approach to identify regulatory targets and related policies. Aviation safety regulation is no exception. Public perceptions of accidents and their causes often make the regulator focus on what the public perceives as the cause (mostly related to a heavily covered accident), and not necessarily on what the industry, the regulator, or expert information and judgment may otherwise suggest.

If the public indeed tends to capture the regulation process in this case, what are we to make of Stigler's *industry capture* argument, which suggests a regulatory bias in favor of a small, well-organized industry group and not in favor of the public? Are these two views contradictory? Is there something in high-profile media-celebrated low-probability risks that makes the public more politically potent? Why would the industry be able to capture the process when it comes to regulating public utility monopolistic rates, for example, but not when it comes to aircraft risks? Moreover, if the industry is aware that the public is misinformed, or otherwise misperceives the "real" risk, why doesn't it attempt to address such misperception?

In the next sections I argue that, in fact, it has been in the best interest of major airlines to accommodate these public and political perceptions and to support inefficient regulatory agendas because they discriminate against smaller and financially weak airlines, raise barriers to entry, and serve other major airlines' interests.

## 2.  IS SOCIETY SPENDING TOO MUCH ON AVIATION SAFETY?

The public perceives aviation safety as a major item on the political agenda and supports aggressive regulatory efforts to reduce aircraft accident risk. Yet it is doubtful whether most people know how many aircraft accidents, incidents, or related fatalities in fact occur and whether such statistical data play a major role in forming the public's perception.

I have asked people (including industry members who are not directly involved with accident statistics) if they view aircraft safety as a matter of national importance and if they know what last year's (or a yearly average) fatality rate for US commercial airlines was. The answer to the first question is overwhelmingly positive—of course people see aircraft safety as important—and the answer to the second question is no. When I ask the same people to guess at the average yearly number of fatalities in commercial jet transportation, the average response is 3,000 fatalities per year. When I ask if their position regarding the importance of aircraft safety would change if the number of fatalities were, in fact, only 300 per year, the response is overwhelmingly negative.

Obviously this informal sampling has only anecdotal value, if any, but surely it is indicative of the nature of the problem. People in general don't know, and don't base their perception of flying risks on the actual number of fatalities or accidents or any other statistical indication of actual industry performance. This is the essence of the regulatory bias argument. According to traditional economic principles, regulatory efforts should accord with objective observations of industry performance. The public, however, seems not to be impressed with such evidence.

### 2.1    Accident Statistics

Some statistics are in order here. Ample empirical evidence indicates that the number of commercial jet aircraft accidents dropped significantly during the 1960s and 1970s and since then has remained at a relatively stable low rate, significantly lower than any other means of transportation. Table 5 shows the number of fatalities, seriously injured passengers, and hull loss per year between 1982 and 1999 for US air carriers operating under 14 CFR 121 as reported by the DOT.[130] Usually accident risks are presented and analyzed in normalized rates (such as accidents per hour, per number of flights, per miles, and so on). Normalized rates standardize the risk to the relative exposure of the various risk categories. I use absolute and non-normalized numbers because they are easier to interpret than the normalized rates, which mask the absolute size of the problem.

During the 18 years period 1982–1999, a total of 2,221 passengers died in aircraft accidents of commercial US FAR Part 121 airlines, an average of 123

---

[130] Source: US Department of Transportation, Bureau of Transportation Statistics; http://www.bts.gov/. Includes 14CFR 121 airlines. Effective March 20, 1997, aircraft with 10 or more seats must conduct scheduled passenger operations under 14 CFR 121. Injuries exclude cabin and flight-crew.

passengers per year (97 during the last five years summarized in Table 5). [131] This is a low absolute number. It becomes even more impressive when one considers the several hundreds of millions of miles flown and the roughly 600 million passengers (enplanements) per year flown during the last few years shown.

*Table 5. US Carriers: Fatalities, Seriously Injured Passengers and Hull Loss 1982-1999*

| Year | Fatalities | Serious Injuries | Fatal Accidents |
|------|-----------|------------------|-----------------|
| 1982 | 210 | 17 | 5 |
| 1983 | 8 | 8 | 4 |
| 1984 | 1 | 6 | 1 |
| 1985 | 486 | 20 | 7 |
| 1986 | 4 | 23 | 3 |
| 1987 | 213 | 39 | 5 |
| 1988 | 255 | 44 | 3 |
| 1989 | 259 | 55 | 11 |
| 1990 | 8 | 23 | 6 |
| 1991 | 40 | 19 | 4 |
| 1992 | 26 | 14 | 4 |
| 1993 | 0 | 7 | 1 |
| 1994 | 228 | 16 | 4 |
| 1995 | 152 | 15 | 3 |
| 1996 | 319 | 19 | 5 |
| 1997 | 2 | 19 | 4 |
| 1998 | 0 | 10 | 1 |
| 1999 | 10 | 36 | 2 |
| Total | 2,221 | 390 | 73 |

Table 6 reflects the distribution of transportation fatalities across major categories during 1993-1998 as reported by the DOT.[132] The chart includes (in addition to FAR 121 air carriers) scheduled commuter airlines operating under FAR 135, air taxis (usually small aircraft in non-scheduled commercial operation), and General Aviation (small aircraft in non-commercial mostly recreational operation). It also includes highway-related fatalities and railroad accidents.

Table 6 shows the total fatalities in commercial aviation (including air carriers, commuters, and air taxi) to be significantly lower than in other categories. General Aviation accounts for the highest number of fatalities in any aviation-related category.[133]

---

[131] Total accidents for the 10-year period 1985–1996 of worldwide jet passenger fleet was 268 with a total number of of 6,156 fatalities (Boeing, 1997).

[132] Extracted from Bureau of Transportation Statistics; http://www.bts.gov/. Due to changes in different reporting procedures and definitions, there are slight inconsistencies. For a clearer understanding of the statistics, see the source.

[133] This category includes small privately owned aircraft mostly used for sport and recreation. The population group that participates in this operation is less averse to aviation risks.

*Table 6. Transportation Fatalities*

|  | 1993 | 1994 | 1995 | 1996 | 1997 | 1998 |
|---|---|---|---|---|---|---|
| Air Carriers | 1 | 239 | 168 | 380 | 8 | 1 |
| Commuters | 24 | 25 | 9 | 14 | 46 | 0 |
| Air Taxi | 42 | 63 | 52 | 63 | 39 | 45 |
| G'en. Aviation | 736 | 730 | 734 | 632 | 660 | 621 |
| **Total Air** | **803** | **1,057** | **963** | **1,089** | **753** | **667** |
| Cars | 21,566 | 21,997 | 22,423 | 22,505 | 22,199 | 21,164 |
| Motorcycles | 2,449 | 2,320 | 2,227 | 2,161 | 2,116 | 2,284 |
| Trucks | 9,116 | 9,574 | 10,216 | 10,553 | 10,972 | 11,375 |
| Buses | 18 | 18 | 33 | 21 | 18 | 36 |
| Pedestrians | 5,649 | 5,489 | 5,584 | 5,449 | 5,321 | 5,220 |
| Other | 1,352 | 1,318 | 1,334 | 1,374 | 1,387 | 1,392 |
| **Total highway** | **40,150** | **40,716** | **41,817** | **42,065** | **42,013** | **41,471** |
| **Total Railroad** | **1,279** | **1,226** | **1,146** | **1,039** | **1,063** | **1,008** |

I do not propose to deal with the general issues of setting social priorities for risk reduction efforts, but rather to illustrate with some descriptive statistics the general regulatory bias argument made by economists. Compare commercial flight risk to ground transportation, for example. In 1998, 41,471 people were killed in the US and 3,192,000 injured in 6,334,000 motor vehicle crashes, amounting to an average of 114 daily fatalities.[134] Moreover, 15,935 fatalities of the 41,471 were alcohol-related motor vehicle crashes, which are considered preventable to a great degree. Furthermore, the average age of drunk driving casualties suggests a high economic value to lives to be saved. Flight accidents by comparison 1) are rare, 2) involve significantly fewer fatalities, and 3) are very difficult and expensive to reduce further. It is therefore worth considering that the next dollar spent on safety would save more lives if it were allocated to reduce drunk driving, for example.

## 2.2    Interconnected Markets

It is important to note that cost-benefit analysis of risk regulation usually takes place in a partial equilibrium static environment. The regulator, for example, attempts to show the direct costs and benefits attributable to issuing a certain rule or regulation. This methodology by its nature ignores the dynamic impact of such regulation in a general system of interactive markets. Any action taken to improve safety also increases cost, and costs are at least partially transferred to the passenger by

---

[134] DOT, Traffic Safety Facts 1998, National Highway Traffic Safety Administration, HS 808 95.

increases in fares, thereby tending toward reduced in demand for air travel (everything else equal).

Passengers' response to increased fares is expected to be stronger, the higher the elasticity of demand is, and the response is related as well to the presence of substitute transportation alternatives (cars, trains) or other services (fax, teleconferencing). The demand response is strongest with respect to short-haul flights where ground transportation is a close substitute for air travel. Consider that strengthening aircraft safety regulation increases fares, which in return increases the public's use of cars and other ground transportation, thereby increasing exposure to ground accidents and the overall extent of fatalities and injuries. A passenger who might have flown for an hour but who resorts to driving to avoid higher airline fares is exposed to car accident risk during close to six hours of driving the same distance.

A prominent example is the FAA action in the shutting down of ValueJet and its subsequent restructuring as a significantly smaller airline at a higher cost. ValueJet operated short-haul DC9 aircraft mostly on shorter-than-an-hour flights. When the airline terminated operations passengers who had enjoyed discount fares went back to driving. The risk of car accidents is higher than ValueJet's specific risk (even though ValueJet's risk was higher than the airline industry average). While the FAA's strong response—influenced by the media, public and politicians—was perceived as raising the industry safety standard, it most likely has cost society in an increased number of fatalities in car accidents.

This is the sort of observation economists like to suggest. Such important observations, however, often escape the public debate of aviation safety. Cost-effectiveness of safety regulation targets is usually evaluated by comparing the cost per human life saved across an *independent regulatory effort*. The problem is not only that a dollar spent on aviation safety can be better used to reduce other risks, but also that the regulatory effort may significantly increase risk exposure if it has the effect of motivating the public to use riskier transportation means.

## 2.3 Questions and Debates

The traditional (normative) approach of economists to risk regulation is based on the presumption that expert observers can specify an "objective" probability distribution of accidents and related costs. The main problem emphasized by economists is information imperfections that are largely attributable to the public not being informed about risk-related information. The regulator's intervention is expected to correct this situation by basing regulation on correct "objective" measurements or by educating the public and fixing its misperceptions regarding such risk. There are several problems with these notions.

### 2.3.1 Risk Approximation

Unfortunately, there is no general consensus regarding whether a "true" and objective risk measurement or estimation is attainable or verifiable. It is also not quite clear to what extent historical industry performance is a good indication of future performance. Accidents, in general, are interpreted as an outcome of complex dynamically unfolding processes, critically dependent on a particular historical sequence of events and chance. The nature of accidents poses fundamental challenges to our ability to generalize and predict risk.

### 2.3.2    Data and Measurement

Even if we assume that a practical approximation of risk is attainable, there are a host of pragmatic problems relating to the ambiguity, uncertainty, and complexity of flight risk, its measurement, and the availability of pertinent data. Experts often disagree on the definition of flight risk, let alone on all the variables that may represent it. Moreover, related information is partial and fragmented. Usually, accident statistics are used, although these reflect only a fraction of the relevant data besides ignoring most of the cases that don't involve accidents.

In addition, since accidents are statistically rare, basing risk assessment on such data is unstable; one accident may be sufficient to turn a given conclusion on its head. A more recent practice is to consider available incident data as well, a step that obviously improves the sample size and data, but still suffers from similar problems.

There are also many problems related to the normalization of risk for the purpose of inter- or intraindustry comparisons. In this case as well, the normalizing variable may change the conclusion quite dramatically. For example, ground transportation may become significantly less risky than flying if accidents are normalized by the duration (in hours) of exposure to the risk of driving compared to flying and not by miles. In addition, numbers of injuries and fatalities are related to the size of an airplane or the number of boarded passengers. Therefore, two cases with "identical risk" may alter a statistical outcome, depending on the number of passengers who happened to be aboard the aircraft.

Most experts seem to prefer to use the number of flights as the better normalizing variable for accidents or incidents. One reason is that accidents are usually concentrated in short time segments—during takeoff and landing—so normalizing by miles flown may distort the conclusion. Using this method, however, makes inter-industry comparison problematic.

All these issues mean that different experts have different opinions concerning the "objective" specification and measurement of risk. Moreover, because of the very nature of the problem, personal judgment is often necessary in the analytical and empirical assessment of flying risk, and it is by no means clear which expert opinion is more "objective" or "true" and which therefore should be used.

### 2.3.3    Public Perceptions

Even if aviation risk experts could somehow agree on an objective scientific measurement of risk, the public might not. It is the essence of democracy that we select priorities through a political process and that expert opinion cannot prevail unless it also reflects the public perception. The public in a democracy could vote to regulate the risk of ghosts in haunted houses, disregarding the unanimous expert opinion that ghosts do not exist. An economist would most probably assign the same cost to the same person dying in a car or an aircraft accident (every thing else being equal). Society, however, may perceive dying in an aircraft crash as deserving a significant premium. In this case the "objective" view, even if it were to exist, is not relevant unless the experts can educate people and change the public perception.

One of the common policy recommendations of economists in this respect is that regulatory bodies should make an effort to inform the public in order to change perceptions to conform to the evidence available. In this spirit, for example, the federal government has made accident and incident data and investigative reports widely available to the general public through the internet or other means.

### 2.3.4    Cognitive Pathology

Finally, statistical theory is only one component in the complex process of forming risk perceptions in society. Economists may tend to see the issue as a technical asymmetry, but cultural, psychological, and social factors are no less important. The question of what part of the public "misperception" is related to these issues is important, since providing "objective" information may not easily change cognitive pathology. Providing information may not necessarily solve the problem, as the public misperception is more complex and rooted in deeper cultural and psychological factors.

In this respect, it is unlikely that the volume of safety information recently made public by the regulator has changed any public perception, partly because the information is statistical and technical in nature, and disregards the way people's perceptions are formed.

## 3.   IS THE REGULATOR EMPHASIZING THE WRONG THREATS?

On December 20, 1995, an American Airlines Boeing 757 aircraft crashed near Cali, Colombia (163 fatalities). On May 11, 1996, a ValueJet McDonnell Douglas DC9 aircraft crashed into the Everglades near Miami airport (110 fatalities). On July 17, 1996, a TWA Boeing 747 aircraft crashed into the Atlantic Ocean near Long Island (230 fatalities). These three major accidents hit the US aviation industry after a relatively long period of low fatal accident rates. They involve three different aircraft types, airlines, and circumstances, but through them we can illustrate certain aspects of the intraindustry regulatory bias.

Only limited media coverage was given to the first accident, perhaps because of its location in the Andes Mountains and its marginal accessibility to television crews. The second and third accidents received unprecedented media and political attention. The TWA accident became one of the most expensive and complex fatal aircraft accident investigations in US history.

The TWA investigation concludes that the aircraft's center fuel tank exploded, although no clear evidence identifying the ignition source or the explosion cause was found. This accident triggered a major political and regulatory response relating first to the prospect of sabotage and terrorism (an initial speculation never supported by hard evidence) and later to possible fuel system and electric wiring vulnerability due to wear and tear.

The direct cause for the ValueJet accident was simpler to figure out, since the explosive materials were identified quite quickly. It appears that hazardous materials (armed aircraft oxygen-generators), which require special handling and care, were delivered by an outside vendor to the airline without the proper preparation, packaging, and identification, and were subsequently loaded into the aircraft cargo compartment. This accident triggered a strong political and regulatory response, including the grounding of the airline.

While most people heard of the ValueJet accident and the TWA accident, the American Airlines accident, which had perhaps the most important safety implications for the industry, escaped the public and political attention. Even a Florida judge's ruling that the American Airlines crew was guilty of willful misconduct, amounting to "extreme deviation from the standard of care under circumstances where the danger of likely harm was plain and obvious" received relatively little public and political attention. [135]

## 3.1  Safety Threats – A Simple Typology

People usually perceive accident causes according to abstract, general categories and relate them intuitively to flying risks by causation that makes perfect common sense, whether or not these conclusions are supported by industry practice and data. The public, in general, associates "older" aircraft and "discount-rate" airlines (traditionally using cheaper/old aircraft and believed to skimp on maintenance costs) with higher accident risks. [136]

According to a Harris poll in 1996, for example, respondents ranked poor maintenance (83%), maintenance error (78%), airplane structural fault (72%), and poor ground control (66%) as more threatening to air safety than pilot error (65%). A Roper poll suggests that 88% of a sample held that "more extensive inspections of the mechanical safety of the airplanes would be worthwhile." [137]

The public notions about safety threats do not match industry data, which attribute most fatal accidents to pilot errors. A review of the US commercial jet fleet accident data during 1987-1996 identifies cockpit crew errors as the major primary cause for hull loss accidents (69.3%). The airplane (including its structure) is identified in 9.7% of the cases, maintenance in 9.7%, and air traffic controller action in 3.2% (Boeing, 1996). 1996 Gallup polls also confirm that the public has more

---

[135] 1997 WL 664964 (S.D.Fla.). Willful misconduct is construed to be necessary for insurance liability under the Warsaw Convention.

[136] This public perception was a major reason for a strategic decision by new startup airlines to acquire new aircraft in the late 1990s (for example JetBlue). Perhaps ironically, public perception that old aircraft are more risky motivated such airlines to acquire new Airbus A320 aircraft with the worst fatal accident history.

[137] Quoted in FAA, "Aviation Safety Data Accessibility Study".

confidence in major commercial airlines than in discount and commuter airlines.[138] Industry data confirm that commuter airlines in general are more risky.[139] But there is no consensus that discount and financially distressed airlines are less safe.[140]

Table 7 identifies six general categories of accident causes. My argument is that public perception and industry strategic behavior resulted in a mismatch between the real challenges facing the industry and the regulatory priorities that were in fact selected. The regulator assigns higher priorities to issues on the right-hand side of Table 7 (discount airlines, old aircraft, and aircraft and maintenance issues mostly related to old aircraft), while in fact the major challenges facing the industry are related to the issues on the left-hand side (major airlines, new aircraft, and cockpit crew issues).

*Table 7. Accident Causes - a Simple Typology*

| Major Airlines | Discount Airlines |
|---|---|
| New Aircraft | Old Aircraft |
| Cockpit Crew Issues | Aircraft & Maintenance |

The right-hand side issues are perceived by the public and pushed by elected officials as the major safety threats on the industry agenda. The major airlines, in general, accept this view, and encourage regulatory initiatives that target these issues, since that serves their strategic interest.

It was to the advantage of the strong major airlines to encourage the public perception that a "major airline flying new aircraft is safer." They thus differentiate their product as part of their marketing strategy. It is also to the advantage of the major airlines to support regulatory initiatives focused on these issues since such regulation increases their rivals' costs, particularly those of smaller and startup airlines that can offer aggressive fare competition. The major airlines support standards-based regulation that mandates high safety costs and imposes proportionally higher maintenance costs and stricter regulatory surveillance and enforcement efforts on discount and startup airlines. Such regulations reduce the cost advantage of startup and smaller major airline competitors and raise entry cost and other barriers to entry.

The fact that the public perception suited the strategic objectives of the strong major airlines may also explain why the airlines have not initiated a major campaign to educate the public or otherwise dispel the public misperception regarding flying risk.

---

[138] FAA, "Aviation Safety Data Accessibility Study".

[139] Uniform safety standards were applied to commuter and non-commuter airlines only in the late 1990s.

[140] This assertion is difficult to verify empirically for several reasons including the fact that more regulatory efforts are focused on the discount and small airlines.

The ValueJet crash involved an old aircraft (DC9) and a discount airline; the TWA crash involved an old aircraft (Boeing 747) and a financially troubled airline; and the American Airlines crash involved a new aircraft (Boeing 757) and a strong major airline. The perception of the first two accidents was framed in terms of Table 7's right-hand side issues, and triggered aggressive political and regulatory attention, while the third accident was seen in terms of the left-hand side issues, and triggered significantly less attention.

After political pressure (allegedly from the White House too), the FAA decided to ground ValueJet. The FAA imposed no "punitive" measures against TWA due to uncertainty regarding the probable cause of its crash and the absence of evidence implicating the airline in wrongdoing. The market, however, reacted quickly, and ticket sales (and revenues) dropped significantly after the accident, inflicting with other accident-related costs severe losses on the airline. Indeed, accident-related costs are quoted as one of the major reasons for TWA's bankruptcy filing and its takeover by American Airlines.

Economists justify airline safety regulation on the presumption that markets do not transmit the proper signals necessary to induce an airline to take proper safety actions. Did the market really fail with respect to the TWA crash? Isn't the market's actual response to the crash sufficient to motivate an airline to take the necessary safety steps?

As for ValueJet, since its market entry in 1993, the public had perceived it as a small, discount-rate airline that used old aircraft. Passengers' willingness to assume a higher risk for deeply discounted fares made the airline an overnight success. After the accident, sales dropped significantly, and further discounts were necessary to induce demand.

This looks like the free market response that economists like to see. Yet the regulator grounded the airline, actually interfering with the market response, instead of leaving it to the market to figure out how much it would be willing to pay (if anything) for a ticket on a "high-risk" airline. Of course, the market response absent the regulator's intervention might have forced ValueJet to restructure or to take other steps to improve safety, or lack of business might even have shut the airline down. Alternatively, the market might also have looked for even lower fares to compensate for perceived higher risk.

For a relatively short time after the accident, the FAA defended ValueJet and stated that it operated within acceptable industry standards. Yet after facing extremely strong political criticism, the FAA changed its course and grounded the airline.[141] It subjected the airline to very rigorous inspection, and forced it to reduce its fleet size and commit to restrict its future growth before restarting operation.

One can obviously argue for or against the FAA policy regarding ValueJet. One thing, however, is clear. Its action helped the major airlines strategically by removing a competitive threat from the market, at least temporarily, and by forcing ValueJet to shut down and reenter the market with significantly higher costs and less of a competitive advantage over the major incumbent airlines. ValueJet was the

---

[141] Political criticism of the FAA with respect to this accident resulted in redefining FAA objective and other changes in the agency.

largest and most significant success of the new market entries in the early 1990s. For many, it symbolized the triumph of the free market mechanism to challenge the power of the dominant established airlines. Critics (including the Department of Justice) have argued that only startup airlines like ValueJet can challenge major hub airline fares. The FAA's supportive attitude toward the airline immediately after the accident reflected this view, but it was forced to change quite quickly thereafter as members of Congress directly blamed the FAA for the accident.

On the other side, critics of the FAA's ultimate decision to ground ValueJet have suggested that the regulator discriminated against ValueJet. Other airlines with worse-than-average safety records have not triggered such a regulatory response. An example is US Airways, which during the seven-year period prior to the ValueJet accident was involved in significantly more fatal accidents than any other single airline (five out of a total of eleven major fatal accidents). In addition, several other accidents involving mishandling of hazardous materials both before and since the ValueJet accident never triggered such a regulatory response despite a consensus that this is an area of industry-wide safety vulnerability.

The American Airlines accident involved a "mega-major" airline and a new-technology "glass-cockpit" aircraft. In fact, prior to this accident the B757 was considered one of the safer (perhaps even the safest) aircraft type in operation. It had never experienced a fatal accident since its introduction to the market more than ten years before the Cali accident. The accident involved a chain of cockpit crew errors and miscommunication with the air traffic controllers, which ended up with CFIT—the most common category of primary accident causes.

Unlike the other two accidents, this accident triggered neither a strong public and political response nor a noticeable market response. Nor did the regulatory dealings with this accident have the sense of urgency and political pressure that accompanied the other two cases.[142]

One explanation may be that because the public understands that accidents are inevitable, and perceives discount-airlines and old aircraft as the major threat to airline safety, it perhaps accepts accidents of the American Airlines kind as an inevitable cost of flying. If this is in fact the case, it is possible that neither the free market mechanism nor the regulator provides the larger major airlines the proper incentives to internalize safety efforts.

The general public perception that the "larger major airline" and "new aircraft" combination is safer may cause the market price mechanism to transmit inefficient signals to airlines in this category and pay them a safety premium that they do not deserve. In addition, in the absence of public and political pressure the regulator tends to allocate fewer resources to these safety threats than desirable. In this case information imperfections cause the market and the regulation to fail for similar reasons. Moreover, considering that the larger major airlines are more powerful vis-à-vis the regulator and the political system, it is arguable that they are not as subject

---

[142] I am by no means suggesting that the industry ignored or did not study the consequences and implement lessons from this and other CFIT accidents. My argument is one of prioritizing and related allocation of resources across regulatory initiatives.

to regulatory scrutiny and enforcement actions as the smaller airlines in proportion to their respective "real" risks.

## 3.2    What Threats Should Dominate the Regulatory Agenda?

Judging by industry statistics and experience, cockpit crew issues in general and their association with new automated technology in particular should dominate the regulatory agenda. A landmark study of the interfaces between cockpit crew and automation concludes that:

> Designers, pilots, operators, regulators and researchers do not always possess adequate knowledge and skills in certain areas related to human performance. It is of great concern to this team that investment in necessary levels of human expertise [is] being reduced in response to economic pressures when two-thirds to three-quarters of all accidents have crew error cited as a major factor (FAA, 1996, p. 3).

These issues have received less public recognition and have therefore attracted less political pressure than the "old-aircraft/discount airlines" elements. They have also not played a major role in airlines' strategic behavior, since they involve fewer rent-extracting opportunities in comparison to the other safety threats.

One of the main ways to combat human factor risks involves developing procedures and training, which usually are associated with industry-wide learning by doing, processing of information, and its internalization in institutions.[143] Activities like these with public good characteristics are often not embodied in tangible transferable products—attributes that make the appropriation of their value in market transactions quite difficult—and therefore there may not be adequate market incentives to invest in them.[144] According to standard economic wisdom, this is a market failure that calls for government intervention. Information problems and interest group structures in this case, however, cause the regulator and the industry to devote less effort to this category of threats. This is a regulatory failure substituting for a market failure.

The introduction of new-technology aircraft presents very difficult issues for the industry. While the industry and regulators have accommodated the politicians' and the public view by targeting old aircraft and their maintenance as an urgent safety threat, the major safety challenge is actually in the opposite direction: where cockpit crew and new aircraft technology interact.

The term "cockpit crew error" is considerably more complex than the mere notion that crew action (or inaction) was wrong, and deserves a more detailed discussion. It includes actions that may trigger an accident in an otherwise perfectly functioning aircraft or a reaction to a mechanical or other system malfunction that can prevent an accident (many times a combination of both). It involves personal

---

[143] Human factors are considered in the aircraft design stage. Once the aircraft is delivered for commercial operation, training and procedures are expected, among other thing, to compensate for design deficiencies.

[144] In general the market provides more incentives to develop machines than to develop procedures and engage in training.

elements, interpersonal interactions among crew members, and crew interactions with automation systems, given operational and institutional environments.

There is an inherent asymmetry in new automation technology that is challenging on numerous levels. Automation makes aircraft operation safer and considerably easier to manage most of the time. On the rare occasions when a serious breakdown occurs, however, extreme demands are imposed on the crew. Moreover, while most of the time automation reduces workload to a level where the performance of duties is almost boring, its requirements may become complex, highly encumbering, and certainly confusing during time-critical periods and crises. Dealing with new automation requires a crew to develop "split personality" skills. On the one hand, flying may become a routine mechanical and supervisory task. Yet when pilot intervention is required, flying requires complete engagement and extraordinary response.

It is this shift from a normal phase of automation control to human intervention that is most critical. Once a pilot decides to intervene (which is by no means an obvious decision), he must be aware of where the aircraft is in the flight path, what the automation has been doing, what must be done now, how to execute the desired intervention (automatically? manually?), and how the automation will respond. These are challenging decisions, requiring actions that must be completed during split seconds and often under conditions of critical time constraints, proximity to terrain, or unusual flight attitudes that demand extraordinary responses, often of a counter-intuitive nature.

The major accident prevention strategy for crew errors in general, and interaction with automation in particular, is to develop operational procedures and training. Yet there are inherent difficulties relating to the nature of automation risk that make the industry actual training efforts less than desirable. First, automated cockpit technology has a complex *mode* structure that pilots must understand and be trained to operate.[145] Since investment in training and related resources is limited, and the need for pilot intervention skills in extreme circumstances is relatively rare, most of the training focuses on "normal" automation operations. Second, flying skills are acquired in training and in an ongoing process of learning by doing during normal line operation. Given that crews have to intervene in extreme circumstances relatively rarely, normal commercial flying experience may not be enough to allow crews to develop the skills necessary for such intervention.

Consequently, pilots' crisis intervention skills are lacking. It seems a minimum regulatory target to require more extensive flight simulator and other training over crew intervention in the case of automation surprise or unusual aircraft behavior and terrain risks. The Human Factor Team, in its landmark research on this issue, concluded that the team "is very concerned about both the quality and the quantity of automation training cockpit-crew receive" (1996, p. 2).

---

[145] Mode refers in general to the manner of behavior of a system and its components.

## 4.   OLD AIRCRAFT AS A SAFETY THREAT–A CASE STUDY

The spectacular landing of a severely damaged Aloha Airlines B737-200 aircraft with a major part of its top missing (April 28, 1988, near Maui, Hawaii) ignited public and political concern over aircraft age as a major safety factor. This accident came to symbolize the risk of catastrophic structural failure due to metal fatigue.

The specific plane involved in the accident was manufactured in 1969, and had logged more flying cycles than most aircraft in commercial service. The public and politicians perceived the accident as aircraft age-related, reinforcing the intuitive notion that older aircraft are less safe to fly. Very soon an aggressive media and political attack was launched on old aircraft, based on the presumption that the older-generation aircraft are prone to accidents. A new term was born: "geriatric aircraft." Politicians reacted aggressively to the public concerns:

> In the months since Aloha, US politicians have been quick to spot an issue. Representative Tom Lewis says that the public ... is tired of tombstone technology. It is not reassuring to know that there may be other types of preventable catastrophic accidents still flying. [146]

Immediately after the Aloha accident, the manufacturers, the FAA, and the airlines launched an unprecedented and aggressive regulation initiative focusing on aircraft structural fatigue as a major safety issue. This initiative yielded a series of structural-related Airworthiness Directives (ADs) that required heavy modification, mostly to Boeing manufactured aircraft, at two thresholds: 20 years of calendar age, and a certain number of landings (cycles). Upon reaching the age thresholds, these aircraft were required to go through expensive maintenance that included replacement of certain airframe structures.

At the end of 1990, the average world fleet was nearly 12 years old, 2,050 out of 8,857 airplanes were over 20 years old, and two-thirds of the airplanes over 20 years old were being operated in the US (Boeing 1991). The US General Accounting Office estimated that between 1,400 to 4,100 airplanes in the US fleet would need to comply with these requirements at a cost of $2 billion. An initial inspection of a 727 aircraft, for example, could cost $500,000 not considering down time and other costs (Boeing 1991). At the time the regulation was issued, it was expected that most of these aircraft would be uneconomical to repair by the time they reached the landing threshold and would have to be retired.

The Aging AD was only the first stage of implementing this ambitious regulation. Parallel to this, the industry developed additional regulatory initiatives including reinspecting previous structural repairs and a corrosion prevention and repair program (CPCP) that, according to Boeing, due to its implementation cost may make older airplanes obsolete (Boeing 1991). Moreover, the same population of aircraft that was affected by the Stage III noise regulation was affected by age regulation. The targeting of these aircraft by the two regulatory initiatives was expected to make most of them too expensive to operate.

---

[146] *US News & World Report*, May 16, 1988.

*4.1    The Industry's View of Aircraft Age as a Safety Threat*

The aggressive regulation initiative that developed in response to the Aloha accident addressed metal fatigue of older aircraft structure as a major safety factor. Empirically, however, the structure of the affected aircraft was proven to be safe and not to justify such aggressive and expensive regulations. Within the industry, it was generally accepted that the empirical evidence and the industry experience did not support assigning such a high priority to efforts concentrating on metal fatigue when most aircraft crashes were known to be related to other reasons, mostly to cockpit crew errors.

Catastrophic (or uncontrolled) decompression due to structural failure was always an item on the industry's general concern agenda, but was never identified as a primary cause for an accident in the US FAR Part 121 jet fleet before the Aloha accident.[147] The industry's dominant attitude toward aircraft age can best be summarized in a few quotations:

> Given proper maintenance and inspection, airplanes can be operated indefinitely. In fact 87% of the hull loss accidents were caused primarily by other factors than the airplane itself or its maintenance ... [cockpit crew] related errors accounted for 72% of the major accidents in the l980s (Boeing, 1991, pp. 48-49).

Most aircraft fatal accidents are related to the generic category of controlled flight into terrain (CFIT), in which case the aircraft structure plays no role.[148] Furthermore, most of the accidents that are related to aircraft involve engines and landing gear failures and not structural failures.

Figure 13 and Figure 14 illustrate the industry standard analysis and presentation of primary causes of fatal accidents.[149] Figure 13 summarizes the industry's perception of the distribution of primary accident causes of the world commercial jet fleet for the 1980–1989 period, at the time the age initiative was launched. Cockpit crew mistakes accounted for more than 80% of world hull losses (72% of major accidents).

---

[147] A similar aircraft experienced a structural decompression in China in 1981. The investigation report found severe untreated corrosion damage. This aircraft, however, was not old, had flown fewer than 40.000 cycles, and was subject to significantly less stress.

[148] CFIT is defined as an event in which a mechanically normally functioning aircraft is inadvertently flown into the ground due to flight crew error.

[149] Sources: Boeing (1991) and Boeing (1996), respectively.

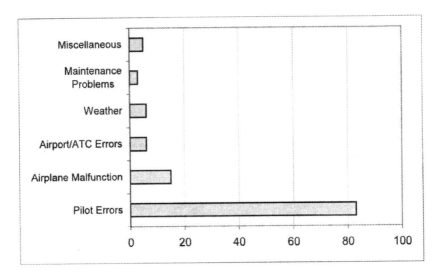

*Figure 13. Primary Causes of Major Accidents World Fleet 1980-1989*

Figure 14 classifies worldwide aircraft accidents by category for the 1988–1995 period. Most accidents (17) were identified as CFIT, which is the major cause of aircraft loss. Since the beginning of commercial flying through 1995, more than 9,000 people have died worldwide as a result of CFIT. Five US fatal aircraft crashes occurred between 1987 and 1995 due to CFIT. The second most frequent cause of fatal aircraft accident was *loss of control in flight* (16 aircraft during 1988-1995). Close to 60% of the world industry fatal accidents during the period from 1988 to 1995 are attributable to CFIT and *loss of control in flight*.

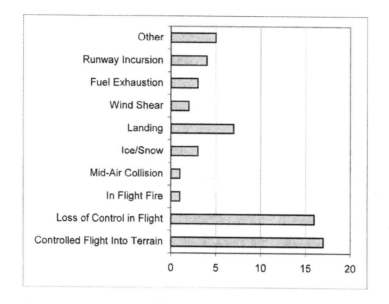

*Figure 14. Fatal Accidents By Type World Fleet 1988 -1995*

## 4.2    The NTSB Report and Major Conclusions

The industry response to the Aloha accident was immediate and unprecedented. US manufacturers, airlines, and regulators took a global leadership role in addressing aircraft metal fatigue as a major systemic safety target. By the time the final NTSB report dealing with the accident was published—more than a year after the accident occurred—an impressive age regulation initiative was already in motion.[150] The regulator and the industry pointed to the new and impressive age-related regulatory initiative, and the details of the accident investigation received only limited attention and minimal public or political exposure.

In its report, the NTSB identified the "probable cause" of the accident to be the failure of Aloha Airlines' maintenance program to detect the presence of significant disbonding and fatigue damage, which ultimately led to significant structural damage and uncontrolled decompression. Contributing factors were: 1) the failure of the airline's management to properly supervise its maintenance force, 2) failure of the FAA to properly evaluate the airline's maintenance program and failure of the airline's inspection and quality control procedures, 3) failure of the FAA to require the full extent of lap-joint inspection as was recommended by Boeing in SB 737-53A1039 in its FAA AD 97-2148, and 4) the lack of a requirement (by Boeing or the FAA) of a *terminating action* fixing production

---

[150] NTSB (July 14, 1989).

difficulties related to 737 cold-bond lap-joints, which resulted in premature fatigue cracking and poor bond durability.[151]

The accident report reveals a poor level of maintenance at every possible level. Both the airline, responsible for developing its maintenance programs and procedures and applying them, and the FAA, responsible for approving the maintenance program and practices and enforcing compliance, completely ignored the condition of the aircraft and the nature of its operation. Moreover, an alarming maintenance evaluation report written several months before the accident by Boeing and identifying major concerns with maintenance and aircraft condition was largely ignored by the airline and was not made available to the FAA prior to the accident.

The aircraft was one of four Boeing 737 aircraft operated by Aloha and among the oldest 737s in the world fleet. At 20 years old, the aircraft had accumulated the second-highest number of cycles in the world 737 fleet (close to 90,000 cycles). Aloha's 737 fleet was exposed to abnormal operational conditions, accumulating cycles at a faster rate than any other operator's (the specific aircraft had an average 2.5 cycles for each flight hour) in a harsh corrosion-prone environment ("island hopping").

These obvious safety-related factors were not reflected in the airline's FAA-approved maintenance program, which called for a 15,000-flight hour interval between major structural inspections ("D" checks)—far beyond normal industry standards—due to the high cycle-to-hour ratio applicable to the airline. Nor was there a corrosion inspection program, despite the highly corrosive environment of Aloha's operations. On top of this, the Aloha structural inspections were phased in 52 segments, which combined B, C, and D check tasks and accomplished during overnight segments. This practice implied that no thorough (daytime) evaluation of the aircraft's airworthiness condition could have been accomplished.

In general, Aloha's aircraft required above-industry average maintenance efforts, but received far less than the prevailing norm. The airline's conduct escaped the regulator's attention on two levels: first, when the FAA approved an inadequate maintenance program for use by the airline, and second, when an overworked and inexperienced FAA representative (PMI) was assigned the day-to-day job of airline surveillance and failed to notice any problem. According to the NTSB, he was not even aware of the high flight time status of the Aloha aircraft.

It is noteworthy that the NTSB concluded that the "*failure* of Aloha Airlines maintenance program to *detect*" (emphasis added) the damage that ultimately led to the catastrophic structural failure was the probable cause of the accident, and not the structural failure itself. The NTSB found the deviations from normal industry maintenance standards and practices, which were designed to detect and repair such structural damages, to be so significant as to constitute a probable cause. The NTSB viewed the accident as mainly representing a *maintenance failure* rather than an *aircraft failure*.

---

[151] The process by which two adjacent skins panels are joined longitudinally. The cold-bond procedure resulted in low bond durability, corrosion, and premature fatigue cracking, and was replaced with a more durable procedure starting with the 737 aircraft line number 292.

A disturbing illustration of the maintenance inadequacy was that the fuselage damage was severe enough to be noticed by a boarding passenger, yet the Aloha maintenance or cockpit crew did not detect it prior to takeoff. Even more disturbing, perhaps, is that the industry in general and Aloha in particular were aware of possible problems with lap-joint bonding that were directly related to a well-defined group of aircraft including this one. Boeing addressed this problem by a service bulletin (SB) issued as early as 1972 (revised in 1974) and upgraded to an Alert status in 1978. Moreover, Aloha had previously discovered in another 737 a 7.5-inch crack along the same lap-joint (S-10L) identified by the NTSB as the origin of the fuselage separation in the accident aircraft.

The NTSB report is critical of both the FAA and Boeing, suggesting an inadequate response to the lap-joint bonding problem as contributing factors. The SB issued by Boeing recommended an inspection of several locations at which the skin panel lap-joint is connected to the fuselage frame (including S-4L+R, S-10L+R, and S-I4L+R in the upper lobe). Boeing's recommendations were translated into a mandatory directive (AD87-21-08) on November 2, 1987, but the AD mandated inspection of only two locations (S-4L+R) of the six recommended by Boeing and excluded the rest (S-10L+R and S-14L+R). The NTSB identified the excluded S-10L as the origin of the skin separation in the accident aircraft. The fact that neither the FAA nor Boeing initiated a terminating action as a final fix to the problem was identified as a contributing cause as well.[152]

## 4.3   Interest Groups

The regulatory response to the Aloha accident is an interesting case study of the interlocking roles that different interests and information structures play in the regulatory process. It is instructive to look at this issue from the perspective of the major players in the regulatory process.

### 4.3.1.   The Public

The public has perceived old aircraft as a major threat. The Aloha accident and its media coverage prompted a strong and unprecedented public and political demand to identify "old" aircraft as a major item on the national airline safety agenda.

### 4.3.2   The Manufacturers

After several years of constant expansion, the rate of growth in orders started to slow down, and the number of orders for new aircraft placed with manufacturers fell significantly. The previous-generation aircraft proved to be reliable and efficient, given fuel prices at the time. Imposing expensive regulation on previous-generation aircraft was expected to accelerate their retirement and positively impact demand for the new generation of aircraft.

[152] Such termination action was mandated only after the accident.

The manufacturers also recognized that "marketing influence (i.e., public perception of older airplanes)" constitutes an important factor in demand for air travel that can impact the service life of an airplane (Boeing, 1991, p. 44).

They used this fact in their efforts to accelerate retirement of older aircraft. In addition, complying with new aging maintenance requirements provided an opportunity for the manufacturers to extract monopolistic rent. The aging AD required the purchase of parts and tools that could be supplied only by the particular (monopolistic) aircraft manufacturer.

It was clear to Boeing that a major cause of the Aloha accident was related to production difficulties of a specific group of Boeing manufactured aircraft. The NTSB report pointed a finger at Boeing in two major respects. First, the origin of the problem was related to the disbonding of lap-joints and tear straps that "originated from manufacturing difficulties" encountered with surface preparation and/or bond material processing "during the construction of the airplane" (p. 71). Second, a terminating action with respect to this problem was "neither generated by Boeing nor required by the FAA." These issues could potentially expose Boeing to liability or at a minimum to bad publicity.

Obviously it was in Boeing's interest to encourage the public perception of this accident in generic terms as aircraft age-related and not as a particular production problem. It is noteworthy that Boeing led the industry in this regulatory initiative, while its competitor MDC did not. In fact MDC age-related maintenance actions with respect to the same vintage DC9 aircraft, for example, came later, and they were significantly less rigorous and expensive compared to the Boeing requirements for 727 or 737 aircraft.

### 4.3.3    The Airlines

The post-deregulation industry had become more heterogeneous, as the financially strong airlines specialized in newer and more expensive aircraft. As a result, the financial burden of age-related regulation was expected to weigh more heavily on the weak airlines, including the new startup airlines that traditionally favored older, less expensive aircraft. The new regulatory initiative required airlines to modify aircraft that had reached 20 years of age, or else acquire new aircraft. At the time this initiative commenced, the weak airlines, including major airlines like Pan Am, Eastern, TWA, and Continental, were facing financial difficulties, and this regulation put their ability to survive further in doubt.

In addition, in the aftermath of the Aloha accident, the public came to attach an increased importance to differentiation of airlines on the basis of aircraft age, using an airline average fleet age or a specific model age as a signal for its expected safety, reliability, and comfort levels. The strong airlines responded to this public perception by placing orders for new aircraft in an attempt to differentiate their service on an aircraft age basis, thus encouraging the age regulation initiative.

The financially weak airlines were the only interest group that had an obvious incentive to inform the public regarding the industry perception of metal fatigue and age-related risks, but it was a losing battle for them to challenge the public perception. It is first of all a difficult task to change such a perception, especially when the manufacturers and the strong major airlines encouraged the public perception. Moreover, by identifying themselves publicly as "old aircraft operators," these airlines could differentiate themselves right out of the market. They had no other choice but to remain silent.

### 4.3.4    The FAA

The FAA can be viewed as a common agency, acting for several principals with diverse interests and information structures, and responding to extremely complex events in an uncertain environment characterized by information failures. The FAA was pressured by the public, by politicians, by the manufacturers, and by the major airlines to focus on age as a major target. The manufacturers and the strong airlines accommodated these public demands, and embarked on this regulatory initiative. The FAA could have either taken a position against the manufacturers, the public, and the strong major airlines, or joined them in accommodating the public will.

It is doubtful that the FAA had any incentive to take any other action than support the age regulation for several major reasons. First, it is objectively difficult to correct such public perceptions, especially in the absence of a unified position by manufacturers and airlines to do so. Obviously, the FAA would be hard pressed to suggest that such an aggressive initiative is not required in disagreement with the industry majority position. Second, if the FAA had defended the safety of old aircraft, the public might have perceived the next accident to be age-related, and the FAA would be blamed for failing to address the problem.[153] Third, initiating an ambitious age-related regulation program provides rent-extracting opportunities for the agency and industry members, along with the potential for increasing budget, personnel, and power. Fourth, it was in the FAA's best interest for the Aloha accident to be perceived as related to a generic age problem, so it could avoid criticism of its failure to prevent the accident, as was later described in the NTSB report.

It was also in the industry's and the regulator's best interest to exert control over the age regulation initiative and try to direct its outcome according to their interests. It is typical for "hot" political processes, as this one turned out to be, to have dynamics of their own. In fact, the US House of Representatives mounted harsh criticism of the FAA, and proposed legislation that would arbitrarily mandate the retirement age of aircraft. The industry and the regulator had to show the politicians major aggressive age regulation in order to preempt alternative initiatives by Congress.

---

[153] By definition, every accident that involves an aircraft that is older than the median or average aircraft age could be interpreted as an age-related accident.

## 4.4    Have Age Regulations Affected Accident Risk?

In 1990 the industry started gradually implementing new and extensive age-related maintenance. Did this regulatory initiative affect accident risk? This question can perhaps never be answered due to the absence of a statistical control group. Figure 15 may have some descriptive merit. It shows the time series of the total accident rate (both fatal and non-fatal) per 100,000 departures since 1990.[154] It is noteworthy that during this period unprecedented numbers of old aircraft were retired and new aircraft were delivered to the industry. The data cannot support a claim that implementing age regulations starting in early 1990 changed the industry accident and incident record in any noticeable manner.

A review of accident and incident data since 1990 reveals that cockpit crew error has continued to be the major primary cause for accidents and that CFIT and *loss of control in flight* account for most of the accidents. Moreover, many of these accidents involved issues of crew interface with the automated technology installed in new aircraft.

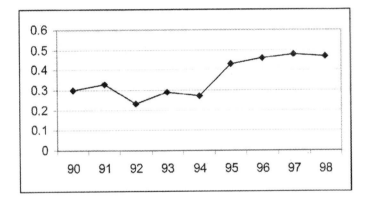

*Figure 15. Accident/100,000 Departures 1990-1998*

In addition, a major aircraft-related safety concern evolved, pointing to a possible problem in Boeing 737 aircraft rudder design. Two similar fatal accidents of 737 aircraft involving *loss of control in flight* occurred during this period (United Airlines, March 3, 1991, 25 fatalities; USAir, September 8, 1994, 132 fatalities). The first crash involved a 737-200A, the second a newer-generation 737-300, suggesting a possible problem affecting 737 families of all generations (including newest technology aircraft) that share the same general design characteristics. According to the NTSB, since the United Airlines accident in 1991, numerous cases of uncommanded roll and yaw events involving 737 aircraft have been reported.

---

[154] Source: US DOT, Bureau of Transportation Statistics; http://www.bts.gov.

## 5.  NEW AIRCRAFT AS A SAFETY THREAT

Approximately two months after the Aloha accident, in June 1988, a chartered Air France Airbus A320 crashed during a demonstration flight in an air show in Habshein, France. The A320 was one of the most advanced digital cockpit aircraft in commercial use. Besides the typical automated flight management system, it was the first in commercial application to be equipped with computerized Fly-by-Wire technology.[155]

The accident was related to problems of cockpit crew interaction with automation. Flying at low altitude, the crew engaged a digital pitch mode that provided a relatively slow thrust response to throttle movement. During the last 25 seconds of the flight, the aircraft decelerated, its pitch angle increased, and it ran out of energy. It flew into the trees and was totally destroyed by the impact and the fire that followed.

For many industry experts, this accident and not the Aloha accident epitomizes the major safety challenges of the era. It involves three major related issues: cockpit crew error, crew interaction with automation, and CFIT, issues that have dominated the industry's safety concerns starting in the 1980s. Yet while the Aloha accident attracted public scrutiny and motivated political pressure on the regulatory agencies, the A320 accident passed almost without notice by the American public.

### 5.1    Pilot Error

Pilot error has been determined to be the probable cause or a contributing cause of the majority of accidents since the beginning of the jet age. Like many casual observers, I used to interpret the generic category of "crew error" literally as an event that is related to a crew member or members taking some wrong action (or not taking the right action), mostly due to inattention, lack of discipline, or incompetence, for which it can be held responsible. This seems like a harmless interpretation at first glance—who among us doesn't make mistakes? A more careful examination of the data, however, reveals that "crew error" involves far more than meets the eye.

Pilot error cannot be viewed as independent of the aircraft and its systems or independent of the organizational and regulatory systems within which pilots operate. In fact, many of the crew error cases identified in accident and incident data relate to the manner in which pilots and automated systems interact, given institutional and operational environments. This problem has became only more complex as automation has assumed more of the pilot's traditional tasks and has become an active interfacing agent between the crew and the aircraft controls. In this respect, many pilot errors in modern airplanes can be viewed as related to deficiencies in the general design philosophy or the specific design of avionics systems.

---

[155] Aircraft control commands are transmitted digitally instead of through cables and hydraulic systems.

It is arguable that most human errors are a result of design deficiencies, because designers should assume accident-prone pilots and make sure that an "idiot proof" machine would take into account and cancel any human error. In fact, it is possible to show that all the accidents attributed to crew error could have been eliminated by an improved machine design. On the other hand, one may argue that at least a certain degree of clumsy automation is inherently inevitable, and it is the task of organizational and regulatory systems to design operational procedures, rules, guidelines, and related training to deal with automation.

While the specific allocation of accident responsibilities across crew, machines, and organizational and regulatory systems is open to debate, it is quite clear that there is a serious problem related to interaction between automation and the crew. Moreover, the regulator has an important role in setting automation standards, certifying technologies, and directing operational and safety procedures and training after such technologies are certified for commercial use.

## 5.2    Increasing Cockpit Automation

A careful review of industry data reveals an increasing rate of accidents and incidents associated with crew interaction with automated cockpit technology, paralleling the increased use of automation in aircraft cockpits commencing in the early 1970s. For example, on December 12, 1972, a TWA Boeing 707-331C aircraft crashed at John F. Kennedy Airport in New York while executing an instrument approach. The accident was associated with crew disengagement of the autopilot at sooner than the minimum authorized altitude. On December 29, 1972, the crew of an Eastern Airlines Lockheed L-1011 aircraft on its way to Miami became absorbed with a possible malfunction of landing gear, while the aircraft was in *control wheel steering mode*. The crew inadvertently disengaged Altitude-Hold and did not hear the altitude alert, and the flight ended in a fatal crash. Approximately seven months later, a Delta Airlines' DC-9-31 crashed while the cockpit crew was preoccupied with questionable flight director information.

Cockpit crew interface with automation and related accidents and incidents has gained particular importance since the early 1980s as more advanced computerized systems have appeared in new generation "glass cockpit" aircraft and as cockpit crew interaction with complex automation has increased considerably.

> Since the widespread application of automation in aviation beginning in the early 1980s, the overall accident rate has decreased slightly. However, this overall decrease masks the existence of a trend in incidents and accidents that are attributable in whole or in part to pilots' interaction with automated systems (University of Texas, 1997).

These accidents share a similar pattern:

> the pilots either do not understand what the automation is doing or do not receive adequate feedback from the automated system.[156]

---

[156] *Aviation Week &Space Technology*, January 30, 1995, p. 52.

At the same time as the American public and politicians steered regulatory initiatives targeted at old aircraft, the commercial aviation industry was struggling with adopting and adapting to the evolving cockpit technology and its special risks. And the new technology posed significant challenges to the industry with respect not only to the design of new aircraft but also to the development of new operating philosophies, procedures, standards, and adequate crew training activities in which the regulator plays an integral and crucial role.

The fatal accidents and the substantial number of incidents related to automated cockpits are related to and are a clear manifestation of joint failures in manufacturing design, regulatory body certification of such design, and the development and enforcement of adequate cockpit procedures and cockpit crew training after approval of a design for commercial use. The regulator's role is extremely important since it involves, through certification, the setting of automation-related standards during aircraft design and development stages. In addition, once an aircraft type is certified for commercial use, the regulatory body approves and controls the operational procedures and cockpit crew training practices that compensate and if necessary correct for design deficiencies.

The critical automation interface problem has developed with little public attention and with no special media or political pressure for several major reasons. In the late 1980s and the beginning of the 1990s, most fatal accidents involving crew-automation interface occurred outside the US and were not widely covered in the US media. There have been several major Airbus A320 accidents besides the 1988 accident in Habshein, France: Bangalore, India (2/14/90); Strasbourg, France (1/2/92); and Warsaw, Poland (9/14/93). In addition, an A300-600 crashed in Nagoya, Japan, in April 1994, and an A330-321 in Toulouse, France, in June 1994, and there were serious incidents with an A310 in Moscow in 1991 and an A310-300 in Paris in 1994. During the same period, the accident rate of US commercial airlines was relatively low and stable, and no high-profile automation-related fatal accident occurred to any US aircraft to attract American public attention to this issue. The crash of an American Airlines Boeing 757 in Colombia in 1995, perhaps the most significant automation-related fatal accident of a glass cockpit aircraft operated by a US carrier, could have triggered strong public and political attention but did not.

Other facts contribute to the absence of major pressures for regulatory initiatives regarding the new technology. Most automated cockpit-related accidents during the late 1980s and early 1990s involved Airbus aircraft. There was a notion that the problem was related to Airbus manufactured aircraft, which involve a somewhat different design philosophy from US manufactured aircraft. Several accidents and incidents involved A320s equipped with *fly-by-wire* technology, a technology not used by US manufacturers at the time. It was thought that perhaps the problem was more specific to this aircraft type, although the accidents were related to computer interface problems and not to *fly-by-wire* technology *per se*. It is also noteworthy that the A320 was not widely used in the US during this period.

These facts were used to suggest that the problem is manufacturer-specific, aircraft-specific, and more relevant to foreign airlines. Obviously, the US manufacturers encouraged this perception, since it provided them with a marketing edge over the European manufacturer attempting to increase its market share. This is in spite of the fact that at the same time, there was clear and ample operational evidence showing there were serious interface problems in the US as well as abroad and in all types of advanced cockpit aircraft of all manufacturers. The major indication was the accumulation of a significant number of reported incidents involving crew interaction with technology.

A survey performed by R. John Hansman of the Massachusetts Institute of Technology over the period 1990 to 1994,

> found 184 mode awareness incidents in the Aviation Safety Reporting System. In these incidents, pilots were confused for some reason about what the automation was doing.[157]

The FAA Human Factor Team, dealing with the same incident reporting system, concluded that:

> These vulnerabilities appear to exist to varying degrees across the current fleet of transport category airplanes in our study, regardless of the manufacturer, the operator or whether the accidents have occurred in a particular aircraft type (FAA, 1996, p. 24).

This body of evidence, however, was related to incident reports that did not concern fatal accidents, were not generally accessible to the public, and did not involve dramatic media coverage. Obviously, the industry had no interest in making the public aware of such a problem. On the contrary, it let the public "obsession" with "tombstone technology" used in "geriatric" aircraft dominate the regulatory agenda and serve its strategic purpose.

## 5.3    Crew Interaction with Automation

The issue of automation and crew interaction with automation and its application to aviation safety is one of the most challenging issues facing the industry. In the following I describe some of the major characteristics of the problem in somewhat more detail. This will also serve as a background for the American Airline 757-200 accident analysis.

### 5.3.1    Automation Surprise

> Automation surprises, where the automation behaves in ways the cockpit crew does not expect or understand, are a too-frequent occurrence on highly automated airplanes (FAA, 1996, p. 33).

Many accidents and incidents related to crew-automation interaction share a similar pattern that is typical to complex dynamic systems. They usually start with a triggering event that appears to be minor, and through a sequence of events—often involving misassessment and miscommunication—the situation unfolds into an incident or a full-blown accident.

---

[157] *Aviation Week & Space Technology*, January 30, 1995, p. 52

Such cases in general are history-specific (path-dependent) and thus often difficult to generalize about or predict. Most of them, however, occur because automation assumes particular manual and cognitive functions that the crew used to perform, and the crew may not be aware of what the automation is doing or that the automation may do something different from what is intended or understood by the crew.

The triggering event of the American Airlines 757 accident in 1995 appears to be the crew's input of a wrong waypoint (beacon) designator into the flight management system (FMS).[158] The pilot accepted the computer-generated default option instead of the one he intended, thus directing the aircraft in a wrong direction. Through a sequence of subsequent miscommunications (among the crew and with the Colombian air traffic control) and misassessments, the crew lost its awareness of the aircraft's location in its environment, and the plane ultimately crashed.

In two cases involving A320 aircraft (San Diego in 1990 and Strasbourg in 1992), pilots inadvertently entered angle-of-descent data while the aircraft was in vertical speed mode, causing the aircraft to descend at a rate of several thousand feet per minute (3,000 fpm instead of 3 degrees). In the first case, the pilots recovered the aircraft; the second resulted in a fatal crash short of the airfield.

In a China Airlines incident (747SP, 1985) near San Francisco, the crew did not notice the autopilot's compensation for an engine's loss of power, and when the captain disengaged the autopilot the airplane went into an unusual high-speed dive, from which it fortunately recovered.[159]

The triggering events in all of those involved unintentional or erroneous input by the crew or unnoticed automation-triggered commands that steer the aircraft in other ways than expected, creating "automation surprise." Software error contributed to the first accident[160]. In the two A320 cases faulty design of a data entry devise (hardware) contributed to the crew erroneous data input. In the last case, automation triggered an action that was unnoticed by the crew. The ability of the crew to prevent an accident in such cases is critically depending on its ability to overcome the surprise and figure out what the aircraft is actually doing.

### 5.3.2    Mode Confusion

> Complex automation interfaces, large differences in automation philosophy and implementation among different airplane types and inadequate training also contribute to deficiencies of cockpit crew understanding of automation (FAA, 1996, p. 33).

The terms "mode management," "mode awareness," and "mode confusion" dominate the discussion of the safety of automated systems in general and of aircraft

---

[158] FMS-an automated system that helps the pilot control the aircraft's lateral and vertical flight path, optimizes performance and monitors fuel.

[159] An American Eagle accident with ATR that suffered severe icing involved unexpected autopilot disconnect initiating an abrupt roll.

[160] Analyzed below.

in particular. Mode issues are a major category of problems in human-machine interaction.[161]

Aircraft automation is an extremely complex, tightly coupled modal system consisting of many subsystems and subcomponents, each with its own set of modes that are interrelated and interact with other systems' modes. The status of a system with respect to its modes including its level of automation at any given time can be viewed as a vector of all active modes. Such a vector of active modes sets the system-specific configuration and operational characteristics at any particular time. Mode switching is obtained manually, automatically, or in combination ("semi-automatically"), by direct commands or in reference to manual or machine-generated target parameters (altitude or speed, for example). Switching one mode may trigger other related mode switches, resulting in changing of the overall system configuration and operation in complex and non-obvious ways. The presence of multiple modes and different interactions of configurations creates complexity and is quite demanding on pilots' cognitive and system manipulation skills.

The human-machine interaction in a modal system is complex, non-trivial, and error-prone. The crew must know and understand how to operate the system and how the system operates. It is insufficient to know how to manipulate the interface input entry devices (a complex task by itself). It is necessary also to know what the systems and the aircraft will do in response. Besides its general proficiency and understanding of the overall system, the crew in flight must be aware of the system's mode status in *real-time* and be able to intervene if necessary or desirable. The crew must remember, understand, and master the operation of each mode, its operational characteristics, and the relationship and interaction among functions across modes. Since the system includes automated supervisory modes, the machine may automatically select and switch modes or reference parameters. Crew members must understand and notice, with the assistance of the display and enunciation devices, what the system does and continually update their real-time cognitive picture of the systems and the situation of the aircraft in relation to its operational environment.

### 5.3.3   Vertical Navigation

> There is a general consensus that these [vertical] modes are the most difficult for flight crews to fully understand (FAA, 1996, p. 33).

A classic study completed for NASA by Weiner in 1989 identifies vertical navigation as the aspect of flight least understood by pilots. In his study of 300 pilots Weiner found about 55% agreed with the statement: "In the Boeing 757 automation, there are still things that happen that surprise me." About 30% agreed with the statement: "There are still modes and features of the B757 that I don't understand." Similar results (67% and 40%, respectively) were obtained by Sarter and Woods (1992). A study by Palmer, Hutchinson, Ritter, and Van Cleemput (1993) of the

---

[161] Mode refers in general to the manner of behavior of a system and its components.

Aviation Safety Reporting System (ASRS) identifies over 8,000 altitude deviation reports over the course of one year.[162]

The Human Factor Team in both June 1996 and May 2000 reconfirms these conclusions and further concluded that while vertical modes are the most difficult for flight crew;

> Yet some operators provide very little training, if any, on the appropriate use of these modes. In these cases, pilots are expected to learn how to use the vertical modes during line operations (FAA, 1996, p. 33).

## 6. AMR FLIGHT 965–ANALYSIS OF AUTOMATION RELATED ACCIDENT

On the evening of December 20, 1995, American Airlines flight 965 originating in Miami attempted to negotiate its approach and landing at Alfonso Bonilla Argon airport at Cali, Colombia.[163] The flight left the Miami gate 34 minutes late and experienced approximately an hour and a half of additional delay on the ground before taking off.[164] On 21:29:23 the captain advised the passengers that he had begun the descent. At about 21:41:28 the aircraft crashed into the mountains north of the airport.

The recovered CVR (cockpit voice recorder) and FDR (flight data recorder) as well as debriefing of Colombian traffic controllers and recovered aircraft systems provide many clues as to what went wrong. There is plenty of material dealing with the accident data and their interpretation, from a variety of sources including: the Colombian government, American Airlines, Boeing, the pilot labor union (APA), parties to a suit in the Southern District of Florida Court and the judge's findings (later reversed on appeal), the NTSB, industry safety and training organizations, and academic researchers.

Although there is a general consensus regarding the major conditions and events that led to the accident, there are somewhat different stories that tie them together.[165] Most differences seem to relate to which element in the chain of events was more important, or distinguishing between what constitute "probable causes" and "contributing factors," or who is liable.[166] There is, however, a consensus that:

1. This was a typical CFIT accident;
2. The majority of aircraft fatal accidents have been in this category;
3. There are many cases of CFIT that do not result in an accident or reported incident due to crew intervention;

---

[162] See, for example, McCrobie, Alkin, Sherry, Feary, Polson, and Palmer (2000).

[163] The flight took off at about 18:34 and crashed at about 21:42. According to the NTSB (1994) most of the accidents reviewed (43%) occurred during afternoon and evening hours (14:00 and 21:59). More than 51% of the reviewed accidents occurred during the approach/landing phase.

[164] 55% of the accidents in the NTSB (1994) study involved flight delays.

[165] Since we will never be able to confirm the full "truth" of what happened, many interpretations are possible. My interpretation of the events is based on publicly available reports, court decisions, and related studies. I did not independently verify the accuracy of the data.

[166] Viewing an accident as a path-dependent chain of specific events makes the "probable cause" method less meaningful for safety regulation policies and instead encourages a systemic rather than a specific focus.

4. CFIT accidents are considered by the industry as preventable to a great extent;
5. CFIT accidents involve problems of vertical navigation, an aspect of flight that has been identified as the least understood by pilots;
6. Most CFIT accidents involve a combination of crew error, management of automation issues, interaction with local traffic control, and violation of operational procedures specifically designed to reduce CFIT risks; and
7. Crew training is a major CFIT prevention strategy.

One of the important clues in the cockpit voice recorder transcript is perhaps not what is in it but rather what is missing. There is no indication that during the last approximately 30 minutes of the flight the pilots performed approach review or briefing, discussed the descent checklist, or otherwise analyzed or were engaged in challenge-and-response (either between the pilots or with the controller) of the approach path and related operational strategies.[167]

Several errors and crew confusion occurring during the last several minutes of the flight seem to be related to inadequate preparation prior to commencing the descent. This is particularly critical in the particular CFIT-prone, operational environment the crew faced, specifically: 1) nighttime approach; 2) terrain-critical airport; 3) instrument approach with no supporting ground radar vector;[168] and 4) a foreign country with non-native English speakers as air traffic controllers.

The Cali airport is located in a valley approximately 43 miles long and 12 miles wide. The published approach path starts at the Tulua VOR and goes generally southbound over the valley; the terrain rises steeply to 13,000 feet to the east and over 6,000 feet to the west. Under these conditions, following the published approach path and maintaining situational (especially terrain) awareness is critical.

Descent review and briefing is a standard procedure, intended, among other things, to help the crew create a mental model of the flight path and the operational environment.[169] During such reviews and briefings, the crew develops a common understanding and a frame of reference that facilitates inter-crew communication and communication with the local controllers as well as a situational awareness that is required if changes in the flight plan or intervention with the automation become necessary.

New glass cockpit technology has full mission automation capabilities that allow one to fly a plane by learning to push the right buttons. Most of the time the crew's role is largely supervisory. The problem is that unanticipated events or changes in the original plan require very high cognitive and flying skills including full aircraft system mode and flight path awareness. While automation significantly reduces crew workload most of the time, it increases workload at time-critical points. The disparity between the normal crew supervisory role and the extraordinary demands

---

[167] The programming of the published flight plan into the FMS may suggest that a briefing was conducted before, but there is no indication in the CVR transcript (including the time after the change in the original plan) that this occurred.

[168] The radar was blown up in a local terrorist action.

[169] According to the NTSB (1994) most primary crew errors (73%), involve lack of adherence to procedures.

imposed on a crew at critical times is quite dramatic. Flight path review and briefing, check list challenge-and-response, monitoring of navigation charts and displays, and related procedures and training must be practiced constantly in order for a crew to be ready and fully alert to intervene if intervention is called for.

In the Cali flight, a series of apparent errors and communication problems between the crew and the local controller occurred during the last stages of the flight. Language and cultural aspects have been singled out as a core problem in analysis of this case. The problems seem also to a large extent related to the crew's inadequate preparation for the approach and insufficient flight path awareness. In particular, one may infer from the CVR transcript that the crew did not recognize or otherwise ignored the importance of flying over Tulua for a safe approach and landing at Cali.

The beginning of the problems in communication between the crew and the controller can be traced to failure of the Bogota controller to inform the Cali controller that the flight was proceeding in a direct route to Tulua VOR. Later, the crew did not follow standard procedures in its first contact with the Cali control at 21:34:44 and did not restate the last position report. Instead, the crew stated only its altitude, which confused the controller. According to the controller, since the crew did not state its route clearance, he cleared the flight at 21:34:59 to Cali VOR and requested "...report, uh, Tulua." The captain confirmed, and stated "direct Tulua." Certain analysts suggest that the use of the words "report ...Tulua" (as opposed to "via Tulua") and the different interpretation of the term "direct" in Spanish created ambiguity. The crew apparently interpreted the exchange with the controller as clearance to fly directly to the Cali VOR without flying over Tulua and starting an ILS approach there. The captain reacted to this exchange immediately by executing a FMS (flight management system) turn toward the Cali VOR, ignoring the required procedure to start the approach from Tulua.[170]

The chain of events so far, although involving errors, misunderstandings, and violations of normal procedures, was not sufficient to cause an accident. One of the consequences of executing the Cali clearance became quite important to the crew later on. Execution of the *direct to* mode on the FMS erased the reference to Tulua (ULQ) from the active database eliminating easy access to this information when it would have been useful later.[171] FMS approach changes usually require a number of keystrokes and are time-consuming (including computer response time); they cannot be properly accomplished in a time-critical environment without work overload. It is an inherent paradox that while the new automated flight system relieves pilots of significant workload in general, it also requires complex and time-consuming procedures if the crew wants to intervene or is forced to intervene, especially during time-critical operational stages such as approach or takeoff.

---

[170] The first officer was the flying pilot. The captain's action violated several operational procedures: He executed the new beacon information before the clearance was read back to the controller, he did not challenge the controller's ambiguous clearance, and he did not wait for the flying pilot's confirmation and advised him about the change only after it was executed.

[171] Selection of Heading Select allows manual steering of the aircraft and disengages the fully automated lateral navigation mode. *Direct to* mode highlights the active destination waypoint but removes the non-active ones from the FMC display.

At 21:36:31 the Cali controller asked the crew to consider an amended direct approach, eliminating the need to execute a 180-degree turn before landing. This change did not require or imply any change in the published approach path toward Cali. Under pressure (perhaps because the flight had already been delayed), the crew accepted this offer quickly, and apparently without the proper analysis as to whether such a deviation was advisable and, if so, how it should be executed. Because the Tulua waypoint was not readily displayable on the FMS, necessary calculations were rather complex and in fact would have required more time than the crew took to confirm acceptance of the route change, which further suggests that the crew accepted this change automatically and without challenge.

According to post-accident calculations, it appears that the aircraft was too high, too close to the runway, and going too fast to execute such a landing. The crew was too quick to accept the change, and the controller too quick to confirm the clearance without stating an altitude restriction as required by normal procedures. By accepting the change in the original flight plan at this point, the crew forced itself into an almost impossible workload within a very limited period.

Attempting to execute the new approach, at 21:36:40, the captain requested a lower altitude clearance from the controller.[172] The controller, consistently assuming the aircraft was flying in the normal published path, and expecting to be informed once it flew over Tulua, cleared the amended approach (but not the altitude) and repeated once again: "Report Tulua VOR." When the captain repeated the clearance wording as required, he stated "... will report the VOR...." The controller corrected him: "Report, uh, Tulua VOR." Despite a controller's clearance that was different from that expected by the crew, and no clearance to a lower altitude, the crew did not challenge the clearance, or try to clear up the apparent ambiguity with the controller. At that point, passing 17,358 feet in altitude, speed-brakes were deployed.

At 21:37:29 the captain requested a non-standard clearance to fly directly to the Rozo waypoint. This request violated the normal procedure for an instrument approach, which required flying over Tulua in order to safely descend over the valley leading to the airport. Remember also there was no ground radar in operation. Such a request may suggest, again, that the captain was not aware of where the plane was in the flight path and operational environment. The controller interpreted this request within the context of using the normal published path starting over Tulua, and in fact repeated his "report Tulua" statement during the exchanges that followed. The captain interpreted the communication as clearance to fly directly to Rozo, and executed accordingly.

The crew apparently understood, or otherwise acted as if it were cleared to a 5,000 foot altitude, in spite of: 1) operational procedures mandating maintenance of the last assigned altitude when operating on an unpublished route; 2) no lower altitude cleared by the controller; and 3) the fact that descent under 15,000 feet required flying over Tulua. Moreover, the plane descended from 15,000 feet without informing the controller regarding the descent (and the controller merely understood that the crew did not "report Tulua" yet). It is particularly notable that the crew did

---

[172] The last (and only) low altitude clearance was given by Cali control at 22:34:47 to 15,000 feet.

not adhere to the American Airlines procedures for operating in this area, which state, for example: "Do not request or accept direct clearance which results in off-airway flying" and "the only safe place to descend below MEA ... is in a published holding pattern."[173]

At approximately 21:37:42 (altitude 16,880) the captain, intending to direct the aircraft toward Rozo, entered what he thought was the Rozo identifier letter "R" from his charts into the FMS. The computer responded by suggesting two pages of NDB identifiers from the navigational database, listing "Romeo," the Bogota beacon, first, and not listing beacons for Rozo.[174] At that point, the captain quickly selected the first option without verifying the coordinates. He apparently ignored the computer display of a modified "provisional" path showing the aircraft's direction more than 90 degrees eastbound into the mountains.[175] The captain neither confirmed the change nor advised the flying pilot of it before executing the command, which surely contributed to the flying pilot's confusion regarding what the aircraft was doing.[176]

The legal battle surrounding this accident is an interesting case study of the legal, political, and public tendency to interpret accidents in black-and-white rather than as complex interacting systems. The legal system above all (and the general public too) usually demands a single "beyond a reasonable doubt" entity to be found liable or to be responsible for an accident. The judge singled out the crew as the responsible target, assigning only marginal importance to the systemic issues of automation and institutional- and regulation-related aspects (he was reversed on appeal). A federal jury hearing an American Airlines lawsuit against the FMS manufacturer, Honeywell Air Transport Systems, and Jeppesen, which supplied the conflicting navigational databases, decided to make these companies liable. Focusing on a probable cause in the legal process tends to divert attention from problems in the system as a whole. It is quite simple to blame a single crew or a software supplier of negligence; it is perhaps even advisable, in the sense that judgments may provide economic incentives to manufacturers and operators regarding desired standards of care. The problem is that aviation safety involves a complex system of built-in overlaps and redundancies and that systems themselves must assume that such mistakes occur and find ways to prevent them from becoming accidents. Effective regulation requires focusing on and fixing the system as a whole, including inadequate regulation, aircraft design philosophies, training, and so on. The judicial

---

[173] 1997 WL 664964 (S.D.Fla.), pp. 8–9. The American Airlines manuals include numerous specific warnings and detailed procedures in anticipation of CFIT of exactly this type. They warn the pilots, among other things, not to automatically accept ATC statements and to challenge their instructions, and exercise special caution regarding situational awareness: "The most important factor, however, is you. You must know what is going on and where you are" (p. 7).

[174] Several inconsistencies between the navigation charts and the computer databases contributed to the confusion. The most significant one is that the chart used [R 247] to refer to both the "Romeo" (Bogota) and the "Rozo" (Cali) beacons. Executing Romeo in the FMS required only "R," but executing "Rozo" required spelling out "Rozo."

[175] The computer shows the new suggested path on a map (visual) display, before it is finally selected, allowing the operator to confirm the provisional path direction with his intended one.

[176] Since one pilot executes the FMS changes, it is a normal rule for him to clear such changes with the flying pilot.

system in its focus on liability and not on prevention targets only elements of the system. In fact, the need to defend against liability and to preserve legal rights may interfere with prevention activities in the industry.

It took the crew over a minute and a half to detect the wrong direction. This is a long time in this context, particularly with numerous clues and indications that the aircraft was flying in the wrong (and dangerous) direction. At that point, the aircraft was at approximately 13,500 feet and a heading of 100 degrees (roughly 90 degrees off course). A series of exchanges among the crew suggest that they had lost their situational awareness and were confused. "Heading select" mode was engaged, and the airplane rolled out of the left turn and began a right turn. After approximately 19 seconds, the ULQ (Tulua) identifier was executed, and the aircraft rolled out of the right turn and began a turn to the left. A 20-degree bank-turn to the right (unknown *heading select* but probably in the Rozo direction) followed, as well as autopilot vertical speed mode selection (for unknown reasons). One of the crew then entered "R" (the Bogota beacon) into the FMS but the heading was not executed so that ULQ (Tulua) remained the active waypoint. The CVR transcript shows clear signs of confusion (21:38:49 "Uh, where are we...." 21:38:58 "...Yeah, where we headed?").

The confusion we find on the CVR, although certainly alarming in this incident, is still not a necessary condition for a flight to crash. Normal operating procedures anticipate such circumstances, and pilots are instructed to immediately discontinue descending. Crews are trained to abort such a descent, especially during night-time, above high terrain, and with no ground radar support.[177] The American Airlines Flight Manual unequivocally requires that once an aircraft is off the published approach path the pilot should not descend below the last assigned altitude. Nevertheless, between the time the captain executed the left turn toward Romeo (the wrong beacon) and the time the aircraft was turned right, it dropped over 5,000 feet. During the approximately four minutes that the aircraft was off-course, the crew continued their descent from an altitude of just under 17,000 to almost 8,000 feet without interrupting it. In fact the pilots never discontinued their descent until the GPWS (ground proximity warning system) alarm went off, even though the aircraft was off-course and the crew seemed confused.

The Florida judge grounded his decision that the crew acted in reckless disregard on this point, finding that:

> no reasonable juror, presented with the record before this court, could find the pilot's decision to continue the aircraft's descent despite being significantly off course at night in an area known for dangerous terrain did not constitute the intentional performance of an act with knowledge that the ... act will probably result in injury or damage.

The GPWS is the final element in a complex system of redundancies that is expected to prevent a normally functioning aircraft from flying into terrain. It is designed to alert the crew approximately 30 seconds before expected impact, a time period that is generally sufficient for the crew to perform an escape maneuver and recover the aircraft. At approximately 21:41:15 (altitude approximately 8,480) the

---

[177] It is not clear if the crew realized that radar coverage was not available during the last few minutes of the flight.

GPWS alert sounded ("Terrain, terrain, whoop, whoop, pull up..."). In response to the alarm, the crew disconnected the autopilot and quickly conducted the escape maneuver. At approximately 21:41:28, the aircraft crashed into the mountains.

Post-accident investigation suggests that the crew left the auto-throttle engaged during the escape maneuver.[178] In addition, the speed-brakes were deployed.[179] In the absence of a visual angle-of-attack indicator, the pilot responded to the stick-shaker, which alerts the crew before a stall, and therefore could not maintain maximum aircraft climb. The aircraft thus could not achieve maximum escape performance.

Accidents and incidents related to the modern aircraft cockpit share a similar general pattern that is typical to complex dynamic systems. They usually start with a triggering event that appears to be minor. Then, through a sequence of events often involving misassessments and miscommunications, the situation develops into an incident or an accident. In hindsight, crew actions often look surprising, and a post-mortem investigator finds it hard to understand how the crew could have missed the handwriting on the wall. The fact of the matter is that the situation was not so obvious to the crew.

Why didn't the American Airlines crew understand what was happening? Why didn't it react in the expected way? They did what was different from normal procedures or different from what was "reasonably" expected in two major ways. First, they continued to use automation-assisted navigation, although it had become confusing and very demanding during a heavy workload stage of the flight. Second, despite being confused and lacking situational awareness, they did not discontinue their descent. It seems obvious that the crew should have reverted to basic radio navigation and discontinued the descent. This is what the design philosophy of the automation assumes and what the operational procedures require. The pilots, however, like other crews before them (and unfortunately crews to come), discontinued neither the automation nor the descent.[180] Instead, they continued to try to resolve their situational confusion using confusing automation–or perhaps they were not aware that they were so confused.

The fact that such crew behavior is by no means unique must raise major red flags about pilot training, design of new technologies and procedures, and their approval and certification by the regulator. Finding pilots or airlines or database manufacturers, or all of them, liable does not address the major safety challenges inherent in the new technology. Instead, it masks them.

---

[178] Automatically adjusting power for climb, cruise, descent, or approach according to computer or manual input. When this mode was engaged, the engines could not reach full thrust prior to impact.

[179] Movable panels on the top portion of the wing that by increasing drag slow the aircraft down and increase decent rate, operated manually.

[180] A 1994 crash of a China Air A300-600 is a tragic example of this principle. The crew was trying to stay on glide slope and land, while the autopilot was engaged in *go around* mode and controlled the aircraft in the other direction. The crew struggled ((literally) with the autopilot for control over their aircraft, but did not push the autopilot disconnect button.

PART 3

# COMPETITION

# CHAPTER 7

# YIELD MANAGEMENT

> I believe that yield management is the single most important
> technical development in transportation management since we
> entered the era of airline deregulation in 1979.[181]

American Airlines' experimentation with *supersaver fares* at the end of the 1970s marks the beginning of yield management (also called revenue or seat inventory management). After the CAB eased its regulation of public charter airlines, the charters enjoyed a significantly lower cost structure, and the major airlines, particularly American, came to view them as a serious threat. How could American—notorious for its high cost structure—cut costs or otherwise produce seats at such a low cost level?

As it thought about dealing with this threat, American's management realized that in fact it was already producing seats that could be sold at a negligible cost. The load factor under the CAB rate regulation was roughly 50%; aircraft in fact were flying half-empty.

> If we could figure out a way to sell those empty seats at the prices the charter guys
> proposed, thought [American's CEO Robert] Crandall, we would make a lot of
> dough.[182]

American's solution was capacity-controlled, restricted, discounted fares. The objective was to keep the high-paying traffic at its current level while selling the otherwise empty seats at a discount. This still reflects the major challenge of revenue management today; *sell as many seats as possible at full fare, and then fill otherwise empty seats with discount fares that exceed your variable cost.*

This story illustrates the essence of revenue management. Seats are produced in the aggregate, in bulk, but sold separately. Production cost is mostly fixed, and high compared to a small incremental cost. Capacity is largely fixed, and determined ex-ante, and demand is uncertain and fluctuating. Seats are perishable—once the aircraft leaves the gate, all unsold seats are gone forever. Passengers are heterogeneous and can be segmented into at least two groups on the basis of their demand elasticity; that is, certain groups are ready to pay more than other groups for the same trip. The airlines' problem is to segment the groups and sell seats at the corresponding prices while eliminating inter-group arbitrage or the possibility that high-paying passengers will cross the group lines to buy at the discount fare

---

[181] Robert Crandal, quoted in Davis (1994).

[182] Robert Crandal, quoted in Cross (1995, p. 446).

(*fencing*). Revenue management deals mainly with segmentation, fencing, and rationing the availability of seats over time.

American's idea at the time was to sell seats that otherwise would remain empty at discounted fares to people who otherwise would not fly. It first used a 21-day advance purchase restriction as a sorting device for segmenting the market, and initially applied a booking limit of 30% for discount tickets across the board.

The airline quickly learned two major lessons. First, demand patterns differ across flights, so different rationing rules should be applied for different flights according to the specific markets served. This spurred a significant trend of focusing attention on estimating demand behavior on a disaggregated basis. Second, it is not simple to decide in advance how many discount tickets to sell. A balance must be struck between the benefit of selling a discount fare ticket today—and by so doing eliminate a potential empty seat in the future (*spoilage*)—and the opportunity cost of eliminating a potential sale to a high-fare paying customer in the future (*displacement cost*).[183]

This trade-off is the core challenge of revenue management. Ideally an airline would book its tickets and fill an airplane with the high fare-payers first. High-paying passengers, however, tend to appear last, and there is uncertainty regarding whether and when they may appear.

Yield management has come a long way since the introduction of the *supersavers* in 1977. American Airlines would use its accumulated experience and increasing computer power strategically in 1985 in response to competition by People's Express. The *ultimate supersaver* fares American introduced at that time required a 21 days' advance purchase but otherwise were priced lower than or the same as seats offered by People's Express. And indeed, People's Express's founder and chair attributed the financial difficulties and the ultimate failure of his airline to American's pricing strategy.

Approximately ten years later with far greater computing power and better analytical tools at his disposal, Robert Crandall—the industry's leader of revenue management—said: "we expect yield management to generate at least $500 million annually for the foreseeable future."[184]

Revenue management became a hot topic in academic and business circles starting in the 1980s. Both academic publications and general interest in this issue have exploded.[185] Collaboration among academic researchers, airlines, consulting firms, and other organizations attempting to develop and profit from this new area has grown dramatically.[186] Any major airline around the world without a revenue management department established one; all the airlines gradually increased their

---

[183] Displacement cost is usually defined as the opportunity cost of booking a seat including all future revenues that may be lost if the booking is accepted.

[184] Crandall is quoted in Davis (1994).

[185] For a literature summary, see, for example: McGill and Ryzin (1999), and Boyd and Bilegam (2003). For an industry perspective, see, for example, *Handbook of Airline Economics* (1995), Section 6.

[186] AGIFORS was established in the early 1960s as a professional society dedicated to the advancement and application of *operational research* within the airline industry. Its contribution to an active interaction between academicians and practitioners on revenue management issues has been remarkable.

computing power, analytical sophistication, and the complexity of their revenue management strategy and decision tools.

Yield management has been widely perceived as a unique success story in which academic concepts of economics, operating research, and computer information science became implemented by industry, and were believed to have directly contributed to a dramatic increase in profits. Other observers, however, see the focus on extracting increasing prices from the group of higher fare-payers—rather than focusing on cost-cutting—as the culprit in the breakdown of the major airlines' strategic model in the early 2000s.

In this chapter on airlines' pricing strategy, I first examine revenue management techniques—what the airlines do, and how they do it. In the second section I review economic concepts of price discrimination and their contribution to an understanding of airlines' practices and their welfare and antitrust implications. Finally, I examine the overall outcome of this strategy.

## 1. REVENUE MANAGEMENT METHODS

Revenue management consists of three major components: 1) product design (or versioning); 2) pricing; and 3) seat inventory allocation. *Product design* specifies a set of service characteristics (flight dates, weekend stayover, and other return flight requirements), purchase restrictions (7, 14, 21 days' or longer advance purchase requirements), cancellation options (refunds, rescheduling penalties), and channels of distribution (direct, travel agent, internet). A certain combination of purchase restrictions, cancellation options, and channels of distribution are grouped to create "products" or price categories (or classes). *Pricing* involves assigning a price to every category defined in the product design stage. Full fare is assigned to tickets with minimal strings attached. Product design and pricing occur ex-ante and are usually rigid (although sometimes they may be changed over time).

*Seat inventory allocation* involves continuing real-time allocation of the available seat capacity over the price categories that are determined in the pricing stage. Yield management models focus on seat inventory allocation, treating the product categories and the particular prices as given.[187]

### 1.1 Expected Marginal Seat Revenue

The publication of Peter Belobaba's Ph.D. dissertation in 1987 is often seen as an important milestone in the evolution of revenue management. Belobaba extended an earlier attempt by Littlewood (1972) of BOAC to figure out an optimal *booking limit* for a simple two-class fare structure. Belobaba's *expected marginal seat revenue*

---

[187] *Revenue management* and *dynamic pricing* are two related theoretical approaches to revenue maximization. The first deals with seat allocation given exogenous prices for fare classes. The second deals with price setting over time given fixed capacity and random demand. Airline pricing strategy is usually dealt with from the first perspective, but real application involves aspects of both views. For a theoretical analysis of dynamic pricing see, for example, Maglaras and Meissner (2004).

(EMSR) idea follows standard concepts of the optimal allocation of limited resources among a variety of uses by comparing the expected cost to the relevant benefit at the margin. The airlines' problem neatly fits into the familiar so-called news-vendor problem—a basic textbook optimization model.

Assume for simplicity two groups of potential passengers: business and leisure. Members of the first group are ready to pay more for the same seat, but make their bookings closer to the departure date in a way that may be summarized by a certain probability distribution function that the airline is able to estimate (or otherwise knows). The airline can fill the aircraft quickly by selling discount tickets to the second group far ahead of time. It can also set booking limits for advance ticketing in order to protect seats for future full-fare business travelers. Selling a discount ticket today implies giving up the opportunity that a business traveler may purchase this seat as the departure date approaches.

The airlines' problem may be described as deciding (ex-ante) how many seats to protect for future high-fare payers (or its corollary, how many low-fare seats to sell). A standard textbook optimization solution suggests selling an incremental seat as long as its revenue value is higher than its expected displacement cost.

## 1.2    Flight Leg Control

As the concept revenue management evolved, the airlines translated it into an enormously large and complex, sometimes dynamically amended, mathematical programming problem. Traditional academic research and business applications focused on optimal allocation of seat inventory among several *fare classes* over a given *flight leg* (a single takeoff and landing). The two-fare class problem illustrated above was expanded first to treat multiple fare classes (airlines usually have the capability of using 5 to 26 classes).[188]

Fare classes (or products), associated with predetermined advance purchase cancellation options and other restrictions, serve as a major inventory control item. Current revenue management systems do not attempt full assessment of each seat-booking request in real time. Instead, control is usually obtained through opening or closing of fare classes (sometimes called *buckets*). The decision variable is therefore which of the fare classes should be made open for sale at any particular time. Fare classes are often *serially nested*—so that a lower-fare class will not be available for booking if a higher-fare class is closed (corollary: if seats are available at a lower-fare class they will also be available at a higher-fare class). Nesting may also be *parallel*—so that two or more classes may be concurrently open for special promotion or bulk wholesaler fare deals—or *mixed,* or changing over time.

Most mathematical formulations of the revenue maximization problem assume serially nested fare classes, a sequential booking pattern (i.e., higher-paying passengers appear later in time), and statistically independent demand for each fare

---

[188] For example: first, business, and coach classes, where the latter class is subdivided into Y—full fare— and B, M, Q, V, and T—different levels of discount.

class.[189] In practice, airlines use a large database available on their computerized reservation system to study and estimate the distribution of demand for each fare class of a leg in order to estimate the optimal level of overbooking and expected displacement cost.[190]

## 1.3    Network Optimization

Augmented computing capabilities and greater sophistication of the reservation system and an increasing concentration and integration of the hub-and-spoke network system in the late 1980s and early 1990s focused attention on the network system aspects of the problem. First attempts in partial consideration of the network aspects used *flight segment* rather than *flight leg* controls. This approach considered multi-leg itineraries as long as the flight was direct and didn't involve connections between different flights. Later attempts used itinerary (or origin-and-destination) controls, which consider network-wide effects of closing an itinerary.[191]

Consider, for example, a passenger wishing to travel from A through B to C. With a single-leg inventory control, each of the AB and AC legs is optimized separately and independently. A passenger can be rejected on the AB leg because another one-leg passenger is ready to pay more for this leg, even if the combined ABC itinerary is expected to generate more revenue for the network if the legs are sold together. This is an important issue since, for example, roughly two-thirds of passengers flying to a major hub connect to other flights. Therefore, booking a reservation transaction in a leg that connects a spoke with a hub may eliminate many potential itinerary combinations.

Looking at the analytical optimization concept from a network perspective does not change the major principle: Accept an itinerary request (network path) if its net value is higher than its expected displacement cost. Implementation, however, is anything but simple.

What is the expected replacement cost of closing a seat in a requested itinerary? Any requested itinerary may be composed of more than one leg and include landing in a hub or otherwise using connecting flights. Closing a seat may eliminate many combinations of possible other itineraries with different expected values. Rejecting a request may generate an amended itinerary by the same passenger of different leg combinations. A full analysis must consider all possible future realizations of the reservation process that are influenced by changing the availability of any of the seats on any of the network's legs.

This is an immensely complex problem in a large network since closing a seat may displace potential bookings with subsequent impacts of their own. And, a return flight component with further network effects is often involved. Also, rejecting a

---

[189] For a possible formulation of this problem with concurrent demand for different classes see, for example, Zhao and Zheng (2001).

[190] Belobaba's formulation is optimal only in a two-fare booking structure. The so-called EMSRb method is an extension of his idea and provides optimal booking limits for single-leg multiple-fare cases. See, for example, McGill and Van Ryzin (1999).

[191] I use the terms itinerary and origin destination (OD) interchangeably.

reservation request may result in a passenger buying up (paying more) or buying down (paying less) in the same network or buying from a competing network, and this often involves goodwill cost. Each one of these responses has different and non-obvious expected costs. Assessment of expected displacement cost must also allow for the dynamics of cancellations, overbooking, and the expected cost of oversold conditions.

Controlling seat inventory by itinerary requires a simultaneous network optimization model that captures all traffic interactions in the network. The objective is to find the seat allocation that maximizes the total expected revenue of the network, subject to capacity constraints on the various legs. The mathematical programming formulation must capture the combinatorial aspects of the network and the specific demand for every leg. The airline's objective function depends on demand distributions; it is not linear or continuous, which makes the size of the problem and its mathematical solution problematical.

Several approaches have been developed in order to overcome this condition and approximate optimal allocation solutions. The various methods yield theoretically optimal solutions only under narrow assumptions or are otherwise only asymptotically optimal. Nevertheless, simulation testing shows the network methods produce better results over the leg-controlled methods. In general, the literature and techniques implemented by airlines for flight leg optimization are in agreement and largely uniform. The network optimization literature, however, is diverse, and several different techniques for network optimization are available and in use by different airlines.

American Airlines developed one approach to approximating network effects starting in the late 1980s that has become widely used. This so-called *virtual nesting* control method was a response to the limited number of controllable booking classes provided in fact by the computerized reservation system. The essence of the approach is that the various origin-and-destination itineraries that flow over a certain flight leg are clustered into a manageable number of (usually six to eight) booking classes (*buckets*) based on value. Subsequently, serially nested buckets (rather than fare classes that flow over a leg) are used to control booking. Various methods are available for clustering (or indexing) the itineraries into buckets of similar approximate value contribution to the network.

A newer method that is gaining popularity is called *bid-price* control (or *continuous nesting*). In this method, threshold values (bid prices) are assigned to each leg of the network, and a requested itinerary is sold only if its fare exceeds the sum of the bid prices of the legs that make up the itinerary. The bid price reflects the displacement or opportunity cost of booking (closing) a seat of a certain leg. The shadow (dual) prices of the capacity constraint in a linear programming formulation of the (non-linear) optimization model are used to obtain near-optimal bid prices.

## 2.   WHAT CAN WE LEARN FROM ECONOMIC THEORY?

Traditional economics divides markets into two major conceptual structures: perfect competition, and monopoly. Under perfect competition, firms cannot affect market prices and are forced to price their homogeneous products at a level that equates marginal cost to consumers' marginal willingness to purchase. In this case, the market dictates a uniform equilibrium price level and makes price discrimination impossible.[192] Products will be priced differently only if they require different direct costs of producing or supplying them. For example, it is expected that a business class seat may be more expensive than a tourist class seat since it involves a higher marginal production cost. Two similar tourist class seats may be priced differently if one is purchased through the internet and an electronic ticket is issued, and the second is not.

Price discrimination with regard to a similar product, absent direct cost differentials, is possible under the assumptions that characterize a monopoly. In this case, the firm possesses market power and sets prices according to demand characteristics and not necessarily on the basis of marginal cost.

This traditional dichotomy of market structures in economics directly associates price discrimination with monopolistic power and its potential inefficiencies. It is on this basis that certain observers claim the airlines' use of revenue management techniques to discriminate prices is by itself a manifestation of their market power and reason enough for government intervention.

It is worth remarking that, while price discrimination is often associated with monopolistic inefficiencies and perceived as unfair—especially in a society that is suspicious of large corporations and reveres fairness and non-discriminatory institutions—it elicits a far more positive response from many economists, who often argue that under certain conditions, price discrimination is more desirable for society than uniform pricing. Moreover, it is debatable whether charging all passengers a uniform price per ticket—which may be perceived fair by some people—is necessarily any more fair than charging passengers according to the specific value they assign to a trip.

Interestingly, while price discrimination by airlines has become a high-profile political issue and a target of widespread criticism, it is in fact quite common throughout the economy. We pay different prices for lunch and dinner; hard cover and soft cover books; peak and off-peak railroad tickets; business and home computers, software applications or telephone use; magazines at the newsstand and by subscription. There are student, senior citizen, labor union, and other organization as well as volume-based and advance purchase discounts. We can self-select whether we pay for a rental car (or a cellular telephone) at a fixed price or on the basis of usage or a combination of the two.

## 2.1 Perfect Price Discrimination

Economists usually distinguish among three major theoretical categories of price discrimination. In addition to analytical convenience, this distinction is quite helpful

---

[192] Firms in this setup are said not to have market power and to behave as price takers. Price discrimination usually refers to charging different prices for homogeneous products on the basis of demand elasticity and not on marginal cost differences.

for interpreting real-life observations of airlines behavior and its possible welfare implications.

A perfect (*first-degree*) discriminating monopolist knows how much the next passenger is willing to pay for a ticket and charges him or her accordingly. It can directly identify and sell each unit of its product to a buyer who is the most willing to pay the highest price, and fully extract *consumers' surplus*.

Note that the perfect competition and perfect discriminating monopoly models provide two theoretically efficient solutions as far as production goes. In both cases, the marginal buyer pays the marginal cost. In the first case, there is a uniform price at the marginal cost level, and consumers keep their surplus. In the second case, every buyer pays a different price according to willingness to pay, and the producer keeps all the surplus.

Information and transaction costs necessary for implementing direct individual discrimination in practice, however, are usually assumed to preclude real-market implementation of first-degree discrimination either by a regulator or a monopolist, so we relegate this notion largely to textbook exercises.

### 2.2    Imperfect Price Discrimination

Selling to each customer at the customer's specific level of willingness to pay is perhaps an unrealistic scenario. But what if the monopoly could segment the market by major groups of buyers rather than the specific individuals that compose it?

#### 2.2.1    Direct Discrimination

*Third-degree* price discrimination describes a firm discriminating interpersonally and directly, so that prices vary across distinct and verifiable consumer groups. The firm is assumed to be able to identify, segment, and fence consumer groups on the basis of their known demand functions. Location-based, senior citizen, student, and other verifiable group discounts are examples. This type of discrimination requires less information than the perfect discrimination alternative, yet the firm must know the demand characteristics of each group.

Is this type of pricing behavior desirable? According to economists, it is surely desirable for the monopolist, since it can be shown that its profits in this case will increase over the uniform pricing alternative. But is this pricing desirable to society as a whole?

The answer to this question is more ambiguous. Sometimes allowing the monopolist to discriminate in pricing may enhance social welfare, and other times it may not. It is important to develop the intuition behind this concept in more detail in order to understand when discrimination is desirable.

Let's look at the American Airlines supersaver story again. Assume that the industry acted as a cartel, and the CAB set a uniform price per seat in order to maximize industry's profits. There is only one (high) uniform price, and at this level only low-elasticity high fare-payer passengers use air travel. A high-elasticity passenger group with a lower willingness to pay (let's say students) does not use air transportation at all.

Assume that the airlines could keep the high fare-payers at the same level of revenues, and sell discount tickets (at any price higher than the average seat cost) only to students (recall that aircraft flew at roughly 50% capacity during the regulation regime). Airlines' total production and profits increase, and students are able to enjoy air travel, which they could not afford before.

This example is a clear-cut welfare-improving outcome, because both the airlines and the students are better off, and the high fare-payers are no worse off. Price discrimination is desirable, because without it students would not have been served at all.

The results become more ambiguous if under uniform pricing consumers from both groups find it attractive to buy tickets. If price discrimination is allowed, it can be shown that under certain assumptions the high fare-payer group may end up paying a higher price and the low fare-payer group a lower price than the uniform price alternative, so the welfare impact on each consumer group is conflicting. The low-payer group is better off and so is the monopolist, since its profits increase. The high fare-payer group—now required to pay more—is worse off.

The necessary condition to make the overall impact of price discrimination welfare-improving is that the production level must increase in comparison to the uniform price alternative. If production shrinks or stays constant, total welfare is diminished (Varian, 2000).

This story makes intuitive sense: Monopolistic distortions are associated with less production than under perfect competition or perfect discrimination. Price discrimination that generates significant production and market expansion compared to a uniform pricing monopoly stands a good chance of being a more desirable alternative (yet is still less efficient than the theoretical ideals of perfect competition or discrimination).

### 2.2.2 Indirect Discrimination

If you look at an aircraft cabin, it is hard not to think that all the seats look the same and feel the same, and therefore should also be priced the same. As we have indicated above, economists—despite this notion—suggest that a profit-maximizing monopolist would try to sell seats for different prices depending on different buyers' willingness to pay, and that this policy may be socially efficient. Now, in a process that may look strange, the airlines have decided not just to price seats differently but also to impose complex restrictions on certain seats, thereby diminishing their value and restricting their use— that is, a passenger must buy a seat so far in advance; she must stay at her destination over the weekend; and the she cannot cancel the trip or change the itinerary.

Why would an airline take similar seats and reduce their potential use and value? Does this make sense? The typical approach to analysis of these issues is called second-degree price discrimination.

*Second-degree price discrimination* is associated with indirect discrimination. The firm is aware of important demand characteristics of consumer groups, but it cannot identify the specific consumers in these groups. It therefore offers a menu of product versions to consumers in order to force them to self-select, and buy the version that best fits their needs. Discriminating firms often use quantity and quality variations including non-linear pricing when the price may vary with the quantity of purchase (a volume discount for example) or its quality, or other product characteristics. This type of discrimination often involves intra-personal discrimination in the sense that the same person may have to pay different prices for similar products and services.

Designing product versions (*versioning*) plays an important role in segmenting the market and sorting consumers under this form of discrimination. Airlines start their yield management operations with product design. In this stage, purchase and service restrictions, cancellation options, and channels of distribution create a product version. For example, it is assumed that business travelers tend to conclude their affairs during the working week and spend their weekends at home. Vacation travelers, on the other hand, tend to stay at a destination over the weekend. An airline's offering of two categories of tickets—one requiring a weekend stay over and the second not—is intended as a market segmentation device.

Assume there are two potential buyer groups; let's say business travelers (who are time-sensitive) and tourists. The firm's objective is to sell as many units as possible of unrestricted tickets to the high-paying business group and the remaining units to the low-paying tourist groups and prevent arbitrage. Since it cannot identify the buyers, it adjusts the good's quality and characteristics and offers two price-quality packages, anticipating that the high fare-payers will buy only the high-priced, high-quality, version (and as many as possible).

This requires clearly distinguishable differences between the versions. If the differences are negligible, high fare-payers may buy the low-priced version, and profits will not be maximized. Generally, an airline is better able to segment or divide the market and eliminate arbitrage, as the quality differences between packages become more significant and more meaningful to the high fare-payers. The restrictions on the lower-priced version may be of little direct benefit to the airline; in fact, they may be costly to implement, and therefore may increase production costs over the high-quality version.

The main purpose, however, is to separate the low-willing-to-pay buyers from the high-willing-to-pay buyers and keep the high-paying segment of the market buying the high-quality, high-priced, version. It is not that the airlines want to take advantage of or confuse discount ticket buyers because they don't care about them, but rather that they want to make the quality and the value of the high fare-payers' seats more distinctive and desired.

This practice is by no means unique to airlines. Economists coined the term *damaged goods* phenomenon to describe producers degrading or damaging a product in order to create a lower-quality version that will help support or maintain the high-quality, high-priced, version. Examples include Intel's elimination of desirable features from its computer processor, IBM's installation of a device that retards the printing speed on its laser printers, Sony's reducing mini-disc playing capacity, and Federal Express's making an extra trip on next-day deliveries, to name just a few. In many of these cases, the lower-grade versions are more expensive to produce but sell for less. The seller makes the high-quality version more valuable and more desirable to high fare-payers by reducing the quality and the usefulness of the cheaper version.

Is this practice socially efficient? Although different in the details of the analysis, second-degree price discrimination models support similar overall welfare conclusions. If under a uniform price only the high fare-payers would buy a product, then permitting discrimination is expected to improve welfare, as it permits the inclusion of new customers who otherwise would not be served in the market. If the two groups buy under the uniform price, the results are ambiguous (Varian, 1997).

## 2.3 *Ramsey Pricing*

In 1927, Frank Ramsey suggested a pricing policy that gained favor with economists, especially in connection with rate regulation of railroads and electric utilities, and that economists now use to explain current airline pricing. The presence of economies of scale and scope and the use of common input facilities in a multi-product scheme in a typically regulated industry work against traditional marginal cost pricing. Ramsey suggested a theoretically attractive way to deal with this situation. This idea is particularly interesting in application to regulating *a strong natural monopoly*, when technology and cost characteristics preclude a perfectly competitive market. The welfare issue, then, becomes figuring out an optimal (rather than ideal) pricing policy (*second-best*) that would maintain production with minimum welfare distortions.

We know that having the marginal buyer pay the marginal cost is a necessary (but not a sufficient) condition for efficiency. It is also required, however, that total revenues be sufficient to cover total costs, including fixed costs, as otherwise production will result in negative economic profits. This is an important point to make clear.

Marginal cost is the additional cost of producing the next unit, so it consists only of variable (avoidable) expenditures. Where there are economies of scale and scope due to high fixed and sunk costs, the result may be a high and declining average cost and a relatively low or even zero marginal cost. Therefore, charging customers at the marginal cost—as advisable under the perfect competition ideal—will not be sufficient to cover the total production cost. The fact that joint facilities or shared capacity are used to produce multiple services or products further complicates figuring out the relevant marginal costs and the allocation and collection of the joint fixed and other costs.

Ramsey's idea is that in order to minimize welfare distortion the total surplus should be maximized, subject to the firm breaking even on its total cost. This yields the *inverse elasticity rule*, which implies in essence that the regulator should set differential prices for each product or service in such a manner that buyers contribute toward covering the joint fixed cost, according to their demand characteristics. According to this rule, buyers who are more willing to pay are charged a premium over high-elasticity buyers. This solution is not (*first-best*) efficient since the price set is higher than the particular marginal cost. The firm, however, will not earn super-normal economic profits since total revenues are equal to total cost.

The inverse elasticity formula must also take into account the interdependence of demand for the various joint products and their related cross-elasticity. Products may be substitutes or complementary, so the pricing of one may negatively or positively impact the demand for the second, and thus cross-elasticity must be reflected in the pricing structure.

Ramsey's optimization is also applied to deal with peak-load pricing, when a fixed production capacity is jointly used to serve variable demand, and buyers are differentiated on the basis of high (peak) and low (off-peak) demand periods. Since peak and off-peak demand are more or less substitutes, discounting off-peak prices, for example, may shift consumption away from peak periods.

One of the interesting implications of this idea is that a profit-maximizing monopoly in a free market and a perfect regulator are expected to adopt the same pricing rule. The objective of a welfare-maximizing regulator is to bring the total surplus to a maximum. This is equivalent to the objective of a profit-maximizing firm.

On this basis, it would have been expected that the CAB would use Ramsey type pricing during the regulation regime. Similarly, it should have come as no surprise that the deregulated industry adopted Ramsey-like price discrimination. The CAB, however, didn't use Ramsey pricing during the regulation regime, and economists *were* surprised to see the deregulated industry adopt price discrimination.

Why didn't the CAB apply Ramsey pricing rules during the regulation regime? Regulators were aware of Ramsey's pricing, and in fact used *value-of-service* pricing in setting railroad rates. The CAB, however, believed that scale economies were not present in airline markets, and therefore deemed this kind of pricing irrelevant.[193]

A quotation from the CAB 1975 report reflects the CAB's perception:

> All airline costs are variable in the long run, and hence constant with respect to output, from which it is deduced that the costs of carrying discount traffic are identical with those of normal traffic and the use of promotional pricing cannot lower average costs in the long run. (p. 70).

Seats were considered homogeneous and the length of a trip a major cost variable. Fares were assumed to be at or about the long-run average cost, so selling additional seats at a discount was expected to generate losses.

The use of price discrimination by the deregulated airlines surprised economists who observed deregulation during the 1970s and 1980s for the same reasons. In hindsight, it seems natural that the industry would price-discriminate according to Ramsey's idea. But most observers believed the industry to be naturally competitive, and therefore did not expect price discrimination.

---

[193] The CAB experimented to a limited extent with discount fares in the 1970s.

A second quotation from the 1975 CAB report reflects the prevailing view of the way pricing was expected to respond to deregulation:

> Prices would presumably be more closely tailored to cost than at present because competition would provide strong incentives for efficient pricing (p. 167).

Economists did expect deregulated price structures to become more complex, but they believed the deregulated industry would follow the perfect competition notion, and that prices would tend to be set according to costs. Instead, the major airlines adopted price discrimination schemes that in many respects resemble Ramsey's pricing rule.

It is interesting to see also that the industry has not earned super-normal profits since deregulation, which may suggest that airlines tend to capture consumer surplus subject to the break-even constraint as suggested by Ramsey.


## 2.4    Price Discrimination Under Competitive Conditions

A common criticism of traditional economics is that it focuses on the extreme metaphors of pure monopoly versus perfect competition, while most real-life cases fall somewhere in between these two extremes. During the last 10 to 15 years, economists have shifted their focus from the traditional bipolar market structure to gain an increased understanding of network economics, oligopoly competition, and pricing. Despite this increasing body of knowledge, we still have not heard a clear-cut answer regarding whether price discrimination is efficient or not, and whether antitrust intervention is in fact desirable.[194]

The theory suggests in fact some examples that are insightful but difficult to generalize and apply to the real world. The results obtained depend on each model's specific assumptions regarding market structure and demand and cost characteristics. The challenge is compounded by the complexity of the market and pricing structures we observe in reality and the not-always-obvious role they play in practice.

Let's look back at the simplest analytical case of a third-degree discriminating monopoly, for example. Price discrimination is expected to increase the monopolist's profits, but has ambiguous overall welfare implications depending on the specific circumstances, particularly demand characteristics that the monopoly faces and that are captured analytically by its elasticity. If one assumes a firm competing with one or more firms, instead of a pure monopoly, the competition's response (cross-firm elasticity) must be considered as well. In this case, extracting a greater consumer surplus may have a conflicting competition response, which further complicates a conclusion and makes it more ambiguous.

If one moves to model second-degree price discrimination, a new set of issues arise as competition response can affect the ability of the firm to offer price schedules that optimally sort and reveal consumer characteristics. In this case, a firm

---

[194] For an extensive review of economic theory literature see Stole (2001).

interacts and must consider strategic responses by consumers as well as by competitors, and the effects may be offsetting.

Reviewing this literature is beyond the scope of this work, but I can point out a few selected interesting conclusions.

### 2.4.1   Increased Production

We have noted that a necessary condition for welfare improvement in the simple monopoly case is a significant increase in production. This is an appealing conclusion with important policy implications. What happens to this conclusion when we move to a competitive market structure?

It can be shown that extending the model to account for an oligopolistic competition structure under quite general assumptions still requires an increase in aggregate production as a necessary condition for welfare improvement.

### 2.4.2   Entry

What is the impact of price discrimination on entry? Small airlines that made new entry into competition with incumbents over hub routes often complain about the unfair use of price discrimination to block entry. Can economic theory on price discrimination shed some light on this issue?

I would like to point to three general concerns in this regard. First, it has been shown in various models and under different assumptions that increased competition is expected to increase price dispersion. This is an important point, because price dispersion is often perceived as evidence of monopolistic power and a call for regulation to encourage entry and competition especially on hub routes. Yet increased market competition may be a *reason* for increased price dispersion. This also further complicates an already complicated issue as to if and under what conditions cutting prices in response to entry is predatory or otherwise not socially desirable.

Second, Armstrong and Vickers (1993) formulate an entry model that includes an incumbent monopolist facing two market segments and a potential entrant into one of the segments. This might be a low-cost airline attacking a low-elasticity market segment over a hub's route. The incumbent's best response to entry is to reduce price in the challenged market. The lower price would make entry more difficult. According to this model, the incumbent could prevent entry under certain assumptions regarding entry costs. In such a case, price discrimination may eliminate entry and be socially undesirable.

Third, economists use the concept of *monopolistic competition* to model markets that consist of many companies with some market power, yet not enough to affect entry or the payoffs of any other firm. Katz (1984) uses this framework, assuming two groups of consumers, and shows that price discrimination could induce more entry than the efficient equilibrium level, and therefore contribute to an inefficient overproduction. If, according to Armstrong and Vickers, discrimination could serve to bar entry and result in too little production, under the monopolistic competition model too much entry and production would be expected.

## 2.5    Uncertain Demand

A relatively new line of inquiry with relevance for our discussion may be traced back to Prescot (1975), Dana (1998, 1999), and Eden (1999).[195] This work relates price discrimination to coping with demand uncertainty. These studies show that—contrary to the traditional view—price discrimination is not necessarily associated with monopolistic power, but may rather reflect equilibrium under competitive market conditions.

Airlines set prices in advance, and start selling tickets long before a flight takes off. At the time of sale, there is uncertainty regarding demand realization at any time before takeoff. There is also ex-post price inflexibility so that prices cannot be adjusted after the tickets are sold according to actual demand behavior.

A theoretical solution is a market for contingent tickets that specifies prices in advance, subject to certain future demand realization (for example, a passenger may get a refund, or pay a premium according to the actual flight load factor). This requires possible states of demand and associated prices to be specified (ex-ante) and verifiable and enforceable (ex-post). Such contingent markets, however, do not exist, and airlines offer instead a menu of outputs at different prices. By doing so, the airlines indirectly discriminate across states of aggregate demand.

When a flight is offered for sale, certain fare categories are open and available. Now assume that an unexpected event is announced in a destination city, resulting in increased demand. The pre-announcement buyers enjoy the lowest fares available at the time, but this category runs out quickly after the announcement is made, and buyers are forced to buy otherwise identical seats at higher prices. This mechanism provides airlines with some pricing flexibility, and lets them adjust to demand fluctuation in an otherwise rigid pricing environment. Revenue management systems that airlines use accumulate and adjust demand information over time, and adjust booking limits to each fare category in response to demand.[196] This practice looks like second-degree price discrimination, but it may occur for a different reason.[197]

The major conclusions of this line of study may be stated as follows:
1. Price dispersion may characterize a highly competitive industry with no market power.
2. Under certain conditions, discrimination may be more efficient than linear pricing.

---

[195] See also Stole (2001).

[196] Airlines pricing strategy is usually dealt with from *yield management* perspective. Real application involves aspects, (or may be interpreted as a) *dynamic pricing*. It is not completely clear if fare classes are different products or different prices for the same product (or perhaps a combination of both).

[197] Aspects of optimal overbooking can also be interpreted in connection with uncertain demand. For example, airlines from time to time pay passengers to switch to another flight if they experience higher than expected demand for a flight.

3. Price dispersion is expected to be greater in a competitive industry than in the monopoly case.
4. Off-peak flights or flights to airports with less demand will not necessarily command lower prices.
5. An equilibrium price under perfect competition assumptions will be equal to effective marginal costs (for a given state of demand), which includes in addition to standard marginal production cost the expected capacity cost. This last point is interesting since revenue management as practiced by the airlines attempts to assess such capacity opportunity (shadow) cost in setting ticket prices.

## 2.6  Contestable Markets Once Again

Recent advances in information technology, particularly their manifestation in the market, have attracted economists' attention. New advanced technology often involves fixed joint and sunk costs and low (sometimes even negligible) marginal costs. The most celebrated example is obviously the technology pattern that characterizes Microsoft.

In fact, this general pattern is typical to many businesses, such as book publishing, restaurants, and airlines, to name just a few. It is costly to produce the first copy of, let's say, a computer software application, but cheap to produce the subsequent copy. Should these products be priced at their marginal cost, fixed and overhead costs cannot be recouped. Analogously, it is costly to produce the first aircraft seat in a network and relatively cheap to add the next one, as most of the cost of maintaining and operating a scheduled network system is fixed.

This is similar to Ramsey's story above, except that while traditional economics viewed the natural monopoly case (utilities, railroads) as a unique grand exception to an otherwise perfect world, this phenomenon seems to have become the norm rather than the exception. Moreover, strong competition characterizes many such industries despite economies of scale that are related to fixed and sunk costs.

Airlines are driven to be large, and some to be huge, yet even the largest airlines constantly battle competition, vary prices with astonishing frequency, and engage in what seems like never-ending strategic planning for survival. They enjoy price-setting power, yet their freedom to set prices turns out to be quite restrictive; it by no means resembles the *price-making* power of a theoretical monopolist.

Airlines pricing responds to demand rather than to marginal cost, and certain passengers and markets pay what are perceived as monopolistic premiums, yet threats of potential and actual entry by startup and incumbent airlines abound. Sometimes such entries become a success, and other times a failure in a manner that is difficult to predict, duplicate, or generalize. Yet, overall industry income is anything but above normal—and paradoxically if any airline shows persistence in generating above-average rates of return it is the discount-fare Southwest, which uses price discrimination to a far lesser extent than other major airlines. Traditional economics portrays the natural monopoly as having maximum market power to *make prices,* and firms in perfectly competitive or contestable markets as being forced to *take prices,* depending on the absence or presence of actual or potential competition. In both cases, economists suggest that markets tend to "settle down" at a stationary equilibrium that responds only to exogenous shocks. These concepts cannot account for our observations of market behavior and need reconciliation.

A market is contestable if entry is quick and easy. Perfect contestability, in particular, requires instantaneous and zero-cost entry. According to this concept, sunk cost is a major entry barrier and an impediment to contestability. It is viewed as a substantial cash outlay that is required for entry, with a significant part of it to be lost on market exit. This cash outlay is considered a detrimental entry barrier not only because an entrant needs to raise it and risk losing it, but also because an incumbent has already invested it, and therefore has a clear competitive advantage over the new entry. It is this asymmetrical impact of sunk costs on an entrant in comparison to an incumbent that impedes competition and may push the market toward monopoly.

Baumol (2002) has modified the traditional contestable markets idea to account for what we see today in market behavior. He focuses on a different type of sunk costs that characterizes innovative industries (and other industries) that routinely invest in organizational, process, and product innovations. In such industries, firms invest fixed and sunk costs that are "substantial, mandatory, and constantly repeated" (p. 162). At the same time, both incumbents and new entrants are required to constantly make and recoup such outlays, so sunk costs may not have the traditional detrimental impact on new entry.

During the early 1980s, economists believed that airline markets tended to be contestable since aircraft, the major portion of airlines' fixed cost, were not market-specific and were therefore non-sunk. According to the new view, sunk costs that are required continually to maintain and develop airline networks are substantial yet not sufficient to bar entry. And therefore, the need for sunk costs and strong competition may coexist. This is a non-traditional theoretical construct that accounts for sunk costs in a competitive market setup.

Together 1) the need to recoup fixed and sunk costs that are large compared to the marginal costs and 2) the presence of strong competition, dictate another non-traditional theoretical combination—above-marginal cost yet competitive pricing. Incumbents must set prices above marginal cost in order to cover their long-term costs, but actual and potential competition forces them to stick to break-even revenues and precludes super-normal profits. Moreover, according to Baumol (2002), maximizing profits under such conditions forces price discrimination:

> It is the need to recover continuing and repeated sunk costs that accounts for the prevalence of discriminatory pricing in the innovative industries (p. 167).

This model offers a non-traditional view of firms that can discriminate in pricing yet are powerless price-takers, forced by the market to adopt a certain set of discriminatory prices in order to extract normal returns and survive. It is free entry into such markets (and not monopolistic power) that forces price discrimination.

One of the important characteristics of this theoretical depiction is that, contrary to the traditional conception, equilibrium is not stationary and is constantly vulnerable to entry (Baumol calls this *churning equilibria*). First, above-marginal cost pricing invites entry since, at least theoretically, an entrant with the same costs can slightly cut prices and still earn profits. Second, price discrimination by itself may invite niche entry into a market segment. Such entry does not require investing the sunk cost necessary to become a full market competitor at entry. This can account for a startup airline's strategy of targeting a niche segment market that is served by a major hub network, for example.

Finally, zero economic profits imply that, all else equal, there is no room in the market for both incumbents and entrants, and therefore successful entry would require exit:

> Consequently, a constant strategic battle for survival must be the order of the day, with the time trajectory characterized by an unending inflow of entrants, followed by a stream of exiting enterprises composed in part of entrants, in part of former incumbents (p. 175).

Over time, and assuming that entry is not too difficult, industry concentration and member firm size would correspond to an efficient cost-minimizing configuration. There may be very-different size competing firms, and industry concentration would not necessarily reflect monopolistic power or super-normal profits.

## 2.7    Policy Implications

What lessons can be learned from the economic principles we have reviewed in this section? First, price discrimination is not necessarily an indication of airlines' monopolistic power. It may help airlines cope with demand uncertainty and recoup joint fixed and sunk costs under highly competitive market conditions. In fact, price discrimination may be the only way to recoup such costs.

Second, price dispersion is expected to increase with increased market competitiveness and entry.

Third, price discrimination may arguably be socially desirable even if an airline possesses monopolistic power. This is particularly the case if discrimination significantly increases production and expands markets over the uniform price alternative.

Fourth, pricing above marginal cost, firm size, and industry concentration are not, in and of themselves, an indication of monopolistic distortions. We must also look at total costs and revenues to see if distortions indeed exist. Persistent returns above average long-run total cost might serve as an indicator of monopolistic distortion and trigger antitrust attention.

These principles all reflect a departure from traditional antitrust thinking. While these conclusions are gaining more favor with economists, they are not widely applied or even accepted, and remain subject to debate. An important question at the end of the day is to what extent the industry structure, particularly the dominant hub-based networks, permits new entry and competitive threats.

On one side of the debate, there are observers who believe the major airlines have monopolistic power and charge monopolistic premiums in hub markets. These observers are familiar with Ramsey, but argue that the conclusion that Ramsey pricing is efficient may hold only in a static context, that the presence of market power and price differentiation limit entry, retard technology progress, and may reduce free market-generated diversity and choice.

Moreover, Ramsey pricing is a *second-best* solution. This means it is desirable only when technology forces a natural monopolistic market, and that in the absence of such a monopoly production would not occur. Yet the operation of competing airlines using linear or simple network structures and their exceptional success may prove this is not the case.

The observers on this side of the debate believe that by dominating a hub airport an airline in fact controls an essential facility and forecloses entry by competition. In this context, discrimination, bundling, tying, and other sophisticated pricing devices are used in a predatory manner to bar entry. The regulator, therefore, must break the hub power by several means: enforcing competition into hubs (such as by making slots available to airlines other than the majors); regulating and limiting strategic pricing and network integration through code-share or otherwise; and rigorously prosecuting predatory behavior.

On the other side of the debate, some suggest that a significant portion of price differences can be explained by cost differences and not by demand elasticity. There are two not so obvious cost elements worth emphasizing. First, it is arguable that the alternative cost of protecting an empty seat for a late booking must be considered as well. The alternative cost of a protected seat changes dynamically over time as the departure date approaches, and must be reflected as a cost element in pricing a seat. In fact, yield management systems determine booking limits by assessing such alternative costs and incorporating them into the pricing.

Second, major airlines use scheduling and increased frequency of flights to attract passengers into their networks. The incremental cost of attracting passengers by adding flights to a network system is high, and may be higher than the average cost per seat. Moreover, the cost of adding frequency may be difficult to allocate because of the network-wide effect of such addition.

But even if there are no cost differences, other observers suggest, the nature of the major airlines' production and cost functions dictates price discrimination, yet market forces eliminate super-normal profits. Indeed, it is widely accepted that airline profits do not exceed (and often are below) normal rates. Moreover, the move to create hub-and-spoke networks and discriminate in pricing came at the same time as a significant increase in airlines production, expansion into markets not previously served, and a general trend of declining average fares.

Furthermore, the need to recoup the substantial costs of investment in upgrading fleets and complying with safety and environmental regulation during the 1990s and the huge losses suffered during the crisis of the early 1990s encouraged price discrimination and widening price spreads during the second half of the decade. These observers point to strong industry competitiveness, network growth, and ongoing technological advances in aircraft and related technology to refute the notion of significant monopolistic distortions.

Airlines use complex pricing schemes with ambiguous theoretical welfare implications. For example, historical purchase patterns and other personal data are stored in airlines' databases, and are sometimes used through direct internet connections in a manner that arguably resembles first-degree price discrimination.

This technique is often used for business and other frequent passenger groups. The use of internet devices, on the other hand, also facilitates transactions that resemble perfectly competitive classic auctions and target internet-savvy passengers. Bulk discounts to specific groups or large-volume buyers, frequent flier arrangements or family discounts have third-degree and often non-linear price discrimination characteristics. These techniques are implemented within a complex framework of service versioning, which corresponds to second-degree price discrimination.

Moreover, consumers' heterogeneity is multi-dimensional and complex. Multiple segmentation devices are used simultaneously so that second-, third-, and other types of discrimination are combined. Segmentation may be direct or indirect using intra-personal or inter-personal differentiation. This includes discrimination on the basis of: marketing channels (direct, internet, travel agents), time (of day and zones), geographic location (a lower price to potential passengers living near a competitor airline's hub), language (to capture ethnic communities), peak/off-peak (daily, weekly, seasonally, and event-related), quality (first, business, tourist, and other restrictions), quantity (bulk discount to travel agency, volume discount for companies and organizations), purchase history, frequent flier (mileage-related discount on future purchase), bundling (with hotels and car rentals, return flights), and more. Moreover, fare classes may be used as a dynamic pricing mechanism to cope with uncertain demand, and therefore certain classes are opened and/or closed in respond to changes in unfolding demand expectations for a specific flight. It is not clear if fare classes are different products (versions), or different fares for the same product and in fact, they may be both.

The complexity of the issues and the consequent ambiguity provide interest groups with theoretical ammunition to argue opposing views. And there are partisans on all sides. Startup airlines attempting entry into major airlines' markets argue that hub airlines are monopolists and their use of price discrimination is predatory. Consumer advocates and high-fare paying passengers criticize airline pricing as being too high and unfair. Both interest groups as well as the regulators believe that encouraging competition, especially into high-fare paying hub markets, is desirable. Yet increased competition and entry—the theory says—may encourage wider price spreads, which is interpreted by certain observers as an indication of monopolistic power, unfair pricing, and a reason to further exert pressure on the regulator to encourage competition.

## 3. BREAKDOWN OF THE DOMINANT YIELD MANAGEMENT MODEL

The dominant business model for the major US airlines in the late 1990s and the early years of the new century has involved high-frequency, integrated hub-and-spoke network systems connected globally through alliances and reliant on complex discriminating pricing schemes to price network components and their combinations to passengers. Passengers relied mostly on travel agents to provide price information. Agents were paid commissions by the majors and used majors-dominated global distribution systems (Amadeus, Galileo, and SABRE) for information and booking. This structure facilitated price discrimination. A typical passenger was presented with a menu of service alternatives and corresponding fares and was expected to select a desirable version according to her willingness to pay. The absence of direct low-cost competition on most routes and an overall booming economy and high demand for air travel, further facilitated segmentation and fencing of passengers into fare categories.

The competing model adopted by the low-fare airlines involves mostly linear or an otherwise simple network structure as well as simple, mostly no-frills products and fare structures with little or limited price discrimination. Fares usually varied dynamically according to expected demand for a specific flight over time and not according to passengers' demand elasticity. Airlines in this category used alternative distribution systems and have made an increasing use of internet technology for product distribution and ticketing.

During the 1990s, the major airlines increased their reliance on price discrimination as a major strategic policy of maximizing revenues. How did this policy affect average fares and profit trends? Figure 16 reflects annual net profits between 1990 and 2002.[198] Figure 17 reflects net profit margins between 1996 and 2003 (domestic and system).[199] Figures 18 and 19 reflect average industry yield index (revenue per passenger mile in real terms) and the composite cost index between 1990 and 2001.[200]

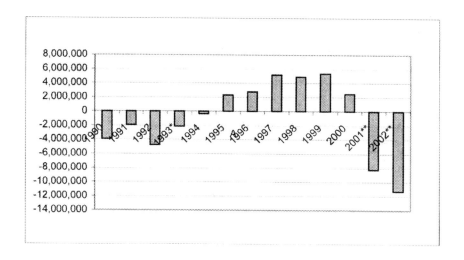

*Figure 16. Annual Profits 1990-2002*

---

[198] Source: Air Transport Association.
[199] Source: DOT BTS Airline Financial statistics http://www.bts.gov/oai/indicators/yrlyopfinan.html.
[200] Source: Air Transport Association.

234

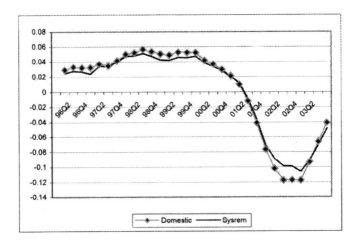

*Figure 17. Domestic and System Net Profit Margins (Quarterly) 1996-2003*

The figures reveal that, despite an increasing use of price discrimination and revenue management techniques, overall industry revenues and profitability trends, while improved over the early 1990s, were anything but super-normal. Average real fares declined during most of the 1990s (adjusted for inflation, average fares declined 25% from 1990 to 1998), while costs were largely stable and rising during the second half of the decade. The gap between average fare and average cost remained largely stable throughout the 1990s, and by no means does it suggest an overall trend of an industry extracting more than its fair share. Note that the net margin trend reversed itself in the year 2000 (before September 11, 2001). The margin for the fourth quarter of 2000 dropped by roughly half relative to the previous year.

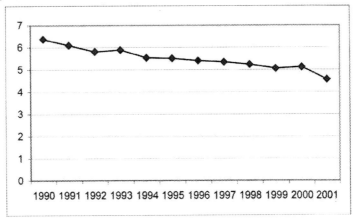

*Figure 18. Real Yield (cents) 1990–2001*

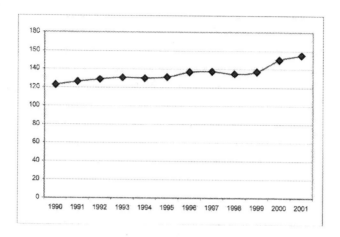

*Figure 19. Composite Cost Index 1990-2001*

Understanding the place and the dynamics of the pricing strategy and its business impact, however, requires detailed examination of specific fares and their different components, not just average trends. We have no such detailed analysis, mostly because of the complexity and ambiguity of pricing practices as well as the unavailability of the specific data required.

The economic studies we have confirm (and I believe there is a general consensus) that:

1. The range of fare spreads has increased in many markets during the 1990s especially during the second part of the decade.
2. The average prices in high-fare ticket categories have increased in real terms, while the average prices in low-fare categories have declined.
3. The higher-fare travelers have paid increasingly more per ticket in real terms, and their share as a group in total revenue has increased during the 1990s. For example, the top-fare travelers (95th percentile and above) in 1992 accounted for 8% to13% of airlines revenue compared to 17% to 18% in 1998.[201]

As a result of the major airlines' pricing strategy, a relatively small group of mostly business or otherwise time-sensitive travelers came to pay an increasing and disproportionate large share of the industry's revenues. The demands of this group, however, are quite sensitive to the business cycle and income effects. When the economy started to slow down, and with the changing fortunes of high-tech companies and their executives in late 2000, demand for full-fare seats diminished, wiping out a significant portion of the industry's revenues.

---

[201] See, for example, Transportation Research Board (1999).

Full-fare monthly revenues for the year 2000 peaked in April, reaching an impressive high of $1,000 million.[202] By December it had dropped to approximately $800 million. By the end of the summer of 2001, just before the events of September 2001, revenues dramatically fell 50% and reached just over $400 million. Then, in September 2001 they dropped to $237.3 million, recovering to $400 million approximately six months afterward (IATA, 2002, p. 6).

The traveling public at the same time became more aware of and discontented with the major airlines' pricing practices. The majors and the group of full-fare-paying passengers found themselves in a peculiar relationship, as in the old song, *you always hurt the one you love*. The airlines needed these passengers' revenue badly, and looked for ways to attract them and tie them into their systems and maintain their loyalty, especially in light of the increasing low-fare competition. Yet, this group of passengers was also the one that was charged increasingly more for their seats, and they thought this too expensive and unfair.

Moreover the availability of fare information on the internet and the eroding importance of travel agents and the traditional distribution networks as booking information providers made price differentiation (and particularly fencing between fare classes) harder to accomplish. By year-end 2000, it had become apparent that many business travelers were not willing any longer to trade off ticket restrictions for the price they commanded, and became low-fare payers. Later it also became apparent that the airlines could not take for granted, that high willing-to-pay buyers would, indeed, self-select and purchase the more expensive product version.

The group of low-fare payers, on the other hand, was hurt as well, and became frustrated with the increasing restrictions and thus the reduced quality imposed on the seats available to them. In some cases, the presence of competition by low-cost carriers meant this group could buy equivalently priced or less expensive tickets with no restrictions or limited restrictions. The major airlines found themselves in a bind when the previously winning policy of restricting the low-fare travelers did not stimulate sufficient full-fare revenues any longer—and at the same time reduced both the demand of and the revenues from low-fare travelers.

By the early 2000s it became apparent that traditional yield management had lost its magic.

The major reasons for the breakdown of the traditional yield management model correspond to the inherent weaknesses of second degree price differentiation that are outlined in basic economic textbooks. Most important, for this strategy to work, seller must find the right balance between the quality attractiveness, and relative prices of the product versions, in order to induce buyers to reveal their real willingness to pay and buy accordingly. That means:

1. The seller doesn't want the inferior version to be too inferior, or else too many low-end buyers will not buy at all. This issue became even more significant when low-fare competition started offering similar service with no such restrictions at all.

---

[202] Including first, business, and non-restricted full fares.

2. The seller doesn't want the perception of the inferior version to be too close to the superior version in quality, or else buyers with high willingness to buy will be tempted to switch. The economic slowdown and subsequent recession and changes in passenger tastes made the differences between the versions less significant and the high-fare payers less willing to tradeoff the prevailing restrictions with lower fares. In fact, many high-fare payers became more sensitive to fares than to the restrictions and have been ready to stay-over weekends or book in advance in order to pay less.

3. The seller doesn't want the price gap to be too wide, or else buyers with a high willingness to pay may be tempted to switch. As mentioned before, fare spreads widened significantly during the second half of the 1990s. Moreover, a wide price gap between two versions is perceived as unfair and makes high-fare payers unhappy and therefore look for their tickets somewhere else.

The disappearance of many high-fare paying passengers eliminated a disproportionally large part of the major airlines' revenues; the devastating impact on revenue was far out of proportion to the group's size. The airlines' reliance on full-fare revenues exacerbated the challenge of falling demand due to the economic cycle and to post-September 11 terrorist threats. The implications of these conditions went far beyond the mere adjustment of capacity to the volatility of a business cycle. They in fact forced the major airlines to rethink their strategic business model.

# CHAPTER 8

# WHAT NEXT?

> We're going to destroy the airline business, as we know it.[203]

The economic slowdown beginning in the middle of 2000, the September 11, 2001, events, and the war in Iraq have affected the industry quite dramatically. But even before the end of 2000 and before September 11, it had become obvious that the dominant business model of the major network airlines, particularly their heavy reliance on revenue management and high-frequency business travel, was losing ground, and that a major revision was necessary. Then September 11th and subsequent events prompted an urgent search for adequate strategic responses, whether a significant adjustment of the old business model or adoption of a brand-new one.

If there is one major lesson to be learned from looking at the industry's evolution since deregulation, it is that forecasts seldom materialize—the market has a life of its own, and firms often show surprising ways to respond and adjust to unfolding events. This observation notwithstanding, what are we likely to see next? To answer this question, it is instructive, first, to take a step back in time and look again at the evolution of the industry's structure since the early 1990s, and then try to figure out in what direction we may be heading.[204]

## 1. EARLY 1990S—INDUSTRY IN CRISIS

At one time in the early 1990s the ability of the major airlines to survive was seriously in doubt. Highly leveraged, crippled by high fuel and labor costs, battered by price wars, and weakened by a poor economy, the airlines' future looked quite grim, and talks about bust, doom, and re-regulation were rife.

A major casualty of the early 1990s crisis was Pan American Airlines. Pan Am was a pioneering airline. It served as the flagship carrier of the nation during the post-WWII era and was early on granted most of the lucrative international flying rights. Pan Am symbolized the US spirit and its presence throughout the world. It enjoyed a unique monopolistic market position, granted by the government and

---

[203] Ryanair's Chief Executive Officer Michael O'Leary, quoted in Reuters Update, June 3, 2003, by Michael Roddy.

[204] I reiterate certain trends in order to keep this chapter coherent on a stand-alone basis.

regulated by the Civil Aeronautics Board. Its demise in 1992 is emblematic of the failure of the archetypal business model of a pre-deregulation airline to adjust to the challenges of free market competition. Surprisingly, American Airlines—once considered the most vulnerable major airline and a candidate for exiting the market—emerged as a leader, and its hub-and-spoke network strategy became the dominant business model for over 20 years.

All major airlines suffered during the early 1990s crisis. Pan Am and Eastern Airlines were liquidated, and TWA, Continental, and America West reorganized under protection of the bankruptcy court. Other majors reorganized and restructured while threatening to file for bankruptcy protection. Cutting costs, reducing capacity, renegotiating debt contracts, changing long-term fleet planning and route structures, and increasing market share and consolidation by acquiring assets from failing airlines were the typical major incumbents' responses.

## 2. MIDDLE 1990s

Improving economic conditions beginning around the middle 1990s, followed by an unprecedented boom into the end of the decade, changed the picture quite dramatically.

### 2.1 Recovery

TWA and Continental Airlines emerged from bankruptcy. TWA was never able to make it, though, and was eventually acquired by American Airlines, joining the list of extinct pre-deregulation iconic airlines: Pan Am, Eastern, and Braniff. Continental—not so long before assigned the least chance to survive among the majors—took advantage of the Bankruptcy Code and successfully restructured its operations and finances. It then surprisingly emerged as one of the most cost-efficient and financially strong major airlines. Northwest Airlines, very highly leveraged and a possible candidate for filing for bankruptcy protection itself, was successful in reorganizing without court help, and emerged as an efficient major airline as well.

A new business model developed, characterized by a complex, multi-hub, global-network system. Capturing dominant domestic market shares provided high-density feed into the complex high-fixed cost, high-frequency network system. Vertical integration agreements with domestic commuter airlines enhanced the system's density. The consolidation of the commuter airlines and their integration with the majors during the late 1980s and early 1990s came at a time of struggle for the commuters. Under-capitalized, hit hard by several tragic accidents, and frequently with poor safety records, their long-run survivability was called into question. But starting in the late 1990s and with the advantage of new 50- to 100-seat jet aircraft, they emerged stronger than ever before, biting off a piece of the majors' traditional market and creating what some observers call the *commuter revolution.*

Code-sharing and other agreements with major foreign airlines extended the system into international markets and created a small number of mega global airlines dominated by United, American, and Delta. These airlines—which had provided mostly domestic travel during four decades of regulation—became the world industry leaders in providing global travel. According to this business model, an airline offers one-stop shopping for many consumers, offering many composite products and attempting to maximize network revenues by demand-based price discrimination through sophisticated yield management and other techniques.

Southwest is a unique case of a successful business model that in many respects reflects a binary opposition, a mirror image of the major incumbents' model. Instead of offering "everything to everyone," it has offered a standard, simple, mostly point-to-point, low-fare, no-frills, travel option in niche markets, consistently generating new demand and expanding markets. Using one type of aircraft, non-unionized labor, and mostly secondary niche airports, Southwest attained the industry's lowest cost structure and highest productivity, consistently experiencing robust growth in market share. Southwest is the only airline that survived the crisis of the early 1990s with no major losses. It has persistently encouraged competition by stimulating new demand as well as attracting passengers from the major network airlines.

## 2.2    Startup Entry

The early 1990s crisis also encouraged the entry of new startups, as aircraft, labor, and other inputs became available at very attractive prices. Most startups attempted to copy the Southwest business model (with some variations) for market entry. In the mid-1990s, it seemed for a while that a few startups had gained market momentum—a very small yet significant critical mass required for initial survivability.

ValueJet was the most promising startup of the time. It became the darling of the regulator—which hoped that low-cost competition would restrain major airline fares; of investors—who speculated that ValueJet would become the next Southwest Airlines; and of passengers—who enjoyed low fares on short point-to-point routes.

The startup business model ValueJet adopted was in many ways consistent with the traditional entry strategy followed during the 1980s. The airline took advantage of the extremely low prices in the used aircraft market at that time, and used non-unionized labor offering low-fare, no-frills service. Unlike Southwest, it also targeted markets that were served by a major airline, attempting to take advantage of its low-cost structure. Using low-cost used aircraft lowered the working capital threshold and the sunk costs of entry into the market. Other low-cost startups appeared as well during this period, taking advantage of available low-cost grounded or retired aircraft, but most of them failed or barely survived.

The tragic accident of a ValueJet aircraft in 1996 put a hold on any meaningful startup entry for several years. The notion that low-cost startup airlines are prone to accidents came to dominate the public view and directed the regulator's policy.

New, more restrictive safety requirements and increased scrutiny were imposed on such airlines; such measures included limiting the number of aircraft a startup may operate as well as its fleet growth. The latter policy was in response to the criticism the regulator mounted in the ValueJet case that too fast an expansion was allowed.

Yet startup airlines needed to build a critical market mass to survive. An entry attempt by somewhat better-capitalized West Pacific Airlines, using a newer generation of 737 aircraft, failed as well during this period.

## 3. LATE 1990s

By the end of the century it had become conventional wisdom that startup airlines were doomed to fail. The market had evolved into two clearly identifiable groups. On the one hand, each one of the major hub airlines offered complex global reach including seamless interlining with network members. In this group, passengers were discriminated along the lines of their demand elasticity. On the other hand, the low-cost, low-fare, group, with only one significant member—Southwest—offered simple fares, on mostly point-to-point travel.

### 3.1 Antitrust Concerns

There seemed to be no significant price competition among members of the major hub airlines group, although there has been limited yet increasing competition between them and Southwest. Fares have been significantly lower in markets that are served by both Southwest and a major airline than in those served only by majors. These circumstances have been expanding along with the consistent growth of Southwest's operation.

During the late 1990s, observers and antitrust regulators questioned whether the major airlines were enjoying market power, earning monopolistic premiums on hub routes, using predatory pricing against low-cost entry, and expanding their market power through code-share agreements. At this time, the government launched an unprecedented number of antitrust regulatory initiatives targeting airlines' competitive conduct. Yet, in spite of the undoubted dominance of the major airline networks, market structure didn't stabilize and the group of major airlines continued their attempts to further consolidate and integrate their domestic and international operations, perhaps into three or four major global networks.

Certain observers interpreted this trend as a move toward increasing network efficiency. Others saw it as a move toward enhancing the majors' monopolistic power. A strong antitrust stance by the government, however, seemed to have halted further integration moves to some extent. The government approved the acquisition of TWA by American in a prepackaged bankruptcy procedure, making American the largest airline in the world. United—the previous largest world airline—pulled out of its agreement to acquire US Airways for several reasons, including the government's position on antitrust-related issues.

A booming economy toward the end of the 1990s resulted in unprecedented demand for air travel among both business and leisure travelers. In 1995, after five years of constant losses, the US airlines started to post positive earnings, and continued to do so during the next five years. It is significant that although profits were robust during the second half of the decade, domestic yield was quite stable at around 13.75 cents per revenue passenger mile. Profitability was obtained by price discrimination and increasing load factors, as the average major airline's load factor broke records and surpassed the 70% mark in every one of the last four years of the decade. In 2000 nearly 650 million passengers boarded planes.

The increased density and use of the network kept earnings positive but declining, and put operational pressure on the system, resulting in congestion, delays, and poorer product quality and passenger satisfaction. Deteriorating product quality attracted political and regulatory attention, framed in terms of protecting passengers' rights.

### 3.2    JetBlue—A New Entry Model

JetBlue entered the market in February 2000, when the major airlines' hegemony was undoubted, and most observers believed the startup entry was doomed to fail. The entry model adopted by this airline defied conventional wisdom and the past experience of traditional entry and raised skeptics' eyebrows. On the low-cost, no-frills, side of the market, JetBlue faced the hurdle of a difficult-to-duplicate Southwest Airlines pattern. On the other side, the powerful majors s posed a serious threat to new entry with their dominant hub structure, global reach, and reputation for aggressive —by some counts predatory—response to new entry.

JetBlue positioned itself as a low-fare, high-quality yet no-frills airline, and selected as its major base the slot-controlled New York JFK Airport—usually shunned by startups— ordering a large number of brand-new, very expensive Airbus A320s as a single aircraft type for its fleet. It planned to start up operations just beyond the peak of the economic cycle, unlike most other new entries, which tried to take advantage of the availability of cheaper outputs during low cycle periods.

This model stands in striking contrast to the traditional entry model, which involves a small number of inexpensive used aircraft for initial market penetration at a low entry cost. JetBlue's entry required substantial initial (mostly sunk) capital in order to cover the cost of obtaining sufficient market mass from both the demand and supply sides. JetBlue was backed by an unprecedented large capital investment, compared to the typical several million-dollar amounts that had characterized traditional new entries. It is worth noting that under-capitalization had been identified as a major cause for all startup failures prior to JetBlue.

A high-quality low-price entry strategy may seem very attractive at first glance. Obviously, an airline, or any startup firm for that matter, is likely to win a market if it can indeed provide a better product for a significantly lower price. Achieving that goal, however, is a very different matter, since high quality usually costs more and requires substantial investment and sunk costs. This is particularly true when it comes to acquiring brand-new aircraft with a normal price tag of $50 million each.

JetBlue took advantage of the fierce competition between Airbus and Boeing and Airbus's aggressive move to gain market share by reducing prices and accommodating startup airlines acquiring new aircraft during their startup period. It accommodated the public perception and the regulator's focus on old aircraft as a potential safety risk. It also took advantage of the "honeymoon" period when maintenance costs of new aircraft are minimal. The combination of a relatively lower new aircraft acquisition cost at favorable terms, non-unionized labor, and initial low maintenance cost provided a highly competitive (although arguably temporary) production cost. Surprise and skepticism as to this strategy not withstanding, it has since then been duplicated by numerous startups over the world.

## 3.3    Economic Downturn

The average airlines load factor peaked in the year 2000, yet earnings—although remaining positive—fell significantly from previous years, due to the softening economy. Industry profitability for the 12 months ending June 30, 2001, declined substantially in comparison to the previous year. The number of business and other full-paying passengers declined quite dramatically, negatively affecting the major incumbents' revenues. The revenues from full-paying passengers fell 50% in the summer of 2001 compared to the summer of 2000.

During 2001, and before the tragic events of September 11, it had become clear that the complex high-frequency network system that the majors had built did not generate enough revenue to be maintained during an overall demand drop, most particularly the disappearance of full-fare-paying passengers. For the first time, the industry experimented with price discrimination during an economic downturn, which set the stage for a significant restructuring, as the major airlines discovered this practice made them more sensitive than the low-cost carriers to the economic downturn. In fact, the low-cost airlines as a group were able to expand operations and maintain revenue growth in spite of the economic trend.

Passengers became more aware of and discontented with the major network airlines' pricing practices, and many business travelers were no longer willing to trade off ticket restrictions for the price they commanded. They joined the group of low-fare payers. The latter group, on the other hand, became frustrated with the increasing restrictions and reduced quality imposed on their seats. The major airlines found themselves in a bind, as the previously winning policy of restricting the low-fare travelers did not stimulate full-fare revenues any longer, and at the same time reduced demand and revenues by low-fare travelers. The effectiveness of the traditional approach to yield management (segmenting and fencing high-fare paying passengers by imposing restrictions) has eroded as passengers have become more sensitive to price and often buy low-fare tickets even if actually they were willing to pay more.[205]

Even before the events of September 11, 2001, it had become all too clear that the dominant business model of the previous decade needed to be adjusted to a new

[205] See, for example, Cooper, Homem-de-Mello and Kleywegt (2004) for the *spiral-down effect*.

reality. This conclusion was amplified by the continuing growth and relative success of the group of low-fare startup airlines.

## 4. CRISIS ONCE AGAIN

The 1990s ended with the notion that the major network airlines had become too strong and used their unchallenged power to limit new entry and extract super-normal profits. The early 2000s, in contrast, started with the notion that the major network airlines may be doomed to go the way of the dinosaur. Calls for government antitrust intervention were replaced with calls for government financial assistance in order to keep them flying. Just several years before believed invincible, the major network airlines were straggling for survival and for the first time since deregulation faced meaningful competition from low-cost mostly point-to-point airlines.

### 4.1    September 11, 2001, and the New Terrorist Threat

Early one morning—after more than ten years when US aircraft had not been involved in fatal crashes due to sabotage—four United and American aircraft carrying passengers and ten tons of jet fuel each were flown into the World Trade Center, into the Pentagon, and into the ground in Pennsylvania. The next morning, we awoke to a new reality that had immediate devastating operational and economic challenges along with substantial new long-term implications.

A mere three months later, an American Airlines passenger was subdued by the cabin crew as he was trying to ignite explosives in his shoe. A number of other aircraft were diverted and forced to land for reasons of anthrax scares. All this reflected the vulnerability of air transportation to biological and chemical terrorism. In this new environment, F-15 and F-16 jet fighters were summoned to follow suspicious commercial flights over US territory. Passengers had to stand in never-before-experienced long lines and wait for security inspections. They were subject to removing their shoes and sometimes even their clothing, and their nail clippers and razors were confiscated. Wide and frequent media coverage of these issues and reports of alleged failures of security systems, as they struggled to adjust to the new reality, did nothing but increase passengers' concerns and exacerbate their fears about flying.

At the end of 2002, a hand-held missile was fired at (but fortunately missed) an Arkeia Israeli Airlines chartered flight of a 757-300 with 270 passengers on board taking off from Mombassa, Kenya. This, with follow-up media coverage of potential hand-held missile risks, demonstrated, that in this new reality, taking proper security steps at airports and on board aircraft might not be enough to prevent terrorist sabotage. Suicide bombings of exotic tourist attractions in Bali and Kenya in 2002 raised travelers' concerns all the more. These are the kind of new exotic destinations that deregulation had made possible for a wide range of people at affordable rates. It was suddenly clear that flying would never again be the same.

## 4.2   *Industry in Crisis*

The industry posted $10 billion in operating losses for the calendar year 2001, $4.5 billion of that generated during the fourth quarter of the year immediately after September 11 alone. Total annual losses were over $6 billion. Operating losses for the calendar year 2002 were roughly $9 billion, and total losses approached $7 billion.

A careful review of airlines financial performance reveals that, although the industry as a whole posted operating losses, the low-cost airlines, as a group, posted operational profits.[206] Financial data confirm a trend that had started before September 11, 2001, that in the new environment major network airlines would suffer proportionally more than the competing low-cost airlines. In fact, in a relatively short period immediately after September 11, several low-fare and regional airlines were able to recover, increase capacity, and actually grow. The major airlines by contrast reduced capacity and consolidated operations, and yet continued to show substantial losses.

The three largest major airlines, once considered invincible, prompting concerns of monopolistic power and the blocking of meaningful entry, were struggling to survive. Large, complex, high-frequency hub-and-spoke networks were slimmed down; flight frequencies were reduced, and flights were spread more evenly throughout the day in order to better use resources and reduce costs. The grounding of many aircraft and switches to smaller planes reduced capacity. Orders for new aircraft were deferred or cancelled.

Revenue management, considered by many to be the success story of the late 2000s, was blamed to a large degree for the majors' failures. The advantage of scope density and scale inherited in a high-frequency, complex, hub-and-spoke network, once considered the majors' source of market power, lost its magic.

In early 2003, United Airlines filed for bankruptcy protection. United had been considered the most financially sound airline during the regulation regime. It was surely thought to have been in the best position to enter deregulation, becoming the largest network airline in the world and one of a group of three major airlines that dominated the industry for more than two decades. In early 2003, industry commentators saw it was conceivable United might even be forced to liquidate, and that American Airlines and possibly other majors would be forced to file for court protection under Chapter 11 of the bankruptcy code.

The September 11 events, the overhanging uncertainty in the US regarding a possible war with Iraq, and continuing terrorist threats only accelerated the economic downturn. All these circumstances had a substantial overall negative economic impact. For the airlines, this represented a form of double jeopardy, because in addition to the general economic recession, they had served as a direct target for terrorist attacks. Unlike the early 1990s' crisis, when the Gulf war ended

---

[206] Particularly Southwest, JetBlue, and AirTran.

in only a few months and oil prices stabilized quite quickly, the new terrorist threat is of an ongoing nature and with long-term structural impact. In addition, oil prices remained high and even increased during the early 2000s. To make things even worse, a new strand of a flu virus (SARS) originating in China appeared in 2003, further affecting passenger demand for flying, and forcing additional reductions in capacity and fares in markets that otherwise seemed somewhat less vulnerable to terrorist threats.

A new type of government security regulation has been imposed on the market. The safety and environmental issues that topped the regulatory agenda during the 1990s gave way to quite new concerns and different public perceptions of terrorist threats and the way to address them. New institutions have evolved to face the new threats. And new questions have been raised as well. How should the economic burden of September 11 and its aftermath be allocated across society? Should airlines be directly subsidized, and if so, on what basis? Who or what sort of agency should be responsible for passenger security? Who should pay for it? Should standard cost-benefit analysis be applied to terrorist threats?

Observing the public and political debate one cannot escape a sense of *déja vu*. As in the previous crisis, perceptions of bust and gloom have triggered renewed calls for re-regulation of the industry. The more severe nature of the industry crisis and the ongoing terrorist threats have been suggested by some to be a reason to re-regulate the industry and even to nationalize it. We should remind ourselves that calls for the regulation or the nationalization of national infrastructure network industries that involve enormous fixed costs and face challenges of volatile demand and cyclical overcapacity are by no means novel, and can be traced to political debates that raged at the turn of the last century.

Yet, on the other side of the debate, one can hear other familiar voices advocating the minimization of government intervention in the market and letting the free market work its course. Such observers argue in favor of continuing the deregulation process through the privatization of airports and the traffic control system and further liberalization of international competition, including on domestic city-pair routes. Proponents of this view expect fewer surviving major hub-network airlines to emerge from this crisis, airlines that have lower costs and are better suited to the new patterns of the public's travel demands. Reduction in costs and increases in market shares of the surviving major network airlines are expected to be the basis of their market strength, once the economy recovers.

## 5. THE LOW-COST AIRLINES PHENOMENON

There is increasing evidence that the so-called *low-cost airlines,* offering mostly point-to-point service, have fared better than the large incumbent network airlines during the economic downturn.[207] After a long time when the major network airlines

---

[207] The term "low–cost" airlines became synonymous with startup airlines or new entry by non-major network airlines. They are also sometimes called low-fare or discount airlines. The main members of this group in the US are Southwest, ATA Airlines, America West, JetBlue, Spirit, and Airtran (previously ValueJet).

were considered invincible and Southwest a singular success story, it appears for the first time after deregulation that new entrants in this group in fact pose a serious and increasing threat to the majors. Many industry observers have interpreted the relative success of this group, especially in the face of the severe crisis affecting the majors, as an indication of the failure of the complex hub network as a business model.

The emergence of the new low-cost airlines is an important phenomenon that deserves further discussion. We should note at the outset that the name *low-cost* that was coined to describe this group of airlines may be somewhat misleading, as these airlines offer a different kind of service, and only segments of the overall service offered by the major incumbents. In fact, the airlines in this group are quite diverse with respect to the specific market opportunities they respond to, their specific market penetration, and their overall business strategies. One striking difference between Southwest and JetBlue, for example, is that the former built its growth on *stimulating* market demand by using low fares and relatively high capacity (several round trips per day), and by becoming a major player in very carefully selected often secondary airports in city-pair markets. The JetBlue entry is more of a market *skimming* nature. It often involves flying a limited number of flights in a relatively dense market without becoming a major player in these markets.

The low-cost group, however, shares certain similarities that are noteworthy. They offer mostly point-to-point linear connections, simpler pricing structures, and a minimal number of traditional frill offerings. They serve short- to medium-range (in the US domestic) markets. They usually (but not always) operate one type of aircraft fleet, employ non-unionized labor, and make extensive use of booking and electronic ticketing (major airlines usually pay 9% sales commissions). They have grown quite dramatically, starting around the beginning of 2001, and have maintained their growth post-September 11, 2001. Atypically of traditional entry models, most of them acquired a large number of *new* aircraft, and have enjoyed very attractive prices, financing, and accommodating terms provided by the aircraft manufacturers.

The low-cost startup entry is a trend that is likely to significantly affect the industry evolution. Several of the characteristics of this trend deserve further discussion and analysis.

## 5.1    A Global Phenomenon

The emergence of this group of airlines is by no means unique to the US. It is in fact being taken as a serious threat by major incumbent airlines throughout the world.

In Canada, for example, WestJet, Canada 3000 (the latter a result of a merger between Royal Airlines and CanJet), and Jetsgo have captured almost 20% of Air Canada's traditional domestic market share since the beginning of 2000 and December 2002. Such a competitive response wasn't considered at all likely in December 1999 when the Canadian regulator announced that for no better alternative it was forced to approve the merger and integration of the ailing Canadian Airlines into Air Canada to create one major airline that would dominate the Canadian market. The regulator was very concerned that such integration might in fact create a monopoly and placed various restrictions on the new Air Canada.

Despite these concerns, competition has actually increased markedly. A significant reduction in overall demand due to September 11, the impact of the economic recession, and loss of market share to the new low-cost startup carriers forced Air Canada to file for bankruptcy protection in 2003. Air Canada introduced its own brand name, Tango, and a subsidiary airline called Zip as answers to this new competition. The low-fare market in Canada may have become too crowded and too competitive.

In Europe, the Irish entrants Ryanair and the British EasyJet are the most significant low-cost carriers to seriously threaten the struggling incumbent majors.

## 5.2 New Aircraft and the Manufacturers' Role

The developing relationship between the aircraft manufacturers and the group of low-cost airlines is a new and very important element in the current dynamics of the airline industry that deserves further discussion. The economic downturn commencing in early 2001 and the financial post-September 11 crisis forced the major incumbent airlines to reduce capacity, ground aircraft, and defer new aircraft deliveries and orders. This, of course, made the major airlines—the traditional buyers of new aircraft—unlikely candidates for acquiring new aircraft.

The manufacturers, however, had built a large (mostly fixed-cost) production capacity, and looked to book sales even at significantly reduced prices. New aircraft deliveries in 2002 dropped to 673 units after four years of between 800 to 900 new aircraft deliveries per year. Deliveries for 2003 were below 600 units. By the end of 2002, more than 2000 aircraft had been removed from service and parked in various storage facilities, most of them withdrawals by major incumbent airlines.

In this reality, the startup airlines became the only game in town for the manufacturers, which would otherwise be forced to practically stop production or store new aircraft off the production line.

The traditional alliance between the manufacturer and the major incumbent airlines has shifted quite dramatically, as the manufacturers started focusing on the emerging group of new airlines as a major market opportunity for their new aircraft. The beginning of this trend can be traced to the crucial role that Airtran (ValueJet) played as the major launching airline for the Boeing 717 (MD95), eventually ordering 59 aircraft.

This trend became more apparent and more significant as the competition between Boeing and Airbus over market dominance increased. Boeing captured American Trans Air (ATA) and facilitated a complete fleet change with new-generation Boeing 737 (37 aircraft) and a new extended version of the 757-300 (12 aircraft). ATA has phased out the older aircraft it operated and has changed its business plan to become an important player in the low-cost scheduled market. JetBlue ordered 78 new Airbus A320 aircraft to provide capacity for its startup operation. This is the first time that a startup airline had committed to such a large number of aircraft at such a substantial cost. In 2003 JetBlue ordered an additional

65 aircraft and placed 50 additional options. In Europe, Easy Jet ordered 120 new A319 from Airbus, and negotiated options for additional 120 aircraft. Ryanair ordered 153 737-800s, and negotiated options for an additional 125 aircraft. Ryanair took over another low-fare airline, Buzz, and in fact has challenged Air France's position as the third-largest airline in Europe after British Airways and Lufthansa.

The detailed terms and conditions of new aircraft acquisition agreements are usually unpublished, but the available information points toward major accommodations by the manufacturers in order to attract low-cost airlines to new aircraft. Average new aircraft prices have been slashed dramatically, in some cases perhaps even by almost half list price. Manufacturers have also taken part in maintenance and financing and in the disposition, residual value guaranty, and trade-in of older aircraft that have been replaced by the new aircraft.

It is this unprecedented drive by the manufacturers to sell aircraft by cutting prices and assuming some of the risks of the startup airlines that has fueled the growth of this new type of airline competition. Moreover, since new aircraft require only minimal maintenance cost during their early lives, these airlines enjoy a (temporary) cost advantage over the incumbent airlines that is surely helpful during their initial penetration stage and building of market share. Passengers, in return, get the best-quality aircraft for prices that were simply not conceivable only a few years before.

The question is, however, how long will this last? Will the new airlines be able to generate sufficient market share, and earn enough once the honeymoon period is over?

## 5.3    Labor Costs

Another important cost advantage of the low-cost airlines is their non-unionized labor and low labor costs. This is an important issue, by some counts the most significant challenge for the struggling major incumbent airlines.

Labor is the largest single category of industry costs. Figure 20 shows that the total labor-related expenditures of the major and national passenger carriers during the second quarter of 2003 were over one-third of the industry's total costs (more than the combined costs of fuel, ownership, interest, insurance, maintenance, materials, landing fees, communications, advertising, and food).[208]

Labor costs have increased consistently since deregulation in spite of the fact that the industry's real yield has dropped (see Figure 21[209] and Figure 18 for labor costs and real yield trends, respectively). Note in particular the increase in labor costs between 1998 and 2002, when revenues dropped significantly. Labor negotiations in the late 1990s and aggressive labor union activity focused on the industry's financial success during the second part of the decade, while ignoring the beginning of a new

---

[208] Source: Air Transport Association.
[209] Source: Air Transport Association.

revenue crunch. But even in the year 2002 and after the dramatic negative economic impact of September 11, labor costs continued to rise.[210]

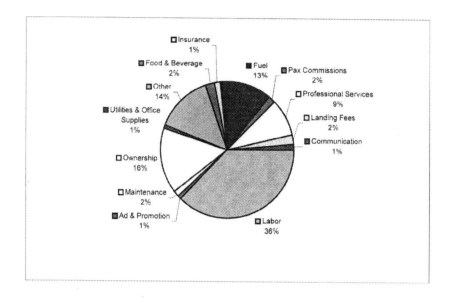

*Figure 20. Cost Allocation 2003*

Most of the increase in labor costs is attributable to the major incumbent network airlines. Figure 22 shows the rate of increase in labor costs per available seat-mile during 1998-2001. During this time, United increased its labor costs by over 25% and American and Delta by over 20% each.[211]

It is important to mention again that the major incumbents entered deregulation encumbered by certain complex, irreversible, and downward-rigid labor-related contractual and institutional arrangements. For example, labor negotiations were and still are regulated by the Railway Act of 1933.[212] Labor agreements have been renegotiated repeatedly since deregulation, yet labor costs have continued to rise. Airline employees, in fact, are compensated at a level nearly twice the average for all US industries.[213]

---

[210] During 1998–2002 one strike, ten non-strike work actions, and four presidential interventions occurred.

[211] Source: United Airlines filings in bankruptcy court (calculations based on US DOT Form 41).

[212] For a detailed analysis see GAO (2003).

[213] See BLS National Compensation Survey July 2002. Available on the internet at http://www.bls.gov/ncs/ocs/home.htm#overview.

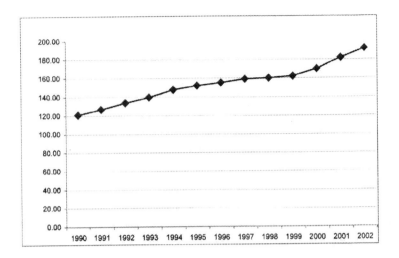

*Figure 21. Labor Cost Index*

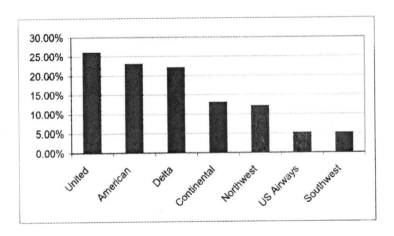

*Figure 22. Increase in Labor Cost per Available Seat Mile, 1998-2001*

The current labor institutional arrangements and agreements of the incumbent network airlines are complex and far-reaching. They touch upon every aspect of an airline's operation and costs in significant and not always obvious ways. Union representatives are directly involved in and influence most of the airlines' decisions. It is common for labor arrangements to affect a vast spectrum of activities covering, for example, the purchasing of paper clips or the purchase or leasing of aircraft. Labor arrangements affect organizational structures, processes, and procedures such as maintenance programs, aircraft operational manuals, and training. They are rooted in every airline's history and became imbedded in its culture. They include aspects that not only dictate direct high wages and costly benefits but also impose highly restrictive work rules and organizational procedures that require more employees and higher costs (for example, minimum monthly pay guarantees and vacation overrides). They also impede an airline's strategic freedom to compete in deregulated markets. Labor agreements, for example, restrict the use of smaller and more cost-efficient regional jet aircraft, limit the scope of code-sharing agreements, and prohibit or restrict outsourcing of maintenance and other services to lower-cost vendors.[214]

As previously discussed, the major airlines' strategic move to create complex hub-and-spoke networks was motivated to a large extent by their attempt to average down their high and rigid labor costs. During the 1990s the strategic combination of high-frequency hub operations and price differentiation, in the face of a relatively limited but growing low-cost competition, accommodated such high labor costs. But the drop in high-fare paying passengers and the expansion of low-cost competition starting in the late 1990s posed a serious challenge to the major incumbents.

Low-cost startup airlines pay their mostly non-unionized labor significantly less per seat-mile. In addition, large-scale layoffs by struggling major airlines during the early 2000s provided the low-cost airlines with opportunities to hire experienced and non-unionized labor to accommodate their expansion. Free from historical labor commitments and constraints, the low-cost airlines pay less for employees who work and produce far more.[215] In addition, the new aircraft's maintenance "honeymoon" period, mentioned before, reduces the need for maintenance labor for new startup airlines like JetBlue, for example.

Figure 23 compares labor costs by airline in 2001.[216] The cost differences between the incumbent network airlines and the low-cost airlines are striking. United and American paid their labor more than double the amount paid by JetBlue per seat. They also paid one and a half times the amount paid by the low-cost incumbent Southwest.[217] Continental Airlines has the lowest labor cost among the major incumbent airlines. This was achieved only after aggressive restructuring efforts mostly during its two bankruptcies in 1983 and 1990.

---

[214] United Airlines Chapter 11 bankruptcy case offers an interesting account of the airline's experience with its labor unions. See, for example, Informational Brief dated December 9, 2002 by United.

[215] Average pay for a United captain, for example, is more than double the pay of a JetBlue captain while the latter spends almost twice the amount of hours in the cockpit.

[216] Source: United Airlines filings in bankruptcy court (calculations based on US DOT Form 41). US Airways reflects pre bankruptcy cost.

[217] The cost differences become even more significant when they are adjusted to stage length. United adjusted cost is 4.75 cents and JetBlue's is 1.95 cents. Southwest is an incumbent low-cost airline and is bound by historical labor commitments that may put it in a disadvantageous position relative to a new startup like JetBlue.

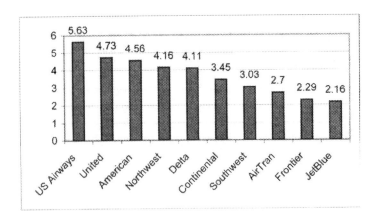

*Figure 23. Labor Cost per Available Seat-Mile (cents) 2001*

One cannot overestimate the importance of the labor issue for the survivability of the incumbent network airlines and the unfolding industry structure. The challenge in this respect is enormous and involves far more than just cutting wages and benefits. It requires a complete change in a complex web of organizations and processes that had evolved during 40 years of regulation. It is clear that in spite of continuing negotiations and changes, labor issues have not properly adjusted to fit the new reality of the deregulated market. They must be radically changed in order for the major network airlines to survive.

## 5.4    Network Architecture

Low-cost airlines operate mainly point-to-point routes. The major incumbents operate complex hub-and-spoke networks. Is point-to-point service in general superior, or does it involve less cost than complex hub networks?

It is important to recall, first, the major advantages of operating a complex network system. Assume that an airline (or a regulator) wishes to figure out the least costly structure to connect a given set of nodes (origins and destinations). Hub-and-spoke networks require, in general, fewer connecting flights to service the same set of nodes compared to direct service to the same nodes. For example, in December 2002, Southwest, the sixth-largest airline in the US, served 68 cities in 31 states with 375 aircraft, mostly by linear point-to-point service. Us Airways, the seventh-largest airline in the US, served 177 cities in 38 states plus 23 international cities with 360 aircraft. US Airways operated 15 fewer aircraft in its complex network to serve 132 more cities, which illustrates the advantage of a complex network structure over a linear structure.

Thus, *everything else equal*, a hub-and-spoke network can be a less expensive production alternative to connect the same nodes. The hub-and-spoke network, furthermore, has the advantage of density and scope. This is important, particularly with respect to nodes that have relatively small city-pair markets. The network structure, in fact, combines passengers originating in various nodes, and channels them through a hub flight to a destination node. Thus, city-pair markets that may not justify a linear direct connection due to a relatively small market size can sustain service through a hub.

Also, adding a node to a hub network has a non-linear system-wide effect, creating many new combinations of service and increasing density. A network structure, however, requires passengers to use connecting flights, which creates bottlenecks and congestion, and requires sufficient hub capacity in order to serve a large network.

Major network airlines offer connections of a wide variety of origins and destinations at high frequencies, by combining complementary legs and increasing aircraft cycles. Integration with regional and international airline through code-share or otherwise further increases the node variety on a global basis. Operating such a network system requires a substantial amount of fixed cost and complex pricing strategies in order to recoup such costs.

Point-to-point competitors usually choose to service a certain market in a certain city-pair. Such a strategy could be called *cherry-picking,* since only certain markets that suit specific operational (primarily aircraft characteristics) and marketing parameters are serviced. In such specific markets, these airlines may have a relative cost or pricing advantage over the incumbents.

We can think of a network airline as a supermarket, offering everything for every taste, and a low-cost airline as a specialty store that concentrates on operating one type of aircraft serving a select market on certain selected legs. A point-to-point operation cannot enjoy the spillover traffic of connecting flights that a hub network enjoys, so it must have a large enough market to provide at least a breakeven load factor and allow for frequent round-trip aircraft operations.

Southwest, for example, implemented its point-to-point strategy by selecting secondary airports, those not usually served by major incumbents, and stimulating demand by relatively low prices. Southwest competed for many years in a general market segment that was also serviced by the major incumbent, but flew to secondary airports and therefore offered a substitute and not equivalent product. Other airlines selected high-density markets, even if served by major incumbents, provided that they had sufficiently large potential markets to support their point-to-point flights.

While the complex network structures have provided the major incumbents economies of scope and enabled their market dominance, such a framework is inherently vulnerable to competitive attack. First, a startup entry may focus on a market niche or a small segment of the network market, and would not have to invest the huge sunk cost involved in being a full-scale competitor, at least during its market penetration period.

Second, price discrimination that facilitates the recouping of joint production fixed costs by a network airline may invite competition in several major ways. The startup might attack the high-paying market segment and offer a competing service at a lower price. It can also compete in the low-paying segment of the market even at the same price by eliminating the restrictions that the major incumbents impose on this segment in order to differentiate their service.

Third, point-to-point competitors may have marketing and cost advantages in offering non-stop service in city-pairs that are served by a network airline but require a connection in a hub (if the market is large enough).

Thinking in terms of general network architecture principles, we are likely to conclude that complex hub-and-spoke networks are effective and expected to persist as a part of any air transportation system. Direct point-to-point type service has its own particular advantages, and it should be expected to coexist along with complex hub networks when the markets served are sufficiently dense to make such operations profitable.

## 6. WHAT NEXT?

The major incumbents are challenged by many circumstances today: economic recession, significant security concerns, and new competition that has accumulated enough market share to pose a serious threat. This is the first time since deregulation that such competition is posing a real threat, a threat that is particularly challenging because of the particular environment today.

A few points are worth reiterating in this regard. First, world-recognized major incumbents (United and American) were singled out in the September 11 events, which besides the direct economic impact prompted the notion that perhaps small startups may attract less terrorist attention and therefore may be a safer travel alternative.

Second, as we have noted, the economic recession pushed overall demand down, but in particular demand for business travel, the traditional market served by the major incumbents.

Third, the global economic downturn, terrorist threats, and fears about SARS reduced more than overall demand but particularly the international trips provided only by the major incumbents.

Finally, because of all these trends, domestic low-fare-paying traffic became the major source of industry revenues, and it is this market that the startup low-fare airlines have targeted.

Under these conditions, the major airlines' traditional high-revenue base contracted, and price discrimination lost its previous effectiveness because high-fare payers are hard to find. Thus, the major incumbents had to reposition themselves to attract that market segment that is price-sensitive, which they had heretofore neglected and which is now also subject to meaningful new competition. The majors must not only compete with airlines that serve this market segment at a lower cost, but also generate enough revenue to cover their accumulated high losses *and* the cost of maintaining their large underused capacity and extensive debt. New startups are spared this burden. They are much more fit to compete and to attack the incumbents when the majors are quite vulnerable and hurting already.

Are complex hub network airlines, in fact, doomed to go the way of the dinosaur, as some observers suggest? Will point-to-point airlines eventually dominate the market? Is the competition we observe now in fact a battle between two competing standards for market dominance? Given the current environment and industry history, which of the airlines in the complex network and point-to-point groups will survive?

How will the market structure evolve? Will the startup airlines stick to point-to-point operation as a long-term strategy, or will they adopt hub network operations? Or a combination of both?

Economists like to imagine a benevolent planner or a regulator that with the help of an understanding of network architecture could design the most efficient manner to connect a given set of nodes, subject to aircraft operational and market characteristics. Will the free market in fact evolve in this direction?

There are many ways the future may unfold, depending on many uncertain factors as well as the specific strategies that players adopt to respond to opportunities and threats. If history is any guide, we may be surprised again. Perhaps an outcome that we have not even thought about, or have believed has only a small likelihood to emerge, will emerge (or maybe not!).

There is no doubt that the startups and the commuter airlines as a group have shown remarkable and perhaps unprecedented success in penetrating the market. This is due, among other things, to aircraft and labor cost advantages, and also to the fact that their market entry coincided with the damage inflicted on the incumbents by the consequences of September 11 and economic recession. Will the startups' successful entry last? What will happen next?

The following are a few important points to consider.

## 6.1  Strategic Response of the Major Airlines

The major incumbents must respond strategically to the startups' entry. Will their strategic response help them defend their market share or otherwise survive? The majors are obviously struggling to survive and to maintain their dominance. They must adjust to the new reality, and find strategies to reduce their average cost or the cost of serving the market segments where they are threatened, or otherwise increase revenues.

This requires direct cost-cutting by renegotiating labor contracts and debt and lease obligations, and rethinking and redesigning their fleet and network structures and hub operations. They must do this with or without bankruptcy court protection.[218] Moreover, since major incumbents are subject to historical labor, debt, and other contractual costs of maintaining their systems, will they be able to radically cut labor costs? They may be forced to further increase concentration and integration through merger, code-share, or other arrangements that would increase their market share and average their costs down. Increasing market share may compensate for their inherent relative cost disadvantages.

---

[218] As of this writing, US Airways had just emerged from Chapter 11, and United and Hawaii Airlines had filed for court protection and were struggling to reorganize.

Delta, for example, responded directly to the low-cost competition by establishing its own low-cost point-to-point airline (Song). United followed suit with its version of low-cost operation (Ted). Previous attempts by major incumbents to start low-cost airlines have not been particularly successful. Will this attempt be any different? American decided to face the competition by changing its fleet configuration and competing within its current structure. Will this strategy work any better?

US Airways had reorganized its affairs and reemerged from Chapter 11 bankruptcy as a smaller lower-cost airline. Shortly thereafter it was forced to seek court protection once again. Will the restructured US Airways—still encumbered with debt and expecting to lose for a while—survive? Will United survive bankruptcy? Will any major airline (American?) acquire the struggling United in its quest to increase market share and reduce costs?

The regional airlines have been expanding dramatically. Equipped with new and smaller jet aircraft, they may be better positioned than the majors to compete in a substantial portion of the same market attacked by the startups. Did the regionals overextend their fleets and order too many aircraft prior to the crisis? What role will they play in the competition against the startups?

Hub operations have also changed in response to the new conditions. High-frequency flight schedules during peak demand periods have been spread more evenly throughout the day in an attempt to reduce costs (*rolling hubs*). High-frequency operation during peak demand periods was traditionally believed to be a major strength to hub airlines—a prime quality indicator that distinguished major hub airlines from the competition. It remains to be seen how this sort of development will affect cost and demand.

## 6.2    Role of the Government.

The government plays an important role through two major mechanisms: antitrust action, and direct financial assistance. It is usually the case that antitrust concerns are assigned less importance during times of financial crisis. In fact, after a relatively long period of indecision, the government approved a marketing integration agreement among Delta, Continental, and Northwest in 2003, an agreement with only a slim chance of approval prior to September 11. Passengers on any of these airlines will be able to integrate frequent flier mileage, which may give these airlines an advantage over startups. Antitrust impact may become very significant if two (or more) struggling major incumbents attempt to merge or if United Airlines, or any major airline for that matter, plans to liquidate and other major airlines might want to acquire its assets.

The distribution of funds from the September 11 financial aid package to airlines has affected their cash flow position and survivability as well. The manner of distribution can directly make or break an airline, and therefore is a target for lobbying and political interest group pressure.

## 6.3    What Will Happen After the Startup Aircraft Honeymoon?

Part of the cost advantage associated with the startups' acquisition and operation of new aircraft is temporary. In not too many years, very expensive maintenance work will be required on these planes. The startups may also face increased lease and debt payments after the end of the initial financial accommodation period provided by the manufacturers.

How long will this honeymoon last? What will happen after the honeymoon period? Will the market share accumulated during the honeymoon be enough to keep operations profitable with increasing costs? Will the future average cost of the startup airlines still be lower than the average cost of the major incumbents? Fares may be forced up with increasing costs; will low-paying passengers continue to be attracted to startup airlines even if fares rise?

## 6.4    The Next Ad Hoc Coalition

The aircraft manufacturers' strategy has been a very important engine driving the evolution of the industry. I argued in previous chapters that during the 1980s and 1990s the manufacturers and major incumbent network airlines formed an ad hoc coalition that impeded startup entry. In this chapter I argued that in the early 2000s the economic crisis have forced major incumbents to reduce fleet capacity and therefore eliminated them, for a while, from the market for new aircraft. Driven by high fixed costs and commitments to labor, and competing over market share the manufacturers have effected the unprecedented dramatic expansion of a new breed of low-cost airlines using new aircraft. In this go around the manufacturers, in fact, hurt the major incumbent airlines—their traditional buyer group. But what will happen next?

The low-cost startup airlines placed a very large number of orders and options for new aircraft acquisition encouraging very optimistic expectation for expansion and overreaction to the potential success of the new-low cost business model. At the same time, the major incumbents are restructuring, regrouping, and repositioning themselves for the new market environment. It is expected that a smaller (but surely leaner) group of major incumbents would emerge from the crisis ready to the next round. And they would most probably be the next major potential buyers for new aircraft. The major airlines are frustrated, perhaps even feeling betrayed by the manufacturers' alliance with the startup airlines. And it is very likely that they would push the manufacturers to further cut the price of new aircraft in the next go-around so that they are better fit for the battle.

It is also interesting to see if the fierce competition between Boeing and Airbus in the long-range and international markets (with their new 7E7 and A380 aircraft) would create a new breed of low-cost startup airlines in theses markets as well. Such startups, if created, might further hurt the major incumbents.

## 6.5    Post-Penetration Strategies

What will the startups' objective and strategic moves be, once they have established themselves and gained initial market share? One of the striking aspects of the Southwest Airlines success is that it has stuck for more than two decades to the same general strategy of mostly expanding its point-to-point operation with one type of aircraft into carefully selected domestic cities.[219] Will Southwest continue this strategy?

JetBlue decided unexpectedly to expand regionally with smaller regional jets. How will this strategy evolve? Will JetBlue expand its operations across the Atlantic? Its location at New York's JFK Airport obviously provides it interesting international opportunities.

One of the interesting opportunities that may unfold is expansion through mergers and takeovers of other airlines or buying assets from other airlines. Low-cost airlines may be able to acquire assets from other major airlines in trouble or facing liquidation, if such sales occur. Perhaps paradoxically—and because of the stock market's peculiarity—startups that become investors' favorites may end up meriting a high market valuation because of very optimistic expectations of future performance, which could facilitate takeovers through acquisition of shares.

In early 2003, Southwest's market valuation was over three times the valuation of the largest five major airlines combined. This perhaps reflects investor community confidence in the continuing success of this airline along with a conviction that airlines that survive the current crisis will prosper in the future.

The stock market also accepted JetBlue very enthusiastically, speculating that it was the next industry's success story. In the spring of 2003, with just over two years in business and operating 40 aircraft, JetBlue's market valuation was already over twice the valuation of American Airlines and higher than American and United combined. Only time will tell whether the market has overreacted or not. Obviously such a significant market valuation could provide JetBlue or any other startup with the potential power to takeover a major incumbent airline or substantial part of its assets if it adopts such a strategy. Will JetBlue pursue a strategy like this?

Will major network airlines go the way of the dinosaur? Probably not. The point-to-point airlines are expected to keep on taking advantage of market opportunities and continue to grow. Some will be successful, and some may not. The major network airlines may be forced to further consolidate and integrate in order to reduce average fixed costs and reposition themselves to withstand the new startups' threats. There will be losers in both camps, and most probably a very small number of winners.

---

[219] With the acquisition of Morris Air as only a relatively small divergence.

# CHAPTER 9

# ON THEORY AND POLICY IMPLICATIONS

> Deregulation has not given us what we wanted, and the conditions it was supposed to rectify are worsening... The result is what we have today—a balkanization of our aviation system—16 major hubs dominated by one carrier. New entry, real new entry is virtually unheard of (Senator Ernest Hollings, July 27, 2000).[220]

> Today, American [Airlines] faces low cost competition on 70 percent of our routes. The challenge now for large network carriers like American is to revise our business model not only to deal with our old rivals, but also to prepare our company for long term success in an environment where newer, lower cost competition represents a much bigger slice of the marketplace (Donald J. Carty, American Airlines CEO, September 24, 2002). [221]

Economists have made remarkable contributions to antitrust and regulation theory and implementation. The influence of economic theory in this area is perhaps unique. Yet economists are often at odds with the way policy is in fact shaped and implemented. They are also often at odds with one another. We can benefit from a look at some major aspects of economic theory and its implications for regulation and antitrust policy issues specific to the aviation industry.

My discussion generally contrasts the traditional view that has dominated antitrust implementation with new or alternative theoretical ideas and conclusions. And, matching the current state of economic thought, my discussion raises more questions and highlight antitrust dilemmas more than it suggests a clear-cut policy menu.

It is well accepted that sound policy advice usually requires not only attractive concepts but also extensive empirical testing as to their validity. Such empirical testing is often difficult to enable. Also, specific industry trends relating to complex market dynamics are often tied to specific history and events, and therefore cannot be deduced from traditional generalized quantitative analysis. In this respect, while the new theoretical thinking is highly appealing on an intuitive basis, the real-life importance of its conclusions may not be clear and is often a matter of judgment.

---

[220] Hearing on Airline Competition, http://commerce.senate.gov/hearings/0727hol.pdf.

[221] Testimony before the Subcommittee on Aviation, House Committee on Transportation and Infrastructure. http://www.house.gov/transportation/

## 7. STATE OF CURRENT THEORY

Economic theory has changed quite dramatically during the last 20 years or so. Better theoretical understanding of strategic behavior and complex dynamics and a wider acceptance and reformulation of evolutionary views of the economy (including neo-Schumpeterian, neo-Austrian, and neo-institutionalist views) allow us to observe, reinterpret, and remodel the market in different and exciting ways. It widens our focus to include—in addition to the traditional static norms of economic welfare—issues of market and competition *processes* and *dynamics*, which have largely remained outside mainstream traditional thought. This new understanding gives the old debates regarding government regulation and antitrust a new life.

The good news is that we now have at our disposal perhaps the richest and the most insightful theory ever, and we can understand and analyze in a theoretical context many observed phenomena that earlier escaped the dominant line of the traditional thinking. The theory also has important policy messages, emphasizing technology, incentives, and institutions. The bad news, however, is that the new theory is different from and often at odds with the traditional views, and that the main issue—the extent and the manner of government intervention in markets—is left largely unresolved and open to further debate and personal judgment. And in fact, one can still find traditional *and* new theoretical foundations for why government intervention should take any position along the political spectrum, as certain economists advocate market socialism and others conservative *laissez faire*, with equal conviction.

The current theoretical map is eclectic, fragmented, partial, and often tentative and evolving. Instead of the dominant traditional view with its universal grand theory, general equilibrium, nature, we now have quite a large number of partial-equilibrium models, illuminating different specific aspects of the market, and in a way that often cannot be generalized. Instead of focusing on a major and well-defined market failure (monopoly), the new models suggest a diverse and widespread array of failures that plague markets in complex ways. Instead of striving for some abstract economy that offers a unique, "best" perfect market equilibrium, we face the challenge of possible multiple equilibria and intertemporal inconstancies. Consequently, economic discourse within the discipline, within industry, within the government, and with the public has become more complex. While it is sometimes discordant, it is also perhaps more pertinent and more relevant to the real world.

The complexity and the conditional conclusions of the new models often make them difficult to communicate or translate into simple general narratives. Moreover, models convey unsettled, ambiguous, and somewhat conflicting general policy messages. Noteworthy are two points that I find particularly important.

First, the theory emphasizes new reasons for potential market failures (asymmetric information, asset specificity, network effects, path-dependence, and other reasons for dynamic inconsistencies) that arguably might cause market breakdowns, lower-than-desirable levels of production quantity and variety, and locked-in inferior outcomes. Yet these claims fly in the face of what we observe in reality.

Second, the theory suggests on the one hand a new and perhaps wider role for government intervention in fixing such market failures, including expansion of the traditional antitrust focus on pricing to issues related to technology creation, standards, and innovation. Yet, on the other hand, it emphasizes complexities and informational, institutional, and political constraints that make the specification and efficient implementation of such intervention policies highly questionable if they are possible at all.

## 8. NON-LINEAR DYNAMICS—SURPRISES ARE INEVITABLE

An observer of the evolution of the industry over more than two decades cannot escape the sense of mistakes and surprises as the basic assumptions, rules, and models we were accustomed to use to interpret the industry's behavior failed altogether to predict the major shifts in its evolution. The most obvious example is that the contestable markets hypothesis that had formed the theoretical foundation in favor of deregulation was refuted. Perhaps ironically, economists advocated for what seems to be the right policy based on the wrong reasoning.

Few observers of the early deregulation experience, for example, expected the complex hub-and-spoke system to evolve the way it did. Observers during the late 1990s focused on hub premiums and price discrimination as signs of market power, but they did not expect it to become both the reason for the collapse of the majors' business strategy in the early 2000s and the source of a market opportunity that attracted new entry. Low-fare startup airlines were not generally expected to emerge as a serious potential threat to the once invincible major incumbents. Who could have imagined during the late 1990s that in a few years industry observers would seriously doubt the continued dominance of American, Delta, and United in the domestic US market? Who would suggest that the complex hub-and-spoke networks might be doomed to go the way of the dinosaur?

We have learned also that the ability of regulators and other observers to gain relevant data, understand the data, and affect market dynamics in real-time is quite limited. One characteristic of complex dynamic systems is that the future may not be uniquely predictable, given the past, and its long-term direction may be clear only with hindsight. It is often the case that our understanding lags real-time events. And sometimes the lags are quite long. Only in the late 1980s, for example, did economists develop and refine concepts of network architecture that the Civil Aeronautics Board could surely have put to very good use during several decades of airline regulation—had they been known then.

Even today, many observers still view airline networks as a linear summation of representative city-pairs, disregarding the basic notion that it is non-linearity that creates network effects; that is, a network's value is not a simple summation of its parts. Also, many economists who conducted empirical studies during the 1990s in order to find the *monopolistic hub premium* missed many aspects of network economics, in particular the understanding of price discrimination and revenue management in this context. Estimations of the average price gap between passengers with low and high willingness to pay—as in several studies—do not necessarily reflect monopolistic distortion in a case of jointly produced, complex combinations of network links and nodes. Economists gained an impressive understanding of these issues during the late 1990s and early 2000s that allows us a better retrospective understanding of pricing strategy in the middle 1990s.

This general line of argument is by no means novel. For decades economists have pointed to uncertainty and imperfect information as the major reasons that government intervention in markets might be more costly than the market failures the intervention was intended to cure. What may be new is that our development of theory during the last decade or so has offered a new analytical interpretation of uncertainty and the way surprise and errors may be inherently built into the *dynamics* of market systems.

According to such market depictions, surprise may be inevitable even if one is able to somehow develop a deterministic model of the market. *Non-linear dynamics* break down the traditional relationships between cause and effect, and at any time the market may be attracted to stable or non-stable structures in a way that may not be predictable ex-ante. According to this view, the fate of the market may be determined dynamically by a combination of specific history and chance.

Our new theoretical perceptions cast serious doubt on the traditional paradigm that views government intervention, whether through regulation or otherwise, as an engineer fixing a machine in order to achieve norms of static efficiency. The new view embraces the notion that the market behaves like a complex, open, and dynamically changing ecosystem, so we now have new questions regarding whether and how the government should intervene to affect such a system. One of the particularly challenging aspects of the new theories is that static universal norms—which we have been accustomed to believing in—may not be relevant in a system ruled by such complex dynamics.

Traditional economists dealing with the issue of "second-best" have emphasized the inherent difficulties in regulating an economy composed of a closely coupled system of partial markets interacting with and affecting each other. Repairing one component of the market system (by regulation or otherwise) often disrupts other markets. The government therefore must consider the overall set of market interactions that would occur in response to a specific intervention policy.

This notion becomes even more challenging if one assumes non-linear dynamic relationships in the economic system. In this case, the government must first guess the market's *natural* direction (can it?); fashion an antitrust policy or a remedy that would move the system in a different and more desirable direction (assuming that such a direction exists and is known); and anticipate the effect of such a policy or remedy on the specific targeted market as well as on the general market system that is dynamically interconnected in complex and unpredictable ways.

This view poses serious antitrust dilemmas. Regulators attempt to anticipate competitive strategic responses and long-term market dynamics in the case of mergers or other integrating moves, for example. Would a merger between two major airlines that achieved horizontal and vertical consolidation necessarily be anti-competitive? Antitrust regulators objected to the proposed United Airlines and US

Airways merger, anticipating that if approved it would significantly reduce competition and increase fares. Would it have? Perhaps such a merger, if approved, could have arguably prevented the bankruptcy of both airlines, as well as creating a more efficient network system by reducing cost, lowering fares, and putting the merged network in a better position to compete with Southwest, JetBlue, and other low-fare airlines—and reduce fares even further.

I mentioned before the merger of the two largest Canadian airlines, Air Canada and Canadian, which raised major antitrust concerns. While many observers perceived this merger as creating a monopoly, the immediate market response was a significant increase in the entry and competition of low-fare startup airlines. And the merger of Boeing and McDonnell Douglas was expected to make Boeing the dominant aircraft-manufacturing firm, controlling more than two thirds of the market.

Yet the competition between Boeing and Airbus in the early 2000s is so far stronger than ever; Boeing has lost its traditional dominance; and new aircraft prices have dropped as never before. Manufacturers of small (50- to 100- seat) commuter jets have begun to capture a part of the traditional Boeing/McDonnell Douglas market. These results could not have been predicted at all before the mergers happened, nor can we either predict with any certainty the unfolding future market structure. Moreover, traditional empirical studies that are based on large samples of universal historical data might not help much in predicting the future because of the specific history and events that in fact determined its dynamic trajectory.

## 9. COMPLEXITY—THE CHALLENGE OF TRADEOFFS AND AMBIGUITIES

Traditional economics tends to be dichotomist in nature, generally emphasizing simple binary-opposite cases for policy implications. Markets may be perfect or monopolistic, for example, and therefore should be left alone in the first case and regulated in the second. If markets fail to follow the perfect market ideal, a perfect government is expected to cure well-defined market failures in the public interest. Monopolistic pricing is usually viewed as inefficient, and therefore must be a major target for antitrust or regulation.

This perspective defines the foundations of the traditional structural-based antitrust view that has dominated government policy and judicial precedent. A big firm with a large market share, for example, must by that characteristic be a candidate for antitrust scrutiny. The fact that a firm is using sophisticated discriminating pricing techniques is a good indication it has market power that must be addressed. In the real world, however, neither the government nor markets conform to the simple abstraction of the traditional approach. Rather than simple dichotomies, what we face are complex trade-offs and ambiguities that usually cannot be evaluated as good or evil.

Market complexity poses serious challenges for antitrust analysts. In fact, the complex trade-offs that often characterize the analysis of antitrust cases are by their nature susceptible to widely varying emphasis, interpretations, and personal judgment. The antitrust statutes consist of broad substantive provisions, and the courts have been given wide discretion in interpretation, which they often base on changing economic theories. Cases brought by the government are by their nature ambiguous, involving complex trade-offs, and therefore often do not fit a simple *per se* interpretation or meet a straightforward *structure-performance-conduct* litmus test.

It is no accident that in every major antitrust case one finds prominent economists arguing opposing views, and emphasizing different aspects of the same complex story, but with equal conviction. Decisions in such cases by their nature entail a measure of arbitrariness and reflect a court's particular judgment. Conceptual debates over antitrust cases by economists and other observers usually outlive court decisions; they are rarely resolved.

## 9.1    The Dominant Hub Dilemma

Major airlines operating dominant hubs, for example, may arguably possess regional monopolistic power and use sophisticated pricing as well as other potential anticompetitive strategies, and therefore have attracted considerable antitrust attention. A large network and high flight frequency reduce average cost through economies of scale, density, and scope, and give passengers the benefits of schedule coordination that allows smooth interlining and connecting of a large number of city combinations through hubs. Code-sharing and other types of strategic alliances and integration permit downstream and upstream local and global coordination and interlining that again create compatible combinations of cities not otherwise available under a structure composed of several competing small rival networks or linear market structure. But they also capture essential airport facilities; limit rivals' access to the hub; possibly reduce competition over certain consolidated routes; likely facilitate vertical foreclosure; and may have other anticompetitive effects.

Economists have shown analytically that the benefits of a large one-standard network that facilitates compatibility and coordination may outweigh the social cost of its monopolistic structure under certain assumptions (Economides, 2004). In this case, size and market concentration cannot be defined as being *good or evil* since the network is composed of a complex mix of both in a manner that may not be simply segregated or aggregated. There is no doubt there are several clear advantages to scale, scope, and standardization of a dominant hub network, but the benefits may come along with conflicting costs, including impediments to new entry and other potential anticompetitive aspects. These complex trade-offs are often difficult to assess and aggregate, and pose challenging dilemmas to antitrust thinking and enforcement.

## 9.2    The Predatory Price Dilemma

Ambiguities abound in pricing. The predatory pricing case brought by the antitrust division against American Airlines offers a fascinating example. Consumers and antitrust authorities love low fares, but when do low fares lose their social legitimacy?

The crux of this problem is that strategic pricing involves dynamic long-term intertemporal considerations that often cannot be inferred from the facts available. Would the predator eventually be in a position to extract super-normal profits? And if the answer is yes, would it in fact charge monopolistic prices? The practical cost-related benchmarks that the courts often use to determine predatory pricing are usually simplistic and static in nature and cannot capture the relevant information. Competition moreover is multidimensional, and includes many aspects not captured by the traditional price-quantity parameters. Airlines may respond to entry by changing travel agents' commissions and other incentives, by increasing frequent flier benefits, and changing network city-pair combinations and capacity. To make things even more challenging, the joint-production, fixed costs, and uncertain demand involved in major hub operations dictate price discrimination and sophisticated pricing techniques that may make detection of predatory or monopolistic pricing very difficult.

This point has important implications for antitrust cases. The court usually has to find that a firm has *market power* before concluding that it charges monopolistic fares. And a firm's ability to charge fares above marginal cost is traditionally associated with the presence of market power. Yet new theory surveyed before suggests that price discrimination and above-marginal cost fares in network systems are not necessarily an indication of traditional market power. Also, figuring out in an antitrust case the relevant definition of a market and the associated costs becomes very challenging in the case of a complex network system.

A little story may illustrate some other ambiguities and certain general antitrust dilemmas regarding predatory pricing in respond to new entry.

It is arguable that low-fare startup airlines use their "honeymoon" cost advantages relating to transient low ownership and maintenance cash requirements to price their product below accrued average cost during their market penetration stage.

> We're going to destroy the airline business as we know it, [Ryanair's] Chief Executive Officer Michael O'Leary told Reuters as he initiated more fare cutting to spur growth, starting with an offer of a million one-way tickets for 19.99 to 29.99 British pounds apiece.[222]

In the fall of 2003, Ryanair even offered tickets for just over $3 a seat on certain flights in Europe.

Is such behavior predatory? It is too early to know the expected outcome of the fierce competition between the low-fare startups and the major incumbent airlines in Europe and the US. It is conceivable, however, that Ryanair or EasyJet, for example, may dominate at least certain European markets in the future. In fact, Rayne operated close to 500 daily flights during the summer of 2003, threatening to push Air France from its position as the third-largest European airline. Similarly, it is conceivable that JetBlue, for example, might dominate certain New York markets in the future. A legal case might be made that the startups' low-penetration pricing meets the static antitrust benchmark of predatory pricing. Will any antitrust authority

---

[222] Reuters, UPDATE, June 3, 9:45 am, 2003, by Michael Roddy.

268

pursue such a lawsuit while passengers are enjoying such a low price to fly high-quality brand-new aircraft, even if only for a short period?

In these circumstances, the major incumbent may have no other choice but to match prices or aggressively set lower prices in response to the startups' attack. Most of a major incumbent's assets are network-specific, and cannot be easily moved to other activities. A substantial part of its cost is fixed and sunk, and its marginal costs are relatively low. These conditions would encourage fighting back by cutting fares.

Again, however, cutting fares to meet the new entry, or increasing capacity or any other competitive response, may also be described as predatory in terms of current benchmarks, especially since the incumbent must respond to the startup's low cost and low penetration price. The startup airlines in this case might cry foul and perhaps even ask for antitrust intervention. Is antitrust action desirable in such a scenario? Who is the predator in this case?

The antitrust authorities and the public are usually more sympathetic to the startup's position, and the incumbent's response is almost automatically viewed as an attempt to consolidate its monopolistic position, whatever the natural strategic response in deregulated markets. To make things even more complicated, a revenue-maximizing network airline is expected to respond to new entry by cutting fares in the attacked market and raising fares in other markets.

The traditional antitrust theory associates price discrimination with monopolistic power. It focuses attention on separate markets and ignores overall network pricing. The theory therefore may view the incumbent as a predator in one market and charging a monopolist premium in another, disregarding the fact that overall it earns no more than normal profits. Pushed by public opinion, the antitrust authority is more likely to pursue a legal case against the major incumbent— but is such an action justifiable in terms of improving economic efficiency?

## 10. NEW ECONOMY

The debate is joined as to whether the *new economy* requires a major revision in regulation and antitrust policies.[223] This issue is relevant for our airlines analysis, because, although aviation is considered a mature industry, it has many characteristics in common with the network industries of the new economy. This includes: high fixed costs relative to low incremental costs; increasing returns to scale and scope in production; and demand-side network effects and innovation-based competition.

The most salient new element is the notion of demand-side increasing returns to scale due to consumption externalities. According to this perspective, goods and services are not consumed in isolation but rather in compatible combinations of nodes and links, so the overall value of adding a node to the network is higher than the direct value of such a node.

---

[223] The term *new economy* is usually used in connection with the computer, and communications industries.

Complex airline networks combine compatible city-pairs and offer many connections of origins and destinations. And a seat on a flight is not consumed in isolation but in combination with other products and services. In fact, transportation services may not have any value on a stand-alone basis. They are consumed in combination with business, leisure, or other personal components, and they are connected to other compatible networks including reservation systems, air and ground transportation, car rentals, hotels, resorts, and so on. Also, an efficient transportation system is important in maintaining an efficient economic system and has worldwide positive spillover effects. Traditional economies of scale and scope in production together with economies of scale and scope in consumption encourage firms to compete on market share, and larger firms to dominate the market. The new network theories provide an additional, demand-side, perspective on why aviation and other network industries are expected to have natural monopolistic (or oligopolistic) characteristics.

Some of the major conclusion of the new theory are as follows: (Economides, 2004).

1. Network effects have a *natural* tendency to produce markets with a small number of dominant firms and unequal market shares and profits.
2. Economies of scale in production and consumption may make it difficult for small firms to enter and survive unless they produce significant innovation.
3. Innovation contests drive competition.
4. Because of network externalities, price may fail to convey the real value of a service or product, and therefore networks may tend to be smaller than desirable.
5. Markets may be locked into dominant technologies, products, or services (*path dependence*). Such locked-in alternatives may be socially inferior to others by static norms.
6. Demand may not conform to traditional negatively sloped demand curves, and prices are expected to differ from marginal cost.
7. Pricing tends to be sophisticated, and price discrimination is expected in order to recoup fixed and sunk costs.
8. A firm may maximize surplus even under a monopolistic market structure.

Two general observations are worth making. First, these conclusions are at odds with the traditional *structure-conduct-performance* approach that dominates antitrust enforcement. Note in particular that a situation that may look inefficient based on the traditional view may in fact mask a highly competitive and socially desirable natural outcome of oligopolistic competition.

Second, the general conclusions of the new economy models may look quite dated because of their general resemblance to the traditional natural monopoly concept. Also, the Sherman and Clayton Acts and their offshoots are perhaps general and vague enough to serve as a constitution-like instrument and therefore may cover the principles of the new economy without change. What is perhaps new is that advances in theoretical developments give us new analytical tools that help us reinterpret the "old" alternative ideas as to the dynamic and process aspects of competition in a new light. They also help us recognize that aspects of natural monopoly have become quite pervasive throughout the economy. This is contrary to the traditional view that a natural monopoly is a unique exception in an otherwise perfectly competitive world, and should be regulated.

Two of the general conclusions of the new economy theory have particular application to our subject matter and deserve further discussion: the first relates to market inequality and the second to innovative-based competition.

## 11. MARKET INEQUALITIES

As we review the long tradition of antitrust debates (but at the risk of generalizing), one cannot help but conclude that antitrust discourse often adopts a simplistic view of market dynamics characterized by two mutually exclusive and conflicting fixed-point *attractors*. The first would be the ideal perfect competition solution, and the second the inefficient static monopoly solution. Firms are perceived as small relative to the market and have access to the same technologies in the first case, so that none of these market participants could reasonably affect market prices, and the distribution of their market shares and profits would tend to be equal. In the second case, the assumption is that firms aim to obtain market power and earn super-normal profits, and one or a small number of big firms would capture all or most of the market.

Antitrust proponents generally believe that the dynamic tendency of the market system is to approach the static monopoly condition and that it is the responsibility of antitrust and other regulatory bodies to direct the system toward the competitive solution. Proponents of antitrust actions believe that, absent antitrust intervention, economies of scale that stem from network effects, for example, and firms' assumed natural drive to create market power might force a market into a fixed-point structure that might as well be a traditional monopoly. According to Joel I. Klein while with the US Department of Justice Antitrust Division, for example;

> The natural state of markets is not to move toward increasing competition. Market power, rather than a competitive market, is something that every business understandably wants—because it allows a business to increase its profitability at the expense of the consuming public (Klein, 1998, p. 6).

Inequality in the distribution of market share and profits is often taken as a major indication of a movement away from the competitive solution. Antitrust authorities often believe that combating inequality in market share and profits is desirable and would move an industry away from a socially undesirable state of static monopoly. They try to encourage new startup entry (by providing slots to startups, for example), to break dominant firms into smaller firms, to combat price discrimination, and also take a strong stance against mergers and acquisitions and other network integration instruments.

There are two reasons this policy may not accomplish its proclaimed objective. The first is a general methodological argument I learned from one of my graduate school economics professors, and it is important to repeat. It is no secret that the underlying assumptions of the perfect competition model significantly diverge from real-life conditions. It is nevertheless acceptable to economists to treat this model as a *predictive or positive* model, and therefore put its prediction power and not the accuracy of its assumptions to the test. In other words, if the predictions a model generates are "good," the model is considered good, even if its assumptions do not match the real world. But one must be very careful turning such a positive model into a pragmatic policy model for decision-making. We can figure out the desirable policy within the abstract model, but this does not mean that the same policy would bring about similar outcomes if it is applied in a real market that does not operate according to the analytic assumptions made in the predictive model.

The perfect competition model associates, for example, economic efficiency under certain specific assumptions (including homogeneous products produced and consumed in isolation, and firms' equal access to the same fixed technology) and the tendency of firms to be of equal small size relative to the market. But these connections or this result by no means support a conclusion that if antitrust authorities forced airlines (for example) to operate small networks of equal size and charge uniform prices the industry would move toward a more efficient perfect state of competition.

My economics professor drew an analogy to make this point clear. A rooster's morning call could serve as a good theoretical positive model to predict that morning has arrived (it will obviously pass the empirical test). But one should not confound the positive role of a theory and its real-life policy application. Using a positive model as a pragmatic policy model is like suggesting killing the rooster in order to force the evening to come in the morning.

The second reason the typical antitrust reactions may not create a perfect competition is that it is the *natural* dynamic tendency of network industries with significant economies of scale in production and consumption to produce a small group of winners and unequal market and profit shares. In such a case antitrust attempts to encourage new startup entry and object to mergers and code-sharing and other consolidation agreements cannot change the market natural tendency to create structures with a small group of winners, and would not lead to perfect competition (Economides, 2004).

Antitrust authorities might perhaps move a system from being attracted to one oligopolistic state to another and cause a different combination of firms to become the dominant winners, but they are not able to force perfect competition, or impose market share equality.

Looking at industry evolution after deregulation, it is clear there have always been a small group of winners as well as inequality in market shares and profits. Several major airlines have failed and exited, and others have grown larger to dominate the market. Most small startup airlines have exited the market or have otherwise barely survived.

Southwest is the only example of an entrant to become one of the major winners. In the early 2000s, in fact, it was the only winner, capturing most of the industry profits while the other major airlines generated losses. Yet the success of Southwest is associated with its continued growth in size to become one of the six largest major airlines in the industry and capturing dominant market positions. It is no coincidence that the most successful post-deregulation competitive response to free entry is emergence of one large airline that has captured a large market base to become a major airline itself, rather than many indistinguishable small airlines as perfect competition proponents would expect. The success of Southwest together with the failure of several major incumbents changed the *composition* of the group of winning airlines, but did not bring about more equality in market shares or profits.

The wave of new point-to-point entry in the early 2000s in the US and Europe mentioned before is characterized by the startups building very large fleets of new aircraft and positioning themselves to compete in order to become major airlines. In the summer of 2003, for example, JetBlue announced plans for a potential growth to around 300 aircraft in only a few years, and Airtran placed orders or options for an additional 100 Boeing aircraft. In Europe, Ryanair and EasyJet—the most noticeable response to airline liberalization in Europe—announced orders and options that would result in each one operating approximately 250 aircraft in only a few years.

All this reflects the inherent natural tendency to create large networks and capture a substantial market share. And therefore regulators' attempts to free up markets and encourage competition and startup entry do not produce a state that is akin to the perfect competition model.

## 12. INNOVATION AND CHANGE

*Creative destruction* is a term Schumpeter coined in the 1940s to describe innovation as an engine of dynamic change in the capitalist economy. According to this perspective, entrepreneurs and firms try to beat their competition by introducing qualitative changes in production, products, and related organizations and processes. Market creativity is destructive in the sense that some winning innovation or change may push a once-winning incumbent technology, firm, or product out of the market.

This idea was bounced around for several decades as an attractive alternative view to the mainstream's focus on a static monopoly as a major cause for market failure. The concept has more recently gained increasing acceptance among economists and has even become a political buzzword, particularly with respect to innovation races that characterize competition in the new economy. But innovation races are not unique to the new economy. It takes but a quick look at the bread or cereal sections of a local supermarket, for example, to see that it is not the price of a homogeneous loaf of bread or bushel of wheat that drives competition, but rather a whole lot of innovations and changes in a product's quality, appearance, and marketing that take center stage.

### 12.1 Competition in or for the Market?

There are striking differences between the traditional perfect competition view—focusing on competition *in* the market—and the one envisioned by Schumpeter and his adherents—focusing on competition *for* the market. The views depict a different world. The first, the perfect competition world, emphasizes price or quantity as the major instrument of competition. In this case, free entry is expected to drive incumbent firms' profits to zero and offer no incentive for new entry or creation of new enterprises. The equilibrium is stationary and may change only in response to exogenous shocks.

The second view, Schumpeter's, suggests a dynamic disequilibrium process unfolding over time, a market always in a state of flux, driven by flows of innovations and the creation of new but transitory monopolies while old ones are destroyed. Firms are driven to win all or most of the market by introducing innovation—by doing or offering something different (even if only slightly different). If a firm is successful in gaining super-normal profits, other firms will be attracted to join the innovation race, and try to do better and take a bite of the winner's apple. And it is the *actual* and *potential* pressures of such a quantitative competitive threat that keep the winner investing in the creation of innovations in order to maintain its position.

A view of the competition process in the aviation industry (and other innovative industries) as *creative destruction* is very attractive. It is no coincidence that this concept, which borrows from biology, caught the imagination of many economists, when it provided a new vocabulary to describe observed phenomena that could not be described using the vocabulary of traditional models.

Firms in a Schumpeterian world *seek* profits rather than *maximize* profits, and competition is associated with a *rivalry* process that involves *learning* and *discovery*. Competition in a Schumpeterian world captures a wide range of observed competitive activities that involve dynamic changes in all the parameters, processes, and institutions that the traditional models implicitly or explicitly assume are fixed or irrelevant. In this respect, the traditional and the Schumpeterian views are mutually exclusive, in the sense that no perfect competition or pure traditional monopoly exists in a Schumpeterian competitive world, and vice versa.

It is important to note that a traditional static monopolistic condition—which proponents of antitrust see as a threat—entails that all firms and entrepreneurs give up any meaningful attempt to challenge the monopoly, and that consumers submit to paying high prices for less than a desirable quantity, quality, and variety of whatever product or service, without looking for substitute products or services. According to this view, dominant hub strategy and integration agreements between airlines may lock the market into monopolistic positions that block meaningful competition and allow major network airlines to charge above-normal fares for less than a desirable level of production, quality, and variety while impeding product or process improvement and change with no free-market challenge.

Schumpeter disputes that such monopolies exist in capitalist markets. According to him, the ability to gain dominance and appropriate super-normal profit is transitory. It is not a result of market power, but rather a direct reward that is incidental to innovation and creates a new added value for society. Moreover, the monopolist must stay ever vigilant, and keep investing in research and development. It must continue to keep innovating and producing changes in order to maintain its position against potential or actual competing innovations. According to Schumpeter:

> a monopoly position is in general no cushion to sleep on. As it can be gained, so it can
> be retained only by alertness and energy (Schumpeter, 1950, p. 102).

Schumpeter's writings imply a complex and unstable dynamic process that generates a flow of changes and innovations, all the while improving on society's overall creative capacity and welfare. Such a process seems unlikely to get stuck at an inefficient static traditional monopolistic point, as antitrust proponents would suggest.

## 12.2 The Airline Industry and Innovation

The traditional structural parameters of the industry during the 1990s reflect a consistent market dominance by the major network airlines. These conditions were the basis for increasing antitrust concerns and enforcement demands by the government and public representatives. But the circumstances hid intensive qualitative competition pressures, of the Schumpeterian type, that could not be seen in the traditional product-market measurements.

The major airlines did not approach their apparent strong market position as "a cushion to sleep on," nor did they take their dominance for granted. They kept expanding their networks domestically and globally; they fought actual and potential entry, and attempted to further increase consolidation and market share. They were always on their toes, engaged in a competitive endeavor of learning and change, despite their apparent market dominance and the failure of meaningful new entry (except for Southwest). They routinely invested in R&D related to innovations and changes in product, technology, pricing, sales, organization, and similar processes. In this market, a company "must do the next big thing or go bust." And in fact, efforts to create the next big thing consume much of management's energy.

The major network airlines created the next big thing when they adopted the dominant hub network system. Their vertical integration with regional airlines and code-sharing with international airlines created an impressive large global network system and market dominance. They invested in R&D to create innovative computerized booking systems, sales, scheduling, pricing, maintenance, and revenue management techniques.

Competitive changes have been experimented with in a very long list of areas, since deregulation. Only a few changes become noticeable and significant. Major incumbents experimented with: different logos and aircraft livery; food service; in-flight entertainment systems; curbside check-in; seat configuration and leg room; first, business, premium, elite, and many other attempts to differentiate classes; frequency; scheduling; route structures; computerized reservation systems; internet booking and electronic ticketing; airline image;[224] ground and air amenities; maintenance, and so on.

Revenue management and pricing was a particularly major area of innovation and experimentation in the late 1990s. Airlines invested substantial R&D resources in developing computerized pricing methods and processes. The activity focused much more on developing concepts, technology, and processes than on price itself,

---

[224] Delta, for example, adopted a feminine image for its low-cost Song subsidiary. Hooter Air includes two Hooter girls in each aircraft crew.

much more on how to structure fares and adjust them dynamically to market changes than on how much to charge. According to information presented in the antitrust lawsuit against American Airlines in 2000, for example, hundreds of thousands of price changes are filed each day. This behavior cannot be reconciled with the notion of price making in the traditional monopoly model.

Deregulation opened the market up to new entry by incumbent and startup airlines. Many planned and actual startups sprung up with new ideas and proposed changes, in an attempt to challenge the dominant business model of the major airlines, to eat into the majors' actual or potential markets. Although the common denominator of most attempts was to offer lower fares (or higher-value) service, the plans included a long and complex mixture of different product and process characteristics. Every business plan responded to specific perceived market opportunities, offering something different or new that was believed to give a new entrant a competitive edge over the incumbents. Most of these startups failed, many even before starting operations.

According to the DOT, between 1989 and 2000, 87 new applications were submitted to start up scheduled passenger airlines, as well as 66 to start cargo and charter airlines. Fifty-six applications for passenger-scheduled airlines were approved, of which 18 started operations in 2000. Fifty-one charter and cargo airlines were authorized, of which 24 operated in 2000. Only a very few of these entries made a market dent or otherwise gained overall market recognition.

The most important early post-deregulation attempts at innovative startup competition included: charter airlines, building a complex, low-cost hub-and-spoke system (People's Express, Presidential), and the attempt to offer a point-to-point type low-fare service (Southwest). Only Southwest survived to become a real "big thing."

A major part of Southwest's success is related to uncovering and responding to a market opportunity that is associated with certain inherent vulnerabilities in the major incumbents' dominant hub strategy. Southwest offers non-stop flights (eliminating the need to connect through hubs) to secondary airports; these flights are less expensive to operate and help airlines and passengers avoid congestion and delays. Southwest discovered that many passengers are ready to substitute lower fares and non-stop flying with some added cost and inconvenience for ground transportation from the secondary airport.

The overnight mail and small package service initiated by Federal Express in the 1980s is also one of the striking innovations that has affected the market noticeably. The transport of mail and cargo has been a traditional revenue source for incumbent airlines since the inception of commercial aviation. The shuttle concept first introduced by Eastern Airlines and later by Pan American Airlines is another important successful innovation (the shuttles are now owned by US Airways and Delta, respectively). Chartered or scheduled all-business class (or first class) operations were tested several times without noticeable success, but this strategy may have gained some momentum post-September 11, 2001. Lufthansa was the latest newcomer to this type of operation in 2003.

The two most important innovations that are expected to affect the industry's structural evolution in the 2000s are the regional airlines (operating new regional jet technology) and the low-fare point-to-point startup airlines. Airlines in these two categories have been gaining significant market share and taking a significant bite out of the majors' traditional pie. In 2000 there were 519 regional jets in the USA. By year's end 2003 there will be nearly 1,300. Capacity of the largest regional airlines grew at an annual rate of over 20%. Low-fare carriers (other than the regionals) grew at about 13% annually, all the while the big six major airlines shrunk by about 15% in three years.[225]

During almost two decades of deregulation, antitrust authorities concerned themselves with the increasing consolidation, concentration, and other potentially anticompetitive strategic moves by hub network airlines. Price discrimination and in particular higher fares on low-elasticity routes were interpreted as the exercise of monopoly power. As the major incumbents faced significantly falling revenues due to the diminishing demand for high fares and the increased competitive threat of low-fare airlines in the late 1990s, they responded by widening price spreads and creating record-breaking load factors, yet average yields remained almost the same. High load factors exerted significant operational pressures on the complex network system, resulting in increasing passenger dissatisfaction with poorer service quality.

The proponents of the traditional antitrust measures did not see the competitive pressures that the majors faced; they ignored the falling revenues and the below-normal trend of rates of return. They instead interpreted what they saw as the epitome of monopolistic evil. They saw only the charging of monopolistic fares on monopolistic routes, predatory fares against new entry, and diminishing service quality. The government and public representatives mounted unprecedented multiple antitrust and regulatory efforts against the major airlines and took a strong stance against code-sharing and other attempts at integration.

Southwest, on the other hand, meanwhile enjoyed almost complete freedom to compete against the majors and came to dominate almost all the airports it serves. It has offered a different product from the majors; it has a significantly lower cost structure, and its relatively low fares have helped to cap the fares charged by the majors. It has used discriminatory pricing (although to a lesser extent than the majors because of its linear structure); it has not been seriously challenged by direct competition from any lower-fare airline, and its long-term profitability has been far above industry norms. All startup attempts to imitate or challenge Southwest's success and high profitability (and there were many) failed.

There is no doubt Southwest has made an impressive contribution to consumer choice and product diversity as well as lower fares than the network airlines. Yet, looking at Southwest from a traditional structure perspective, we see it has the dominant positions in almost all the airports it serves; it enjoys economies of scale; and it has earned super-normal profits.[226]

This is, however, what Schumpeterian competition is all about. Southwest has captured a significant portion of the potential incumbents' market and has earned above-normal profits in return for its innovative value-added activity. Southwest's

---

[225] Dan Reed, *USA Today*, July 25, 2003.

[226] In 1999, for example, Southwest's operating margin was 16.5%, while the major airlines' margin averaged 6.8%.

competitive pressures on the major incumbents and the potential entry of other players—searching for market opportunities and for weaknesses in the major incumbents' strategy in order to introduce creative changes—keep the majors on their toes.

The wave of low-fare startups in the early 2000s was a response to a new set of market opportunities and weaknesses of the major incumbents. It is worth emphasizing again that the startups responded to market opportunities that were created particularly by: 1) the majors' price discrimination strategy; 2) the cost advantage of using internet rather than standard booking and travel agencies; and 3) unprecedented low new aircraft prices.

The issue of internet booking is important and deserves further comment. An important element in the major airlines' competitive strategy has been their computerized reservation systems (CRS) and agent commission overrides. Antitrust authorities were concerned that the CRS and ticket agent practices impede competition, and thus targeted these two issues for antitrust efforts. Yet, low-fare startup airlines ended up adopting new internet technology that has significantly reduced ticketing and booking costs, avoids agent commissions, and directly informs passengers about market fares. The ability of the majors to manipulate the CRS and agents to foreclose competition has diminished considerably. Moreover, by using internet technology the startup airlines avoided the high commissions that the majors had paid agents (often 9%), and obtained a significant cost advantage relative to the majors. The easy availability of fare information on the internet as well as the use by the low-cost airlines of simpler *(priceable)* dynamic fare strategies made demand segmentation and fencing by the major incumbent very challenging and forced them in many cases to drop or amend traditional yield management methods.

This new wave of point-to-point airlines is threatening not only the major network incumbents but also for the first time potentially threatening Southwest's hegemony as a low-fare airline. The new startups that will succeed are expected to earn super-normal income in return to their ability to innovate, and such success, if it occurs, may take a bite out of both the majors' and Southwest's actual and potential market and income.

The major incumbents must obviously respond to increasing actual and potential competitive threats and to the evolving post-September 11 market. For this reason, the regulator should give them the same freedom to compete that Southwest has enjoyed for more than two decades. The significant post-September 11 expansion of the low-fare airlines occurred in concert with diminishing overall traffic demand and increasing costs (such as for security and fuel) that affected the major incumbents disproportionately. One of the possible responses is increasing domestic and international consolidation and integration among the majors in order to reduce the average cost of maintaining their complex global high-frequency networks. Such a strategy may increase the market share of surviving airlines in this group—a condition that the regulator has traditionally objected to—but this is a natural competitive response that should not be viewed as an attempt to monopolize the market and appropriate economic rents.

## 13. SUMMARY AND CONCLUDING COMMENTS

The year 1938 marked the beginning of the commercial airlines business. Equipped with break-through aircraft technology (the new DC3s), the industry could for the first time financially sustain its operations independently of mail subsidies, and arguably start to freely compete. Instead, economic regulation was imposed following the public utilities concept, eliminating price and entry competition for the next 40 year to come.

At the foundation of the political debates and scandals that led to the regulation in 1938 stood two conflicting views of the economic nature of the industry. On one side of the debate—and supported by the small independent carriers—was the view that the industry is naturally competitive and that the big major airlines conspired with Postmaster General Brown in the Spoils Conference to extract super-normal profits at the public expense. This view was reflected in the short-lived Airmail Act of 1934, which in the trust-busting tradition imposed competitive and open-to-all route franchise bidding, broke down the vertically integrated airlines and aircraft manufacturing firms, and emphasized horizontal competition over routes.

On the other side of the debate—and supported by the major carriers—Brown believed the industry had natural monopolistic characteristics, and therefore awarded route franchises to major large airlines that could exploit economies of scale subject to public utilities type regulation. Eventually, the 1938 Act imposed such a regulation scheme. This generally bipolar view of the industry has not been resolved to this day, and still tends to frame much of the political debate (not to mention the interest structure) as to government intervention in the airlines industry.

Is the industry naturally competitive? Proponents of deregulation in the 1970s believed it is, and that regulation in fact served the airlines' interest and not the public's. The conventional wisdom was that there were no economies of scale and no significant sunk costs in the airline business, and that potential competition would discipline prices. Therefore, regulation is a source of inefficiency and must be done away with.

The industry, however, evolved in a different direction from that expected by most observers: into an oligopoly with a small number of dominant airlines. There seems now to be a wide consensus regarding several major issues. First, economies of scale have played an important role in pushing the industry toward heavy concentration among only a few major players. Second, the success of deregulation really represents a mixed bag—but its overall benefits outweigh its costs. Third, although there is no agreement regarding whether the evolving industry structure justifies any type of government intervention, there is widespread agreement that traditional price and entry regulation failed, and that the industry should not be re-regulated.

### 13.1 Antitrust

In the following I would summarize a number of important general lessons for public policy that can be drawn from the analysis.

First, while it is evident that the natural tendency of the industry has been to create a small group of winning airlines, the evolving industry is anything but approaching a static monopoly state. With hindsight, it is clear that the antitrust concerns, especially during the late 1990s, were over-reactions. The history, so far, confirms the general notion that static monopolies are an endangered species, if they exist at all, in a non-regulated free airline market.

Second, a major reason for the antitrust overreaction is attributable to the traditional focus on structural parameters in the product market while not paying enough attention to qualitative competition and its dynamic aspects.

Third, it is important to recognize that innovation races always existed and have potentially threatened the winners of the day. The fact that only a few of those who attempt innovation and change emerge as new winners should not be interpreted to say that there are not enough participants in the race, or that the competition is not rigorous enough. It is the continuing stream of *potential* and *actual* attempts to innovate and change that drives the industry. Moreover, it is not the number of winners that counts but rather the impact of innovation on the market. Southwest has been the only significant new winner for more than two decades, but its impact on fares and many other aspects of the market has been enormous.

Innovative competition has directly targeted and attacked the major strategic strongholds of the dominant incumbent airlines, and the main targets of this competitive innovation have also topped the regulators' antitrust agendas. The hub-and-spoke concept, long considered the source of the majors' monopolistic power, became the target of the nonstop point-to-point alternative. Price differentiation, once considered a manifestation of monopolistic power, became a target of low, simple, and fairer fares. The computerized reservation systems and agent commission over-rides that gave the major incumbents a unique advantage became almost irrelevant when the startups began to use internet booking and ticketing, thus avoiding agents and related costs. The major airlines' traditional advantage in acquiring new and expensive aircraft and their use of this fact to differentiate their services from low-cost startups, was turned against them in the 2000s. These observations confirm the view that free market creativity either disciplines or destroys temporary monopolies, so antitrust enforcement may not be required.

Four, above marginal cost pricing as well as the complexity and sophistication of the fares must not be automatically interpreted as a manifestation of unwarranted market power. The network nature of the airlines, high fixed and sunk costs, and uncertain demand dictate such pricing. Moreover, increased competition—and not market power—may encourage increase in price spreads. Traditional benchmarks used to determine predatory pricing by the courts are not adequate for the industry. Persistent returns above average trends of long-run total cost might serve as a better indicator of monopolistic distortion and trigger antitrust attention.

Fifth, the industry is highly cyclical. Upheavals and periodic crises are common. Up periods are associated with relatively high production rates and utilization of resources, higher earnings, and low or no new entry. It is during the latter periods that antitrust concerns gain momentum. Down periods are associated with significant overcapacity, financial crisis, and a significant startup entry taking advantage of oversupply of inputs and the financial weakness and contraction of incumbents. It is during the latter periods that concerns regarding industry survival take over and antitrust concerns are largely ignored. Policymakers should look at long-term trends and avoid a policy roller coaster.

Sixth, the negative skepticisms underlined by the complex dynamics view of the industry must seriously be considered. Caution must be used especially in guessing the future evolution of the industry and in attempts to impact its course. Biologists know quite well that it is extremely challenging—if at all possible—to predict specific patterns of evolution. Predicting the long-term future of an industry or affecting its direction may be just as challenging.

## 13.2    Regulation

Price and entry deregulation—although not perfect—has proved to be a success in fixing many of the regulation regime's failures. Yet the deregulation movement seems either to have stopped or to have lost its momentum, and while airlines are free to use price and entry competition they are still very heavily regulated.

Deregulation did away only with the Aeronautics Board and most of its economic regulation activity. Economic fitness and safety certifications are still issued by the Department of Transportation and the Federal Aviation Administration, and are necessary in order to start up an operation. The requirement for certification affects startup entry and often limits the number and type of aircraft a startup may operate. All the other elements of the system's ownership, control, and regulation have survived deregulation and still exist. Moreover, increasing environmental and safety concerns have significantly increased noise regulation and supported additional pressure to expand and impose noise and emission regulation. Airline network globalization has imposed a new set of safety and antitrust regulatory concerns and restrictions, and there are new challenges inherent in the international interest structure. The US government made significant steps in the 1990s to liberalize international service under the US Open Skies policy, but much is left to be desired. New security regulations were imposed in the aftermath of September 11, 2001, and the new federal airport security agency (TSA), the Department of Homeland Security, and the FAA are involved in security regulation.

Paradoxically, while the Deregulation Act is perceived in general as a significant move toward reducing government intervention and enhancing market liberalization, a new and complex set of regulations have been imposed on the industry.

We can draw a number of important general lessons for public policy.

First, more than two decades of deregulation have proved that market forces can sustain rigorous competition. While the current condition is by no means ideal, deregulation cured many of the previous regime failures. Policymakers should resist all calls to re-regulate the industry. Such calls usually emerge during a cyclical industry crisis. If circumstances result in a determination that government intervention is necessary, policymakers should focus on subsidies (with neutral competitive effects) or other incentive schemes and avoid traditional regulation.

Second, privatization of the air traffic control and airport systems has been on the deregulation agenda for a long time, yet no significant progress has been made in this direction. These systems are not priced according to market signals and therefore are inefficient in terms of standard economic principles. Policymakers should focus on deregulating these systems.

Third, privatizing of the airport systems and opening them up to free competition or otherwise increasing the number of major airports could significantly increase competition and improve consumer welfare. In the event that policymakers would be persuaded that the market is smaller than socially desirable due to network effects, it is advisable to consider subsidies or other incentives for private development of new airports.

Fourth, the uncertainty and controversial nature of noise and safety regulation issues create opportunities for diverse interest groups to participate in a complex political scenario of rent seeking and bargaining. The regulatory outcome usually has a great deal to do with the basic information structure and the specific balance and dynamics of political power of the various interest groups and not necessarily much to do with standard economic principles, or rational social prioritization. Policymakers should focus on internalizing otherwise missing social costs into the market system. Environmental and safety regulation can be improved by using incentive schemes including effluent tax or quantity incentives (tradable permits).

# EPILOGUE

Twenty-five young industry executives were staring at me. Each had a laptop, a sophisticated cellular telephone and a smart challenging look; no one was wearing a suit or tie. I recalled my first meeting with Pan Am's management 25 years earlier. They looked different. They were wearing suits (mostly gray) and ties and had sharpened yellow pencils and yellow pads. The whole industry looked different then. All the same, I could not avoid a sense that the market had outsmarted both groups. How could I put more than two decades of my experience in the turbulent airline industry into a short speech to this group of eager executives?

"I have bad news and good news" I started with a standard cliché. "The bad news is that we are part of the most problematic, the most impossible industry ever. This industry is cursed with every possible plague, some of them of mythological proportions. Not only do we have to put people in the air, but we also have to fight bad weather, epidemic diseases, and terrorists bent on blowing up aircraft or flying them into buildings." I got some curious looks from my audience.

"This industry," I continued, "is full of contradictions. It is high-tech and capital-intense; yet it is also labor- and fuel-intensive. In fact, one-third of our costs pays for labor and another third fuel and aircraft. The industry is very sensitive to the economic cycle, to oil prices, and to world security crises. Since the 1960s, economic downturns, oil crisis, and security crises have occurred together, causing demand to plummet as fuel prices increased, sending our costs through the roof just when we needed them low. Labor and equipment costs are mostly fixed, rigid, and hard to cut. To make a bad situation even worse, it is usual during the last gasps of high cycle periods that our relatively good financial condition incites labor to demand and forces managements to agree to pay increases and to place large orders for new aircraft capacity, just to find out soon thereafter that we could not afford them. And if this situation is not challenging enough, certain competitors enjoy the benefit of non-unionized or otherwise lower paid labor and more favorable aircraft deals, which surely gives them a significant competitive edge.

"Most airlines seem as if they possess market power, which traditionally is associated with monopolistic pricing and above-normal profits. Yet overall profits are lower than normal. In fact, it takes only one cyclic downturn to wipe out the total industry profits accumulated from the beginning of commercial flight. This happened in the early 1990s and again in the early 2000s. And then, ignoring abundant evidence of failures, chronic overcapacity, and enormous losses, new entrepreneurs and market entry remain attracted to the market. There are always some people out there who believe that can do something better than you and gobble a piece of your market. This tendency is stronger during times of recessions and industry crisis when demand cannot support the incumbent airlines' capacity, let alone new entries. Usually they fail; sometimes they succeed; but in either case they take a piece of the incumbents' revenues. Because of chronic over-capacity, losses, or otherwise lower-than-normal profits, successful startup entries or expansions by incumbents have forced other airlines to shrink or exit the market.

"We use similar aircraft to produce seats that look quite the same and focus endless efforts on differentiating our service by trying to build our airline's (or service) unique image or otherwise create or influence passengers' perception. Image building, which has become a key element in airlines' strategic success, is not only difficult and expensive to build, but is also extremely easy to lose. It might take only one unfortunate marginal slip in an otherwise perfectly functioning and extremely complex and successful flight operation to alienate passengers. And we are judged by criteria that have nothing to do with, and in fact contradict, our main task of providing an inexpensive and efficient transportation service. It may be the quality of our cuisine, or the china on which it is served (are we a restaurant?), our flight attendants' uniforms or hair styles (are we a beauty pageant?), the material of the seat covers (why is a leather seat considered more desirable?), our ability to predict passengers' tastes regarding audio and video entertainment (JetBlue bet on passengers attachment to their normal channel TV programs and won), or the art work on our aircraft's tails (British Airways quickly removed its quirky artwork after media criticism).

Quality competition of this type requires continued innovation, is contagious, and tends to push costs up. It is sufficient that one airline introduces a new idea, to force all other airlines to imitate it or come up with another in order to maintain their market position. Moreover, this type of innovative competition involves—in addition to physical or material elements—extremely difficult challenges of reading the minds of passengers and anticipating their complex reactions.

"As an economist, I invested many years studying the ideal theoretical world of *perfect competition.* In this model, certain assumptions are associated with an economically efficient and stable market outcome. I believe none of these assumptions is related to our industry and its evolution is anything but stable. Instead, it is plagued with every possible market failure and it behaves in a manner that is better described by evolution concepts than traditional mechanical Newtonian ones. Most of our costs are fixed or otherwise non-avoidable and are very high relative to our low marginal costs. We produce non-divisible network of scheduled flights, but sell separate seats. We must maintain our service and costs even if only a few seats are sold. This further encourages intense price competition. Seats are perishable—once an aircraft takes off, the unsold seats are gone forever. An unsold seat goes down in value and therefore is better to be sold at any price. Yet, on the other hand, according to industry experience, high-fare paying passengers tend to appear closer to takeoff (do they?). Should we protect seats for late bookings at higher fares? Should we overbook? How many early seats should we sell? Should we try to segment passengers based on demand elasticity? Or vary fares dynamically based on demand realization?

"There are economies to scale, density, and scope in our production. In addition, production scale and airline size play a tricky role in demand, since increasing scheduled frequency and network size impact the perceived quality of service and therefore not only affect the quantity demanded but also shift the demand curve. This motivates airlines to increase capacity and size. Our service is not consumed in isolation but rather in combination with business, leisure, and other network products and services (hotels, car rentals, and trains), creating consumption externalities. Complex networks are also characterized by joint production of services and therefore further make direct cost allocation and marginal pricing extremely challenging if at all possible. Moreover, air transportation impacts world economies, and our operation and growth have strong global spillover effects.

"And there are information asymmetries regarding safety and other quality characteristics and production externalities due to missing markets for noise and other pollutants and heavy government regulation affecting every step we make.

"Finally, it is not only difficult to survive and live in this industry, but it is also quite difficult to die, or otherwise exit it. In fact, high sunk costs, the combination of high fixed costs and low marginal costs, and other high exit costs coupled with the available protection of the bankruptcy laws encourage life after death. Protection of the bankruptcy court allows airlines to extend their life by generating cash flows at fare levels that cover immediate operations but do not justify long-term survivability. This obviously hurts the competitors. If successful, an airline may emerge from bankruptcy for a second life, better fit to compete than ever before. Ironically, there is an enormous power in being weak. A failed airline that emerges from bankruptcy may be better positioned for the next go-round than a strong successful one that survived a downturn without bankruptcy. Being financially weak may give a struggling airline more bargaining power to negotiate down its costs and survive as an efficient airline relative to a strong one."

At this point my audience seemed puzzled, perhaps even depressed. "But there is also good news," I quickly said before losing their attention. "The good news is that in spite of this long list of challenges and the sense of doom and bust, there are always clear winners in our game. Throughout the history of aviation there always are a few winning airlines that were able to survive and prosper, even if only for a round or two. And I believe that each one of us has a chance to become such a winner. The secret for success is easy to define and seems obvious in general abstract terms, yet it is quite difficult to copy or implement. All winners were *creative* and *innovative* and developed new ideas and concepts that made them the 'next big thing' in the strategic battle of innovation for survival. These airlines, whether incumbents or startups, recognized and pursued market opportunities for profitable changes, in response to passengers' needs and tastes, new technologies, and their competitors' strengths and weaknesses.

"Everyone is talking these days about the low-cost airlines phenomenon as the next big thing in the making. Suddenly everyone is either already starting or trying to start or become a low cost airline. And undoubtedly most members of the group of so-called low-cost airlines are doing better than the major incumbent network airlines. But one must be cautious in reading the unfolding market. The-low cost airlines are surely affecting the industry in very significant ways, but it is still quite early in the game and the verdict is still not in regarding which are going to be the winners or losers. One thing, however, must be emphasized; the low-cost entry is a creative response to new and unprecedented set of market opportunities. What made these groups of airlines succeed so far is not cutting costs *per se*, but rather their discovery of and response to market opportunities for a profitable change—doing something new or differently from the competition—in a manner that reduces costs or increases the market value or its perception by passengers. And their creative response, no doubt, has been destructive to the dominant strategic model of the major incumbent airlines of the late 1990s.

"What are the most important market opportunities that were identified and targeted by the low-cost airlines? They are: 1) lower-paid mostly non-unionized labor; 2) less expensive new aircraft; and 3) new internet technology. But in addition, they have directly responded and attacked the inherent weaknesses of the complex hub network system: 1) They offer a simple nonstop (point-to-point) service that most passengers prefer (everything else equal); 2) they cherry-picked and attacked specific point-to-point markets or certain desirable segments that can be more efficiently served by a linear connection with one type of aircraft, avoiding the need for the large fixed cost of building and maintaining a complex hub-and-spoke system; and 3) they attacked the inherent vulnerability of the major incumbents' price differentiation strategy, in fact impairing their ability to segment and fence high-fare paying passengers. It is important to remember that above-marginal cost pricing and price differentiation invite price competition in certain segments of the incumbents' network. Note also that most of the low-cost startup entry occurred after September 11 while most major incumbents were weak, struggling with enormous losses and demand drop. They were also entangled with historic commitments and constraints that take time to adjust. A bleeding prey usually attracts the predators.

"Finally, what are some of the important lessons in a nutshell?

"*For the airlines*: Innovation and change is a matter of life and death in the battle of economic survival. A successful introduction of the next big thing destroys or at least damages the previous one. No successful airline is immune from losing its market position and therefore must constantly fight a strategic battle for survival. This requires continuous learning and discovery of new opportunities focusing on passengers, new technology, and rivals' and an airline's own strengths and weaknesses. This is a challenging task for a management that is usually busy running day-to-day tasks and putting out never-ending fires.

"The major incumbent networks face an enormous challenge, far beyond the necessary defensive move of directly cutting costs. Their future depends to a large extent on their creative offense in response to the unfolding new competition and changing market environment. They must think outside the box, and adjust to the new reality in a creative way. In this respect the major network airlines (or any other incumbent or startup airline) must resist the natural tendency to copy or imitate the low-cost rival's strategy. Instead they must respond by taking advantage of their own strengths while attacking their rivals' weaknesses. The current success of the low-cost linear market model should not be interpreted in simplistic terms as a general failure of the complex hub network architecture. Instead the advantages of economies of scope and density that are inherent in such architecture must be emphasized and put to work. Major network incumbents should specialize in serving markets that can be more efficiently served using this structure. This may require changing focus from relying on revenues from high-fare paying point-to-point passengers to connecting passengers. Their global reach as well as their control over and affiliation with regional airlines are also important strongholds that should play an important role in their creative response.

"*For economists and antitrust authorities*: The history of the deregulated industry shows that it is better interpreted by the rules of the jungle than the abstract rules of Newtonian physics. Economists have not been blind to this condition, and in fact have offered alternative market views and new formulation of complex dynamic systems that increase our understanding of the industry and cast serious doubt on the validity of many of the traditional structural foundations of mainstream antitrust thinking and implementation.

"I believe there is a general consensus that a pure textbook monopoly is bad for society and must be busted by the antitrust authorities. Such monopolies, however, don't seem to exist in deregulated airline markets. Therefore if an antitrust agency is sure that a pure monopoly is about to be created absent its intervention—as was the case during the late 1990s—it may be wrong, or else it should better let the competition bust it."

# REFERENCES

Air Transport Association of America. *The Airlines Handbook*. http://www.airlines.org/publications.

*Air Transport World*. (1990, October). "Here We Go Again." pp. 61-64.

_____. (1990, October). "Aircraft Operating Data." p. 150.

_____. (1990, October). "Editorial: Style, Substance and Competition." p. 2.

_____. (1992, May). "Living Beyond Their Means?" pp. 70-77.

_____. (1992, December)."The Price of Retribution." pp. 54-58.

_____. (1993, March). "The Red Zone." p. 5.

_____. (1998, March). "Is Bigger Better?" pp. 31-33.

_____. (2000, April). "Stalling for Time." pp. 47-57.

*Airfinance Journal*. (1991, October)."Stocks Rise But Lessons Wary as American Cuts." No.131, p. 6.

Armstrong, M., & Vickers, J. (1993). "Price Discrimination, Competition and Regulation." *Journal of Industrial Economics*, vol. 41(4), pp. 335-359.

*Aviation Week & Space Technology*. (1992, April 6). "Airlines Fiscal Morass Erases Profits and Crimps Fleet Plans." pp. 36-38.

_____. (1999, January 18). "Airlines Temper Rhetoric in Last Winter Fare War." p. 33.

Baumol, W. J. (2002). *The Free-Market Innovation Machine Analyzing the Growth Miracle of Capitalism*. Princeton, NJ: Princeton University Press.

Baumol, W. J., Panzar, J. C., & Willig, R. D. (1982). *Contestable Markets and the Theory of Industry Structure*. NY: Harcourt Brace Jovanovich.

Berry, S., Carnall, M., & Spiller P. T. (1996). "Airline Hubs: Costs, Markups and the Implications of Consumer heterogeneity." NBER Working Paper No. w5561.

Bingaman, A. K. (1996, January 25). "Consolidation and Code-sharing: Antitrust Enforcement in the Airline Industry." Presentation by Assistant Attorney General, Antitrust Division, US Department of Justice.

Boeing (1991). *Current Market Outlook, World Market Demand and Airplane Supply Requirements*. Boeing Commercial Airplanes Group.

_____. (1992). *Current Market Outlook, World Market Demand and Airplane Supply Requirements*. Boeing Commercial Airplanes Group.

_____. (1996). *Statistical Summary of Commercial Jet Airplane Accidents*. Boeing Commercial Airplanes Group.

_____. (1996a). "Avoiding Controlled Flight Into Terrain." *Airliner*, The Boeing Company, Seattle Washington, April – June 1996, p.11

Boyd, E. A., & Bilegam, I. (2003). "Revenue Management and e-Commerce." http://www.prosrm.com/articles.

Breyer, S. (1993). *Breaking the Vicious Circle: Toward Effective Risk Regulation*. Cambridge, MA: Harvard University Press.

CAB (1975). *Regulatory Reform: Report of the CAB Special Staff*. Washington, D. C., B-74R.

Coase, R. (1960). *"The Problem of Social Cost."* J. Law & Econ. 3, pp. 1-44.

*Commercial Aviation Report*. (1990, October). "Boeing Lends to UAL." p. 3.

_____. (1990, November)."Continental Obtains Backstop Boeing Aid." p. 8.

_____. (1990, December). " 40% of US Airlines Will Be Bankrupt." p. 10.

_____. (1991, November). "Paying for Aircraft: US Fears Increase." p. 1.

_____. (1992, September). "US 1992 Losses Will Rival 1991." p. 6.

Cooper, W. L., Homem-de-Mello T. & Kleywegt, A. J. (2004). "Models of the Spiral-Down Effect in Revenue Management." http://www.business.uiuc.edu/research/020119paper.pdf

Crandall, R. L. (1995). "The Unique US Airline Industry." In *Handbook of Airline Economics*. Aviation Week Group, NY: McGraw-Hill, pp. 3-8.

Cross, R. G. (1995). "An Introduction To Revenue Management." In *Handbook of Airline Economics*. Aviation Week Group, NY: McGraw-Hill, pp. 443-458.

Dana, J. D. (1998). "Advance purchase Discounts and Price Discrimination in Competitive Markets." *Journal of Political Economy*. 106(2), pp. 395-422.

_____ . (1999). "Using Yield Management to Shift Demand When the Peak Time is Unknown." *RAND Journal of Economics*, Fall, pp. 456-474.

Davies, R.E.G. (1964). *A History of World Airlines*. London: Oxford University Press.

Davis, P. (1994). "Airline Ties Profitability Yield to Management." SIAM News. Vol. 27, No. 5.

Dempsey, P. S. (1995). "Dysfunctional Economics and The Airline Industry." In *Handbook of Airline Economics*. Aviation Week Group, NY: McGraw-Hill, pp. 185-200.

_____ . (1997, November 5). Testimony before the Committee on Judiciary of the U.S House of Representatives.

Dempsey, P. S., & Hardaway, R. (1992). "Airlines, Airports and Antitrust: A Proposed Strategy for Enhanced Competition." 85 *Journal of Air Law & Commerce*, pp. 455-507.

Department of Transportation (2001). "Domestic Aviation Competition Series: Dominated Hub Fares." http://www.airlinecompetition.com/Hub%20Final%20Paper.htm.

Dixit, A. K. (1997). *The Making of Economic Policy: A Transaction-Cost Politics Perspective*. Cambridge, MA: MIT Press.

Economides, N. & White, L. J. (1994). "Networks and Compatibility: Implications for Antitrust." *European Economic Review*, vol. 38, pp. 651-662.

Economides, N. (2004). "Competition Policy in Network Industries: An Introduction." http://www.stern.nyu.edu/networks/.

FAA. (1996, June 18). *Human Factor Team Report on: The Interface Between Flightcrews and Modern Flight Deck Systems*.

_____ . *Aviation Safety Data Accessibility Study Index: Public Concerns About Aviation Safety*. http://www.asy.faa.gov/safety_info_study/pubconcerns.htm.

Freedman, M. & Freedman, R. (1990). *Free to Choose: A Personal Statement*. NY: Harcourt Brace & Company.

Gallagher, M. J. (1995). "ValueJet Airlines: An Analysis." In *The Handbook of Airline Economics*. Aviation Week Group, NY: McGraw-Hill, pp. 37-44.

General Accounting Office. (1993). *Higher Fares and Less Competition Continues at Concentrated Airports*, GAO/RCED-93-171.

_____ . (1996). *Airline Deregulation–Barriers to Entry Continue to Limit Competition in Several Key Domestic Market*. GAO RCED-97-4.

_____ . (2001). *Airline Competition Issues Raised by Consolidation Proposals*. GAO- 01-370T. http://www.gao.gov/new.items/d01370t.pdf.

_____ . (2003). *Airline Labor Relations–Information on Trends and Impact of Labor Actions*. GAO-03-652.

Goranson, G. & Miller, M. (1989, June 21). *Aging Jet Transport Structural Evaluation Programs*. The 15th Symposium on the International Committee on Aeronautical Fatigue. Boeing Commercial Airplanes Group.

IATA. (2002, September, 16). Air Transport Outlook 2002. Conference Proceedings. Madrid, Spain.

Kahn, A. E. (1998). *The Economics of Regulation Principles and Institutions*. Cambridge, MA: MIT Press.

Katz, M. (1984). "Price Discrimination and Monopolistic Competition." *Econometrica*, 52 (6) pp. 1453-71.

Klein, J. I. (1998, January 29). *The Importance of Antitrust Enforcement in the New Economy*. Presentation before the New York State Bar Association.

Laffont, J. & Tirole, J. (1993). *A Theory of Incentives in Procurement and Regulation*. Cambridge, MA: MIT Press.

Levin, M. (1996, August). "Goodbye, Model Railroad." *Air Transport World*, p. 46.

Lynn, M. (1997). *Birds of Prey, Boeing vs. Airbus: A Battle for the Skies*. NY: Four Walls Eight Windows.

Maglaras, C.& Meissner, J. (2004). "Dynamic Pricing Strategies for Multiple-Product Revenue Management Problems." http://www.meiss.com/download/RM-Maglaras-Meissner.pdf.

McCraw, T. K. (1984). *Prophets of Regulation*. Cambridge, MA: Harvard University Press.

McCrobie, Alkin, Sherry, Feary, Polson & Palmer (2000). Enhancing Vertical Navigation Performance in Glass-Cockpit Aircraft. ttp://human-factors.arc.nasa.gov/IHpersonnel/ev/OSU97_MD-11_Survey/OSU97_MD-11_survey.html

McGill, J. I. & Van Ryzin, G. J. (1999). "Revenue Management: Research Overview and Prospects." *Transportation Science*, Vol. 33, No. 2 (May), pp. 233-256.

Morrison, S. A. & Clifford, W. (1995). *The Evolution of the Airline Industry*. Washington, D.C.: The Brookings Institution.

Noll, R.(1989). "Economic Perspectives on the Politics of Regulation." In, Schmalensee, R. & Willig, R. (eds.), *Handbook of Industrial Organization*. Amsterdam: North-Holland, pp. 1253-1287.

NTSB. (1989). *Aloha Airlines Flight 243 Boeing 737-200, N73713 Near Maui Hawaii April 28, 1978*. NTSB/AAR-89/03

____. (1994). *Safety Study*. NTSB/SS-94/01 Notation 6241, Washington, D.C.

Olson, C. V. & Trapani, J. M. (1981). "Who Has Benefited from Regulation of the Airline Industry?" *Journal of Law & Economics*, vol. 24, issue 1, pp. 75-93

Perelman, M. (1994). "Fixed Capital, Railroad Economics and the Critique of the Market." *Journal of Economic Perspectives*, vol. 8, issue 3, pp. 189-195.

Peterson, S. P & Glab, J. (1994). *Rapid Descent*. NY: Simon & Schuster.

Petzinger, T. (1995). *Hard Landing: The Epic Contest for Power and Profits That Plunged the Airlines into Chaos*. NY: Times Business, Random House.

Pollak, R. A. (1995). "Regulating Risk." *Journal of Economic Literature*. Volume 3, March, pp. 179-191.

Reed, D. (1993). *The American Eagle: The Ascent of Bob Crandall and American Airlines*. NY: St. Martin's Press.

Schumpeter, J. A. (1950). *Capitalism, Socialism, and Democracy*. NY: Harper & Brothers Publishers.

Stole, L, A. (2001, November 7). "Price Discrimination in Competitive Environments." (Forthcoming in Handbook of Industrial Economics, available at http://gsblas.uchicago.edu/papers/hio-distrib.pdf).

Telser, L. G. (1994). "The Usefulness of Core Theory in Economics." *Journal of Economic Perspectives* 8, no.2, Spring pp. 151-164.

Transportation Research Board, (1999). *Entry and Competition in the US Airline Industry: Issues and Opportunities*. Special Report 255, National Research Council.

University of Texas, (1997). *Air Crews Evaluation of Flight Deck Training and Use*, Aerospace crew research project. http://www.bluecoat.org/reports/Sherman_97_Aircrews.pdf.

Van der Linden, F.R. (1995). "Progressives and the Post Office." In Trimble, W. F. (editor), *From Airship to Airbus: The History of Civil and Commercial Aviation*. Washington, D.C.: Smithsonian Institution Press, pp. 245-260.

Varian, H. R. (1997). "Versioning Information Goods." University of California, Berkley. http://www.sims.berkeley.edu/~hal/Papers/version.pdf

Vietor, R. H. K. (1991). "The Hubris of Regulated Competition: Airlines, 1925-1988." In High, J. (editor), *Regulation Economic Theory and History*. Ann Arbor, MI: University of Michigan Press, pp. 19-58.

White House Commission on Aviation Safety and Security. (1997, February 12). *Final Report of Vice President Al Gore's Commission*. Washington, D.C.

Williamson, O. E. (1968). "Wage Rates as a Barrier to Entry: The Pennington Case in Perspective." *Quarterly Journal of Economics*, 82 (February), pp. 85-116.

____ . (1985). *The Economic Institutions of Capitalism*. NY: The Free Press.

____ . (1996). *The Mechanisms of Governance*. NY: Oxford University Press.

Zhao, W. & Zheng, Y. (2001)."General Dynamic Models for Airline Seat Allocation with Diversion and No-Shows." *Transportation Science*, 35, pp. 80-98.

# INDEX

# Studies in Industrial Organization

1. H.W. de Jong (ed.): *The Structure of European Industry.* Revised edition, 1988: see below under Volume 8

2. M. Fennema: *International Networks of Banks and Industry 1970-1976.* 1982
ISBN 90-247-2620-4

3. P. Bianchi: *Public and Private Control in Mass Product Industry.* The Cement Industry Cases. 1982
ISBN 90-247-2603-4

4. W. Kingston: *The Political Economy of Innovation.* 1984, 1989: 2nd printing
ISBN 90-247-2621-2

5. J. Pelkmans: *Market Integration in the European Community.* 1984
ISBN 90-247-2978-5

6. H.W. de Jong and W.G. Shepherd (eds.): *Mainstreams in Industrial Organization-Books 1 and 2, Book 1. Theory and International Aspects Book 2. Policies: Antitrust, Deregulation and Industrial.* 1986
ISBN 90-247-3363-4

7. S. Faltas: *Arms Markets and Armament Policy.* The Changing Structure of Naval Industries in Western Europe. 1986
ISBN 90-247-3406-1

8. H.W. de Jong (ed.): *The Structure of European Industry.* 2nd revised ed. (of Volume 1) 1988
ISBN 90-247-3690-0

9. I.L.O. Schmidt and J.B. Rittaler: *A Critical Evaluation of the Chicago School of Antitrust Analysis.* 1989
ISBN 90-247-3792-3

10. B. Carlsson (ed.): *Industrial Dynamics.* Technological, Organizational, and Structural Changes in Industries and Firms. 1989
ISBN 0-7923-9044-X

11. Z.J. Acs and D.B. Audretsch (eds.): *The Economics of Small Firms.* A European Challenge. 1990
ISBN 0-7923-0484-5

12. W. Kingston: *Innovation, Creativity and Law.* 1990
ISBN 0-7923-0348-2

13. B. Dankbaar, J. Groenewegen and H. Schenk (eds.): *Perspectives in Industrial Organization.* 1990
ISBN 0-7923-0814-X

14. P. De Wolf (ed.): *Competition in Europe.* Essays in Honour of Henk W. de Jong. 1991
ISBN 0-7923-1050-0

15. C. van der Linde: *Dynamic International Oil Markets.* Oil Market Developments and Structure 1860-1990. 1991
ISBN 0-7923-1478-6

16. D.B. Audretsch I and J.J. Siegfried (eds.): *Empirical Studies in Industrial Organization.* Essays in Honor of Leonard W. Weiss. 1992
ISBN 0-7923-1806-4

17. R.J. Gilbert (ed.): *The Environment of Oil.* 1993
ISBN 0-7923-9287-6

18. H.W. de Jong (ed.): *The Structure of European Industry.* 1993   ISBN 0-7923-2160-X

19. D.K. Round (ed.): *The Australian Trade Practices Act 1974, Proscriptions and Prescriptions for a More Competitive Economy.* 1995
ISBN 0-7923-3228-8

20. A. van Witteloostuijn (ed.): *Market Evolution, Competition and Cooperation.* 1995
ISBN 0-7923-3350-0

# Studies in Industrial Organization

Printed in the United States
54024LVS00002B/31-45

9 780387 242132